THE RISE AND FALL
OF
OLYMPIC AMATEURISM

MATTHEW P. LLEWELLYN
AND JOHN GLEAVES

D1411685

University of Illinois Press
URBANA, CHICAGO, AND SPRINGFIELD

Library of Congress Cataloging-in-Publication Data
Names: Llewellyn, Matthew P. author. | Gleaves, John, author.
Title: The rise and fall of olympic amateurism / Matthew P Llewellyn,
    John Gleaves.
Description: Urbana : University of Illinois Press, 2016. | Series: Sport
    and society | Includes bibliographical references and index.
Identifiers: LCCN 2016003056 (print) | LCCN 2016024625 (ebook) |
    ISBN 9780252040351 (hardback) | ISBN 9780252081842 (paperback) |
    ISBN 9780252098772 (e-book)
Subjects: LCSH: Olympics. | Olympics—Social aspects. |
    Professionalism in sports.
Classification: LCC GV721.5 .L59 2016 (print) | LCC GV721.5 (ebook) |
    DDC 796.48—dc23
    LC record available at https://lccn.loc.gov/2016003056

For James and Christopher

For Tomasz and Henryk

CONTENTS

ACKNOWLEDGMENTS

Like so many other historians, we have leaned heavily upon the expertise of numerous patient and skilled archivists, colleagues, and friends throughout the completion of this book. Our sincere thanks go out to Wayne Wilson at the LA84 Foundation in Los Angeles; to Regula Cardinaux and Nuria Puig at the International Olympic Committee Archives in Lausanne, Switzerland; and to all of the excellent and diligent archival staff at the University of Illinois in Urbana, Illinois, the British Olympic Foundation in London, United Kingdom, and the International Association of Athletics Federation in Monaco. Also, it would never have been possible to visit these archives without the generous financial support and assistance of California State University, Fullerton. We thank Dr. Shari McMahan, former Dean of the College of Health and Human Development, for providing much needed institutional support to create the time to write this book.

We owe a debt of gratitude to many others. Our sincere thanks go out to Tina Duffus, David Martinez, Ben S. Bevan, and David J. Lunt for their help in translating numerous French, German, and Spanish language sources. It has also been to our great advantage to have sought and been given advice by numerous scholars and friends throughout the writing of this manuscript. We have leaned heavily upon the expertise of Mark Dyreson, Alison Wrynn, Toby Rider, Stephen Wenn, Ron Smith, Chad Carlson, Norrie Baker, Marcel Reinold, Emanuel Hübner, and Erik Nielson. We are also extremely grateful to have been surrounded by a team of willing and able graduate students at California State University, Fullerton. Charles Siegel, Tanya Jones, Paulina Rodriquez, and Emmanuel Macedo helped conduct research, scour through archives, and offer their own critical insights.

Both Willis G. Regier and his successor in the role of acquisition editor at the University of Illinois Press, Danny Nasset, have been a constant source of support throughout this entire process. They thoughtfully responded to our endless e-mails and have both been remarkable advocates of our work. We also offer our hearty regards to both Randy Roberts and Aram Goudsouzian, the editors of the Sport and Society series, and the peer reviewers for their constructive comments and suggestions.

Finally, we thank our families for their love and unwavering support. They offered a valuable distraction from the rigors of research and writing. Their endless love and encouragement is the reason that we managed to complete this work at all.

THE RISE AND FALL
OF
OLYMPIC AMATEURISM

INTRODUCTION

The Olympic Games stand as the largest sporting phenomenon of the twenty-first century. Attracting the world's premier sportsmen and sportswomen from 205 representative nations, as well as global television audiences soaring upward of 4 billion viewers, the Olympics are a cultural, economic, and political colossus.[1] Under the leadership of the International Olympic Committee (IOC), which has grown to become a billion-dollar multinational bureaucracy, the Olympic Games are a highly attractive commodity. Television networks engage in high-stakes bidding wars for the right to broadcast Olympic images around the globe, while exclusive corporate partners such as Coca-Cola, General Electric, McDonald's, Samsung, and Visa avariciously engineer ways to exploit the Olympic brand.[2] Eager to reap the political riches of the Olympics, governments pledge considerable financial resources in the hopes of staging the games before the eyes of the world. The Olympics are an unprecedented political showcase, a platform for nations to demonstrate their power, prestige, ideologies, and cultural diversity, or even to seek validation as a member of the international community.[3]

At their best, the Olympics are a powerful symbol of international peace, unity, and reconciliation, a global forum for promoting national prestige, civic pride, tourism, urban development, and commercial growth. Olympism, the humanistic and educational philosophy that runs through the heart of these games, inspires the promotion of universal ethical principles, global solidarity, and fair play.[4] At their worst, the Olympics are sites for political boycotts, nationalistic rivalry, bribery, terrorism, doping, and scandal. They incite global condemnation, as well as accusations of hypocrisy, sexism, elitism, commercial exploitation, and political favoritism.[5] Through a critical lens, the Olympics and the secretive, autocratic bureaucracy that oversees them are repudiated as a manifestation of commercial excess, a platform for

Western political and cultural propaganda, or a vestige of an earlier imperial and aristocratic age.[6]

Polarizing, provocative, and prosperous, the Olympics, in their winter, summer, Paralympic, and now youth variations, represent the apogee for elite athletes from all corners of the globe irrespective of nationality, race, ethnicity, gender, or religious affiliation. Under the intensive spotlight of the world's media, the motto of the Olympics, *Citius, Altius, Fortius* (faster, higher, stronger), thrives as Michael Phelps splashes to record victories in the pool, Ethiopian marathoner Tiki Gelna swiftly traverses 26.2 miles of London's landmarks, and British Paralympian Tanni Grey-Thompson challenges ableist notions of human limits. The quadrennial games are a global sporting village, a showcase of professional athletic excellence. Although some Olympic sports are largely noncommercial, composed of athletes who will not become wealthy from their sporting endeavors, the principal events hold significant financial riches. Within the Olympic stadiums, pools, and arenas, or even on synthetic beaches, professional swimmers, basketballers, gymnasts, figure skaters, and volleyball players vie for gold medals, international recognition, lucrative commercial endorsements, and other financial rewards.

The professional, commercial, and bureaucratic realities of international Olympic competition obscure the modest origins of the games. Established in 1894 by the Frenchman Baron Pierre de Coubertin, the modern Olympic Movement represented a brand of politically conservative internationalism—a counter to socialism on the left and nationalism on the right. The early Olympic Games experienced a slow and piecemeal development; they were devoid of the pomp, universality, and organizational efficiency that characterize twenty-first-century Olympian spectacles.[7] Spread out over many months, the games were remarkable for their glaring mismanagement, low international turnout, bizarre assortment of events, and an almost exclusively male roster of participating athletes. The nascent Olympics differed in another important regard: The games were a celebration of *amateur* athletes. Olympic sportsmen and sportswomen were forbidden from profiting personally, in any capacity, from their sporting exploits—a far cry from some of the lavishly subsidized and financially driven contemporary Olympians. These financial prohibitions even extended to indemnities for time away from the workplace. In opposition to the degree of specialization, dedication, and professionalism implicit in *Citius, Altius, Fortius*, amateur restrictions also limited the length and duration that an Olympic athlete could train in preparation for the games. Coubertin's embrace of amateurism came to dominate the Olympic Movement, influencing and dictating the IOC's attitudes toward issues such as commercialism, television revenues, performance enhancement, globalization, and political interference. For more than seven decades, no other force played such a significant role in shaping the world's largest regularly scheduled multisporting event.

DEMYSTIFYING OLYMPIC AMATEURISM

Amateurism came into the Olympic Games as a cultural object that had long since occupied what the philosopher Roland Barthes considered the mythologies of daily life. These cultural myths—the Tour de France cycling race as Homeric epic; the Eiffel Tower as symbol of Parisian travel—provide the feeling of "naturalness" or a "what-goes-without-saying" obviousness.[8] Both the bicycle race and the Eiffel Tower achieve their mythical status by obscuring how they are in reality historically rooted, culturally tethered, and utterly contingent. These myths are sustained by a general neglect for how they are socially constructed and whose interests such narratives serve. Barthes argues, however, that by obscuring its contingency a myth provides the feeling of naturalness, familiarity, inevitability, and thus ultimately becomes the dominant view. Yet, as Duncan explains, Barthes shows that when myths are placed back into their historical context, demystified and exposed, their profound ideological implications emerge.[9] They perpetuate, for Barthes, an idea of society that adheres to the current ideologies of those in power. They stifle dissent, for who could object to what is natural, and thus they preserve the status quo by making the values laden in the myth—as Marxist scholar Antonio Gramsci argues—appear to be common sense so that dominance by the group in power is continually rewon, reproduced, and sustained.[10]

Regarding the mythology of amateurism, this Victorian sporting ethos pervaded (at least within the British Isles) upper- and middle-class culture prior to Coubertin's reimagination of the Greek sporting festival as a modern Olympic Games. Amateurism rose to prominence within Britain at the same point in time when the British Empire exerted its greatest political and cultural influence around the globe. It offered its adherents cultural advantages through its links to muscular Christianity, gentlemanly refinement, and the British public-school ethos of "good sportsmanship" and "fair play." When Coubertin deliberately bound amateurism to the Olympic Movement, the ideology was imbued with a feeling of permanence, a natural fit for the "invented traditions" of his modern Olympic revival. Throughout the twentieth century its assumed status as a revered sporting tradition allowed those in power to use amateurism to protect their vision of sport and to decide who could compete (and how) in sport. As those who controlled elite sport—notably, the IOC and the international federations—discovered amateurism's inconveniences (i.e., its disavowal of commercialism and profiteering), aspects of the ideology were jettisoned as their interests demanded. Even today, amateurism's ethos still occupies much of mainstream sport's cultural common sense. Youth sport is venerated and defended through the idealization of sport as character-building, ennobling, chivalrous, and robust, healthy physical leisure. Similarly, the public condemns professional athletes who use performance-enhancing substances as immoral cheats (the worst insult to those who deify fair play) who fail to adhere to the true spirit of sport.

But viewing amateurism as mythology is precarious because myths are themselves inherently unstable. As Barthes warns, "if we penetrate the object, we liberate it but we destroy it; and if we acknowledge its full weight, we respect it, but we restore it to a state which is still mystified."[11] In delving into amateurism's history, we are not attempting to write *the* history of Olympic amateurism, as if there were only one history and we have written it. Rather, we are balancing the desire to understand an ideology that has taken on a mythic air of naturalness, to see it for what it was rather than how it is imagined, with an understanding that the amateur mythology powerfully shaped not just the Olympic Games, but through the Olympic Games, the way people around the world understood sport. We show how the people defending amateurism often failed to understand the ideology's historical contingencies, that amateurism's "goes-without-sayingness" led to policies and rules that had little to do with Coubertin's vision of the Olympic Games, and that the changing currents of culture shifted what amateurism meant but that the ideology always served those who called the shots. At the same time, the simple fact that amateurism was not what people imagined it to be does not mean that it lacked power. In truth, its imagined properties made the ideology more powerful. Amateurism could be at once fluid and pliable while retaining the feeling of authenticity. By making itself out to be a naturally pure form of sport, a humanistic and moralistic ethos with links to ancient Greece, amateurism has woven itself into the very fabric of how much of the world imagines sport still today even though the Olympic Games has dropped amateurism as a criterion for eligibility.

The Rise and Fall of Olympic Amateurism tells the story of those in power. It is not a history of marginalized or mass culture, though such histories are important. It uses material from institutional archives and preserved media, which overly represent the voices of privileged educated, wealthy, and powerful (mostly) men from predominantly Anglo-American societies who ran and controlled international sport. In particular, the research that informs this book has drawn heavily on archival materials housed at the IOC's Olympic Studies Centre, the International Amateur Athletic Federation, the British Olympic Foundation, and the voluminous records found in the Avery Brundage collection.

Critics might contend that using archives that privilege the discourses and texts of the people and the institutions that propagated and benefited most from amateurism is inherently fraught with methodological dangers. What can we know about the past if we simply use the winners' version of history? How much can we know if we use only what the wealthy and privileged wrote down and saved? Such concerns are important. We acknowledge that these metaphors of power are political institutions that might have manipulated and distorted evidence for self-preservation and self-interest.[12] Archives are not straightforward repositories from which absolute truths can be retrieved. As informed by our historical training, we have cautiously and critically interrogated sources in order to view the evidence in its broader social, cultural, and political context.[13] We contend that by examining the attitudes and actions that these organizations took to be perfectly normal, the primary sources that inform this research provide significant insights into how the power brokers of elite international sport preserved amateurism. That is not to say that those who resisted amateurism, such as Tommy Smith, who famously placed his Puma running shoes on the medal podium during his 1968 Mexico City protest as thanks to his sponsor's under-the-table payments, or those who had prohibitive and exploitative amateur regulations used against them, such as Jim Thorpe and Karl Schranz, are absent. These stories are told, too. Rather, by examining amateurism through the lens of those who controlled it and shaped it, we hope to challenge its cultural naturalness by showing what it was for those who lived it, how it changed and for what reasons people changed it, and how it continues to shape attitudes about both the Olympic Games and sport today. Most important, we hope to show that much of what is assumed to be true about Olympic amateurism—the narrative that we think we know—is in actuality a mythologized narrative that ignores amateurism's contingent history, one heavily shaped by changing political, economic, and cultural forces far larger than sport.

To realize this feat, consider for a minute what you, the reader, know about amateurism in the Olympic Games. You most likely know that amateurism emerged some time ago (whether in ancient Greece or Victorian Britain, perhaps; you can't be sure) and forbade athletes from receiving payment for playing in sport. Most likely, you also know that amateurism used to be an eligibility requirement for all Olympic athletes but has since disappeared from the Olympic Games. You may believe that the IOC crafted one set of amateur regulations and applied them consistently and enforced them rigorously across all Olympic sports; and that a long line of IOC presidents such as Coubertin and Avery Brundage fought bitterly to keep their cherished ideal alive even as the Olympics entered into an age of commercialized, televised, high-performance sport. Perhaps you also are aware of its political and social implications: that it privileged wealthy athletes from predominantly Western nations; that it carried enormous racial, gender, and social-class biases; or that it became a pawn in a totalitarian and later Cold War nationalistic battle for hearts and minds. As this book will argue, some of these beliefs rest on a large corpus of evidence while others match what Eric Hobsbawm coined, "invented traditions."[14]

You also likely assume that amateurism has been thoroughly researched. Perhaps, if you've spent much time reading historical works about sport, you think the topic has been done to death and doubt that anything new can be added to the literature, especially not in a work as broad and expansive as this one. How could an ideology so central to not only the Olympic Games but modern sport not have received significant scholarly attention, especially since we know so much about it? Indeed, sport and Olympic-themed research pervade the academic fields of economics, history, media and communications, philosophy, political science, and sociology. The Olympic Games alone have been the subject of an enormous volume of scholarship encompassing a broad range of issues and thematic approaches.[15] Yet remarkably, no historical monograph in any language has dealt comprehensively with amateurism within the Olympic Games, or sport in general for that matter.[16] Such an omission is significant.[17] In that sense, *The Rise and Fall of Olympic Amateurism* represents the first detailed work on the most important ideal of the Olympics Games. This book presents a richly contextualized global history of the role of Olympic amateurism, from Coubertin's Olympic revival in 1894 through the presidency of Juan Antonio Samaranch and the advent of open professionalism during the late 1980s and 1990s.

REIMAGINING OLYMPIC AMATEURISM

Examining the history of Olympic amateurism reveals a far more complicated narrative than many would assume. The social origins of amateurism sprung to life not from ancient Greece, but from Victorian Britain, where an upper-middle-class (and to a far lesser degree, aristocratic) desire to set themselves apart from the perceived morally corrupt working classes employed amateurism as a legitimating ideology for elitist sporting preserves. Amateurism represented a tool for those who held power to reassert control in times of social disorder and political subversion. But amateurism was both exclusive and inclusive. It also was a philosophy of moral improvement and gentlemanly refinement (as sport served at this time as a "manly preserve"), and maintained a doctrine of active competition.[18] Built upon the chivalrous Greco-Renaissance concept of manhood, along with the aggressive spirituality of muscular Christianity, amateurism was a broad and dynamic concept that carried social, moral, economic, health, and aesthetic connotations. The British spread this diffuse ideology through its vast empire and beyond via a series of interrelated channels. Its social acceptability and quasi-historical traditions proved a perfect elixir for Coubertin's fledgling international sporting festival.

As the baron soon discovered, however, the broad dimensions of amateurism made it impossible to legislate the status of an amateur on a global scale. The IOC failed repeatedly to establish a universal definition of an amateur to govern all Olympic sports. Thus, Coubertin and his colleagues entrusted the international sports federations to define amateurism on a sport-by-sport basis. The consequences of this decision proved deleterious: what constituted an amateur in one Olympic sport was considered a professional in another. Confusion reigned. For Coubertin, the issue of amateurism grew tiresome. Privately, he opposed strict Anglo-American antiprofiteering amateur regulations. He viewed amateurism as a moral, aesthetic, and spiritual ideal rather than a series of exploitative and prohibitive regulations. Losing interest in the issue, Coubertin delegated the full regulation and enforcement of Olympic amateurism to the growing nexus of international sports federations and national Olympic committees. Still, the question of amateurism refused to abate in intensity.

The participatory and universal growth of the Olympic Games in the ensuing decades precipitated the emergence of political and commercial forces within the Olympic arena. The encroachment of governments eager to exploit the games for propaganda rewards, as well as commercial interests seeking to peddle products stamped with Olympic insignia, sullied the avowed sanctity of Olympic amateurism. Time and time again, the IOC proved powerless to stem the flow of money and governmental influence. Olympic athletes increasingly moonlighted as commercial spokespersons, while others were transformed into governmental proxies, trained, indoctrinated, and funded by the state. A string of Coubertin's successors endeavored to combat these growing threats, establishing a series of general conditions concerning amateur eligibility and, with each passing decade, debating new regulatory changes to the *Olympic Charter*. Even under the leadership of Avery Brundage, the person accredited as being a fanatical and uncompromising defender of amateurism, the IOC's efforts proved largely in vain. Brundage's dogmatic desire to operate the Olympic Movement on the basis of gratuitous service ensured that the IOC lacked both the financial and bureaucratic capability to defend and enforce amateurism. It would be 1971 before the IOC formed an investigatory and enforcement Eligibility Committee, and, even then, Brundage and his successors failed to provide it with the necessary funding to ensure its success. "Shamateurs" and "state-sponsored amateurs" flooded the Olympic Games. Few honest amateurs remained.

In reality, the Olympic Movement's embrace of amateurism stood in opposition to its core philosophical ideals. Coubertin and his apostles of Olympism preached equal opportunities for all people and all nations, yet the IOC's promotion and preservation of amateurism reads as exclusionary, elitist, and racist. Few athletes, particularly those from the Third World, could afford the lengthy travel and time away from the workplace to train and compete in distant Olympic venues. Coubertin imbued the Olympic Movement with an internationalist ethic but created an institutional structure based on national representation. Governmental officials inevitably seized upon the Olympic Games as a platform for political aggrandizement, stoking the flames of nationalism and eroding any semblance of pure and honest amateurism. Coubertin embraced the amateur dictum "sport for sport sake" alongside the motto of *Citius, Altius, Fortius*, which taken to its logical conclusion implied specialization and professionalism. Olympic athletes, regularly supported by the state, strove to attain Olympic gold. Rising levels of global participation elevated the standards of elite performance, thus forcing Olympic athletes to pursue sport as a full-time vocation. Perhaps most fatally, Coubertin committed the Olympic Movement to a noncommercial ideal in an age of rapidly expanding commercial possibility. While philosophically disavowing gambling, gate-taking, sponsorship, and profiteering, the IOC proved powerless (and eventually became complicit) as corporations and marketing agencies devised elaborate ways to use Olympic athletes to sell their products, and cinematic newsreel and television networks vied to secure Olympic broadcast images. As this book will reveal, the Olympic Movement, and the contradictory philosophical tenets that it espoused, sowed the seeds of amateurism's decline and fall.

Ultimately, the power brokers of international sport sealed the fate of Olympic amateurism, but only at the precise moment that it benefited them the most. The transformation of the Olympics into a televised, highly commercialized global spectacle altered the IOC's ideological compass. The IOC steadily transformed into a modern corporation; financial concerns and brand recognition grew paramount. Eager to sell Olympic broadcasting and commercial rights to the highest bidder, the IOC faced heightened pressures to promote an unrivaled product. The Olympic program had to comprise the most popular sports; the best athletes, amateur or otherwise, had to compete. The "shamateur" ruse that had allowed athletes to cash in while ostensibly remaining amateur no longer suited any party. Things had to change. Though tennis, ice hockey, and association football (soccer) explored early forays into an "open" Olympics, Michael Jordan and his Dream Team of U.S. basketball superstars ushered in the full transformation of the Olympic Movement from an amateur affair to the professional enterprise it has embraced in the 21st century.

1 THE ANATOMY OF OLYMPIC AMATEURISM

On 23 June 1894, sporting dignitaries and administrators from across the globe gathered in the grand auditorium of Paris's Sorbonne University as part of an International Athletic Congress to discuss the notion of reviving the Olympic Games of classical Greek antiquity. French aristocrat Baron Pierre de Coubertin, the Congress's chief architect and financier, seduced the seventy-eight administrators from nine countries in attendance with modern sporting exhibitions, extravagant banquets, and frequent allusions to antiquity. The baron's charm worked favorably as delegates voted unanimously to revive the Olympic Games and to institute the International Olympic Committee (IOC), a permanent bureaucracy whose members would serve as ambassadors of Olympism in their respective homelands.[1] Blending ancient Greek custom with themes of contemporary internationalism, Coubertin proposed ambulatory games to be staged quadrennially in rotating cultural capitals of the world. Demetrius Vikelas, a prominent Greek man of letters and former London University student then residing in Paris, was appointed as the inaugural president of the IOC.[2] Vikelas's appointment appeared a blatant move by Coubertin to win Greek favor, particularly since Athens had beaten out motions in favor of London and Budapest to serve as host of the first modern Olympic Games, scheduled for 1896.[3] After an absence of nearly fifteen hundred years, the Olympic flame would be rekindled in the ancestral homeland of physical culture.

For Coubertin, the revitalization of the Olympic Games was the product of decades of personal endeavor. Born in Paris on 1 January 1863, Coubertin grew up in the aftermath of Napoleon's stunning 1815 defeat at Waterloo that led the French empire into a decline that reached its nadir with their capitulation in the Franco-Prussian War of 1870–71.[4] A crippling sense of degeneracy, together with an impassioned search for the root cause of the malignancy, pervaded French life in the postwar Third Republic. Traumatized, as was his entire generation, by the humiliation of defeat, Coubertin became absorbed with finding a remedy to the debility and turmoil that gripped the nation. France had fallen behind her imperial rivals in the quest for overseas expansion; her foreign trade plummeted; crime, mental pathologies, and venereal diseases soared; and the nation's birthrate declined at an alarming rate. Coubertin identified a lack of physical training in French schools as a major cause of his nation's rapid decline. Rejecting the military, diplomatic, and legal careers expected of a member of France's old aristocracy, he devoted his life to overseeing the physical and athletic development of his nation's youth. An aspiring social theorist (or "applied psychologist" in the parlance of the era), he sought to invigorate his demoralized, unpatriotic, and socially fragmented countrymen through a sport-based educational reform.[5]

Eschewing the German model of regimented, paramilitary gymnastics—*Turnen*—that had long proven popular on the European continent, even in France, Coubertin embraced Britain's amateur sporting traditions as the cornerstone of his pedagogical ideology. His fascination with British competitive sport derived from reading Thomas Hughes's totemic fictional novel *Tom Brown's School Days*.[6] Reading *Tom Brown* as a work of detailed and contextualized history, Coubertin mistook Hughes's fictional version of Thomas Arnold, the legendary headmaster of Rugby school and a champion of muscular Christianity, as the person responsible for the significance accorded to competitive sport in English schools.[7] After a pilgrimage to Rugby and other leading bastions of English education, Coubertin returned convinced that Britain's sporting traditions were the keystone of her empire, a vast collection of transoceanic realms that covered more than one quarter of the world's landmass "upon which the sun never set."[8] He hypothesized that if France adopted a British sporting culture it would revitalize French society, consolidating the ruling classes and restoring the nation to its former status as arbiter of Western civilization. The French body politic was in distress; British competitive sport its elixir.

It is unsurprising that Coubertin's educational mission put him at odds with many of his Anglophobic countrymen, who held a strong distaste for the British and their wild sporting pastimes. Paschal Grousset's overtly nationalistic Ligue Nationale de l'Éducation Physique captured the virulent tone of opposition against reforming French education through British sport. The baron proved resilient in the face of Gallic prejudices, producing a constant stream of publications in support of a British educational system and even founding a number of sports organizations on the British amateur model, the most notable of which was the Union des Sociétés Françaises de Sports Athlétiques.[9] While chauvinism stymied Coubertin's ambitions for overhauling the French educational system, a new objective had captured his attention: the revival of the Olympic Games. Inspired by the German excavations of ancient Olympia, as well as a broad series of regional and national Olympic festivals—nostalgic interpretations of the games of Greek antiquity—dating to the seventeenth century, Coubertin broadened his pedagogical ambitions by seeking to unite athletes across "all games, all nations" through a modern Olympic revival.[10]

In spite of the baron's claims arising from a strong tendency toward personal aggrandizement and historical revisionism, he was not the first to conceive of an international Olympic Games.[11] Utilizing his own political and social connections, as well as a persuasive arsenal of charm, passion, and intellectual rigor, he should nevertheless be credited with bringing the project to its successful fruition. Coubertin was a man of lofty ambition and consummate dedication. He was independently wealthy, resourceful, and culturally astute—a *fin de siècle* internationalist in the age of modernity. A citizen of the politically explosive Third Republic, he gazed cautiously into the globalizing winds of change noting that the rapidity of transcontinental travel and communication and the complexity of global commerce marked a period of dangerous historical transition as well as unparalleled possibility. The growing interdependencies between nations, Coubertin opined, could either stir cultural rivalries and antagonisms or fuel the spread of healthy democracy and mutual understanding.[12] Harnessing a belief in the educative and moral properties of sport, he envisioned a modern Olympic revival as an effective conduit for the easing of international hostilities, as well as a universal platform for fostering peaceful prosperity and respect among nations. The games, he hoped, would represent a vehicle for the promotion of universalism, equity, peace, and human rights amid a period of dramatic change in Western civilization.[13]

Coinciding with the birth of other leading idealistic international movements such as the Red Cross (1863) and the Esperanto movement (1887), Coubertin's Olympic revival represented both the promise and the trepidation of the late nineteenth century.[14] The games also reflected the cultural biases, social ideas, relationships, and practices of the era, notably those favoring privileged male elites from predominately Western nations. Rooted in traditional exclusionary values, the Olympics subordinated groups on the basis of gender, race and ethnicity, and social class.[15] Based on pseudo-scientific theories of physical vulnerability, as well as Coubertin's own patriarchal attitudes toward female athleticism, women were originally excluded from competition; like the games of Greek antiquity, the modern Olympics of Coubertin's imagination would be a strictly masculine affair. The predominance of Western imperialistic thought within the IOC, much of which was grounded in prevailing notions of racial inferiority, initially marginalized nonwhites (particularly Blacks and Asians) from the Olympic arena. The Olympic Games of this era further discriminated along class lines. Reflecting the Anglophone sporting culture upon which Coubertin based his movement, as well as misguided claims of ancient Greek amateurism, the modern revival prohibited professional sportsmen. The Olympic Games were to be for amateurs, the baron proclaimed, reserved for an elite of male competitors who shunned the lure of monetary reward in the pursuit of bodily perfection, the bestowing of national prestige, and the promotion of peaceful competition.[16]

THE SOCIAL ORIGINS OF AMATEURISM

Though often misattributed to ancient Greece, amateurism was a distinctly modern invention born in Great Britain during the latter half of the nineteenth century.[17] Emerging out of a complex series of social, economic, and political changes in British society, amateurism came to influence sport—first within the Anglophone world and then beyond—for nearly a century. A holistic and loosely articulated set of ideas, beliefs, and practices, amateurism is commonly defined as being "about doing things for the love of them, doing them without reward or material gain or doing them unprofessionally."[18] The amateur played the game for the game's sake, disavowed gambling and professionalism, and competed in a composed, dignified manner. The amateur stood modest in victory, gracious in defeat, honorable, courageous, not fanatical or too partisan and avoided elaborate training or specialization. In practice, amateurism functioned as both a legitimating ideology for an elitist, anticommercial sporting system, as well as a broader philosophy of moral and aesthetic improvement. Amateurism not only dictated *who* could play, but also *how* they played.[19]

Later popularized, internationalized, and safeguarded by the Olympic Movement, amateurism was originally conceived in opposition to the commercial orientation and open professionalism that characterized nineteenth-century modern British sport. Prior to the 1860s, the amateur-professional dichotomy did not exist. Sporting culture in late Georgian and Victorian Britain was pluralistic, often transcending class and political divisions.[20] Fueled by gambling interests, open interclass competition regularly filled the British sporting landscape. Wealthy upper-class patrons, as well as publicans and clergymen, provided the financial sponsorship and moral legitimacy for dockworkers, artisans, bank clerks, factory hands, and grocers to compete openly for monetary purses.[21] Within this commercially driven environment, every actor—rich or poor—qualified for the role of athlete in a host of popular sports such as horse racing, rowing, pugilism, football, pedestrianism, swimming, and wrestling.[22] Even in cricket, landed "gentlemen" and lower-class "players" competed side by side, albeit symbolically divided by the prevailing class prejudices of the time.[23]

By the late 1800s, British sport underwent a structural transformation as commercialized spectator sport gained in prominence. Traditional, agrarian forms of popular recreation such as animal baiting and mob football were increasingly eclipsed within an overall search for "rational recreation," by large-scale, regularly organized, gate-money sport. Fueled by the twin forces of industrialization and urbanization, sports entrepreneurs seized upon concentrated markets. Codified, bureaucratized, specialized sports emerged on a national level along the cash nexus, aided by technological advancements in transportation.[24] Grounds were fenced off, stadia erected, and gate money charged. In association football (soccer) and rugby union, cup competitions developed under the aegis of new governing bodies such as the Football Association (1863) and Rugby Football Union (1871), contributing to the prevalence of payments in kind, padded expense accounts, wagers, and lucrative cash prizes. The concurrent growth of first-class county cricket and the gradual inception of a county championship expanded the commercial dimensions of British sport.[25]

The rampant commercialization of Victorian sport heightened opportunities for participation, particularly amongst the urban masses. Through factory legislation and trade union pressure the working classes reaped, albeit unevenly across occupations, the economic benefits of industrialization. A rapid rise in real earnings, followed by the passage of industrial labor laws (i.e., the 10 Hours Act), the granting of an annual one-week (unpaid) holiday, and the creation of Saturday half-day holidays presented the masses with greater opportunities to recreate. With more time, modest disposable incomes, and renewed energy—through the wider availability of cheap meats and grain, as well as new methods of industrial production—the working classes surged into the sporting arena.[26]

The growing influx of working-class players and teams posed a direct challenge to upper-middle-class hegemony. In soccer and rugby union, public school–based clubs and players were gradually eclipsed by their social inferiors, particularly proletarian teams from the northern industrial regions of England.[27] Winning was vitally important to the professional middle classes, men imbued with a public school "games ethic" that connected competitive sport with national and imperial interests.[28] Across a variety of popular British sports, Victorian gentlemen went to great lengths, often blatantly circumventing the rules of the game, in their quest for victory; evidently, the middle classes were not the bastions of Victorian respectability that many have traditionally claimed.[29] The prevalence of violent and disorderly conduct, outright gamesmanship, and regular monetary rewards illuminates the seriousness with which businessmen, accountants, clerks, and other middle-class professionals pursued victory. Public school–based clubs even disbanded after a string of embarrassing losses to save the risk of further humiliation.[30] Defeat dealt a symbolic blow to the middle classes, undermining both their self-confidence and their paternalistic leadership claims.

Even off the field, the rise of enormous crowds of working-class spectators posed a threat to the established social order. Large throngs of unruly spectators—congregated in masses, drinking, gambling, and widely gesticulating—offended middle-class sensibilities. Spectators became the targets of vehement criticism. Reports of open fighting among fans, threats of physical abuse aimed at referees, as well as deafening cascades of foul language and derision, heightened middle-class anxieties toward mass industrial sport.[31] Once the shared, albeit unequal, preserve of all layers of male British society, modern sport began to fracture under the weight of commercial expansion.

The growing prevalence and dominance of the working classes in the sporting sphere, both on and off the field, coincided with broader destabilizing shifts in British society. During the mid-nineteenth century, Victorian Britain experienced profound social, economic, political, and cultural changes.[32] The urban-industrial revolution, and the mass waves of democratic reform that it inspired, heightened the stratification of British society through the creation of a growing and aspiring working class.[33] Despite systematic socioeconomic differences, burgeoning industrial capitalism, and the achievement-oriented, competitive culture that it engendered, presented new opportunities for social mobility. The Parliamentary Reform Acts of 1867 and 1884, which expanded the electorate from 1.3 million to 5.6 million men, coupled with the opening of higher education through the passage of the Education Act in 1870, further elevated the visibility and prominence of an increasingly literate and self-confident British working class. The rise of trade unionism, employees' federations, militant strike actions, and the 1893 formation of the Independent Labour Party underlined the growing social and political influence of the masses.[34]

The transformation of Britain into an increasingly meritocratic, democratic, and financially oriented society offended the sensibilities of the gentrified middle classes. Rising liberalism, democratization, and the success of laissez-faire economics irreversibly altered the moral, political, and economic fabric of British life. In this dynamic Victorian culture, challenges to the established political hierarchy and social order sparked hysterical alarm. Instability, class disorder, and indicators of moral decay lurked at every turn. Fears of social unrest and national decadence prompted the middle classes, in alliance with a fraction of the old landed aristocracy, to act in a defensive and isolationist manner, particularly within the sporting realm. [35] In times of social disorder and political subversion, hierarchy needed defending and reasserting. It is in this climate, amid social struggles and a middle-class desire to set itself apart from the money-oriented, morally corrupt working classes, that amateurism was born.

As an invented tradition, amateurism represented both a rejection of corrupting capitalistic impulses and a bold proclamation of the immutability of the British class system. The professional middle classes disavowed the commercial orientation and pluralistic traditions of British sporting culture in favor of a new vision of sport. Derived from the basic Latin root meaning "to love," amateurism represented a refined, moderate, and exclusive model of organized competition; an alternative to the violent, socially disruptive, and commercially driven spectator sports of the industrial masses. Blending insurgent middle-class Puritanism with romanticized aristocratic notions of valor and chivalry, the Victorian gentlemen was reimagined as an honorable, dignified sportsman who played the game vigorously, but for personal satisfaction rather than pecuniary gain. The amateur celebrated the team over the individual, the athlete over the spectator, and the all-rounder over the specialist. Amateurism represented a pastiche of principles and beliefs (repudiation of profit making, abolition of gambling, acceptance of common rules, and an emphasis on participation), enveloped by a wider set of values commonly referred to as the ethos or "spirit of sport."[36]

PERIOD OF READJUSTMENT

Prior to the 1860s, amateurism existed in a relatively inchoate form, an amorphous, loosely articulated set of values, beliefs, and practices. Aiming to curb the threat posed by incipient professionalization, private clubs and bureaucratic organizations of British sport began aggressively codifying, propagating, and regulating the amateur ethos. Closed, self-perpetuating voluntary institutions such as the Amateur Athletic Club (AAC), the first sport organization to ever use the word "amateur" in its name, and the Amateur Rowing Association (ARA) suddenly dispensed with cash prizes in favor of symbolic awards and, more drastically, restricted participation on the basis of social status. Founded in 1866, the AAC—a forerunner to the Amateur Athletic Association (AAA)—excluded from amateur eligibility any man who "is a mechanic, artisan, or labourer."[37] The ARA later embraced a variation of the infamous "mechanics clause," denying amateur status to any oarsman "who has ever been employed in or about boats or in manual labour for money or wages," and "who is or has been by trade or employment for wages a mechanic, artisan, or labourer, or engaged in any menial duty."[38] Amateurism took on immediate class connotations; it became synonymous with the professional middle classes. Professionalism, it was stated, transformed play into work, consumption into production, and a leisured pursuit into a matter of serious endeavor.

The early crystallization of amateurism into a class-based legitimating ideology failed to apply across more populist British sports. In swimming, rugby union, and soccer, mass working-class interest in those sports meant that exclusion based on social status was out of the question.[39] The Associated Metropolitan Swimming Clubs, an umbrella organization of city of London baths, drafted its first set of amateur laws in 1869 across pecuniary rather occupational lines. The Amateur Swimming Association, which grew in 1886 out of this earlier group of London-based clubs, codified antiprofit regulation on a national level, proscribing payments, prizes, or inducements, monetary or otherwise.[40] The prevalence of working-class players prompted the Rugby Football Union (RFU) to also pass similar antiprofessional rules that same year. Chastened by the example of soccer, which in 1885 had succumbed to commercial forces by legalizing professionalism, the RFU declared any payment (notably, those to compensate workers for wages lost while playing or traveling) illegal—a decision that created an irreconcilable schism in the sport and ultimately led to the establishment of northern rugby league.[41] The establishment of British governing bodies of swimming, boxing, and lawn tennis throughout the late nineteenth century proclaiming amateur status, in various terms and degrees specific to the sport or regional class dynamics, strengthened the middle-class campaign against professionalism.

The codification of socially exclusive, antiprofit regulation masks the progressive and inclusive nature of amateurism. Evolving from the evangelical project of the mid-nineteenth century, amateurism also represented a philosophy of moral improvement. Belief in sport as a civilizing moral force can be traced to the Victorian rational recreation movement.[42] Evangelists joined forces with liberal moralists in seeking to reform the violent, less respectful leisure pursuits of the working classes, notably the unholy trinity of alcohol, gambling, and sex. Reformers promoted uplifting middle-class leisure activities in an effort to instill temperance, self-improvement, self-respect, and social responsibility among the urban masses.[43] Although Victorian public campaigns to replace the music halls, brothels, public houses, and violent animal baiting with rational recreation proved ineffective against the popular waves of commercial leisure, belief in the moral and civilizing properties of middle-class sport persevered.

The British public school played a significant role in the articulation and cultivation of the moral dimensions of amateur sport. Traditionally the exclusive preserve of the aristocracy, the Victorian public school system had been transformed under the currents of industrial expansion. Reflecting the modern realities of British public and political life, the sons of aristocrats, new industrialists, and wealthy merchants were consolidated within and indoctrinated in a new vision of masculinity. The British gentleman was recast as a self-disciplined, functional, responsible member of the elite capable of leadership in a more modern society—in contrast to the traditional effeminate image of the rural country patrician. It was on the playing fields that this new elite model of masculinity was forged. Built upon the chivalrous Greco-Renaissance concept of manhood, along with the aggressive spirituality of muscular Christianity, a "cult of athleticism" dominated the British public school system. Through organized team sports such as soccer, rugby union, and cricket, a coterie of influential public school headmasters maintained that students acquired important character traits such as equanimity, bravery, and honesty—qualities deemed central to the development of patriotic, imperialistic, and devout British gentlemen.

The public school use of sport as a medium for redefining masculinity and behavior, as well as achieving broader militaristic and imperialistic ends, heightened beliefs in the moral and pedagogical dimensions of amateurism. The amateur ethos promulgated civilized, regulated, and vigorous competition designed to meet the shifting conditions of modern industrial and commercial British life. Although competition was heralded as a moral and important force fueling British global and economic dominance, the professional middle classes (ironically, the drivers of free-market capitalism) recognized that it had to be regulated and contained. Ethical participation remained paramount. Axioms such as "playing a straight bat" and "it's not cricket," formed part of an elaborate sporting ethos that translated into broader guidelines for social intercourse. Amateurism provided a sense of civility, sociability, and cordiality in an increasingly turbulent, competitive, and industrialized world. It stressed fair play, decency, honesty, self-control, and respect for opponents and officials, as well as graciousness in both victory and defeat.[44] It was this vision of amateurism, as a transformative moral elixir, that prompted the liberal aristocratic Pierre de Coubertin to reunite and invigorate the French citizenry (and eventually the wider world) through sport and Olympic competition.

Evidently, amateurism was a highly complex phenomenon, a paradoxically exclusive and inclusive, reactionary and progressive social, moral, and educational force. It also carried work, health, and aesthetic connotations. Amateurism arose (in part) out of changing patterns of middle-class work, a shift in Victorian attitudes toward personal and public health, as well as the emergence of a new aesthetic of masculinity.[45] Forged in the highly competitive, yet increasingly sedentary, climate of urban-industrial Britain, amateurism represented a doctrine of active competition. Bolstered by shifting medical attitudes toward the importance of vigorous exercise, amateurism called for Britons to escape the dark, claustrophobic, and poorly ventilated industrial workspaces and commuter trains for suburban playing fields, public parks, and open spaces.[46] It called for Britons to move their bodies freely, energetically, and competitively, but in accordance with a particular style and aesthetic—balanced, cultivated, and refined. Excessive physical and muscular development violated the neoclassical Hellenistic image of the well-proportioned athletic body, a British paragon of masculinity and aesthetic beauty throughout the Victorian and Edwardian ages.[47] Striving, training, and specialization—hallmarks of the professional—were strongly abhorred as crude, impure, and tainted.[48] From his physical appearance, clothing, posture, expressions, and even his technique and playing style, the amateur personified an aesthetic of gentlemanly British refinement.[49]

The complex, variegated, and contradictory realities of British amateurism undermine prevailing scholarly efforts to comprehensively theorize this phenomenon. Amateurism cannot be satisfactorily explained as an apparatus of bourgeois hegemonic persuasion,[50] nor equally, as a manifestation of a wider civilizing process that gradually transformed Western Europe into more orderly, peaceful societies.[51] In both ideology and application, amateurism represented more than a mere alternative to professionalism, a refuge from and reaction to modernity, or a counterforce to the erosion of the human play spirit engendered by industrialism, vulgar commercialism, and mass democracy.[52] Amateurism was many things: broad and elusive, fluid and dynamic. It was an amalgamation of professional middle-class principles and voluntary structures with a romanticized aristocratic code of chivalry and honor. Amateurism was a distinctly modern conception, grounded in material interests and social struggles, and shaped by ethical, economic, medical, and aesthetic forces.

THE GLOBAL DIFFUSION OF AMATEURISM

From its institutional seedbed in Victorian Britain, amateurism traveled the sporting globe, from the cosmopolitan Dominion cities of Cape Town, Sydney, and Toronto to distant British imperial outposts in sub-Saharan Africa, the Caribbean, Southeast Asia, and beyond. Like the spread of modern sports and games, the British diffused amateurism via a series of interrelated mechanisms: notably, the public schools, the economic and industrial system, the imperial British army, the evangelical and muscular Christianity movements, and a vast literary network of sporting journals, male adventure stories, and imperial tracts. In the Pax Britannica—an age of unrivaled British commercial, cultural, and naval power—sailors, merchants, schoolmasters, clergymen, and expatriates introduced British sporting pastimes to foreign lands, established the organizational and bureaucratic framework that ensured their diffusion, and inspired local traditions and patterns of play. The British reveled in their role as the leaders of modern sport, espousing and legitimating their own chivalrous ideology of amateurism.[53] Through their dominance and control of bureaucratic organizations and private clubs such as the Football Association (1863), the Marylebone Cricket Club (1787), and the Royal and Ancient Golf Club (1754), the British provided the formal codification and national—and in many cases, international—administration that elevated amateurism as a global sporting ideology.

Although far from hegemonic, amateurism left an indelible mark on all sporting cultures that it came in contact with. From Bombay and Brisbane to Buenos Aires, wherever British influence reigned, amateurism (i.e., its principles, voluntary structures, and social ethos) was appropriated, imitated, codified, and enforced—although often not in the manner, language, or form or with the same intensity that British sporting leaders imagined. Britain's bureaucratic and cultural dominance opened the channels for its far-reaching diffusion, but amateurism's true success lay in its complexity, plasticity, and breadth. Amateurism spread so pervasively—eventually taking hold within Fascist dictatorships, Communist regimes, and progressive liberal democracies—because it was not an iron-clad, highly specific, fully elaborated ideology. It was malleable enough to fit divergent social, political, ideological, and sporting landscapes. Its broad and elusive nature allowed the professional middle classes, athletic ideologues, and political opportunists alike to employ amateurism either as an emblem of social exclusivity, a tool for moral improvement and national rejuvenation, or a platform for political aggrandizement.

To concentrate on amateurism's vast geographical reach and pliability is to exaggerate its importance. Outside the Olympic Movement, as well as a handful of sports such as track and field, rugby union, and rowing, amateurism paled in significance and popularity to its professional counterpart, particularly beyond the British Isles. Stripped from the unique social, cultural, and ideological fabric of Victorian Britain, amateurism failed to enjoy the same degree of success and legitimacy on foreign soil; in France, Italy, and Spain, professional cycling took root during the same era as Britain's diffusion of amateurism. In most instances, a small coterie of colonial, Anglophile elites—wielding an inordinate amount of power through the sporting bureaucracies, clubs, and colleges they governed—implemented amateur regulations in opposition to both popular sentiment and established professional sporting structures. In the individualistic, democratic, and materialistic United States, where professional baseball and a host of commercially driven recreational activities dominated the sporting landscape, British-style amateurism failed to capture the American imagination. The rhetoric and posturing of early amateur apostles such as influential sportswriter Casper Whitney, Amateur Athletic Union (AAU) chief James E. Sullivan, and Yale University's Walter Camp ensured that amateurism appeared healthy and prosperous on the surface, but in reality a general disconnect there existed between the anti-profit regulation passed in committee meetings and realities on the ground.[54] Amateurism was the overarching ideology that governed and legitimatized AAU and collegiate sports, but most U.S. athletes and officials boldly violated the amateur code.[55] A similar tradition of paying only lip service to the high ideals of amateurism long characterized Scandinavian track and field, South American soccer, and French and Australasian rugby union.[56]

Globally recognized but not universally enforced, amateurism's success and longevity rested in part on the shoulders of the Olympic Movement. The formation of the IOC in 1894 provided the bureaucratic framework that stimulated the diffusion of amateurism on a far-reaching scale. As an institution of remarkable homogeneity, the IOC drew its members from exclusively aristocratic and upper-middle-class circles, tethered together on the basis of an elite education and a strong proclivity for amateur sport. The thirteen original male members of the IOC—many of whom did not even attend the 1894 Sorbonne Congress—were handpicked by Coubertin for their wealth, social status, and geographical sphere of influence.[57] Ever the shrewd tactician, the baron sought to elevate the prestige of his fledging movement. The placement of military aristocrats, wealthy tradesmen, and acclaimed diplomats to seats on the IOC worked to legitimize amateurism as a global sporting model. Influential amateur sporting figures and inau-

Pierre de Coubertin and the original members of the International Olympic Committee. The membership would diversify slowly over time, thus bringing in more progressive views on amateurism. Left to right (seated) Pierre de Coubertin, Demetrius Vikelas, Aleksey Boutowski, (standing) Victor Balck, Karl August Willibald Gebhardy, Ferenc Kemeny, Jiri Guth Jarkovsky. (Courtesy of the International Olympic Committee)

gural IOC members such as Charles Herbert, secretary of the prestigious English AAA, former New Zealand amateur cricketer Leonard Cuff, and Swedish military colonel and gymnastic expert Victor Balck lent credence to the Olympic project. They possessed the sporting acumen and influence to mobilize their respective national amateur governing bodies to participate in the quadrennial summer games.

As the IOC gradually expanded across geographical boundaries and the Olympic Games rose to become the world's largest multisporting event, amateurism achieved almost global bureaucratic dominance. Participating Olympic nations, and their affiliate network of national governing bodies of sport, were forced to adhere—in theory, often not in practice—to the IOC's current amateur policies. Yet the bureaucratic monopoly that amateurism enjoyed fails to satisfactorily explain its global success. From a philosophical perspective, amateurism proved to be deeply appealing.[58] Its numerous practical technicalities, hypocrisies, and exclusionary policies aside, amateurism invoked a higher ideal of physical cultural expression. Free from the trappings of vulgar commercialism and single-minded professionalism, amateurism transformed sport into a highbrow, civilized, and regulated contest. The allure of pleasurable, noncommercial, and relatively self-controlled physical activities transcended national boundaries, elevating amateurism, within the Olympic Movement and beyond, to a position of international prestige.[59]

ADVOCATE OR ANTAGONIST?

The IOC heightened amateurism's global reach and prosperity well into the twentieth century, but the amateur sensibilities of its principle founder, Coubertin, are difficult to comprehend. Coubertin was a man of paradoxical extremes. He was a passionate democrat who once said that the triumph of democracy was an innovation that history would have been better off without. He was a *revanchiste* who sought to avenge France's crushing defeat and the loss of its provinces of Alsace and Lorraine who was simultaneously an internationalist who promoted global reconciliation and the easing of political conflict between nations.[60] Coubertin freely permitted himself many conceptual liberties. In the spirit of his intellectual masters, Thomas Arnold, Hippolyte Taine, Frédéric Le Play, and Alexis de Tocqueville, he trumpeted the values of formal equality, fairness, and justice for all. He fought for workers' rights and free universal and compulsory education, but he believed in a clear aristocratic elite class and expressed a deep distaste for the Jacobin revolutionary impulse and socialism; the storming of the Bastille and the threat of the guillotine tempered his democratic leanings.[61] He was, in the words of one historian, a "pseudo- egalitarian"; moderate, ambitious, conservative, and progressive all in one.[62] His public proclamations on the subject of amateurism appeared equally conflicting and contested. At the 1894 Sorbonne Congress he heralded the "noble and chivalrous" nature of amateur sport and warned against the "spirit of gain and professionalism" that threatened its existence.[63] Yet in a later declaration he denounced amateurism as "an admirable mummy that could be presented at the museum of Boulaq as a specimen of the modern art of embalming!"[64] His inconsistency obscures his true sentiment.

Amid his many ideological contradictions emerges a shrewd pragmatist and tactician. Coubertin was a political opportunist who seized upon amateurism as a means of currying favor with influential European and North American sporting elites who could heighten the success of his fledging initiative. At the 1894 Sorbonne Congress, Coubertin employed amateurism as an inspirational ruse. Recognizing the importance attached to it in influential sporting circles, he disguised his Olympic revival ambitions by calling sporting officials from across the globe together for an "International Congress of Amateurs"—only upon arrival in the Parisian capital were attendees made aware of any discussion of reviving the games of classical Greek antiquity.

Invitations, bulletins, and the program of events were altered at the last minute to reveal the baron's true intentions.[65] He later conceded as much. Writing in his memoirs years later, Coubertin remarked candidly, "Today I can admit it; the [amateur] question never really bothered me. It had served as a screen to convene the Congress designed to revive the Olympic Games. Realizing the importance attached to it in sporting circles, I always showed the necessary enthusiasm, but it was enthusiasm without real conviction."[66]

An openly professional, commercial event, the baron astutely calculated, would fail to inspire support among the ruling European aristocracy upon whom he believed the legitimacy of his Olympic project rested. "I felt that the British would vote for the restoration of the Olympic Games only on the condition that the participants answered the definition of amateurism," he later disclosed.[67] Amateurism stood as the keystone of his Olympic revival ambitions, an invented tradition that claimed a long but "largely fictitious" historical lineage in order to confer social and political capital.[68] He aggressively propagated the myth of ancient Greek amateurism in an effort to link Olympism with the prestigious themes of Hellenism, as well as to promote an imagined continuity between the glorious past and present epochs of Western civilization.[69] Nostalgic idealizations of ancient Greek Olympians—like Milo of Croton, a fearsome, highly specialized, lavishly rewarded wrestler—as amateurs in the Victorian sporting tradition heightened justification for a modern Olympic revival.[70] It fueled the British obsession with both philhellenism and the Victorian games ethic of chivalry and fair play, cultivating a ripe enough atmosphere to develop his Olympic project. Amateurism functioned as an important ideological and motivational cog in Coubertin's early Olympic operations. It inspired the revival of the games, consolidated the movement's influential support base, and lured high-ranking dignitaries and officials to serve on the IOC.

Political posturing aside, Coubertin did find considerable value in the moral and aesthetic dimensions of amateurism. He embraced the spirit of amateur sport but responded indifferently to the socially exclusive, antiprofit regulation espoused by his Anglo-Saxon contemporaries; rigid British elitism failed to resonate with this Third Republic moderate republican. Ignoring the intricate and contested debates over amateur policy, Coubertin dreamt holistically. The broad and elusive nature of amateurism granted him such freedom. He viewed amateur sport not as an endless labyrinth of financial rules and regulations designed to exclude and marginalize, but as a social panacea, a moral force that actively inculcated important character traits and attributes. Free from the "business spirit" that marked professionalism, he rhapsodized that sport served as a restorative agent that could contribute to the betterment of the lower classes and the moral progress of his nation and eventually the entire world. Sport, he argued, when pursued as an avocation rather than a vocation, served as a formative and developmental influence.[71] In seeking to fulfill his paternalistic responsibilities—the centuries-old function of the aristocracy stressed the duty to guide and guard the lower rungs of society—Coubertin embraced amateur sport as a social stimulant that promoted class cohesion, as well the holistic development of the French citizenry. Positive characteristics acquired in amateur sport, he believed, would extend to nonsporting areas as well.[72] This theme of moral and social rejuvenation through sport, which ran so pervasively throughout *Tom Brown's School Days* and became embedded within the ethos of the British public schools, the muscular Christianity movement, and the global nexus of Young Men's Christian Associations, occupied a central position within his movement's philosophy of Olympism.[73]

For Coubertin, Olympism represented a transcultural ideology that promoted "international understanding, peaceful coexistence," and the harmonious moral, physical, and spiritual development of man.[74] It was a modern religion complete "with church, dogmas, and ritual . . . but most of all religious feelings."[75] He envisioned Olympism as a humanitarian doctrine based on an adherence to the ideal of superior life and the pursuit of perfection. It would bind together athletes from all corners of the globe, regardless of nationality, race, ethnicity, geopolitical affiliation, and religion, in the name of peaceful cooperation, cultural tolerance, and friendly competition. Blending ancient Greek notions of mind–body equilibrium with British sporting ideas of peace and fair play, Olympism was immersed in the spirit of amateurism. Despite Olympism's many ideological inconsistencies and exclusionary values, Coubertin clearly considered amateurism a moral and aesthetic force. In this context, he should be read as a political pragmatist, possessing a selective vision of amateurism, one that ignored strict Anglophone social and economic interpretations, in favor of its broader spiritual dimensions. Whatever Coubertin's personal beliefs, amateurism became the IOC's dominant regulatory value, but, as the early editions of Olympic competition would soon demonstrate, it was an ideology without regulation, comprehension, conviction, or luster.

A STRUGGLE FOR SURVIVAL

The establishment of the modern Olympic Games reflected the techno-logical progress and globalizing transformations of the late nineteenth century. Burgeoning transoceanic travel and communication, through the opening of steamship lines, the installation of the telegraph, and the development of the modern media, fueled the mass movement of peoples on an international scale. Free trade, foreign investments, and the broad-ening dimensions of global commerce illustrated the greater connectivity and intermingling between nations.[76] It is in this moment of heightened cultural intimacy that Coubertin's internationalist project took hold. Like other concurrent transnational organizations proclaiming pacifistic ends, the Olympic Games promised to break down cultural barriers by provid-ing a means of communication and contact between nations. The baron grounded his global athletic gathering in another peaceful fin-de-siècle nation-building project: world exhibitions in science, technology, and ag-riculture. The Third Republic hosted three of the most important trade fairs of the late nineteenth century (1878, 1889, 1900), providing Coubertin with a blueprint for staging mass international spectacles.[77] Intertwined with the global discourse of empire, commerce, and industry, the modern Olympic Games reflected the internationalist spirit alive in modernizing Western societies.

Although bold in virtue and ambition, Coubertin's Olympic revival proved difficult to implement. As globalizing forces transformed Western societies into modern, industrialized nation-states, sport remained in a state of relative infancy. From its organizational birthplace in Britain, modern competitive sport traversed the globe through the currents of imperial trade and expan-sion. Yet British sport failed to enjoy anywhere near complete hegemony during the late nineteenth century. Existing cultural movement practices, coupled with a vocal chorus of colonial and nationalistic opposition, col-lectively stifled the spread of the "English disease," as British sport was often called, across the European continent and beyond. Even in the Anglophone world, organized and competitive league and cup competitions, at both the amateur and the professional level, were few and far between. National and international bureaucracies—a valuable organizational pipeline linking sports, national federations, and the IOC together—also were scarce and limited in both authority and reach, ensuring that contact and cooperation between and within sports was virtually nonexistent. Consequently, ad hoc rules and regulations, as well as patterns and traditions of play, remained largely fragmented, inconsistent, and culturally relative. By the conditions

and standards of the time, Coubertin's plans to institute a large-scale, multisporting international event appeared extremely ambitious.[78]

The inaugural modern Olympic Games held in Athens in 1896 reflected
the largely unstandardized and embryonic state of modern sport. Despite
Coubertin's lofty vision of Olympic universality, the Athens Games proved
to be a rather small-scale affair—only 241 athletes from fourteen nations
participated in the Greek capital.[79] As it happened, only a small number of
European and North American nations possessed the structural, organizational, and financial capabilities to participate in early Olympian spectacles.
The Athens Games, stymied by a lack of publicity, haphazard organization,
and a low international turnout, illustrated the experimental nature of early
Olympics. In tennis, Britain's (or rather, Ireland's) John Pius Boland won the
doubles event playing alongside his partner, Germany's Friedrich Adolph
Traun. Another mixed-nationality pairing, Britain's George Stuart Robert-
son and Australia's English-born representative Edwin "Teddy" Flack (who
won when competing in both the 800- and 1500-meter track events), were
eliminated in the opening round; more definitive guidelines for national
representation were still to be introduced. Similarly, the sporting program
in Athens, which included obscure events such as a rope-climbing contest
and a 100-meter swim for sailors of the Greek Royal Navy, combined with
the absence of gold, silver, and bronze medals (which were not introduced
until the 1904 games in St. Louis), further reinforced the haphazard and
piecemeal development of Coubertin's quadrennial Olympic festival.[80]

Counterintuitively, as the initial phases of globalization promoted greater
uniformity and standardization through the erosion of distinct cultural practices and values, amateur rules and regulations governing modern sport
remained widely contradictory and diverse. At the 1894 International Athletic
Congress in Paris, sporting administrators from across the globe gathered primarily—at least so Coubertin hoodwinked them into believing—to establish
a mutually agreeable international amateur definition. Because of the fluid
and malleable nature of amateurism, along with its broad economic, moral,
medical, and aesthetic dimensions, the congress's task proved laden with
difficulty. Administrators discovered firsthand that, as a matter of motive, attitude, or spirit, amateurism defied regulation. As a social-cultural construct,
it stood open to vast international interpretation. Between and within nations,
bureaucracies, and sports, disagreement and dissension ensued. The English
ARA lobbied the congress to accept its socially exclusive mechanics clause, effectively barring the working classes from Olympic competition.[81] Reflecting
cycling's professional heritage, the Ligue Vélocipédique Belge and the Union
Vélocipédique de France took a far more populist position, proposing that

amateurs and professionals be allowed to compete together under certain circumstances. The Union National des Sociétés de Tir raised the necessity of cash prizes for amateur marksmen. The Racing Club of Paris made an equally liberal proposal, advocating the full reimbursement of an athlete's travel and housing costs—a proposal strongly denounced by the English ARA. [82] Amid the many striations, interpretations, and points of contention, the congress eventually passed, after four days of lengthy debate, an amateur definition riddled with concessions and exceptions:

> [An amateur is] Any individual who has never participated in a competition open to all comers, nor competed for a cash prize, or for a prize of any amount of money regardless of its source, specifically from admissions to the field—or with professionals—and who has never been, at any time in his life, a teacher or paid instructor in physical education. [83]

The congress conceded that this definition, rooted in the Anglophone tradition, would not apply to all sports. Revealing the aristocratic bias of the congress members, horse racing, shooting, and yachting were excluded because of their deep-rooted practices of awarding financial prizes. [84] The IOC later granted fencing a similar dispensation, allowing "masters"—paid fencing instructors or professors of gentleman rank—to compete in Athens. Through the creation of policies and loopholes that implicitly favored the wealthy, the IOC's self-professed moral overtones were already giving way to matters of expediency.

The IOC instituted its amateur code at the 1896 Athens Olympics alongside the rules and regulations of select national and international sports federations. [85] Since the games were experimental in nature, it would be naïve to suggest that Olympic amateurism was effectively enforced. In its infancy, the IOC lacked the jurisdictional and technical authority, not to mention organizational capability, to verify the amateur statuses of Olympic athletes. In the absence of national Olympic committees—a significant ally (and hindrance) in the future fight against shamateurism—as well as the inadequacy and inexperience of the Greek organizers, no mechanisms or checks and balances were in place to enforce the amateur purity of the Athens games. This is especially true when you consider that some participating athletes were wandering tourists, unaffiliated with any particular club or association upon which an official amateur status could have been bestowed. As a result, allegations of professionalism and amateur violations emerged. Spyros Louēs, a local Athenian peasant and winner of the inaugural marathon event, received promises of financial and material reward—including lavish monetary purses, free meals, haircuts, and even offers of marriage. [86] Evidently, the Greeks did not fully understand, or likely appreciate, the strange Anglophone notion of amateurism. Attempts by British visitors to get two of their own countrymen, cyclists Edward Battell and Frederick Keeping, disqualified on the grounds that they were salaried employees of the British Embassy in Athens, and thus not "gentlemen amateurs" in the Victorian tradition, also failed to resonate with the Greek organizers.

THE "UNHOLY UNION"

As the 1896 Athens Games concluded to mixed international reviews, Coubertin moved the Olympics to his native Paris, where they were to be held in conjunction with the Exposition Universelle planned for summer 1900, beginning the Olympics' brief but troublesome association with world trade fairs. The pairing of Olympics and expositions appeared to make logical sense, fusing the Baron's fin-de-siècle internationalism with the mechanical, material, and athletic achievements of Western civilization. To Coubertin's chagrin, enthusiasm for the second edition of his Olympic spectacle proved relatively scarce among his fellow countryman. The Union des Sociétés Françaises de Sports Athlétiques, of which Coubertin served as secretary-general, fiercely opposed his plans. The exhibition organizers proved equally averse, pushing the newly appointed IOC president and his Olympic sports to the periphery of their grand industrial and cultural celebration of Western civilization.[87]

Practical and organizational difficulties aside, the connection between Olympism and world fairs proved ideologically troublesome. For an organization committed to the noncommercial ideal of amateurism, the IOC had seemingly sacrificed one of its core principles by forming an "unholy union" (as Coubertin would later describe it)[88] with commerce, trade, and industry—the antithesis of British-style amateurism. The IOC's high-minded appeals to "sport for sport's sake" suddenly appeared shallow when placed in the backdrop of one of the largest commercial fairs in world history. British IOC member and vocal amateur proponent Reverend Robert Stuart de Courcy Laffan agreed, insisting that the decision to unite the Olympic Games with a world fair "is not made to enhance the dignity of them."[89] Yet the IOC was hardly teeming with viable alternatives. The Olympic Games were still largely unknown to the wider world, and if they were known, they faced frequent ridicule as a "ghastly parody" of Greek antiquity or a trivial and debased festival of athleticism.[90] Unlike the Olympic Movement of the twentieth-first century, in which cosmopolitan capital cities engage in multimillion dollar bidding wars to stage the games, the formative IOC was forced into making significant organizational and philosophical compromises just to ensure that the games took place.[91] The consequences would prove disastrous.

Spread out over a period of five months with no opening and closing ceremonies, and containing a bizarre assortment of events, including underwater and obstacle swimming races, balloon racing, live pigeon-shooting, as well as special handicap contests, the Paris Games—renamed by the French exhibition organizers Concours Internationaux d'Exercices Physiques et de Sport—were so disorganized that some athletes were shocked to later discover that they had competed in the Olympic Games.[92] The foreign press proved equally perplexed, with many media outlets referring to the event, which attracted an impressive 997 athletes from twenty-four nations, as an "international championship" or "international meeting," rather than an official cycle of Olympic competition.[93] Under such farcical conditions, the visible internationalism of the Athens Olympic Games reemerged in Paris, obscuring claims of national representation. An Australian-British combination won the 5000-meter team race, the British-USA Foxhunters Hurlingham Club won the polo, and a British-Bohemian pairing secured third place in the mixed doubles lawn tennis event. Mixed international combinations also were present in the soccer, rowing, and tug-of-war events.[94]

Reflecting the spirit of Pierre Waldeck-Rousseau's radical French government, the Paris exposition organizers effectively repealed the IOC's existing prohibition on female participation.[95] Led by Britain's Charlotte Cooper—the first woman to ever become an Olympic champion after her victory in the lawn tennis singles event—twenty-two female athletes entered the Olympic arena in the golf and tennis events. With its authority usurped, the IOC's amateur code also came under severe attack. In an openly commercial ambience, the exhibition organizers instituted Olympic events for professional athletes in several sports, notably fencing, shooting, and yachting. Even the amateurs in Paris openly violated Olympic antiprofiteering regulations reinforced at the 1897 IOC Congress at Le Havre. In a number of events such as automobile racing, motorboating, and equestrianism, successful amateurs received lucrative prizes such as monetary payments, art objects of various value, goblets, and medallions.[96] Although some historians have tried to discredit the legitimacy of events in which professionals took part and cash prizes were awarded—largely by applying modern criteria and standards—all events that constituted the official program of the world exposition should be considered Olympic.[97] The professional and commercial realities of the Paris Games dismiss contemporary beliefs that the advent of professionalism in the Olympic arena was a modern phenomenon, ushered in by the retirement of IOC president Avery Brundage in 1972.

A TARNISHED IDEAL

In 1904, Coubertin's Olympic Movement took another faltering step toward dissolution as the IOC repeated its disastrous association with world fairs.[98] The Games, originally scheduled for Chicago, home of the recent Columbian Exposition, were eventually diverted to St. Louis, Missouri, after limited financial resources and vocal opposition from powerful American athletic officials scuttled Chicago's organizational efforts.[99] The choice of St. Louis, a city already in the midst of preparing a vast centennial celebration of the Louisiana Purchase, hardly provided the baron with a cosmopolitan cultural capital in which to cloak the third celebration of his Olympic festival.[100] Unenthusiastic about the prospect of a long and expensive transatlantic voyage followed by a thousand-mile train ride to what they perceived as a backward outpost in the western U.S. frontier, many European nations decided to stay away. The inconvenient schedule, once again spaced out over five months, plus a bizarre assortment of pseudoscientific anthropological days, special handicap races, as well as open competitions for juniors, novices, and high school students, plunged the St. Louis Games into chaos.[101]

Cloaked in the commercial trappings of trade and industry, the predominately all-American 1904 games further penetrated the IOC's leaky amateur code. As in Paris four years earlier, professional cyclists openly competed in official Olympic events.[102] A number of athletes, including U.S. marathon winner Thomas J. Hicks, reportedly received expensive prizes in direct violation of the IOC's amateur regulations.[103] To Coubertin's credit, he worked diligently in the years prior to the St. Louis games trying to salvage his movement's amateur credentials. In April 1902, the IOC developed a brief questionnaire that it disseminated to national sports federations across Europe and North America in an effort to establish a consensus on the amateur issue.[104] Arousing little international interest—only a small handful of federations bothered to even respond—the IOC president deferred the question of amateurism to the 1905 congress in Brussels, where again, it failed to inspire any meaningful action.[105] "The question of amateurism remains where it was," a frustrated Coubertin acknowledged. "Nobody dares to forge past the stalled and confined issue of outdated regulations and the terms of the definition are both insufficient and teasing."[106]

Floundering on the brink of obscurity, the Olympic Movement emerged from the humiliation of St. Louis fighting for its immediate survival. As the IOC battled renewed Greek efforts to establish Athens as the permanent site of all future Olympic competition, Coubertin cast the issue of amateurism to the periphery. Fearing for his dream of staging the Olympic Games in various capitals and cultural centers of the world, he accepted a brokered political compromise: two separate series of Olympic competition that would be celebrated alternately between Athens and other major international cities on a two-year rotation.[107] Although the 1906 Intermediate Games (or Intercalated Games) were heralded as an organizational success, Coubertin looked to Britain, the birthplace of his personal athletic philosophy, to restore international respectability to his tarnished movement.[108]

2 A UNIVERSAL DILEMMA

From its institutional seedbed in Britain, amateurism would become an enduring ideology that influenced the Olympic Movement for nearly a century. The early editions of Olympic competition, however, revealed that amateurism operated as an effectual regulatory ideal. Since the revival of the Olympic Movement in 1894, Coubertin and his fellow IOC patriarchs labored in vain to unify European and North American nations behind a consistent, workable definition of an amateur. As the IOC discovered, it proved difficult to draw a consensus on an issue that defied clear explanation and remained open to wide interpretation. Reflecting on his movement's earlier muddles in Athens (1896), Paris (1900), and St. Louis (1904), where—in some instances—amateurs competed against known professionals and for monetary prizes, the IOC president noted vexingly: Amateur "rules, which seem simple enough, are more complicated in their practical application by the fact that definitions of what constitutes an amateur differ from one country to another, sometimes even from one club to another."[1] Along its broad social, ethical, economic, and aesthetic dimensions, amateurism was a fluid and dynamic concept seemingly defiant of definition and firm categorization.[2] The sheer breadth and malleability of the ideology of amateurism meant that it proved to be impossible for the IOC to regulate the status of an amateur on a global scale.

Even within Britain, the progenitor of an amateur sports culture, the leading governing bodies of sports produced widely conflicting definitions of an amateur. During the first decade of the twentieth century, soccer granted amateur status to former professionals, rowing enforced its prohibitive mechanics clause that barred manual laborers from competition, and yachting allowed professional crew members to compete under amateur captaincy.[3] Some sports, such as rugby union and cricket, failed altogether to explicitly define an amateur.[4] Under the most severe interpretations, sports made no distinction between money as wages, prizes, gifts, legitimate expenses, and money for endorsements or advertising. Other British definitions included strict prohibitions against the participation of instructors, disobeying officials, engaging in unruly behavior, and competing with or against professionals.[5]

Since the British failed to even come close to a uniform agreement on what constituted an amateur, amateurism freely evolved into an organic and malleable construct. As it spread and diffused around the globe, amateurism modified and adapted itself to fit the needs of divergent national cultures and sporting practices. Although prevailing historiography has almost exclusively viewed the transmission of amateurism as being a unidirectional process enforced on foreign or indigenous peoples via British subjugation and bureaucratic dominance or even as a concept willingly embraced through cultural imitation, the diffusion of amateurism can be better understood as a broader, multidirectional, globalizing process.[6] In the age of global communications, transoceanic travel, and the establishment of worldwide agencies and sporting bureaucracies, amateurism was transformed into a by-product of "cultural interchange," a fusion of British and foreign beliefs, values, and practices.[7] The high-minded and moralizing tenets of the British amateur ethos met with diverging social, political, class, and sporting conditions to produce contrasting legislative amateur standards. By the late nineteenth and early twentieth centuries, amateurism was no longer an exclusively British construct but a multifaceted global sporting philosophy stamped with various regional and cultural nuances whose degrees of family resemblance varied widely.

With diverging interpretations and broad applications came inevitable conflict. Ironically, in the age of increasing codification and standardization in sport, in part through the gradual establishment of national and international sports federations, amateurism proved resistant to consistency and strict universal regulation. In the years prior to World War I, Coubertin and the IOC endeavored to finally resolve the contested terrain of what constituted an amateur. Their difficulties in establishing an international consensus reaffirmed that amateurism was not a monolithic, hermetically sealed ideology that nations explicitly understood, legislatively applied, and rigorously enforced.

A BRITISH OLYMPICS

The award of the 1908 Olympic Games to the city of London marked a pivotal moment in the history of the modern Olympic Movement, a chance for Coubertin to resurrect his fledging organization after its disastrous association with world fairs in Paris (1900) and St. Louis (1904) and the rival Greek Olympian spectacle in Athens (1906).[8] The IOC originally awarded the games of the Fourth Olympiad to Rome, but the eruption of Mount Vesuvius coupled with vocal governmental opposition scuttled the Eternal City's ambitions. Britain, initially a reluctant partner in the Olympic project, rushed to the IOC's late rescue. Connecting the Olympic Games with the Franco-British Exhibition, a grand industrial and cultural event held concurrently in London during the summer of 1908, the British promised to transform Coubertin's Olympic revival into a legitimate global sporting spectacle.[9]

With less than seventeen months in which to prepare, the British busily undertook Olympic preparations. They drafted a detailed program of sporting events and began construction on the vast five-thousand-ton steel, 110,000-seating capacity Shepherd's Bush stadium—the world's first purpose-built Olympic facility. With only a skeleton staff at their disposal, the British Olympic Association (BOA) wisely adopted a system of devolution, delegating the official management of each branch of the games to the corresponding English governing body of sport.[10] The British sought to standardize and rationalize further aspects of Olympic planning and preparation by lobbying the IOC to award full judging responsibilities to the host organizers. Not only did the IOC grant the British permission to enforce the rules, but they also gave them permission to write them. Under the leadership of chairman William Henry Grenfell, Lord Desborough, the BOA compiled the first comprehensive international rulebook for sport ever produced.[11] Containing rules for more than twenty forms of sport and published in three languages (English, French, and German), the BOA's codification efforts highlighted the nation's desire to avoid the organizational pitfalls of previous Olympic and commercial festivals.

In spite of British attempts to establish a universal consensus on rules, the IOC still lacked a clear-cut definition of an amateur. At the IOC Congress held in Brussels in 1905, members revived a resolution passed at the Sorbonne eleven years earlier that prohibited Olympic amateurs from competing with or against known professionals, competing for prize money, or serving as teachers or professors in their chosen specialty.[12] The IOC acknowledged that this definition was not definitive—as the Paris and St. Louis Games forcefully testified—but expressed the hope that it would assist federations in determining their own amateur standards. For the 1908 London Olympics, the IOC, in the absence of an all-encompassing regulatory definition, approved the various interpretations of an amateur upheld by Britain's leading governing bodies. "The definition of an amateur is a delicate and complicated matter," Lord Desborough explained. "A universal definition of an amateur, indeed, being at the present moment impracticable, a definition applicable to each sport has been drawn up, and fully set forth in the published regulations which deal with each of the competitions."[13]

The IOC's decision to grant full autonomy to the BOA created a quandary, as twenty-four British governing bodies published widely contrasting amateur definitions. For instance, in rowing, arguably the most socially divided of all British sports, the highly exclusive Amateur Rowing Association (ARA)—like the Amateur Motor Boat Association—enforced their prohibitive "mechanic's clause," which denied amateur status to any oarsman "who has ever been employed in or about boats or in manual labour for money or wages," and "who is or has been by trade or employment for wages a mechanic, artisan, or labourer, or engaged in any menial duty."[14] In yachting, another distinctly aristocratic pastime, the Yacht Racing Association granted permission for "professional crew members" to compete under amateur captaincy.[15] The Amateur Fencing Association, another powerful bastion of gentlemanly amateurism, outlawed its amateurs from engaging in, assisting in, or teaching "any athletic exercise as a means of pecuniary gain."[16] The Hockey Association took a more liberal stance, refusing to blacklist its instructors and coaches as professionals.[17]

In other Olympic sports the confusion deepened. The Amateur Boxing Association granted amateur status to boxers who had fought exhibitions with "professionals," while the English Football Association permitted requalified amateurs (former professionals) to compete in London.[18] The powerful governing body of football also allowed Olympic players to receive expenses to defray the cost of housing and transportation, a policy strictly prohibited by the Amateur Athletic Association (AAA).[19] The AAA, stubborn in its opposition toward standard expenses, oddly allowed its amateurs to compete with or against "professional" rugby, football, and cricket players in competitive club or cup competitions—the amateur fencing, golf, horse racing, swimming, and wrestling associations made a similar concession.[20] The complexities and peculiarities of British amateurism ensured that for the purposes of the London Olympics an "Olympic amateur" was not a homogeneous term. As a testament to the gradual and piecemeal development of the early Olympic Movement, an amateur in one Olympic sport could be considered a professional in another.

The IOC's system of amateur regulation contributed to the growing quandary. In a move to strengthen the bond between citizenship and Olympic qualification, the 1907 IOC Congress at The Hague granted national Olympic committees—often via their affiliate federations—sole authority to verify amateur statuses and disqualify amateur violators for their own representative competitors. In the case of the 1908 London Olympics, the BOA requested that national Olympic committees provide guarantees that their respective athletes met the prevailing British amateur standards. Even for the most scrupulous and law-abiding federations, complying would have proved a logistical headache, especially since their own amateur codes often did not align with the more rigorous and socially prohibitive British definitions. The Union Belge des Sociétés de Sports Athlétiques, which had long provided compensation for daily travel and lodging expenses, could hardly verify that Belgian track and field athletes were amateurs in accordance with English AAA policy. Similarly, the Fédération Française des Sociétés d'Aviron could not suddenly conform to antiquated English ideals and bar French amateur oarsmen on the grounds of low social rank.[21] In light of such contrasting international standards, it would be naïve to suggest that only pure amateurs according to the British tradition competed at the 1908 Olympic Games.

"FOR KING AND COUNTRY"

The IOC's decision to empower national Olympic committees as the gate-keepers of Olympic amateurism would prove ill-advised. Though celebrated as a universal code of fairness and equality, national Olympic committees often crafted, manipulated, and abused amateurism in the interest of national expediency. The gradual fulfillment of Coubertin's dream of Olympic universality in the years prior to World War I elevated the nationalistic importance attached to sporting success. The Olympic Games, like all international sporting events between nation-states, served as a means of measuring national vigor and gaining international prestige. Victory in Olympic competition was deemed a testament to the strength and vitality of a nation, while failure was considered symptomatic of national decadence and decline.[22] Coubertin's inspired motto, "The most important thing . . . is not to win but to take part," failed to truly resonate with national Olympic committees and governments navigating the expanding propaganda possibilities and pitfalls of Olympic participation. Amateurism, supposedly a hymn to equality, morality, and character development, had connected itself to the contradictory project of nation building. Lies, deceit, and the violation of Olympic amateur rules and regulations ensued. The expectation that participating nations could remain immune to the forces of nationalism and genuinely uphold the strictest amateur standards began to prove overwhelmingly myopic.

The case of Canadian marathoner Tom Longboat illustrated the tension that existed between honest regulation and an insatiable thirst for Olympic victory. Longboat, a member of the Onondaga tribe from Ontario, stood as the world's premier amateur long-distance runner.[23] Success and international recognition inevitably brought question marks about his amateur status. After a ten-mile exhibition race in Boston in the build-up to the London Olympics, the U.S. AAU declared Longboat a professional for allegedly padding his expense accounts. James E. Sullivan, president of the U.S. AAU, promptly notified the BOA of Longboat's disqualification in a move to bar the gold-medal favorite from competing in London.[24] The prospect that Longboat would be unable to don the Maple Leaf and represent Canada in its first official Olympic involvement aroused widespread national outrage. James G. Merrick, chairman of the Canadian AAU, took to the pages of the *Montreal Daily Star* to vigorously denounce U.S. charges as being politically motivated. Merrick accused Sullivan and the AAU of subterfuge, a deliberate plot to prevent the gold-medal favorite from clinching the laurels of victory in the marathon. Longboat's "removal would open up for United States' runners a chance for a much cherished victory in the chief Olympic event," he blustered.[25]

U.S. ambitions received a considerable boost when vocal support for Longboat's disqualification came from the Amateur Athletic Federation of Canada, a Montreal-based breakaway group that had long vied with the Canadian AAU for control of Canadian athletics.[26] With the nation's two amateur athletic bodies bitterly divided over Longboat's Olympic participation, the newly established Canadian Olympic Committee (COC) was forced to take decisive action. After an internal investigation that allegedly revealed no conclusive evidence of wrongdoing, the COC officially verified Longboat's amateur credentials.[27] In accordance with new IOC policy, the British organizers willing accepted the COC's certification, a decision that prompted one bemused U.S. official to question Britain's "much-talked of desire to have purity in athletics."[28]

Whether Longboat violated amateur guidelines or was merely a pawn in a broader bureaucratic or nationalistic battle is uncertain; either way, Canadian Olympic officials faced overwhelming pressure to ensure their nation's leading athlete could compete for gold. Because other nations would inevitably face similar temptations, the IOC's system of amateur enforcement left the fox guarding the henhouse. As Swedish IOC member Sigfrid Edström later warned, "National authorities are so anxious to have efficient athletes take part in the Olympic Games, that they verify the amateur status of an athlete even if his amateur status could be earnestly questioned."[29] Without a definitive amateur policy, nor its own independent body to verify and scrutinize amateur statuses (the IOC's Amateur Eligibility Commission was not established until 1971), the IOC rendered itself effectively powerless against amateur encroachments.

As Western nations awoke to the propaganda utility of Olympic competition, Olympic arenas, stadiums, and pools inevitably became sites for fierce nationalistic struggles. The 1908 Olympic Games in London, the largest, most representative, and most successful Olympics up to that time, illustrated the political realities of modern sport as host nation Great Britain and its transatlantic cousin the United States engaged in a desperate battle for Olympic mastery.[30] Coubertin's dream of promoting international goodwill through Olympic competition faded into sodden London skies as U.S. officials launched a cascade of protests against the British organizers, with complaints ranging from the system of drawing heats, illegal coaching by British officials, and the use of illegal spiked footwear by British athletes in a tug-of-war quarterfinal. The controversial British decision to disqualify U.S. competitor John C. Carpenter in the 400-meter final, for allegedly impeding the advances of Britain's Lieutenant Wyndham Halswelle, along with the dramatic conclusion to the marathon event, which witnessed the exhausted Italian runner Dorando Pietri being assisted across the finish line by British officials, soured sporting relations for decades to come.[31] Like most serious points of contention in broader Anglo-American relations from slavery to imperialism, both sides accused each other of grotesque hypocrisy. U.S. charges of biased British officiating were met by the British insistence that U.S. athletes were scheming professionals who embraced the maxim "win, tie, or wrangle" in their pursuit of Olympic glory.[32]

Much of the nationalistic squabbling in London stemmed from radically different interpretations of how to "play the game." Unlike the British, who generally displayed intransigence toward modern techniques and athletic training, the Americans took a businesslike, scientific approach to amateur sport.[33] In the highly structured and competitive U.S. collegiate environment, professional coaches actively recruited talented athletes, rewarding their sporting performances by financing (to various degrees) their studies and cost of living. Emboldened by a win-at-all-cost mentality, U.S. universities established and promoted a comprehensive scientific basis for improving sporting performance. Albert G. Spalding's extensive *Library of American Sports* provided coaches with up-to-date information on innovative training methods and techniques.[34] Efficiency, specialization, organization, precision, and strategy—the U.S. apostle of scientific management Frederick Winslow

Taylor's watchwords for producing thriving U.S. industries—were embraced as the guiding principles of U.S. amateur sport.[35] U.S. coaches were world leaders, preaching the habits of drill and discipline while exploring the natural laws that governed athletic performance. To the deep and longstanding criticism of British observers, shamateurism prevailed on U.S. university campuses in the form of monetary prizes, neglect of academic studies, training tables, and payments to private tutors. From a legalistic perspective, U.S. athletes were Olympic amateurs, but they did not "play the game" as the British understood it.[36]

As the furor surrounding the 1908 Olympic Games testified, amateurism resisted definition; there was no single characteristic common to all cases of amateurism, no unifying thread or clear bright line that linked all definitions or interpretations. For the London *Sporting Life*, this "unquestionably chaotic position" necessitated a "universal definition" to govern all future Olympic sports. "The uninitiated would doubtless presume that in the [Olympic] games an indisputable amateur definition was laid down, and no entry accepted from athlete who did not conform to that definition. But such is not the case," the popular British sporting daily opined. Reacting to the fallout from the London Games, *Sporting Life* invited contributors from all over the globe to offer their thoughts toward the feasibility of crafting a singular amateur definition aimed at preserving the sanctity of Olympic sport.[37]

THE AMATEUR MUDDLE

In the months after the 1908 Olympic Games a marathon craze swept throughout Europe and North America. Fueled by the highly dramatic conclusion of the marathon event in London, avaricious sports promoters attempted to propel foot racing into a commercial ambience. Lured by the offer of huge race purses, Italian Dorando Pietri, American Johnny Hayes (the eventual Olympic gold-medalist), and other leading marathoners such as the controversial Canadian Tom Longboat switched from the amateur to the professional ranks—marking the first attempt made by early-twentieth-century Olympians to transfer their athletic fame into monetary rewards.[38] The migration of some of the world's most prominent amateur athletes into the lucrative professional racing circuit symbolized the commercial impulses sweeping modern sport in the years prior to World War I.

As professional leagues and commercial ventures flourished across Europe and North America, *Sporting Life* took up the task of placing amateurism back upon the pedestal from which it had allegedly fallen. *Sporting Life*—Britain's oldest and most prestigious sports newspaper (after absorbing *Bell's Life in London and Sporting Chronicle*)—offered coverage of amateur sporting contests throughout the British Isles. The popular British daily had been a keen Olympic chronicler, dedicating considerable space to the 1908 Olympic Games, including a flurry of negative media reports condemning the presence of foreign (notably American) professionals competing in London. "The existence of so many sham-amateurs among Olympic athletes," as well as the decision by marathoners Dorando, Hayes, and Longboat to "gain every possible pecuniary advantage from their exalted position as champion athletes," infuriated *Sporting Life*.[39] Amateurism needed to be governed and enforced to ward off professional and commercial encroachments. The solution, *Sporting Life* hypothesized, was a universal amateur standard—clearly defined, explicitly understood, and rigidly enforced by all national and international sports federations. It proposed a full-scale effort, with the help of the general public and sporting administrators, to collect and distil the various amateur interpretations down to one single definition.

During the coming months *Sporting Life*'s proposition generated an enormous volume of correspondence from across the globe. A highly polarizing discourse ensued. BOA official Theodore Andrea Cook best articulated the primary strain of opposition against the ambitious project. Citing the insoluble nature of British amateurism, he argued that "each individual sport already finds it difficult enough to legislate for its own amateurs, and can only just face the task of legislating for amateurs who play the same sport in different countries."[40] The former Oxford rowing Blue (as athletes who represented Oxford and Cambridge universities were called) pointed to the example of soccer, a game controlled in England by two competing governing bodies who proclaimed opposing amateur codes—a similar bureaucratic bifurcation characterized English rowing.[41] The Amateur Football Association (AFA), a small group of disaffected London suburban and Old Boys' clubs, seceded from the Football Association (FA) in 1907 in opposition to the perceived evils of professionalism afflicting the national game. Though its working definition of amateurism avoided specific reference to excluded trade and social groups, only clubs of approved class standing were welcomed within the AFA's ranks—a far cry from its more democratic rival, the FA.[42] If one sport in one country could not come to a consensus on amateurism, a pessimistic Cook reasoned, you cannot expect the entire sporting world to unite behind "one cast iron definition which shall govern every form of sport."[43]

A phalanx of leading British amateur sporting personalities poured further scorn on *Sporting Life*'s codification initiative, but for an entirely different reason. The technical feasibility of a universal amateur standard paled in significance to the broader class ramifications. The adoption of a comprehensive amateur definition would erode (or make obsolete) the gentleman amateur distinction that had traditionally governed some British sports. The old guard amateur institutions such as the ARA and the AAA would have to embrace a more inclusive and democratic ethos. Already sidelined by the advance of professionalism and retreating before the subsequent transformation of sport into a form of commercial mass entertainment, the prospect of further populist reforms sparked a chorus of patrician and upper-middle-class condemnation. Walter Rye, a famous athlete from the 1860s and founder of the Thames Hare and Hounds running club, pontificated: "In my opinion there are, and always must be, two classes of amateurs, the division being a social one." Rye pointed to "the indiscriminate mixture" in sports such as soccer, rugby union, golf, and tennis as proof that "men who are 'gentlemen of position or education' (to use the old formula) should not mix with the rougher and uneducated lot, or have them in their clubs."[44] Rye's class bias found a sympathetic audience across the Atlantic in the form of U.S. football guru Walter Camp. The prominent Yale football coach expressed an attitude befitting an Ivy League elite when he discredited *Sporting Life*'s scheme on the grounds that "men should compete with their own class."[45]

The prospective passage of a universal (and inadvertently, democratic) amateur code coincided with broader challenges to patrician hegemony in Edwardian Britain. For landed gentlemen and the gentrified upper middle class, the early decades of the twentieth century proved to be a period of remarkable change and uncertainty. The rise of the urban masses, aligned with the growing tide of liberal radicalism and democratization, and the assault on the propertied order—as exemplified through the passage of the Parliament Act—triggered a grave sense of crisis and impending disaster among members of the British elite. Extensive land and social reform, collectivism, the growth of governmental bureaucracy, free trade, taxation on personal wealth, antilandlordism, and the founding of the Labour Party made the ruling classes even more fearful for the future.[46] It is in the backdrop of elevated class tensions that British opposition toward a universal amateur sporting definition should be situated. Mindful of the perilous dynamics of the British social order, Frantz Reichel, vice president and acting secretary of the Union des Sociétés Françaises de Sports Athlétiques (USFSA), mused that the "one cause of delay in arriving at a solution is the particular attitude of England." Unlike in his native France, where the demarcation between amateurism and professionalism was drawn across pecuniary rather than occupational lines, Reichel observed that in England "there are different kinds of amateurs—notably the gentleman amateur who will not row against a man earning his living by the use of his hands."[47] The layered and complex social nature of British sport significantly undermined *Sporting Life*'s codification efforts.

With seemingly little international support, *Sporting Life* went on the offensive, publishing a long, perplexing litany of amateur definitions currently in use throughout the sporting world. Its extensive collation of international codes illustrated that amateurism was a cross-cultural construct, transforming itself within and across national boundaries. *Sporting Life* revealed that in France, the USFSA permitted teachers and paid instructors to compete in amateur competitions outside their chosen specialty. In Australia and New Zealand, the Amateur Athletic Union of Australasia allowed its amateurs to "compete with or against professionals in any game for which no prize money is offered." The Dansk Idraets-Forbund, a broad federation of 384 Danish amateur sports clubs, approved of its amateur sailors, horse riders, and marksmen competing openly for monetary prizes, but it imposed strict ethical rules prohibiting amateurs from engaging in disorderly behavior, incurring personal debts, and boasting a "bad reputation."[48] North of the Jutland peninsula, the Swedish Football Association commissioned the payment of generous daily travel and housing allowances. Across the Atlantic, the National Collegiate Athletic Association took a far more draconian approach, outlawing every single one of these foreign practices.[49] The sheer diversity and lack of international agreement on what constituted an amateur emboldened the London sporting newspaper in its pursuit of crafting an Olympic amateur definition.

"WHAT IS AN AMATEUR?"

As a result of the broad and malleable nature of amateurism, the task of establishing a standard for all Olympic sports appeared insurmountable. Disheartened but not defeated, *Sporting Life* turned over its voluminous report to the IOC for further consideration, urging Coubertin to treat "the matter as being one of the greatest importance to the thousands of amateur athletes whose ambition it is to crown their athletic careers with Olympic laurels."[50] Coubertin found the Anglophone fascination with strict amateur legislation "childish." He wondered, "Why disqualify an amateur athlete because he had competed with a professional, because he had taken part in events open to all comers, or because he was a sports instructor."[51] Ever the shrewd tactician, the IOC president veiled his personal apathy by assuring *Sporting Life*'s readership that since "the present regulations are unjust, and cannot be properly enforced [an] inquiry is exactly what is needed to make the position of the question understood by everyone."[52] He forwarded *Sporting Life*'s findings, compiled in a one-hundred-fifty-file document, to his cousin, Baron Albert Bertier de Sauvigny, a respected French representative to the IOC.

After examining *Sporting Life*'s comprehensive report, Sauvigny addressed the amateur issue at the 1909 IOC session in Berlin.[53] For him, the whole amateur question proved particularly vexing, especially in regard to the widespread disparity that existed on the issue. With a view toward establishing definitively what an amateur is, the Frenchman formulated a survey predicated on the "four main elements of the problem": travel reimbursements, contact with professionals, instructors competing as amateurs, and the recovery of one's amateur status. After much heated debate, the IOC approved a watered-down, five-question version of Sauvigny's original survey:

1. Are you of the opinion that a man cannot be an amateur in one sport and a professional in another?
2. Are you of the opinion that a professor can compete as an amateur in sports other than those he teaches?
3. Are you of the opinion that when an amateur becomes a professional he cannot recover his amateur status? Do you allow any exceptions to this rule? What are they?
4. Do you allow amateurs to receive their traveling and hotel expenses? Up to what limit?
5. Are you agreed that a man loses his title to amateur by simply competing against a professional?[54]

The IOC commissioned the creation of a three-man committee, composed of Britain's Theodore Andrea Cook, American William Milligan Sloane, and Hungarian Jules de Musza, to oversee the distribution of questionnaires to national federations in Europe, the British Empire, and the North American continent. The survey marked the IOC's first significant attempt, since the 1894 congress at the Sorbonne, at addressing the problem of amateur regulation.

Optimism quickly turned to disillusionment as IOC chiefs were forcibly reminded of the puzzling, incongruent, and volatile nature of amateurism. Circulated to national sports federations across the sporting world, the IOC's amateur survey aroused little international interest or support; only eleven federations from eight, predominantly European, nations responded to the questionnaire.[55] Whether as a result of Theodore Andrea Cook's previous outspoken opposition to the project, a broader national apathy toward the Olympic Movement, or perhaps an unwillingness to align their regulatory policies with those of foreign nations, not one federation from Britain and its dominions answered the IOC's amateur survey.[56] It appeared that even the British had long accepted that amateurism was a subjective term, relative to each nation, region, and more specifically, each sport.

Of those who did respond, a disgruntled Coubertin inveighed, "the answers were widely contradictory. Neither in the same country from one sport to another, nor in countries for the same sport, did there seem to be even the slightest agreement."[57] On the issue of whether an athlete can be an amateur in one sport and a professional in another, only the Nederlandsch Gymnastiek, the Fédération Belge de Gymnastique, and two unnamed U.S. sport associations answered in the affirmative. Greater divisions emerged over one of the most contested issues in international amateur sport: the role of paid sports instructors, or as they were more commonly known on the European continent, professors. As a testament to the long European tradition of paid amateur ski, gymnastic, and fencing instruction, the Nederlandsch Gymnastiek, the Fédération Belge de Gymnastique, and a broad collation of Norwegian federations—excepting tennis—supported the idea that a professor can compete as an amateur in sports other than those he teaches. The Association Suisse de Football, the Sports-Club d'Alexandrie (Egypt), and the Società Podistica Lazio (Italy) expressed an equally supportive position.[58]

The requalification of former professionals aroused similar international disparity, underlining Coubertin's protestation that the IOC's survey generated "mere statements; no reasons. Pure fantasy; nothing concrete."[59] The Federazione Atletica Italiana, the Nederlandsch Amateur-Schermbond, and the Dansk Idraets-Forbund were among those that agreed that "contaminated" athletes could recover their amateur licenses after an approved waiting period; predictably, federations failed to agree on the specific length of the waiting period.[60] Nations displayed a greater degree of consensus in supporting the payment of standard travel and housing expenses to amateur athletes but stood divided over the daily amount awarded and the mechanism for distributing remunerations. The Egyptian Sports-Club d'Alexandrie proposed daily allowances of 10 francs when competing in Europe, Asia, and Africa and 15 francs for distant transatlantic competitions in North America.[61] The Norwegian federations advocated a more liberal amount covering travel and housing costs, as well as meals and incidentals.[62] The Federazione Atletica Italiana, like its compatriot the Società Podistica Lazio, took a hard-line approach, regulating that reimbursements must be covered only when "strictly necessary" and never "paid directly to the athletes."[63]

If the IOC needed any further proof that nations failed to agree on the fundamental ingredients of amateurism, then the issue of contact between amateur and professional athletes would provide it. Contests between the two categories of athletes had long been at the heart of British sport. In English county cricket, gentlemen amateurs openly competed with and against professional players. In a host of other British sports, such as track and field, golf, and swimming, amateurs were free to compete against professionals from other sport backgrounds. Amateurism exponents were quick to dismiss such practices as a corrupting influence that would lead amateurs down the path toward full-blown professionalism. The Fédération Suisse de Notation, the Società Podistica Lazio, and the Norwegian federations agreed, disavowing all contact between amateurs and professionals.[64] The remaining federations adopted a more populist position but stood significantly apart over the exact nature of the contact. The Association Suisse de Football overlooked spontaneous meetings between amateurs and professionals, but clamped down against contests set up in advance and undertaken for the pleasure of a "paying audience."[65] The Sports-Club d'Alexandrie drew a clear pecuniary distinction, disqualifying amateur athletes who competed against professionals for monetary reward.[66] The Federazione Atletica Italiana and the Dansk Idraets-Forbund allowed amateur–professional contests on the condition that athletes receive prior bureaucratic approval.[67]

The IOC's amateur survey offered conclusive proof that amateurism was a vibrant, variegated term possessing chameleonlike qualities. From British origins, amateurism appeared to have been lost in translation. But what exactly were foreign nations translating? After all, British amateurism was conceived as a vague compilation of attitudes, ideas, and beliefs; it was a legitimating ideology that excluded the lower social orders from the play of the leisure class, as well as a broad moral and aesthetic philosophy expressing how one should "play the game." Within sports and between sporting organizations, however, not even the British could produce a regulatory definition of an amateur. The British failure to clearly define an amateur, as well as account for numerous legislative technicalities and changing sporting circumstances, ensured that the notion evolved without restraint across national boundaries. With no consensus or central authority to provide a definitive blueprint for defining an amateur, nations with no history of regulating sports were free to create definitions as they saw fit. As the IOC discovered, by the beginning of the twentieth century the consequences were staggering: amateurism—never monolithic—was now undefinable, contradictory, and glaringly polarizing; its plasticity allowed nations to freely mold definitions of an amateur to fit the needs of their respective sporting and political cultures. At the 1910 IOC session in Luxembourg, British representative Theodore Andrea Cook conceded as much, revealing that "a universal definition of all sports is today impossible." He concluded that "at this time it is impossible that all associations agree to a simple formula that would define the status of amateur in a way accepted by all."[68]

The IOC's failure to craft a universal amateur standard for all Olympic sports stemmed in part from the Olympic Movement's legislative weaknesses. Unlike the powerful IOC of the twenty-first century, Coubertin's fledging movement still lacked any real authority in the world of international sport. Rival Greek Olympian spectacles and the disastrous association with world fairs in Paris and St. Louis had left the IOC in a less than favorable position. The baron also faced successive U.S. coup attempts, dating as far back as their support for a permanent Greek Olympic Games in 1896, to wrest control of the IOC from his clutches.[69] As the IOC battled for legitimacy, and even for its continued existence, it had no choice but to respect the bureaucratic autonomy of better-established, and in some cases more powerful, national federations. The survival of the IOC hinged on the continuing support of the federations. Without the quadrennial appearance of British soccer players, U.S. track and field athletes, and French swordsmen, the Olympic Games would prove short-lived, an ephemeral blur in the increasingly crowded sporting landscape. Cook acknowledged the IOC's limited bureaucratic reach: "Trying to fix [an amateur code] with too many facts and with too much rigidity in order to unify could offend federations," he reasoned, "so we can only offer advice and support, but we cannot impose our rules or orders."[70] The IOC's fundamental dependency on national federations helps explain its longstanding failure to craft and regulate a definitive amateur policy.

The emergence and consolidation of international sports federations further complicated this delicate bureaucratic power dynamic. As modern sports diffused steadily throughout the globe, stimulated by developments in transcontinental travel and communication, international federations were established to standardize patterns of play. The French, frustrated by Britain's insular sporting attitude and bureaucratic arrogance, took the lead in the setting up of international federations. Fourteen international bodies, including the Union Cycliste Internationale (1900) and the Fédération Internationale de Football Association (1904), were established in the years prior to World War I.[71] At first these organizations possessed scarce financial resources and wielded little bureaucratic authority. Foundering on the brink of obscurity at the outset, international bodies worked diligently to align national federations under one organizational umbrella. In the case of swimming, eight national federations met in Paris in the aftermath of the 1908 London Olympics to establish the Fédération Internationale de Natation (FINA).[72] The gradual transformation of international sports federations into powerful institutions, imposing their own rules and regulations, steered them inevitably onto a collision course with the Olympic Movement.

A complex bureaucratic web had emerged in which the IOC occupied an increasingly marginalized position. Not only did Coubertin have to navigate the treacherous political terrain with the national federations, but now also had to contend with their more powerful international parent bodies. Burgeoning international sports federations sought increased control in determining both the technical rules of the Olympic Games as well as the program of Olympic events. FINA, the newly established international swimming federation, was quick to flex its bureaucratic muscle by threatening to boycott the 1912 Stockholm Games unless the IOC recognized its own distinct rules and amateur regulations.[73] Coubertin held the weakest hand in this relationship. Refusing to recognize the international sports federations' heightened authority would likely result in a widespread Olympic withdrawal and the cancelation of principal Olympic events—a devastating scenario from which his flagging games would likely not recover. This unfavorable power dynamic stifled the IOC's attempts to establish a universal amateur standard. It would not be until the 1930s, after the transformation of the Olympic Games into a global sporting mega-event, that the IOC could attain a stronger footing in this interorganizational power struggle.[74]

For Coubertin, the IOC's failure in unifying the growing nexus of international and national federations behind a standardized amateur definition proved the last straw. "From that moment on I lost even the little interest I had had in the question of amateurism," he later admitted. The IOC president returned to an earlier proposal: an oath to be sworn by athletes as a remedy against the lies and hypocrisy of shamateurism. "An oath, not a mere public formality for show, but detailed and signed," he hypothesized, "is the only way of being sure about a man's sporting past."[75] Like the ideology of amateurism itself, the oath allowed athletes to agree to an ideal without committing to specifics. It was both high-minded and practical while also being ambiguous and without real force. Within the leadership ranks of the IOC, Coubertin's proposition was considered idealistic. The Reverend Robert Stuart de Courcy Laffan, the long-serving secretary of the BOA and one of the baron's closest confidants, strongly dismissed the idea. An "amateur oath," he counseled, "will certainly be received with disfavor and will create the impression that we are a body out of touch with the views and feelings of the athletic world."[76]

Although roundly denounced and dismissed, Coubertin's advocacy of a sworn oath appeared the only alternative solution—aside from the complete abrogation of amateur legislation altogether—to a vexing conundrum. Without a uniform standard for all Olympic sports, he believed that amateurism was simply impossible to govern. It was a zero-sum situation. Either employ an enforceable, universal amateur definition or simply entrust the athletes to regulate themselves; anything in between, the IOC president cautioned, would simply continue to expose the Olympic Movement to inconsistency, hypocrisy, ridicule, and strife. As the IOC turned its attention toward the 1912 Olympic Games, scheduled for the Swedish capital, Stockholm, Coubertin's insights would ring prophetic.

THE BIRTH OF THE SHAMATEUR

As a conclusive, or at least coherent, definition of an amateur remained in abeyance for future discussion, the 1912 Stockholm Games elevated the Olympic Movement to a position of respectability and prominence. Although celebrated globally as an organizational success, the Stockholm Games further underlined the hypocritical and exclusionary nature of Olympic amateur policy. Despite the Olympic Movement's self-professed moral overtones, the IOC—along with its affiliated network of national Olympic committees and federations—often employed amateurism as a self-serving bureaucratic reflex. The Stockholm Games proved that the British were not the pristine purveyors of amateurism that they sanctimoniously claimed. In a special plenary meeting of the BOA after the 1912 Olympics, J. M. Andrew, president of the London Polytechnic Harriers (an affiliate of the English AAA) revealed that his club openly awarded "broken-time" payments—monetary compensation to help defray the costs of time way from the workplace—to his athletes competing for Britain in Stockholm. "Some of the men were mechanics working by the hour," Andrews recounted, "so I did not mind breaking some of the rules [by ensuring] that each of the Polytechnic men who went to Stockholm received what was equivalent to his wages." The British response to such a blatant transgression of the IOC's antiprofiteering amateur rules was now suddenly muted. In fact, BOA officials voted to forget the matter entirely.[77] Wherever amateurism reigned, hypocrisy hovered nearby.

Authoritative power rested overwhelmingly on the side of the IOC and its affiliated federations: They possessed the ability to both turn a blind eye to (and often even encourage) shamateur practices in the pursuit of Olympic laurels and selectively punish athletes for transgressing their blurred amateur standards. The federations, it seemed, turned their enforcement of amateurism on and off like a tap. Throughout the early twentieth century, amateur athletes were forced to navigate this inconsistent regulatory terrain, at times receiving payment and then being investigated for taking payment by the same individuals. They were rendered powerless, subservient to the will and authority of the bureaucrats who oversaw their Olympic participation.

The infamous case of decathlon and pentathlon Olympic gold medalist Jim Thorpe (in his native language, Wa-tho-huck, 'Bright Path') struck at the very heart of the inconsistent and hypocritical nature of amateurism. The superlative Thorpe, an Oklahoma native, was stripped of his amateur status and subsequently forced to return the Olympic gold medals that he won in Stockholm for violating the IOC's amateur regulations. His crime: playing in a professional baseball league in North Carolina during his summer vacation away from the Carlisle Indian School in Pennsylvania.[78] American AAU president James E. Sullivan, the power broker of U.S. amateur athletics and a man who earned a small fortune peddling A. G. Spalding sporting goods, personally oversaw the handling of Thorpe's disqualification. Sullivan was a highly polarizing figure within Olympic circles, revered by some for his many contributions to U.S. athletics, but in most cases disliked for his unrefined and brash manner. Sullivan's relationship with Coubertin was tumultuous at best, evidenced by the baron's refusal to award him a coveted membership to the IOC.[79] The Thorpe case offered Sullivan a reprieve, a chance to restore his reputation and counter longstanding allegations that the AAU openly sponsored professionalism. Sullivan promised to leave no stone unturned in investigating the allegations. "If [Thorpe] is found to have broken the rules, as stated, he will be stripped of all of his records; his name will be taken from athletic annuals, and he will be compelled to return all the prizes he has won since his infraction," he warned.[80] Sullivan, the chief architect of the 1904 St. Louis Games, which included openly professional events for cyclists, positioned himself as the champion of Olympic amateurism. The irony was stark.

The complete and thorough investigation that Sullivan promised took all of one day. There was no trial, no investigation, and no hearing. Thorpe had no money, no lawyer, and no opportunity to mount a defense. The AAU, in unison with Thorpe's mentor and varsity football coach, Glenn "Pop" Warner, waxed pious, insisting that they had no knowledge of his professional ventures. Eager to resolve themselves of any allegations of wrongdoing, Sullivan and Warner coerced Thorpe into writing a full, or rather scripted, confession. "I was not very wise to the ways of the world and did not realize that this was wrong, and it would make me a professional in track sports," he pleaded somberly.[81] The AAU committee overseeing the case issued an immediate letter to the Swedish Olympic Organizing Committee, advising that Thorpe "is deserving of the severest condemnation for concealing the fact that he had professionalized himself by receiving money for playing baseball." Illuminating the racist overtones enveloping the case, the AAU rationalized Thorpe's actions "on the grounds of ignorance." "Mr. Thorpe is an Indian of limited education in the ways of other than his own people," AAU officials proclaimed.[82] An illiterate, nonwhite, non-Christian native was an easier target for disqualification than the untold number of U.S. Olympic athletes, such as the Irish Whales Martin Sheridan and John Flanagan who found well-paid nominal employment and received under-the-table appearance fees and prize money.[83]

Two observations are particularly pertinent in the AAU's pursuit of Thorpe's disqualification. The Olympic Movement had no firm, hermetically sealed definition of amateurism; at the 1912 Stockholm Games the IOC again recognized the contradictory amateur rules of the host nation's governing bodies.[84] In shooting, yachting, and gymnastics, Thorpe's pecuniary gain from his sporting exploits would have been tolerated. What is more alarming, the statute of limitations (30 days after the award of his medals) for the claim made against his eligibility had lapsed—the announcement of Thorpe's professional baseball career occurred in January 1913, almost six months after the conclusion of the Olympic Games. In accordance with General Rule 13, Thorpe's disqualification was completely unwarranted. The IOC, oblivious to its own amateur rules, and indifferent to mounting international public opinion, decided unanimously to revise the results of the pentathlon and decathlon, expunge Thorpe's records, and award the gold medals to Norway's F. R. Bie and Sweden's Hugo Wieslander during its 1913 annual session in Lausanne, Switzerland. Jim Thorpe earned the unenviable title of being the first athlete charged, convicted, and punished for violating the IOC's amateur regulations. The blade of amateurism had finally come down—illegally, inconsistently, and punitively.

The collective bureaucratic mishandling of the Jim Thorpe case served as a considerable source of embarrassment for Coubertin. The IOC president sympathized with Thorpe and took his disqualification as a call to action. "There is a pressing need to revise the regulations on amateurism," he argued. The existing rules "have become a network of weak links, and for some time now it has allowed professionals to be called amateurs, while holding back sportsmen whose amateur status is quite clear, labelling them professionals."[85] Writing on the pages of *Révue Olympique,* Coubertin revisited the idea of implementing an amateur oath, citing the Thorpe case as an example of its potential utility. If Thorpe "had been called upon to swear on his country's flag that he had never committed any infraction of the regulations of amateurism," he pondered, "would he run the risk of swearing a false oath?"[86] Coubertin also proposed the creation of an international amateur license, to be "granted by a single, independent, and permanent tribunal."[87] Although attractive in theory, this concept would prove bureaucratically impossible amid the jurisdictional power wrangling that existed amongst sports federations. Coubertin grew frustrated, even desperate. The persistent interorganizational squabbling over amateur definitions, as well as the chorus of global condemnation directed at the IOC for its disqualification of Thorpe, had driven him to the breaking point. As the Olympic Movement headed to Berlin, the selected scene of the 1916 Olympic Games, he raised the notion of an "each to their own method" of amateur regulation; a drastic measure that he explained would permit "any amateur presented as such by his fellow citizen" entrance to the Olympics.[88]

Exhausted by the bureaucratic struggle, Coubertin and his Olympic Movement eventually agreed to relinquish the IOC from all regulatory responsibility on the amateur issue. At the 1914 Olympic Congress in Paris, IOC members voted to empower the international federations and, in their absence, the national federations, with the task of governing amateur eligibility sport by sport.[89] This decision, although strengthening the federations' claims to overseeing all technical aspects of the games, ensured that a patchwork of often widely conflicting definitions of an Olympic amateur would prevail. Under Coubertin's leadership, the IOC was clearly not an organization devoted to upholding the strict precepts of British amateurism.

"POLITICAL PATRIOTISM"

The gradual transformation of the Olympics from a mere athletic sideshow into a legitimate sporting spectacle heightened the political dimensions of Olympic competition in the years prior to World War I. In the absence of a World Cup tournament in soccer—an initiative not introduced until 1930— and similar major global sporting events, the most powerful nations turned to the Olympic arena as an ideal platform for trumpeting national vitality. The transcendent power and universal appeal of international Olympic competition enticed political leaders to use the Olympics to project a positive image of their nations to an increasingly global audience.

The United States, more than any other nation, embraced the Olympic stage as a medium for constructing, propagating, and maintaining images of national prowess. Aiming to defend their Olympic track-and-field crown, U.S. Olympic officials launched a scheme to raise U.S.$150,000 to cover the costs of training and preparing a team for Berlin.[90] Convinced of the role that cultural propaganda, and in particular sport, could play in the pursuit of national interests, the German government appropriated 300,000 Deutschmarks ($73,000) from the imperial treasury to train athletes for the first Olympics to be held on their home soil.[91] The czar of Russia also recognized the nationalistic importance of the games, issuing an imperial edict creating a ministry of sport charged with preparing athletes for Berlin.[92] The French

National Committee of Sports lobbied their parliament for 400,000 francs
($78,000) and also received an additional $100,000 donation from Basil
Zaharoff, a Greek arms trader and proprietor of the popular French daily
newspaper *Excelsior*.[93] Even the British, for all of the nation's pretentions
to "sport for sport's sake," were preparing themselves for a titanic sporting
confrontation in the German capital by proposing to revolutionize British
amateur sport. In the backdrop of escalating Anglo-German antagonism,
British Olympic chiefs launched a staggering £100,000 (some $11.5 million
in current values) appeal for public subscriptions in order to underwrite
the cost of an ambitious policy of Olympic reform. The proposed scheme
included professional coaching, state-of-the-art training facilities, and the
creation of a British imperial squad, unifying King Edward VII's subjects into
one representative Olympic team.[94] The rising competiveness of international
sport leading up to World War I illuminates the increasing manner in which
the Olympic Games had become a matter of prestige among nations, a viable
propaganda medium, and a useful barometer of national vitality.

Although the *Olympic Charter* proclaimed that the Olympic Games are
contests between individuals, not nations, the IOC created an institutional
structure based on national representation, a decision that opened the door
to frequent displays of nationalism and political aggrandizement. Coubertin's
call for peaceful "internationalism" was lost amid nations appropriating the
Olympics for political and ideological ends and as a way to promote national identities. The Olympics celebrated the primacy of the nation-state.
Symbols, credentials, and protocol were highly charged, with athletes seen
as nationalist proxies—tangible representations of their "imagined communities."[95] Early IOC policy even encouraged this tendency by charting
national performances in medals (up to 1921). The games provided a viable
platform for inculcating national feelings and fostering an oppositional "us"
against "them" mentality. National anthems, colors, and flags were displayed
as cultural artifacts to reinforce similarities and accentuate differences. The
infrequency of the Olympic Games heightened anticipation and exaggerated
patriotic expression.

The nationalistic currents enveloping the Olympic Games served as a
considerable cause of anxiety for Coubertin. The IOC president vocally denounced the emergence of "patriotic professionalism," labeling state subsidies, professional coaching, and extended training camps as a serious "harm
[to] true athleticism."[96] "It gives off a whiff of professionalism," he later added,
"and forces us to recall that a whole swarm of false amateurs is involved in all
sports."[97] Backed by an alliance of federations driven more by nationalistic
reward than a fidelity to amateurism, he warned that the Olympic Movement

peered over the precipice of a revolution that would endanger its existence. Ironically, Coubertin feared one of the very forces that would ultimately heighten his movement's longstanding popularity; the political and propaganda rewards of Olympic participation and success fueled the global reach of his Olympic brand. Yet as the Olympic Games expanded across national borders and increasingly became occasions for competitive national self-assertion, the amateur ideal would, as Coubertin predicted, come under an unrelenting attack.

The rising nationalistic forces that engulfed the Olympic Movement would soon plunge Europe into a devastating war after the assassination of Archduke Franz Ferdinand II, heir to the Austro-Hungarian throne, by Serbian terrorists. As the escalating Balkan crisis spilled onto the wider European stage, it gradually became obvious that the 1916 Berlin Olympic Games were doomed. Fearing the realistic possibility of the Olympics being lost forever, Coubertin fled to neutral Switzerland and the city of Lausanne, where he established the IOC headquarters and worked fervently to keep the Olympic flame alive throughout the remainder of the war. With the war staggering into a devastating four-year struggle, there was every chance that the baron's idealistic Olympic Movement would perish in the crossfire.

3 THE RISE OF THE SHAMATEUR

World War I brought calamity and destruction. The sheer totality of warfare and the unprecedented levels of violence, as exemplified by the mass battles of the Somme, Ypres, and Verdun, left Europe in both physical and psychological tatters. Modern technology and weaponry claimed the lives of more than nine million soldiers and precipitated the collapse of four empires.[1] The absolute destruction that characterized World War I significantly undermined the importance and power of idealistic international movements like the Olympic Games.[2] The International Olympic Committee's (IOC) mantra of promoting international understanding and heightening global stability through athletic competition had clearly failed to help stave off one of the darkest and most violent epochs in modern history.[3]

Amid the smoldering of ash, dilapidation, and lost lives, Pierre de Coubertin sought to reestablish a place for his Olympic Movement in the postwar world. The IOC president lost no time in restoring the Olympic Games. In recognition of Belgium's bravery during World War I, the IOC awarded the games of the Seventh Olympiad to Antwerp at a meeting on 5 April 1919, in Lausanne, Switzerland. For Coubertin, the choice of Antwerp, a city recently liberated from German occupation and oppression, provided an ideal setting for the first postwar games.[4] Symbolism emerged as a central facet of the revived Olympic ritual. In a move to reestablish Olympism as a powerful force for fostering peaceful international relations and understanding, Coubertin created an Olympic flag with five interlocking rings, signifying the union of five continents. The IOC also introduced an Olympic oath for competitors to be sworn prior to the commencement of the games. Coubertin vied to reposition the Olympic Games, and its invented traditions and unifying symbolism, as a peaceful contrast to the trench warfare and violence that had engulfed Europe.[5]

Like the baron's Olympic festival, Western civilization reemerged from the shadows of World War I transformed. Socialist and Communist movements, fueled by the 1917 Bolshevik revolution, swept across the European continent. Ideological upheavals gripped the Middle East and the Indian subcontinent as large-scale, newly organized nationalist movements emerged upon the disintegration of the Turkish Ottoman Empire.[6] Loosening the shackles of patriarchal oppression, the Suffragette Movement secured the post-WWI granting of enfranchisement to women in Germany, the Netherlands, Great Britain, and the United States. Debilitated postwar economies, high rates of national debt, and swelling ranks of unemployment ensured that mass trade unionism and political and social unrest simmered dangerously on both sides of the Atlantic. Europe's old aristocracy, left ravaged and reeling from the destructive capabilities of modern technology and weaponry, faced a more devastating threat as the currents of liberalism and capitalism threatened to topple the propertied order, the traditional political hierarchy, and the entrenched economic system.[7]

In this era of widespread social and political upheaval, the dominant traditions of amateurism came under assault. The aristocratic, patriarchal, and Eurocentric power structure that sustained and legitimized the amateur ethos was rocked to its core. Populist-minded Western and non-Western nations, in concert with a small band of international sports federations, pushed for a gradual loosening of the amateur restraints throughout the 1920s. Acknowledging the expanding global and commercial dimensions of the Olympic Movement, as well as the subsequent rise in international standards of sporting performance, they urged Coubertin and his colleagues on the IOC to reform amateurism along more democratic and egalitarian lines. The privilege amateurism afforded wealthy athletes over their working-class counterparts seemed irreconcilable, they argued, with not only the postwar cultural zeitgeist but the Olympic Movement's own values. As the baron edged toward retirement, the IOC debated whether it would realize its philosophical promise of universalism and inclusivity, or whether it would continue to deter participation on socioeconomic grounds through a more stringent defense of amateurism.

GLOBALIZING AND DEMOCRATIZING SPORT

The postwar years witnessed a tremendous explosion in the popularity of sport. Advancements in transoceanic travel and communication, the technological infrastructure that was put in place during World War I, stimulated the diffusion of modern sport on a global scale. The English disease reached out from beyond the confines of Europe and North America, "stifling or co-opting" other traditional forms of physical culture and becoming inextricably linked with notions of nationhood and national prowess.[8] Western imperialist sentiment, racism, and ambition, as embodied by colonial administrators and Young Men's Christian Association missionaries, carried sport across Africa, Asia, and Latin America as a tool to civilize and enlighten the non-Western world.[9] The emerging internationalization of sport was paralleled by its soaring popularity across Europe and North America. The wartime embrace of organized sport to stave off boredom and maintain national levels of fitness heightened its popularity in civilian life after the cessation of hostilities.[10] Throughout the Western world, governments appropriated and educators promoted sport for its health, fitness, and recuperating benefits. The construction of large sporting arenas, notably London's Wembley stadium (1919), and those in Munich (1924), Frankfurt and Düsseldorf (both 1925), and Rome (1928), propelled sports such as soccer, baseball, boxing, and track and field into mass public spectacles.[11] Sport immersed itself in Western popular culture. Sportsmen—and, to a far lesser extent, sports-women—became celebrities, competing before the watchful eyes of huge audiences, avaricious promoters, and an expansive global media apparatus.[12]

The rising bureaucratization and standardization of sport through the development of powerful international sports organizations further fueled sports' rapid postwar growth and diffusion. As sport put down roots around the globe, international federations were gradually founded—typically through French initiative—to oversee their regulation. Only fourteen were in existence prior to World War I, including the International Amateur Athletic Federation (IAAF). These nascent federations were politically weak, with the IOC maintaining sharp control over international sport and offering de facto world championships. In the postwar years, however, the international federations gained in strength, developed a degree of autonomy and status, and moved to assert their place and policies within the sporting world—eight new federations were created between 1918 and 1932. The IOC's reliance on international federations to establish the technical regulations of the Olympic Games enhanced the legitimacy of these bodies.[13] The Fédération Internationale de Football Association (FIFA) best exemplified the postwar growth, consolidation, and expansion of international federations. From seven founding members in 1904, FIFA expanded its membership on the eve of the 1928 Amsterdam Games to forty-three nations, including the South American states of Brazil, Uruguay, Paraguay, Argentina, Chile, Peru, Bolivia, and Ecuador.[14] Other federations followed similar trajectories. Despite the persistence of local inflections, a global sporting culture emerged—a *lingua franca* aligning modern rules, regulations, and patterns of play.

The postwar development and consolidation of competitive sport altered the Olympic landscape. As sport took hold on an increasingly global scale, Coubertin sounded his universalistic rallying cry of "all games, all nations." He sought to broaden the reach and elevate the influence of the Olympic Games. "Every sport for everyone," the baron declared, "that is the new and by no means Utopian aim which we must devote ourselves to achieving."[15] His universal vision of an Olympics open to all participants irrespective of social class, race, ethnicity, nationality, religion, and political affiliation led him and his successor in the IOC presidency, Comte Henri de Baillet-Latour, to undertake proselytizing tours of South America in the 1920s. Coubertin's efforts to spread Olympism proved successful as he oversaw the establishment of five National Olympic Committees in the region, as well as the appointment of eight new Latin Americans to the IOC.[16] He also recruited representatives from Asia. Jigoro Kano of Japan, Dorabji Tata of India, and Dr. C. T. Wang of China served on the IOC throughout the interwar years.[17] Coubertin expanded—with some noted reluctance—the global dimensions of the Olympic Movement even further by adding a separate winter edition of the games, first held in 1924 in the glamorous French resort town of Chamonix Mont Blanc. The incorporation of distinctly Scandinavian and Alpine sporting events into the Olympic Movement added further momentum to Coubertin's global aspirations.[18]

The development of a Winter Olympics, coupled with the postwar emergence of Latin American debutants Argentina, Brazil, Ecuador, Mexico, and Uruguay; the new European states of Lithuania, Poland, Romania, and Yugoslavia; and African and Asian newcomers Egypt, India, and Turkey challenged the Western domination of the Olympic Movement. The Oxbridge, Ivy League, and hereditary European elites, who composed the original Olympic contestants in Athens in 1896, had been gradually replaced by a more socially, racially, ethnically, and geographically diverse body of athletes—an impressive 2,883 sportsmen and sportswomen from forty-six IOC member nations competed at the 1928 Amsterdam Olympics.[19] Even at the bureaucratic level, the Olympic Movement boasted more heterogeneity: By 1928 the IOC comprised sixty-seven members from forty-seven nations. The IOC also proved somewhat more socially inclusive: Only 41 percent of its members were of European nobility, in comparison with 68 percent in 1908.[20]

The postwar growth and expansion of the Olympic Movement, however, obscures the paradoxes and limitations of Coubertin's universal agenda. Despite the incorporation of non-Western nations and representatives into the Olympic family, the IOC—in its outlook and structure—remained a distinctly

Eurocentric Old Boys club. Throughout the 1920s the IOC continued to be governed autocratically, with self-appointed members serving unlimited terms, closed voting procedures, and wealthy Western powers dictating Olympic policy. Disavowing the one-country, one-vote system adopted by the League of Nations, a postwar contemporary of the IOC, Coubertinian policymaking ensured that some established Olympic nations (that is, Britain, France, Switzerland, and the United States) had two or three representatives on the IOC, while others had none. Under Coubertin (and beyond), the IOC remained an ideologically conservative, patriarchal establishment that reflected the needs, interests, and beliefs of a privileged elite of white Western gentlemen.[21]

The persistent homogeneity of the IOC carried enormous participatory and regulatory implications. Coubertin's unrelenting abhorrence of female athleticism, an attitude consistent among nineteenth-century European aristocratic men, ensured that the entry of sportswomen into the Olympic Movement occurred along limited, controlled, and gender-appropriate lines that conformed to the leadership's Victorian sensibilities.[22] Although the exclusively male ranks of the IOC continued to voice serious concerns about the physiological and psychological strain of high-level competition for women, interest among female sporting enthusiasts skyrocketed during the 1920s. The growing political assertiveness of the European and North American feminist movement, aligned with the introduction of mass education, served as the catalysts for greater female participation in sport. Under the leadership of Alice Milliat, a respected French authority on women's sport and founder of the Fédération Sportive Féminine Internationale, the first Women's Olympic Games were held in Paris in 1922—a one-day event in which athletes from five nations competed in eleven events (six more than the IOC allowed).[23] Coubertin and his colleagues on the IOC greeted these rival games, as well as the broader emancipatory spirit of the suffragist movement, with vehement disdain. They worked to stymie the development of women's sport throughout the interwar period.[24]

The baron's paternalistic attitude toward African postwar participation further exposed the thin veil of Olympic universalism and inclusivity. Born into the French aristocracy during a period of active colonialism on the African continent, Coubertin displayed the attitudes of an "enlightened colonialist."[25] In an address at the 1923 IOC session in Rome, he expressed sympathy, superiority, and altruism toward Africa. Coubertin spoke of bringing sport "to a retarded continent, to populations still deprived of basic culture." He invoked the stereotype of the "lazy African" and prescribed the civilizing properties of Western sport as an educative and moral elixir.[26] Coubertin dreamt of a universal, multiracial Olympics but failed to stimulate the development of sport in sub-Saharan Africa and to facilitate the entry of colonial African nations into the Olympic Movement.[27] Instead, he proceeded to promote a separate African Olympics for non-Europeans (Jeux Africains) as a platform for imbuing indigenous athletes with the lofty principles of Olympism.[28] In effect, Coubertin implemented a form of "sporting apartheid" that forced African, as well as other colonized peoples, to the periphery of the international sporting community.[29]

In the language of social Darwinism, which evinced biological and anthropological racism, Coubertin believed that the Hutu, Hausa, Somali, and Zulu lacked the requisite psychological and social attributes needed to compete in full Olympic competition. Assuming the racial and temperamental superiority of Westerners, Coubertin maintained a relatively narrow framework of what constituted an "Olympic athlete." Amateurism thus took on important racial (and gender) dimensions in the postwar years. It privileged Western (and masculine) values, principles, and beliefs. The archetypal Olympic amateur was, in Coubertin's imagination, a male athlete who possessed the moral and intellectual capacity to harness the enlightened spirit of fair play, moderation, and sportsmanship. The case of Native American Jim Thorpe earlier revealed the social, racial, and sexual parameters of Olympic amateurism. Thorpe's coach, Glenn "Pop" Warner, blamed the athlete's racial background for the misunderstanding that resulted in the IOC infamously stripping him of his Olympic gold medals. "The boys at the [Carlisle] Indian School were children mentally and did not understand the fine distinction between amateurism and professionalism," Warner claimed.[30] This practice of constructing and fortifying amateurism along racial lines was common outside the Olympic Movement. As Colin Tatz has shown, aboriginal athletes were often denied amateur status by Australian sporting authorities because they were considered incapable of understanding the rules and core values of amateurism.[31]

Despite a gradual and controlled expansion during the 1920s, the IOC remained a predominately conservative, patriarchal, and elitist organization that perpetuated a Western socially constructed model of amateurism. The oppressive realities of postwar Olympic competition aroused significant opposition among the emerging Communist and Socialist left. The Soviet Union, the pariah of the international sporting community during the interwar years, displayed contempt for the avowed apoliticism and internationalism of the Olympic Games. In an era of Stalinist isolationism, the Soviets rejected the games as an inherently capitalist and exploitative bourgeois invention that served the interests of decadent and corrupt Western imperial powers. Soviet leaders denounced the Olympic Movement for excluding the proletariat through the enforcement of socially, racially, and sexually restrictive amateur regulations.[32] Eschewing the Anglo-American focus on individualism, specialization, and achievement, the Soviets formed the Red Sport International (Spartakiad) in 1921 to promote revolutionary class consciousness through mass participation in sport, pageants, parades, and military events.[33]

The Soviet abhorrence of Olympic competition, along with other elite Western amateur sporting events, received support from Socialist groups across Europe and North America that emerged after the social democratic split in the aftermath of the Russian Revolution. Reflecting a similar antibourgeois blend of radical class consciousness, the Workers' Sports Movement arose to promote sporting and recreational opportunities to all irrespective of one's social class, gender, race, ethnicity, or skill.[34] The inclusive and mass participatory traditions of workers' sport stood in ideological contrast to the competitive and class-based exclusivity of the Olympic Movement.[35] The *Daily Worker*, the chief organ of Socialists in Britain, condemned the IOC for its philosophical and legislative defense of amateurism. "This so-called amateur sport is rotten to the core," it derided. "Its chief supporters are the bourgeois gang, who see in it one of the chief instruments for doping the workers into submission to worsening conditions."[36] The *Daily Worker* also regularly exposed the hypocritical realities of amateur competition, claiming that "the number of amateurs who make money, mostly indirectly, out of their sporting achievements and skill, is nauseating when they are paraded before the public as gentlemen."[37] Favoring the mass participation of less privileged national and social groups, the global nexus of workers' sports federations united to stage a series of "worker Olympics," held on two occasions between 1925 and 1932, as a counterforce to the aristocratic, commercialized, and increasingly chauvinistic tone of Coubertin's Olympic Games.[38]

THE AGE OF THE "SHAMATEUR"

The cries of inequality and hypocrisy emanating from the Communist and Socialist left certainly held a perceptible grain of truth. As the Olympics spread across national boundaries and came to include a larger and more representative pool of athletes, the standards of sporting performance became higher and the pursuit of excellence more demanding. The rising nationalistic and political importance of postwar Olympic competition emboldened athletes in their pursuit of *Citius, Altius, Fortius.* Quantified, regimented, and scientific training practices emerged, as famously embodied by the British Olympic sprint champion Harold Abrahams (of *Chariots of Fire* fame). Reflecting on the 1920 Antwerp Olympics, the *Daily Express* acknowledged that the traditional amateur dictum of "sport for sport's sake" had eroded under the progressive modern realities of postwar competition. "The amateur status of the competitors has been as questionable as ever," the British newspaper bemoaned. "For the most part they have been nothing better than hired gladiators, specially trained to snatch a particular prize."[39]

In theory, the IOC's strict antiprofiteering regulations imposed severe restrictions on the pursuit of excellence. Olympic athletes, particularly those from non-Western nations, lacked the financial means, time, and energy to dedicate themselves exclusively to the rigors of achieving Olympic gold. With Olympic victory garnering greater political and commercial reward, however, participating athletes faced unrelenting pressures to violate the IOC's amateur policies. The age of the "shamateur" was born. Professional coaching, appearance fees, expense accounts, nominal employment, and broken-time payments emerged with increased regularity during the 1920s to challenge the IOC's claims to amateur purity. Finnish Olympic champions Paavo Nurmi and Ville Ritola perhaps best exemplified the "shamateur" spirit of the postwar years. "The Flying Finns" exploited the benefits of under-the-table cash payments, as well as paid employment in local factories; generous Finnish benefactors effectively granted the middle- and long-distance champions license to train full-time outside of critical gaze of Olympic officials.[40] New Zealander Jack Lovelock, along with an untold number of other leading postwar Olympians, also contravened their amateur statuses by engaging secretively in profitable professional practices.[41]

The continued rise of capitalism and global commerce and the popularity of cultural products such as music, film, and sport further undermined the legitimacy of the IOC's philosophical defense of amateurism.[42] Coubertin committed his movement to a noncommercial ideal in an age of rapidly expanding commercial possibility. Throughout the 1920s, amateur athletes faced increasingly alluring commercial and monetary pressures. As the Olympic Games developed into a global sporting spectacle, successful Olympians were recruited as celebratory pitchmen (and women) for an expanding array of consumer products; they were positioned as lead actors in Hollywood movies, burlesque aquacades, and vaudeville-inspired shows; and they were even recruited to write their opinions in newspapers and popular literary sources. Clever sporting moguls exploited the commercial potential of amateur sport even further, aggressively pursuing Olympic athletes (often via the promise of pecuniary reward) to compete in athletic meets and special exhibitions before the gleeful hordes of paying spectators. Even the IOC and Olympic Organizing Committees were not immune to these commercial pressures.

The lure of financial revenue inevitably heightened the Olympic Movement's money orientation, its focus on spectatorship, gate-taking, spectacle, and the promotion of an Olympic "brand." The 1920s witnessed the creation of exclusive rights for still and motion-picture images of Olympic competition, as well as the advent of corporate sponsorship. Coca-Cola began pushing carbonated sugar water through Olympic advertisements, and a host of rival global conglomerates also exploited the growing potential of Olympic product placement.[43] The age of for-profit Olympic amateurism had arisen.

The rising currents of commercialism and professionalism merged during the 1920s to expose the growing hypocrisy of amateurism. To all but the most recalcitrant observer, the "shamateurism" taking hold within the Olympic arenas, stadiums, and pools was obvious. Some of the most decorated Olympians of the postwar era stood at the forefront of this professional and commercial shift. American Charley Paddock, the first to be dubbed the "fastest man in the world," parlayed his amateur sporting success into financial reward and commercial opportunity. Paddock's athletic feats, which included two Olympic gold medals in Antwerp and numerous world records, propelled him into a popular celebrity icon. The U.S. sprint king found creative ways to profit, moonlighting as a newspaper columnist, editor, and nationally syndicated expert on sport, starring as an actor on the Hollywood silver screen, and accepting under-the-table appearance fees for running in amateur events throughout Europe and North America.[44] Like Paddock, a host of postwar Olympians made money from their celebrity while maintaining their amateur status. "Flying Finn" Paavo Nurmi, French-Algerian marathoner Abdel Baghinel El Ouafi, Italian fencer Aldo Nadi, U.S. swimming "mermaid" Aileen Riggin, tennis star Helen Wills Moody, and most famously, swimmer Johnny Weissmuller, bartered their Olympic success for the glitz and glamour of Hollywood, or the financial riches of public appearances and commercially packaged athletic shows and exhibitions.[45] Even the new Winter Olympians cashed in on their newfound global celebrity. Norwegian figure-skating starlet Sonja Henie translated her Olympic gold medals into international commercial fame and monetary reward, Nordic and alpine skiers peddled winter sporting equipment, and winter ski resorts vied to exploit the Olympic brand in order to boost tourism and trade.[46] Money flowed and hypocrisy reigned, much to the chagrin of British IOC member Courcy Laffan, who labeled the postwar Olympics as a "nursery for professionals."[47]

Reflecting the democratic and egalitarian spirit sweeping Western societies, media scribes placed amateurism under the public microscope. Its ascribed tenets (antiprofiteering, anticommercialism, and sport for sport's sake) were exposed to the realities of postwar sporting competition. On paper, amateurism remained socially exclusive and prohibitive; in practice, it appeared unenforceable and hypocritical. A populist call rang out for a more relevant, realistic, and enforceable amateur code. Unlike the Communists and Socialists who championed the abolition of amateurism altogether, postwar observers favored moderate, liberal reforms. Stirred by the decision to deny U.S. Olympic gold–medal rower John "Jack" Kelly entry to the Henley Regatta because of his occupational background as a manual laborer, the *Times* of London and the *Manchester Guardian* attacked the Amateur Rowing Association for its ongoing enforcement of a mechanics clause.[48] The *New York Times* denounced the U.S. collegiate sport system and its prevailing culture of restricting membership on teams "to men who are able to pay their way."[49] The *Times of India* condemned the prohibitive cost of international participation, especially for "first class [athletes] who are not rich men and have scruples about accepting private hospitality."[50] Aristocratic, socially exclusive amateur values no longer held unquestioned sway.

The Olympic Movement, the global bastion of amateurism, inevitably attracted close scrutiny. In light of rising athletic standards and vast distances between Olympic host cities, prohibitions against training and travel expenses, living stipends, and financial prizes enforced by most international federations functioned as a mechanism of class exclusion. Olympic training, travel, and participation required a significant outlay of time, energy, and money. In an era in which both Western and non-Western governments failed to ruthlessly exploit the propaganda potential of sport and Olympic victory, state intervention remained minimal. Thus, aspiring Olympians were forced to pay their own way or, at least, raise funds from family and friends. Those who were unable to acquire the money or secure time away from the workplace could not participate. Striking a populist tone, the French publication *Liberté* challenged the IOC to loosen its amateur restraints, particularly in an age of greater global participation. It advocated for the allowance of broken-time payments as a means to stimulate participation among the lower classes, as well as athletes from emerging sporting nations. You cannot "expect amateurs, however pure they might be, to spend about three months, going, staying, and coming back from the [Olympic] games . . . within the narrow frame of pure amateurism," it exhorted.[51] Henri Desgrange, one of the principal founders of the Tour de France, also called upon the IOC to tackle the postwar realities of dishonest hypocrisy and class-based exclusion. Writing on the pages of the French sports newspaper *L'Auto*, for which he served as editor, Desgrange proposed the creation of an international class of Olympic athletes as a solution to the troublesome amateur and professional binary distinction. This new class, he explained, would receive compensation for missed labor and travel but will abstain from outright professional behavior. It would heighten participation among all global and socioeconomic lines, while allowing the IOC to uphold its sacrosanct, antiprofiteering principles.[52] Such imaginative proposals reflected the postwar impetus to revise and reform amateurism along more democratic, globally representative lines.

REVISITING THE AMATEUR QUESTION

By the 1920s, the IOC had grown into an established institution: It possessed a charter, held annual sessions and periodic congresses, disseminated a publication (*Revue Olympique*), and occupied an administrative headquarters in Lausanne.[53] Despite its steps toward organizational maturity, the IOC still failed to coherently define and systematically enforce amateurism across all Olympic sports. The baron, a philosophical opponent of socially exclusive antiprofit regulation, continued to excuse the IOC from any administrative responsibility. Lacking the philosophical conviction, let alone the financial and bureaucratic capacity, he persisted in delegating the task of governing amateurism to the international federations on a sport-by-sport basis.[54] Confusion and inconsistency reigned. At the 1920 Antwerp Olympics, the definitions of an amateur again varied widely across Olympic sports.[55] The international federations of equestrianism, modern pentathlon, shooting, and yachting sanctioned the award of cash prizes but simultaneously prohibited (or, at least, discouraged) working-class participation. The International Lawn Tennis Association (ILTA) awarded amateur status to former professionals ("contaminated" amateurs), but the IAAF proscribed the payment of training and travel expenses. FIFA bestowed amateur status to soccer players who had competed openly alongside professionals, a progressive policy also adopted by the Union Cycliste Internationale (UCI).[56] The amateur question remained as vexing and troublesome as ever.

The steady postwar globalization and growth of the Olympic Movement necessitated that the IOC revisit its position on amateurism. A larger, more representative Olympics, comprising athletes from North Africa, Asia, and Eastern Europe, exposed some of the harsh socially exclusive realities of existing amateur polices. For these new Olympic entities, the cultural nuances and ideological beliefs and practices of amateurism were simply alien. Lacking an established professional sporting structure (and thus a clear distinction between amateurism and professionalism), far removed from the chivalric, muscular Christian virtues of Anglo-Saxon moral superiority, these new Olympic nations considered class-based exclusionary policies—as well as prohibitions against travel and living expenses, broken-time payments, and financial prizes—as jejune and outdated. Unlike their wealthy Anglo-American rivals, athletes from less affluent sporting nations struggled to bear the financial burden of lengthy transcontinental journeys to compete in

Olympic competition without monetary compensation. The amateur code, still a symbol of white Western privilege and exclusivity, demanded rethinking. Acknowledging the globalizing realities of international sport, the *Sydney Referee* exhorted IOC officials to "abandon all their predilections to humbug, and . . . meet the facts of modern life without hypocrisy or sham."[57]

As an increasingly multinational body, the IOC needed to be more astute politically and more sensitive to a diverse range of cultural attitudes and sporting practices. The popularization of the Olympic Games illuminated the philosophical and ideological gulf between the traditional hegemonic powers and the new batch of Olympic nations. Throughout the immediate postwar years, the IOC and its newly formed executive board addressed the calls for legislative order and greater equality. The executive board, a product of the rising bureaucratization and standardization of Olympic affairs, had been established at the 1921 Olympic Congress in Lausanne. Coubertin feared that the IOC had grown too unwieldy; therefore, he created a small nucleus consisting of some of his most dedicated and trusted followers to oversee the administration of IOC affairs and create policy pertaining to both the Olympic program and amateurism.[58]

With a view toward the 1925 Olympic Congress, a periodic meeting between the powerbrokers of international sport, the executive board sought to help guide the IOC and its affiliated international federations toward a clearer, more relevant and enforceable definition of an amateur. The executive board prepared a fifteen-question survey to assist the congress attendees in formulating a new policy on amateurism.[59] The IOC addressed the survey at its 1923 annual session in Rome. Although still a decidedly conservative body, the IOC did express some sympathy with the populist demand for amateur reform. Italy's Carlo Montù championed the introduction of broken-time payments, adding that the IOC must acknowledge democratic developments and refrain from legislating in the opposite direction. De Courcy Laffan took a more moderate position. The long-serving British representative argued that before "condemning" the introduction of broken-time payments and other liberal reforms completely, "we must think we are in a time of democratization where the general point of view towards amateurism is evolving."[60] After a brief discussion, IOC members moved to suspend any further discussions on the subject until the forthcoming Olympic congress.

EMBOLDENING THE AMATEUR IDEAL

Writing on the eve of his retirement in 1925, Coubertin foreshadowed the impending debate over Olympic amateurism. The baron, whose own attitude toward amateurism long oscillated between ambivalence and apathy, acknowledged that the burgeoning popularity of sport across the globe placed the traditional British concept of amateurism on an inevitable collision course with a more progressive and democratic Latin concept. He envisioned a titanic clash of sporting cultures, a "struggle between the haves and the have-nots." The British, aided by "strength of tradition . . . and long-standing routine," would face a leadership challenge from continental European, Scandinavian, and Latin American nations, who were not raised in a British public school amateur ethos and who displayed "zealous national passions." Coubertin, a vigorous supporter of *les sports anglais*, admonished that an ideological battle could be averted only if the British ceased priding "itself on dogmatic superiority in . . . the practice of fair play" and embraced the increasingly egalitarian tone of modern sport.[61]

The perfect storm that Coubertin predicted arrived in the form of the Olympic broken-time controversy. Battles over the awarding of reimbursements for lost time away from the workplace gained momentum in the aftermath of the 1924 Paris Games, particularly after the flood of negative media reports condemning the presence of foreign shamateurs competing in Paris.[62] In the soccer tournament, for instance, critics complained that South American champion Uruguay had openly awarded indemnities to their players without sanction. FIFA, the international federation responsible for overseeing the Olympic soccer tournament, did not officially permit broken-time payments, but it did seemingly turn a blind eye to the unscrupulous practices of its member national soccer federation from South America. The British, who had abstained from the Paris soccer tournament in protest, urged the IOC to finally impose a stringent and encompassing amateur definition at the forthcoming 1925 Olympic Congress.[63] The *Times* of London took a more vigorous stance, condemning what they considered the open professionalism (as well as the scenes of flagrant nationalism) on display in Paris as proof that the Olympic Games were "doomed."[64]

The eighth Olympic Congress marked a renewed attempt on behalf of the IOC to tackle the persistent problem of amateurism. Within the elegant halls of the Prague National Museum, IOC members were accompanied by representatives from twenty-seven international federations and forty national Olympic committees to address various technical aspects of the Olympic Movement. Amateurism dominated the proceedings. Central to the debate were two opposing propositions: the British favored the creation of a uniform definition of an amateur for all Olympic sports, while the French and the UCI called for the international federations to be empowered with crafting and enforcing their own amateur standards.[65] The IOC stood at a difficult crossroads: Would it pursue complete governance over amateur rules and regulations, or, alternatively, continue to cede power to the international federations to verify the amateur standing of Olympic participants outside its purview as agreed at the 1914 and 1921 Olympic congresses in Paris and Lausanne.

The fractious interorganizational relationship between the IOC and the international federations significantly influenced the Prague Congress's decision.[66] For some within the IOC, the postwar emergence of powerful international bureaucracies confirmed Coubertin's earlier fears that they were "instruments of tyranny," designed to supplant the IOC and leave the organization redundant.[67] The baron's homeland, France, a driving force in international sporting bureaucracy, frequently challenged the IOC's legitimacy and its amateur tradition during the postwar years. Keen to wrest full control over the governance of international sport from their Anglo-American counterparts, French officials and federations established an International Sports Committee, a centralized nexus of amateur and professional international federations, as a democratic countermodel to the IOC.[68] Progressive, financially and commercially ambitious French-controlled international federations also maintained notoriously loose amateur standards: L'Union Internationale de Tir (International Sport Shooting Federation) refused to draw a distinction between amateurs and professionals, while the Fédération Internationale de Ski permitted paid ski instructors to compete in its amateur events. The UCI also adopted a liberal stance by opening its World Road Championship to both amateurs and professionals.[69] FIFA took an even more liberal stance. Under the leadership of Frenchman Jules Rimet, the world governing body of soccer constructed plans to launch a World Cup tournament open to professionals.[70] The proliferation of international sport, coupled with the growth of democratically minded international federations, marked a significant challenge to the IOC's hold over amateur sport.

Fearful that unbridled federations would transform the Olympics into a shamateur event, the IOC adopted an alternative proposal. Congress members proposed that the amateur statuses established by the international federations should be respected for the admission of Olympic participants on the condition that all athletes "must not be a professional in any branch of sport; must not have been reinstated as an amateur after knowingly becoming a professional; and must not have received compensation for lost salaries."[71] This was a calculated move aimed at appeasing international federations by granting them a degree of autonomy while maintaining a minimum, but consistent, amateur standard for all Olympic entrants. Under this ruling, former and current professionals, as well as athletes accepting compensation for time away from the workplace, would be prohibited from participating in future Olympic competition. Tennis players, soccer players, and cyclists who conformed to the rules of their respective international federations would now be ineligible to compete at the 1928 Summer Olympic Games in Amsterdam.

The Prague Congress passed a further series of resolutions designed to strengthen amateurism against the democratizing winds of change. Reviving a proposal first conceived by Coubertin, the IOC stipulated that all Olympic participants must sign an official oath declaring that they were "an Amateur according to the Olympic Rules of Amateurism."[72] With a view to preventing perjury, national Olympic committees were instructed to countersign the certificate confirming their athlete's eligibility. This affirmed the national Olympic committees as the primary gatekeepers for amateur enforcement, inadvertently opening the door even further for nationalistic bias and bureaucratic foul play. Long, drawn-out journeys to competitions also were discouraged. The IOC imposed a ban limiting athletes to no more than twenty days of travel per year, with the exception of participation in the Olympic Games.[73] For those fearful of democratic reforms, the Prague Congress was heralded as an overwhelming success. A relieved Gustavus T. Kirby, a long-serving member of the American Olympic Committee (AOC) and an active participant at the Prague Congress, enthused that the congress's amateur rulings proved that "sport for sport's sake really meant something" and that "the replenishing of one's pocketbook was not as important as the satisfaction of one's ideals."[74]

It is no coincidence that the IOC finally sought a role in the administration and defense of amateurism at the precise moment that Coubertin stepped down as IOC president. The baron's private opposition to limiting participation on social and financial grounds had undoubtedly driven the IOC's existing apathetic stance on the issue. As Coubertin long feared, the passage and enforcement of strict amateur conditions sparked vehement opposition from continental European nations and more liberal-minded international federations. Opponents charged that the IOC's rulings, particularly the broken-time clause, fortified the social-class barriers that traditionally prohibited the lower social orders from the play of the leisure class. In an era in which statutory holiday arrangements did not exist, even in industrialized nations, aspiring Olympic athletes were forced to take unpaid leave or even resign from their jobs if their employers refused to compensate them for time away from the workplace. For working-class athletes, especially those who were financially responsible for a family, the IOC's prohibitions against indemnities carried enormous implications: Olympic competition would remain the preserve of affluent athletes from powerful Western nations. Representatives from the Dutch and Norwegian national Olympic committees denounced the "undemocratic ruling" on the grounds that "75% of [its] athletes . . . cannot travel without this."[75] Eager to assuage the dissenting voices, the IOC agreed to curtail the unwieldy Olympic program (the 1924 Paris Games ran for nearly three months) in an attempt to limit an athlete's time away from the workplace. By the time Coubertin stepped down as IOC president, the edifice of amateurism remained intact, but his predicted battle over the future direction of amateur sport had only just begun.

THE BATTLE OF THE SYSTEMS

The election of Comte Henri de Baillet-Latour to an eight-year term as IOC president during the 1925 IOC session in Prague represented an important landmark in the history of Olympic amateurism. Baillet-Latour, a wealthy Belgian racehorse owner and IOC member since 1903, stood as the baron's natural successor. Urbane, politically conservative, and well connected, Baillet-Latour perfectly fit the Coubertinian model for IOC membership. His successful staging of the 1920 Olympic Games in his native Belgium, a nation ravaged by World War I, endeared him further to the baron and ensured his elevation through the ranks of the IOC. Throughout his sixteen-year tenure as IOC chief executive, Baillet-Latour strove to strengthen his organization's philosophical and regulatory commitment to amateurism.[76]

Baillet-Latour's career as IOC president met with immediate challenges, as belligerent federations fought to repeal the Prague Congress's amateur rulings. Tensions were inevitable, especially when you consider the contradictions that existed between the exclusive criteria adopted in Prague and the widely divergent (and often liberal) definitions of amateurism employed by the international federations. The International Lawn Tennis Federation (ILTF), the international governing body of tennis, launched the first major attack, threatening to break away from the Olympic Movement in protest. Robert Gallay, secretary general of the ILTF, issued Baillet-Latour a bold ultimatum: Either the IOC recognizes his organization's more liberal amateur definition or lawn tennis would not appear on the Olympic program in Amsterdam.[77] Like most French-controlled international federations, the ILTF's amateur code ran contrary to the strict rules conceived in Prague, in that former professionals could be reinstated as amateurs after a waiting period of as little as one year. The IOC, on the other hand, now took an uncompromising stance toward professionals, banning them for life. Since 1896, tennis had consistently appeared on the Olympic program, albeit in a somewhat diminished role. The gradual professionalization of tennis, coupled with the poor tournament conditions and the frequent scheduling of Wimbledon during the Olympic fortnight, ensured that Olympic tennis failed to capture the world's imagination. Despite the tournament's marginalized role and consistently poor gate receipts, the possibility of a tennis boycott still posed a threat to the fragile legitimacy of the Olympic Movement.

While Comte Baillet-Latour worked to salvage the Olympic tennis tournament by undertaking a massive letter writing campaign,[78] the IOC became embroiled in a similar debate with FIFA. On 3 May 1926, during its annual congress in Rome, FIFA approved a resolution (12 votes to 8) permitting national associations to award broken-time payments to those amateur soccer players denied paid holiday leave by their employees.[79] FIFA's ruling, a clear violation of the IOC's amateur code as outlined at the Prague Congress, marked an attempt to restore a sense of equality and purity to international soccer, the sport of the lower social strata. FIFA officials strove to uphold soccer's democratic status as the world's game by granting players supporting families with indemnities of up to 90 percent of their maximum salary; bachelors would receive 75 percent of salary. Rules stipulated that compensation would be paid only in "special circumscribed cases," namely travel to international games and national championships for a period not exceeding twenty days.[80]

Sensing a flood of condemnation, FIFA honorary secretary Charles Hirschman rushed to defend his organization's democratic ruling. "If these open and controlled payments of compensation for broken time would not be allowed," Hirschman explained, "it is not unlikely that pocket money would be paid . . . secretly, uncontrolled and unlimited."[81] Reports from South America, revealing that the Chilean soccer federation openly awarded more than $10,000 in illicit cash payments to its amateur players during the recent 1926 continental championship, strengthened Hirschman's argument.[82] Again, Baillet-Latour was placed in a difficult predicament: The IOC must either loosen its amateur restraints to admit broken-time payments or enforce the resolutions of the Prague Congress and eliminate soccer, the most financially lucrative and commercially attractive Olympic sport.

The soccer tournament, the de facto World Amateur Championship, had long established itself as the greatest source of revenue at the Olympic Games. At the 1924 Paris Olympics, the soccer tournament yielded more in gate money than the entire track and field program, and even exceeded the aggregate receipts of swimming, rugby union, tennis, cycling, wrestling, gymnastics, and fencing.[83] By 1928, the prospect of the reigning Olympic gold medalist Uruguay and fellow South American power Argentina pitting themselves against some of Europe's strongest soccer nations at the Amsterdam Olympics heightened the IOC's expectations that profits would reach unprecedented levels. Trapped between the lure of growing spectatorship and windfall profits on the one hand, and appeasing its most vocal amateur allies on the other, the IOC faced the harsh realities of maintaining an increasingly outmoded amateur ideal in an era of broader democratic reform.

Responding to the escalating crisis, the IOC voted during its 1926 annual session in Lisbon to grant its executive board "full powers to deal with the difficulties that might arise . . . with the Football and Tennis Federations."[84] On 8 August 1927 Baillet-Latour and his fellow executive board members, Theodor Lewald (Germany), Godefroy de Blonay (Switzerland), the Marquis de Polignac (France), Sigfrid Edström (Sweden), and Brigadier General Reginald J. Kentish (Britain), met in Paris to seek a conciliatory resolution with the renegade international federations. Football appeared first on the agenda. Fearing that the Dutch organizers would relinquish hosting the games if the lucrative soccer tournament were absent from the Olympic program, members voted in agreement (4–2) with the principle laid down by FIFA at Rome in favor of awarding broken-time payments to amateur soccer players during the Amsterdam Olympics on the condition that monetary payments "will be placed in the hands of the employers, the athletes having no direct contact with any compensation for lost salary."[85] The authorization of broken-time payments not only contravened the IOC's existing rules on amateurism but also officially sanctioned a practice long considered anathema in many leading Western sporting nations.

Curiously, the executive board proved far less accommodating with the ILTF. Members voted unanimously that the IOC would not modify the amateur principles established in Prague, and that as a consequence, former professional tennis players were not eligible to take part in future Olympic competition. The executive board ruled that unless the ITLF realigned its amateur definition in accordance with IOC code, lawn tennis would not appear on the program in Amsterdam. [86] Perhaps it was lawn tennis's mediocre gate receipts and lukewarm popularity with the fans that made losing the ILTF an easier pill to swallow. In the months building up to the Amsterdam Olympics, Baillet-Latour persisted in trying to reach a compromise, but to no avail.[87] Olympic tennis would be sacrificed in the name of amateurism. In fact, the sport would remain in the Olympic wilderness (despite two appearances as a demonstration sport in 1968 and 1984) until 1988, when it was restored as a full medal sport.

THE END OF THE AMATEUR IDEAL?

News of the IOC's broken-time soccer ruling triggered an avalanche of criticism within amateur sporting circles. The British, the self-perceived moral guardians of gentlemanly amateurism, passionately led the charge. In a private correspondence to Baillet-Latour, BOA chairman George Kemp, Lord Ro-chdale, threatened a full national Olympic withdrawal.[88] Dominion sporting officials also coalesced in opposition to the executive board's ruling. James "Pa" Taylor, the president of the Australian Olympic Federation, warned that unless the ruling were immediately overturned, Australia "will decline to send competitors to Amsterdam."[89] The AAU of Canada took a similar hard-line approach, insisting that "there can be no such thing as payment of an amateur for loss of time [because] an amateur is one who plays for the sake of the game."[90] The South African Olympic Games Committee added to the mountain of acrimonious correspondence, demanding that the IOC immediately overturn this "totally irregular principle."[91] Across the Atlantic, the other leading bastion of amateurism, the United States, also expressed its disdain at the IOC's concession. AOC president General Charles Sherrill stridently condemned the provision of sinecures as "dangerous and contrary to all concepts of American sportsmanship and amateurism."[92]

The most vocal opposition emanated from the globe's traditional sporting powers, Britain (and its white Dominions) and the United States. After enjoy-ing decades of invincibility on the playing field, thanks largely to advantages in tradition, experience, wealth, resources, and living standards, Britain and the United States looked on as smaller, less experienced nations began to catch up. The emergence of Algerian-born marathoners, Argentinean boxers, Finnish long-distance runners, Japanese swimmers and triple jumpers, Indian field hockey players, and Uruguayan soccer teams proved that Olympic glory was no longer the exclusive preserve of Anglo-American athletes.[93] The execu-tive board's passage of broken-time payments effectively promised to level the playing field further (in soccer at least) by offering less affluent nations the opportunity to subsidize its best athletes for time away from the workplace. George Nicol, a former English Amateur Athletic Association quarter-mile champion and member of the more progressively minded Polytechnic Har-riers Athletic Club (of Sam Mussabini fame), celebrated the introduction of an indemnity for lost earnings as "merely another step away from an ideal which is no longer practicable so far as international sport is concerned."[94]

British and U.S. officials remained steadfast. Recoiling toward ultra-con-servatism, they dismissed the executive's board's ruling as the first step down the nefarious path toward full-blown professionalism. The British country gentlemen's newspaper *The Field* presaged, "If payment for part time is rec-ognised in Association Football . . . similar payments will inevitably be made in connection with other games and sports."[95] Britain and the United States' own recent sporting history had shown that once concessions were made and the amateur seal was penetrated, it was impossible to withstand the inexorable forces of professionalism. Soccer provided compelling testimony to the fact. The growing prevalence of northern amateur clubs awarding excessive broken-time payments to their players, particularly those recruited from Scotland, eventually forced the English Football Association to recognize professionalism in 1885.[96] Mass spectatorship and growing commercialization fueled the emergence of professionalism in a host of other sports on both sides of the Atlantic, including U.S. football, baseball, horse racing, and golf.[97]

In the weeks and months after the executive board's ruling, reports mounted that Britain, the founding nation of an amateur sports culture, would boycott the 1928 Amsterdam Olympics in protest. The prospect that Britain, accompanied by its imperial allies, might abstain from the games forced the IOC back to its natural recourse: appeasement and reconciliation. In one of a series of impassioned appeals to Lord Rochdale, Baillet-Latour reassured the BOA chairman that the "decision of the Executive Committee of the IOC is not final [and] if the ideas of the FIFA do not meet with the approval of a future Congress, football will have to go out of the programme of the Games."[98] After months of uncertainty, Rochdale eventually backed down. During a special plenary meeting of the BOA, he declared that "each individual sport in this country is justified—if its Governing Body so de-sires—in supporting its own section of the Olympic Games."[99] It is interesting to note that not all British sporting federations were willing to support the decision. Fearing that the amateur game was slipping into the pernicious hands of professionalism, the English, Northern Irish, Scottish, and Welsh soccer associations agreed that a representative British Olympic soccer team would not compete in Amsterdam.[100] The four British soccer associations decided to take a more drastic step, revoking their memberships in FIFA.[101]

REVIVING THE AMATEUR IDEAL

When the Amsterdam Olympic flame was finally extinguished, the IOC re-turned to address the controversial broken-time issue at its 1930 Congress in Berlin. The award of the 1932 Olympic Games to Los Angeles ignited British fears that broken-time payments would soon be introduced to all Olympic sports in order to offset greater travel costs to the distant North American Pacific Coast location, as well as a more prolonged period away from the workplace.[102] These fears were heightened as Belgian sporting authorities vied to repeal the exclusive amateur criteria adopted in Prague; a move that, if passed, would officially sanction FIFA's, and other like-minded interna-tional federations,' policy of remunerating amateur athletes. Sensing that the floodgates could be thrown open to all forms of shamateurism, Britain's representatives and imperial allies presented an amendment to the Belgian proposal. Reviving the resolutions passed in Prague five years earlier—and recently reaffirmed by the IOC at its 1928 session in Amsterdam—the British proposed that Olympic athletes should be considered amateur only if they are "not or knowingly have become, a professional in the sport for which he is entered or in any other sport" and have "never received re-imbursement or compensation for loss of salary." By a vote of 90 to 20, congress attendees approved the British amendment, dealing a crushing blow to advocates of broken-time payments and a more democratic interpretation of the amateur ideal.[103] Incensed by the decision, FIFA subsequently scrapped the soccer tournament at the forthcoming 1932 Los Angeles Olympics and removed all passages relating to amateurism from its statutes. FIFA also persevered in its plan to create a World Cup tournament open to professionals, scheduled for summer 1930 in the Uruguayan capital, Montevideo.[104]

The Berlin Congress's ruling marked a pivotal moment in the preservation of Olympic amateurism. As democratizing and globalizing forces threatened to revolutionize modern sport, the prohibitions against broken-time payments symbolically halted the march of progress. The IOC passed up a seemingly righteous and momentous opportunity to open the Olympic Games up to a broader range of participants, irrespective of one's economic and social standing. Olympic competition would remain the preserve of privileged Western athletes who possessed the financial means to spend weeks away from the workplace in the pursuit of Olympic glory. Herein lay the inherent contradiction of Olympism: Coubertin's rhetoric spoke of universal ideals and equal opportunities for all people and all nations, yet the broken-time ruling and the IOC's renewed pledge to maintain its views on amateurism can be read as exclusionary, elitist, and racist.[105] The call of Olympism as "sport for all" clearly had its limitations; the IOC's decision during the 1930 Berlin Congress to confine women's participation to a mere five sports reaffirmed this truism.

The Berlin Congress's ruling is particularly surprising in light of the fact that the IOC sacrificed the most profitable feature of the Olympic Games in order to preserve its amateur ethos. Evidently, the IOC was not driven purely by financial motives: The soccer tournament at the 1928 Amsterdam Games had generated windfall profits for the Dutch organizers, yielding more than double the revenue (538,860 gilder) of track and field (278,576 gilder), and even exceeding the aggregate receipts of equestrianism, swimming, cycling, hockey, boxing, gymnastics, rowing, fencing, wrestling, yachting, and weightlifting combined.[106] With the benefit of hindsight, it is easy to portray IOC officials as being elitist, obstinate, and insensitive to calls for democratic reform. Under Baillet-Latour's leadership, the IOC clearly believed in the assumed moral virtues of amateurism and fought tirelessly to uphold the sanctity of its cherished ideal. Throughout the 1930s, Baillet-Latour and a cadre of like-minded Olympic officials sought to defend their vision of pure amateurism against the rising profitability, as well as the commercial and political viability, of Olympic competition.

4 "AMBASSADORS IN TRACKSUITS"

Against the backdrop of a global economic crisis that mercilessly drove financial systems to their knees and sparked surging rates of unemployment, the 1932 Los Angeles Olympic Games proved an unprecedented success. Connecting the Olympics with the glamour and stardom of Hollywood, as well as harnessing their full commercial potential as an attractive commodity, the Los Angeles organizers provided the blueprint for transforming the Olympics from a relatively marginal and elitist event into one of the world's most important entertainment extravaganzas.[1] Print, radio, and newsreel media chronicled Olympic feats; silver-screen celebrities and studio moguls flocked to Olympic events; and U.S. companies such as Coca-Cola, Kellogg's, and Helms Bakery avariciously engineered ways to exploit the Olympic brand.[2] The Los Angeles organizers also set new standards in event management by perfecting the modern bid process, boasting an impressive array of sporting infrastructures, including the recently renovated 105,000-seat Los Angeles Coliseum, celebrating the achievements of Olympic medalists in a formal victory ceremony, and housing male athletes in an Olympic Village.[3] Drawing upon the organizational, salesmanship, and promotional skills that had made the United States the world leader in mass culture, and Los Angeles one of the world's fastest growing cities, the 1932 Olympics overcame the gloom of a global depression to achieve economic solvency, recording a surplus of $1.5 million, and more important, ensuring the future stability of the Olympic Movement.[4]

The visible maturation, rising popularity, and internationalization of the Olympic Movement produced a tremendous increase in the political dimensions of Olympian spectacles during the 1930s. Emerging from the economic ruins of the Great Depression, authoritarian and totalitarian regimes in Europe, Asia, and Latin America spurred a substantial rise in governmental involvement in international sport. Though the British were among the first to forge the linkage between competitive sport and national interests, training and shaping the views of an imperial governing class through masculine exertion of the playing fields, their Fascist and militaristic rivals fully exploited the value of physical culture by positioning sport as the centerpiece of their foreign policy.[5]

The appropriation of elite, international sport by authoritarian regimes heightened the popularity and legitimacy of the Olympic Games. After successfully defending amateurism against the threat posed by broken-time payments, IOC chiefs embraced the support of powerful right-wing governments. Their initial hope soon turned to despair as it grew apparent that their authoritarian "allies" had transformed the Olympics into a ruthless game of *realpolitik*. Reports (both fictitious and otherwise) of state-run training camps, financial subsidies, and lavish cash prizes engendered a firm response from the IOC. On the eve of the world's descent into the cataclysm of another total war, Henri Baillet-Latour and his colleagues began working on specific issues designed to protect Olympic amateurism from corrupting practices. The results would be a series of soon-forgotten amateur reforms as authoritarian states shifted from the playing fields to the battlefields and the IOC suspended the games for a second time.

AMATEURISM STRIKES BACK

The expanding global and commercial dimensions of the Olympics during the 1930s presented amateur athletes with more opportunities to parlay their sporting talents into economic reward. The lure of financial riches led an untold number of prominent sportsmen and sportswomen into the shamateur underworld of padded expense accounts and under-the-table black money. Spectator demand and pressures to win on the international stage fueled the professionalization of training and competition.[6] European and North American sports clubs, federations, and race officials were willing to pay huge sums (surreptitiously and often through a middleman) in order to attract the world's leading amateur athletes to their meets and championship events. Ironically, the IOC's prohibitions against broken-time payments as enshrined at its congresses in Prague (1925) and Berlin (1930) served to heighten the scale of these illicit practices. Rising financial reward and an ever-increasing roster of participatory nations elevated the standard of competition, which in turn also pushed amateur athletes inexorably toward specialized and scientific methods of training and preparation. The perennial Olympic champion, the United States, continued to pioneer the "science of sport."[7] Film analysis of technique, training manuals, physical education periodicals, and laboratory studies of physiology and diet were among the new ways that Olympic coaches readied their amateur athletes for the strains and demands of elite competition.[8]

For the IOC, the rising competitive currents of interwar sport and the growing frequency of amateur violations necessitated stricter regulation and closer enforcement. Unlike his predecessor, the philosophically flexible and politically pragmatic Pierre de Coubertin, Baillet-Latour took a far more spirited role in his organization's governance and defense of amateurism. Coubertin employed amateurism as a philosophical ruse to inspire support and attain legitimacy for his Olympic revival ambitions; the Belgian strove to transform the amateur ideal into definable and enforceable legislation. Coubertin favored the spiritual, moral, and aesthetic dimensions of amateurism over the Anglo-Saxon penchant for socially prohibitive, antiprofit restrictions; Baillet-Latour forged an administrative path that sought to reconcile romantic idealism with dogmatic codification. "Amateurism is a state of the soul—not a law," he exclaimed in a tone resembling the baron's. Unlike the long-serving IOC president, however, Baillet-Latour believed that the amateur "soul" had to be governed and constrained. "In order that it may develop in the heart, athletes must live in a special environment," he averred. "The atmosphere must be purified and the general conditions of sports entirely changed."[9] Whereas Coubertin relinquished the IOC from all regulatory responsibility on the amateur issue, Baillet-Latour asserted that idealism had to be governed and enforced. Athletes who transgressed Olympic amateur rules, he cautioned, were to be punished.

The 1930s would mark a pivotal turning point in the history of Olympic amateurism. Under Baillet-Latour's leadership, the IOC appeared more attuned to both the professional and political realities of elite, international competition, as well as the mounting bureaucratic responsibilities of Olympic governance. A new generation of Olympic leaders had emerged. Baillet-Latour and his vice president, Sigfrid Edström, were dedicated administrators armed with a strong devotion to the amateur ideal. Born of wealth and privilege, both men saw it as their paternalistic duty to guide—via strict regulations and punishments—amateur sporting culture.[10] In a departure from Coubertin's long-held skepticism and mistrust toward the nexus of international sports federations, they sought a more conciliatory and intimate relationship. They recognized that the international sports federations would play a pivotal role in aiding the Olympic Movement in the fight against professional encroachments. At Baillet-Latour's behest, the IOC commissioned the creation of a consultative council of international sports federations, the Conseil des Délégués des Fédérations Internationales, as an open forum to address technical and legislative issues pertaining to the Olympic Movement.[11]

An emboldened IOC, in conjunction with its more closely affiliated international federations, moved to tackle the growing stain of Olympic shamateurism. In the build-up to the 1932 Olympic Games, amateur officials undertook a widespread crackdown on semiamateurs who wished to take part in Los Angeles, including Finland's Paavo Nurmi, the nine-time Olympic champion and one of the most celebrated athletes in the world during the 1920s and 30s.[12] "Paavo the Peerless," as he was more affectionately known, long boasted a reputation for his scientific approach to training as well as his brazen acceptance of excessive appearance fees. Nurmi's much-publicized tour in the United States in 1925 generated widespread suspicions that he demanded and pocketed under-the-table money. Reports circulated that the Finn requested (via his personal fixer, Hugo Quist) a $1,000 fee to appear in the annual Drake Relays, a sum far in excess of the U.S. AAU's allotted $10 for daily travel and housing expenses.[13]

Rumor and innuendo followed the fleet-footed Finn wherever he competed around the globe, prompting one anonymous U.S. official to intone: "Nurmi had the lowest heart beat and the highest asking price of any athlete in the world."[14] Even U.S. AAU president Avery Brundage, an emerging force in the global fight against shamateurism, was aware of Nurmi's transgressions. "There is absolutely no question that there were numerous irregularities during Nurmi's first visits to the United States," Brundage later confided, but the AAU was "never in a position to proffer charges against [him]."[15]

The Flying Finn was not the only prominent athlete on the radar of amateur officials. Polish long-distance runner Stanislaw Patkiewicz and France's reigning Olympic 1500-meter silver medalist Jules Ladoumègue were both stripped of their amateur statuses by the International Amateur Athletics Federation (IAAF) prior to the 1932 Olympic Games for violating its anti-profiteering regulations.[16]

Bigger scalps awaited, and they did not come any bigger than the most iconic Olympian of the first half of the twentieth century and the holder of more than twenty world records, Paavo Nurmi. Amateur officials hoped that the disqualification of Nurmi, who was scheduled to compete in the marathon event in Los Angeles, would send a powerful warning to ethically suspect and financially motivated Olympic athletes, a symbolic *coup de grâce* against shamateurism. IAAF president and IOC vice president Edström personally led the investigation into Nurmi's amateur status. Upon receipt of incriminating evidence from the German Athletic Association, indicating that Nurmi received an appearance fee of 1,000 Marks (allegedly well short of the 2,500 Marks he originally requested) during a recent European tour, Edström and the IAAF moved to suspend the Finn indefinitely at a board meeting in Berlin on 3 April 1932.[17]

The headline news that Nurmi would be absent from the roster of participants in Los Angeles sent shock waves around the globe, particularly in his native Finland. Amid all the angry Finnish editorial voices, the Helsinki *Uusi Suomi* condemned the IAAF's decision as "a miscarriage of justice" and a "triumph for diplomatic plots."[18] The *Helsingin Sanomat* waxed defiant, arguing the common refrain that "all potential medalists could have been banned for similar offences."[19] Urho Kekkonen, president of the Finish Athletic Association, shared the belief that inaccurate "second-hand information" and "suspicions" had been used to sacrifice Nurmi on the altar of pure amateurism. Kekkonen blasted the IAAF's ban as unconstitutional—only national track-and-field federations had the power disqualify amateur violators—and demanded that they "revoke the suspension" with immediate effect.[20] Edström and the IAAF executive board stood firm, even in the face of Finnish threats to boycott the Olympic Games in protest.[21] During its annual congress in Los Angeles on 28 July 1932, the IAAF simply amended its by-laws, expanded its remit of power, and promptly banned Nurmi from competitive action for two years, essentially ending the Flying Finn's decorated career.[22]

While a sullen Nurmi watched the Los Angeles Olympics from the Coliseum stands, much to the dismay of U.S. organizers eager to cash in on the appearance of a global superstar, Olympic officials celebrated a major victory in the fight against semiprofessionalism. For the first time since the infamous Jim Thorpe affair in 1912, the IOC proved that amateurism was more than just lofty ideological rhetoric and inane regulations, but a sporting model that could be actively defended and enforced. Nurmi—while likely guilty of all accusations—represented the fall guy in a deliberate scheme on behalf of Olympic officials to halt the black market semiprofessionalism that had overrun amateur sport after World War I. "Nurmi's methods were spreading all over Europe," Edström later recollected, but "by putting [him] out of business we have cleared up the matter and have now a very good standing with all our athletes."[23]

As the global economic depression slowly lifted, Baillet-Latour and his fellow Olympic apostles moved to tighten the noose around the necks of amateur violators. The IOC president called a June 1933 meeting of the Conseil des Délégués des Fédérations Internationales to address the troubling advance of semiprofessionalism in amateur sport. In a forthright speech, Baillet-Latour chided the federations for their excessive emphasis on commerce through the promotion of gate-taking tournaments, meets, and championships. He also targeted the national Olympic committees, national sports federations, coaches, and the media for their complicity in falsifying amateur statutes and elevating the importance of victory to dangerous heights.[24] In conjunction with Edström, Baillet-Latour formulated a series of far-reaching propositions designed to eliminate semiprofessionalism entirely.[25] At the 1933 annual session in Vienna, the IOC ruled that Olympic amateurs were now forbidden from competing against professionals except in "very exceptional cases," organizing and negotiating their own personal participation and travel, or competing overseas for a period exceeding twenty-one days (with the exception of the Olympic Games). Reimbursements for travel and expenses were no longer to be paid "in cash," but in the form of train tickets, meals, and accommodation, and at a cost not exceeding one British pound per day. The tripartite alliance of amateur regulators, which included the national Olympic committees, national federations, and the international sports federations, also were encouraged to play a far greater role in combating shamateur practices. The IOC requested that member federations solemnly enforce the signing and countersigning of the Olympic oath, as well as better educate amateur athletes about the "high moral and sporting force of the Olympic Games."[26]

"MUSSOLINI'S BOYS"

The IOC's heightened efforts to stamp out professionalism within the Olympic arena soon faced a more serious foe than unscrupulous athletes, corrupt officials, and greedy promoters. The 1930s witnessed the alarming encroachment of European, Asian, and Latin American governments into the apolitical realm of Olympic sport. Western nations had long awoken to the political utility of major international events. With the exception of small state subsidies and indirect organizational support, governments traditionally maintained a policy of noninterventionism in Olympic affairs. Born in the ashes of economic decline, Fascist and military regimes emerged across the globe during the 1930s, pulling Olympic sport under the umbrella of foreign policy and transforming major international sporting events into an affair of the state. Through the lens of radical Darwinism, the Fascist and military right manipulated the Olympic Games for propaganda purposes, equating victories on the field of play with national dynamism and ideological superiority.[27]

The Italians, under the grip of its Fascist dictator Benito Mussolini, arose as the first nation to ruthlessly exploit the value of physical culture for the purposes of propaganda and political gain.[28] Mussolini's Fascist Party transformed bourgeois competitive sport into a nationalistic enterprise and an agent of diplomacy. Mussolini, himself a competitive athlete and a self-professed model of Italian virility, embraced major international events such as the Olympic Games, the Tour de France, and the nascent FIFA World Cup as vehicles for binding the linguistically and culturally diverse Italian populace together, promulgating Fascist doctrine, and reaffirming the physical and moral development of Italy under his new regime.[29] Under the aegis of the Fascist Party, all Italian sporting agencies, including the Italian Olympic Committee (CONI), were aggressively propagandized and lavishly subsidized.[30] The government assumed complete authority over every facet of Italian sport. Through new appointments and ideological coercion, the Fascists occupied all major positions within amateur sporting organizations. Lando Ferretti, the president of the CONI and a committed Fascist, was a Mussolini appointee. Il Duce even succeeded in placing Augusto Turati, the secretary general of the Fascist Party and his own fencing partner, as the Italian representative on the IOC.[31]

Wielding complete authority, Mussolini and his Fascist Party established a centralized and comprehensive state-run elite sport system designed to attain success in international competition. At the 1932 Olympic Games, a large, well-prepared, and well-equipped Italian team stunned the world by clinching twelve gold medals and finishing second in the unofficial table of nations. "Mussolini's Boys," as the Italian team was known in the U.S. media, enjoyed substantial government support in their quest to showcase the athletic and military strength of Fascist Italy to the world.[32] The regime facilitated lengthy pre-Olympic training camps, funded the team through a special state-run national lottery, bestowed substantial privileges on Olympic athletes, and rewarded champions with financial prizes. Mussolini even personally cabled victors honoring their success.[33] The state-run media heralded the performance of Italian athletes in Los Angeles as evidence of a new, more powerful, and virile Italy. *La Gazzetta dello Sport*, under the editorship of CONI president Lando Ferretti, celebrated the triumph of the "blue ambassadors of Fascist sport in the theatre of the X Olympiad."[34] *La Stampa*, another organ of Mussolini's Fascist Party, proudly extended "the first salute to the blue veterans in Los Angeles."[35] For their feats of courage, discipline, endurance, and strength, Italian Olympic athletes like Luigi Beccali, gold medal winner in the 1500 meters, were presented as paragons of "Latin athleticism," archetypes of the *Italiano nuovo* (new Fascist man).[36]

The Italian system of elite, state-run sport would serve as a model to other Fascist and military governments in the years preceding World War II. Italian victories in the Olympic arena, the dominance of Italian cyclists in the Tour de France and the Giro de Italia, and successive Italian FIFA World Cups in 1934 and 1938, inspired the Yugoslav military government to nationalize sport as a means to boast its own prestige and legitimacy.[37] Similarly Spain's Fascist government established a Ministry of Sport, Consejo Nacional de Deportes, composed exclusively of Franco appointees to govern and promote national sporting affairs.[38] Like their right-wing European allies on the continent, the Japanese government also sought to demonstrate their nation's substantial sporting advances through sporting and Olympic victory—a policy that paralleled their aggressive territorial schemes highlighted by the September 1931 invasion of Manchuria.[39] Replicating the Italian interventionist model of state control, the Japanese government established a special training camp to prepare their elite athletes for the 1932 Olympic Games, and, according to some U.S. observers, transgressed the "spirit of sport" further by allegedly providing its swimmers with "dope" (in the form of purified oxygen) in an attempt to maximize performance.[40] The politicization of Olympic sport assumed near-global dimensions during the 1930s, as evidenced by the interference of Latin American governments into sporting affairs. Reporting upon a recent visit to the region, American Avery Brundage warned the IOC that the governance of Olympic sport is "entirely political." Brundage, a key figure in the later birth of both the Pan American and Central American games, advised Baillet-Latour that in countries such as Brazil and Colombia "very little is accomplished in any field without the assistance of the government." Olympic teams, he decried, were selected, organized, and subsidized by the state.[41]

Even democratic governments, while not as systematic as their right-wing rivals, abandoned the traditional ideology of laissez-faire in order to meet the new political realities of elite sport. Broadening the ambit of state influence, the Swedish government revived a policy first introduced at the abortive 1916 Berlin Games by conscripting all Olympic-caliber male athletes for a six-month "refresher in military training" (i.e., a pre-Olympic training camp). The government also donated 450,000 kroner (approximately $100,000) to finance the Swedish Olympic team in Los Angeles.[42] The governments of Finland, France, Norway, and the Netherlands also frequently tampered with sporting affairs during the interwar years, offering sizable subsidies to cover the cost of training and transporting their Olympic athletes to Paris (1924), Amsterdam (1928), and Los Angeles (1932).[43] The state use of sport conflicted with the IOC's belief that amateur sport should be run by private, voluntary associations composed of mostly unpaid individuals and free from government interference.

The encroachment of right-wing (and democratic) governments into the realm of Olympic sport failed to stir a noticeable response from IOC officials. Even though Coubertin first identified the threat that nationalism and state intervention posed to the Olympic Movement's avowed apoliticism in the years prior to World War I, the IOC remained surprisingly reticent. Any official proclamations on the subject of government-run training camps, state subsidies, and performance-based cash incentives were decidedly passive. At the 1925 Prague Congress, the IOC merely "expressed the wish" that governmental involvement be "exclusively devoted to the organization of the games and not to the training of national representatives."[44] The IOC's passivity on such an important issue needs to be viewed in an appropriate context. After all, the postwar IOC remained a financially and bureaucratically weak organization; beyond rumor and innuendo, Olympic officials had no real way of knowing the full extent of governmental intervention. What's more, the Olympic Games were still an emerging spectacle; the IOC tacitly enjoyed the support of Fascist and military governments in elevating the importance, prestige, and financial prosperity of the Olympic Games.

From an ideological perspective, the IOC displayed a strong predilection to Fascism and right-wing political thought. As an institution of remarkable homogeneity, the IOC was composed of members from countries (Italy, Germany, and Spain) whose governments and sports organizations "lurched definitively to the right," as well as European and North American aristocrats and businessmen who shared a similar ideological disdain for Communism and an ingrained antipathy toward Jews.[45] In truth, the bourgeois elites who ran the IOC considered Italy's Benito Mussolini and Nazi Germany's Adolf Hitler as influential partners in the fight against professionalism, vulgar commercialism, and Communism. Historian John Hoberman argues that this ideological compatibility between the IOC elite and emerging Fascist governments was based on a "shared ideal of aristocratic manhood and the value system derived from their glorification of the physically perfect male as the ideal human being."[46] The cult of vigor, power, and strength, and a concomitant detestation of weakness—implicit in *Citius, Altius, Fortius*—bound Olympism to the political and military ambitions of right-wing totalitarian regimes. This ideological and aesthetic fusion of Olympism with Fascism and Nazism would reach unparalleled heights during the 1936 winter and summer Olympic Games in Garmisch-Partenkirchen and Berlin, Germany. Replicating the Italian model of realpolitik, Hitler's Nazi government—after initial reluctance—seized control of the Olympic spectacle to the further detriment of the amateur ideal.

THE NAZIFICATION OF THE OLYMPIC SPECTACLE

In 1931, the IOC awarded the Olympic Games of the Eleventh Olympiad to the Weimar Republic as a gesture of reconciliation and a symbol of Germany's reintegration into the international community. Under the guidance of IOC member Theodor Lewald and Carl Diem, the leading functionaries from the world of Weimar sport, Germany undertook initial preparations to stage the winter and summer festivals. Adolf Hitler's unanticipated ascent to the chancellorship of Germany's ruling National Socialist Party on 30 January 1933, however, threw Olympic planning into disarray. Hitler's outspoken disdain for internationalism prompted Lewald to warn the IOC that the Nazis would be "absolutely opposed" to staging the Olympic Games.[47]

Despite Hitler's private opposition, Josef Goebbels, the Nazi minister of propaganda, succeeded in convincing the Führer of the political value of hosting the 1936 Olympics. He encouraged Hitler to embrace Germany's preparations as a platform for national propaganda, an opportunity to dazzle the world with the financial solvency and power of the new militaristic German state.[48] Despite pledging to oversee a German cultural renaissance, Hitler eschewed the nation's regimented system of *Turnen* gymnastics and embraced westernized sporting practices and models of internationalism—yet, paradoxically, in the diplomatic arena he controversially reoccupied the demilitarized Rhineland and ordered Germany's withdrawal from both the League of Nations and the Lausanne Disarmament Conference. From the Nazi perspective, the Olympics represented a powerful form of political and cultural capital, an unparalleled platform for positively shaping world public opinion, combating mass unemployment, and promoting sport among German youth. Overseeing Olympic preparations with the same intensity as he put into Germany's other grossly nationalistic and grandiose celebration of Nazi strength and vitality, the Nuremberg Rallies, Hitler commissioned the expenditure of lavish sums, estimated by one account at 100 million Reichsmarks, for the construction of state-of-the-art sporting and media facilities, as well as an Olympic village—signaling the first time in Olympic history that a state provided substantial resources toward hosting costs.[49]

The appropriation of a supposedly neutral and internationalist sporting event by an authoritarian and openly anti-Semitic state sparked threats of a global Olympic boycott.[50] Hitler's strident policies of racial and religious persecution, aligned with his government's revocation of Jewish citizenship through the Nuremberg Laws passed in 1935, gave further cause for nations to reconsider their participation in both Garmisch-Partenkirchen and Berlin.

Press reports throughout Europe and North America told of the reprehensible manner in which German Jews were excluded from national sports clubs and institutions, prohibited from using public facilities, and forbidden from competing at the forthcoming Olympic Games.[51] The United States took the lead in denouncing the Nazi's discriminatory policies. At the annual IOC session held in Vienna in June 1933, Brigadier General Charles Sherrill, a U.S. member of the IOC, demanded that the Germans immediately rescind their policy of racial discrimination and allow non-Aryans to try out for the German Olympic team. Although Karl Ritter von Halt, a Nazi Party member and IOC representative, balked at the U.S. demands, the IOC eventually secured an official governmental pledge that Germany would not violate the principles of Olympism by barring the participation of Jewish athletes.[52] Hans von Tschammer und Osten, the Nazi regime's inaugural *Reichssport-führer* and a former regional leader of Hitler's brutal Sturmabteilung forces, regularly reassured the IOC hierarchy that the "participation of Jews will be scrupulously observed."[53] The ideologically sympathetic and anti-Semitic IOC leadership was assuaged.

As Communist, Jewish, worker's, religious, and black lobby groups across Europe and North America collectively convulsed in horror at the growing fanaticism and anti-Semitism of Nazi ideology, Germany heightened its preparations for the staging of the 1936 winter and summer Olympic Games. Organizational efficiency, crowd management, and spectacle were hallmarks of the Nazi regime; elite international sport, however, was an unknown quantity. As in other fields in which the Nazis did not really know how to run the country, they turned to Fascist Italy for guidance in formulating an effective organizational sports policy.[54] Presiding over a fragmented sports movement, Hitler followed Mussolini's lead, dissolving Communist, Socialist, and religious groups, eradicating Jewish organizations, and centralizing German sport under the protective arm of the state. Under the close scrutiny of the *Reichssportführer,* German sports federations were relocated to Berlin and all presidents and representatives were appointed from above. The Nazi state took over more charges that had previously been the preserve of private and voluntary sporting bodies, prompting British trade unionist leader and fierce Nazi critic Sir Walter Citrine to inveigh that German sport was firmly "under the heel of Hitler."[55] The complete interpenetration of governmental and civil agencies in German sporting affairs violated the political independence enshrined in the *Olympic Charter*. While Lewald and Diem maintained the illusion of political independence, the 1936 winter and summer Olympics represented a government-run enterprise.

After nearly three years of international condemnation and threats of a global boycott, the Winter Olympic Games, the largest and most expensive winter festival at their time, held at a cost of over 2.6 million Reichsmarks, opened in the twin Bavarian towns of Garmisch-Partenkirchen. Despite their celebrated success, it was the 1936 Summer Olympics in Berlin, or Nazi Olympics as they have been more commonly labeled, that captured the world's attention. Against the backdrop of Hitler's much-publicized diplomatic and military confrontations, a staggering 3,963 athletes from forty-nine nations participated in Berlin.[56] Hitler's late concession to select the former Olympic gold medal fencer Helen Mayer, a "half Jew" under the Nuremburg Laws then living in California, onto the German team appeared to placate international anxieties and helped to avert a U.S.-led boycott.[57] The sporting world seemed to turn a blind eye to the fact that out of the twenty-one German Jews nominated as candidates for the Olympics, none was selected.[58] With both international opinion and the *Olympic Charter* in mind, the Reich went to great lengths to keep the games free of any pernicious anti-Semitic overtones. Anti-Jewish signs, books, and newspapers were removed, and the German people were exhorted to treat visitors, including Jews, amicably—a series of measures proposed by the Ministry of Propaganda to hoodwink foreign guests into leaving Berlin with a favorable impression of life under the Third Reich.[59]

In its main aim, the 1936 Olympics proved to be a remarkable success. Attracting more than three million people (more than double the attendance figures recorded in Los Angeles), the 1936 Berlin Games could rightfully claim, as the historian Barbara Keys put it, the title of being the "best Olympic Games ever"[60] up to that time. Under the skillful guidance of Olympic choreographer Carl Diem, general secretary of the Olympic Organizing Committee, doves flew, the Olympic flame burned brightly, and sonorous overtures of peace and international harmony rang throughout the Olympic fortnight. The scale of precision, organization, publicity, symbolic inventory, and spectacle was unprecedented. Journalists attended in droves, providing blanket radio and newspaper coverage to global audiences. Before the gleeful eyes of Hitler and Goebbels, German sportsmen and sportswomen stood atop the unofficial table of nations for the first time, claiming an impressive haul of eighty-nine medals.[61] The Nazi Party newspaper, *Der Angriff*, exclaimed in delight at the repetitive sight of the Swastika flying high above the Olympic medal podium. "It is truly difficult to bear so much joy," it enthused.[62]

REREADING NAZI SPORT

The propaganda success of the 1936 Berlin Olympics, where German sportsmen and sportswomen won the medals competition against their North American and European democratic rivals, has blurred historical thinking about the structure, aims, and extent of the Nazi sports apparatus.[63] Like much scholarship on Nazi Germany, historiography on the Berlin Olympics has been written through the lens of later history. Images and accounts of genocide, war, scientific and medical experimentation, and military barbarity have led scholars to cling to convenient mythology when unraveling the role that the Nazi government played in preparing its athletes for Olympic victory.[64] The general scholarly consensus holds that Hitler's government undertook not only the financial guarantees to underwrite the cost of the games but went even further and directly paid for the selection and preparation of German athletes.[65] According to this line of thought, Nazi officials identified potential Olympic medal winners and afforded this elite corps special privileges ranging from free travel, food, and accommodation (via "Olympic passports"), as well as broken-time payments to cover the cost of time away from the workplace. Reviving plans for selecting and developing talent first crafted in preparation for the abortive 1916 Berlin Olympic Games, in this line of thought, Nazi officials violated IOC regulations further by sponsoring lengthy training camps and granting German athletes access to expert coaching and medical treatment.[66] The degree of state intervention appeared so strong, some scholars speculate, that Nazis doctors even administered hormones and stimulants (broadly labeled "dope") to their athletes in the hopes of attaining a German team victory on home soil.[67]

Did the Nazis government flagrantly flout IOC amateur regulations in the pursuit of Olympic gold and the propaganda riches that such victories bestowed? Nazi Germany's ideological and sporting rivals at the time argued in the affirmative. Beliefs in the existence of a highly specialized and grossly politicized Nazi sporting system fueled waves of opprobrium across Europe and North America. BOA vice president John Beresford, Baron Decies, condemned the manner in which the Nazis seized upon the training of German athletes. The British "can no longer possibly compete on equal terms with men who have been withdrawn from ordinary life and carefully trained for months," he groused.[68] Like their British allies, the United States argued that the intervention of the Nazi state ran contrary to the spirit of amateurism. The *New York Times* told of German athletes removed from their occupations and placed in extensive six-month training programs under orders of the government.[69] In a familiarly acerbic tone, the Communist *Daily Worker* also recounted stories of German Olympians kept in state-run "rigid training units" many months before the commencement of the games.[70] "The Berlin Games this year are an absolute prostitution of the wonderful ideals that true Olympics involved, and Hitler is making them a gigantic parade of Nazi propaganda," it protested.[71] The *Deutsche Diplomatische-Politische*

Korrespondenz, the press release of the German Foreign Ministry, rejected Western and, notably, Communist accusations. "There is no thought of exploiting the Olympic idea as was done in a red 'Workers' Olympiad,'" it wrote in defense.[72]

Facing mounting public pressure, Baillet-Latour investigated the rumors of Nazi state intervention in the build-up to the Berlin Olympic Games. He wrote a letter to his personal friend Dr. Theodor Lewald, president of the Berlin Olympic Organizing Committee, asking for clarification on the issue. Lewald rushed to placate the IOC president, insisting that the Nazi government was truthfully upholding the Olympic Movement's noninterventionist and amateur principles. He cited a correspondence with Tschammer und Osten, in which the *Reichssportführer* reassured that

> He has abandoned the original intention to proceed with the training of the Olympic athletes in training camps. Training is being pursued in the homes of the athletes by trainers. As much as the collaboration of the *Reichstrainer* is taken into consideration, he is involved with meeting with only some athletes, with their local trainers, during the weekend and one time per month. In cases where, in some sports, the athletes follow a course of training of a maximum duration of 21 days, that happens one time per year, in the middle of their regular vacations. The expenses of these camps are supported by the relevant federation. There is, in all cases, no question of allowances whatsoever in currency for the loss of salary or other subsidies which would be spent on the participants or on their families.[73]

Through the lens of later history, it is easy to read the *Reichssportführer's* disavowal of Western allegations of impropriety as a case of Nazi political brinksmanship and misdirection. His statement appears carefully scripted, designed to inspire the belief that the preparation of German athletes was a voluntary enterprise in strict keeping with the amateur rules and regulations of the international sports federations. Baillet-Latour appeared satisfied. He expressed his contentment in a private missive to Brundage.[74] Rumors "have been spread now and then about every sport, in those countries, where sport is under the leadership of a dictatorial government," he argued, but "they have also been proved to be untrue every time."[75]

Unlike the IOC elite at the time, scholars of Nazi sport today are incredulous. The sheer thoroughness, efficiency, and capital outlay expended by the Nazi government on staging the Olympics, the centralization of German sport by the state, as well as the gold-medal performances of German athletes, suggest that the Nazis ignored the IOC's prohibitions against broken-time payments, extended training camps, and monetary rewards. Beyond the conjecture of Germany's ideological and sporting rivals, evidence to substantiate this position is sorely lacking.[76] The exact role of the German government in selecting and preparing its athletes needs some deconstruction, even though it contradicts our deeply rooted assumption that the Nazis stopped at nothing to achieve success in every field of endeavor. As John Hoberman has argued, elite sport was considered a subsidiary affair, inferior to German economic productivity and military preparations. The single-minded specialization that Olympic success demanded, Hoberman contends, also contradicted the racial collectivity spirit of the German Volk.[77] Hitler's focus on militarism and collectivism, as well as his intense desire to demonstrate Nazi organizational mastery, likely trumped any interest in achieving Olympic success. A review of Germany's past Olympic performances justified Hitler's preference for hosting rather than winning.[78] The lowly ninth-place finish of German athletes at the 1932 Los Angeles Games provided little evidence for Nazi officials to believe that they could reap the rewards of Olympic success in Berlin.

A detailed examination casts further doubt on prevailing beliefs that German athletes were prepared for the 1936 games within a clearly structured, centrally organized, and state-financed high-performance sport system. Documentation reveals that in bigger cities, *Trainingsgemeinschaften* (training communities) were organized for the best German Olympic athletes to train together. Some *Trainingsgemeinschaften* asked the local authorities for subsidies, but these requests generated little response. The introduction of a sports ticket sales tax (*Sportgroschen*) to help finance the training centers also appeared to fall on deaf ears. In some sports, the Nazis did (as Tschammer und Osten confirmed) provide *Reichstrainer*s, but the level of their involvement remains open to debate.[79] Nazi authorities also considered providing financial subsidies exclusively for poor and needy athletes (*Patenschaften*), but evidence indicates that they jettisoned this initiative out of fears that it conflicted with the IOC's amateur rules. Instead, the Deutsche Reichbund für Leibesübungen (governing body of German sports) or the *Reichssportführer* asked the local authorities to provide prospective Olympians with employment. The local authorities, in turn, asked the employers of the athletes to create favorable conditions that would guarantee them enough money and time to train—the final decision, it appears, rested with the employer. The *Reichssportführer* did initiate a "search for the unknown sportsman" (*Suche nach dem unbekannten Sportsmann*). This was not a systematic review of pupils or students. Rather, sports competitions were arranged to which all interested Aryan athletes were invited. These competitions were divided according to sports. The success of this campaign, however, was very low: The only German Olympic athlete who was discovered in this way was middle-distance runner Rudolf Harbig.[80] Elsewhere, the Wehrmacht, the German unified armed forces, did prepare its athletes for the Olympic Games in special courses (*Lehrgänge*) under the direction of competent trainers, but these courses were intermittent and short in duration.[81]

Overall, documentation appears to validate, however counterintuitive, the *Reichssportführer's* insistence that there was no central system of German state support for top athletes or strict government instructions to professionalize an athlete's training.[82] Similarly, evidence has cast doubts on the use of systematic doping, especially anabolic steroids, among German athletes for the 1936 Olympics.[83] German sportsmen and sportswomen were appropriated, indoctrinated, and propagandized as symbolic representations of the Third Reich, but they were not the unscrupulous professionals of our popular imagination.

NO MORE WINTER GAMES!

While the Western media launched accusatory barbs at the victorious German team and their authoritarian allies, the IOC worked behind the scenes to strengthen relations with the international federations. After the success of its inaugural World Cup, FIFA gestured that it wanted to return to the Olympic fold. The renegade world governing body of soccer abrogated its Olympic tournament in Los Angeles upon the IOC's ruling against broken-time payments at the Berlin Congress. Under Jules Rimet's leadership, FIFA suddenly adopted a more conciliatory stance. The IOC was also keen to restore the world's most popular and economically viable sport to the Olympic program. The issue of eligibility remained, particularly since FIFA had removed all passages concerning amateurism from its statutes—a decision that technically deferred responsibility to the national federations of soccer. At its 1934 session in Athens, IOC members agreed to modify its own rules (for soccer only), which had specified that the international federations were the bodies charged with governing amateur eligibility within the overall rules of the IOC.[84] In an unprecedented move, the IOC entrusted the national soccer federations to take over this role, thus clearing the way for soccer's reappearance on the Olympic program in Berlin. Welcoming news of FIFA's return to the Olympic Movement, a jubilant Edström remarked "that even the federations that earlier had tended towards a lenient understanding of the amateur problem now are returning to true amateurism."[85] Little did Edström and his colleagues know that this special dispensation would effectively grant partisan, often state-controlled, soccer federations free license to tarnish the amateur ideal.

After pulling FIFA back within its organizational sphere, the IOC pursued better relations with another French-led federation: the Union Internationale de Tir. The IOC excluded shooting from the program of events at the 1928 Amsterdam Olympics because the French organization had a policy of awarding valuable material and cash prizes to amateur rifleman. Under pressure from Olympic officials, the shooting federation agreed to conform to the IOC's amateur standards, promising to bar those competitors from Berlin who had recently accepted monetary rewards. The Fédération Equestre Internationale intimated that it also would take steps to proscribe payments to its amateur equestrian riders.[86]

The IOC sought to formalize relations with the international federations even further. At the 1934 meeting of the Conseil des Délégués, the international sports federations agreed to establish a subcommittee on amateurism tasked with achieving what the British *Sporting Life* had earlier failed: a universal definition of an amateur applicable to all Olympic sports.[87] Hope inevitably turned to disappointment. By the 1936 IOC session in Berlin, Baillet-Latour reported that the international sports federations had gotten nowhere in their quest to solve the age-old problem of amateurism.[88] Once again, bureaucratic power-wrangling lay at the heart of the issue. The federations believed that they should be the sole arbiters of athletes' eligibility, and the IOC insisted that it had the right to establish certain general conditions for those who wished to take part in the Olympics.[89] In the build-up to the Berlin Olympic Games, the Fédération Internationale de Gymnastique (FIG) and the Fédération Internationale de Ski (FIS) sparked a bureaucratic storm by voting upon definitions of an amateur that did not conform to the IOC's basic eligibility requirements.

The IOC dealt with the international federations inconsistently and case by case. The FIG's decision to grant "teachers of a sport" amateur status provoked a fierce response from newly elected IOC member Avery Brundage. With a pugnacity that would typify his administrative career, the U.S. firebrand considered competitive gymnasts who sought employment as sport instructors as professionals and advised Baillet-Latour that they should be prohibited from competing in Berlin.[90] Carl Diem, the general secretary for the Berlin Olympic Organizing Committee, waded into the debate. With the Berlin Olympics fast approaching, Diem cautioned Baillet-Latour that the exclusion of gymnasts (specifically, German gymnasts) would create "enormous difficulties" because "gymnastics competitions in Germany represent an important branch in the field of physical education."[91] After months of deliberation, the IOC and FIG reached an agreeable middle ground: Elementary school teachers who taught gymnastics as part of ordinary teaching would qualify as Olympic amateurs, but those who specialized in teaching gymnastics or coached the sport at a competitive level would not meet Olympic eligibility requirements. The FIG accepted this brokered compromise and amended its amateur statutes before the 1936 Olympics.[92]

The winter sport federations proved less amenable. The FIS, which was formed at the inaugural Winter Olympic Games in Chamonix, clashed with the IOC throughout the 1930s over its desire to qualify paid ski instructors as amateurs. The post–World War I Alpine ski boom had created many opportunities for talented ski racers to profit by teaching wealthy European tourists how to slide down the Alps. Although this type of instruction was a far cry from the slaloming of the Olympic Games, the IOC remained unconvinced by the distinction. With the slating of several downhill skiing events to appear on the Olympic program in Garmisch-Partenkirchen for the first time, the stage was set for an administrative battle. Norwegian IOC member Thomas Fearnley brought the issue to the attention of his colleagues, advising that FIS's stance on amateurism contravened Olympic regulations.[93] Infuriated by such an affront to the IOC's authority, members urged Baillet-Latour to advise the upstart federation that paid ski instructors would not be permitted to compete in future Olympics. On the eve of the 1936 Olympics, the FIS executive council eventually abandoned its principles and agreed to participate under IOC rules—essentially forcing the exclusion of many of the world's leading ski racers.[94]

This proved to be only a temporary concession. At its 1936 congress, FIS president Nicolai Østgaard declared that alpine skiing will appear on future Olympic programs only "on the condition that the FIS Rules for International Competitions are used."[95] Baillet-Latour was incensed. The commercial ambience enveloping the Winter Olympic Games served as a source of considerable anxiety for the IOC president. Ski manufacturing, tourism, ice rinks, and mechanized ski lifts made winter sport athletes heavily reliant on commercial operators.[96] Determined to eliminate the scourge of commercialism and profiteering, he advised his colleagues on the IOC to stage the 1940 Winter Olympics without the alpine and slalom ski competitions.[97] After the Fédération Internationale de Hockey sur Glace approved a series of measures granting amateur ice-hockey players freedom to capitalize financially on their fame, Edström proposed a more radical motion: the elimination of the winter games altogether.[98] Although the IOC defeated this suggestion (26–1), it revealed the tension that would long exist between the purportedly noncommercial Olympic Movement and the commercial realities of winter sport.[99]

COMBATING AMATEUR ABUSES

For Baillet-Latour, ongoing confrontations with recalcitrant, commercially oriented international sports federations, as well as the growing governmental takeover of international sport, necessitated the formation of a new IOC commission to "study the question of amateurism."[100] In the period leading up to the 1937 session in Warsaw, the IOC president wrote an essay on amateurism in which he identified seven key issues that, he feared, had the potential to bring about the "ruination of the Olympic Games."[101] He addressed the "question of professors," the "situation of sporting professional writers," and the participation of amateurs who compete as professionals in other sports. In view of the politicized tone of interwar sport, he also devoted considerable space to the "nationalization of sports in various countries," alongside a series of other related, government-sponsored practices such as extended training camps, state subsidies and gifts, and the "doping of athletes."[102] His ruminations served as the template for a debate of the topic among IOC members in Warsaw. After a lengthy discussion, the IOC voted to appoint an ad hoc amateur commission, consisting of vice president Edström, Avery Brundage, high-ranking Nazi official Karl Ritter von Halt, and the Italian count Alberto Bonacossa, to prepare a report and present it to the 1938 IOC session in Cairo.[103]

After two private meetings in Cologne and Paris, the amateur commission brought its findings before the IOC in the Egyptian capital.[104] Brundage, the only native English speaker on the committee, appeared to take the lead in drafting the report. After his 1936 appointment to the IOC, a reward—in some measure—for his fierce opposition to the U.S. Olympic boycott movement, Brundage quickly established himself as a dominant voice in the amateur debate. The commission's report reflected Brundage's philosophical devotion and contradictory attitudes on the subject.[105] The amateur commission denounced as a "danger" the "nationalization of sports for political aim." Government-run extended training camps, state subsidies, and monetary prizes were deemed "not in accordance with the idea of the Olympic Games." On the other hand, the commission welcomed "with universal approval" the manner in which governments adopted programs of "collective physical education with a view to perfecting popular sport." Herein lay an inherent contradiction. The IOC extolled the governmental appropriation of sport and Olympism (and the benefits that this afforded the Olympic Movement) but opposed the methods authoritarian regimes adopted in the pursuit of national aggrandizement.[106] The post-1936 embrace of the Nazi government reflected this paradox. The IOC awarded the Olympic Diploma to Leni Riefenstahl for her cinematic capturing of the Berlin Olympics; the "Strength through Joy" (a Nazi leisure organization) won the Pierre de Coubertin Cup in 1938; Carl Diem was granted permission to establish an International Olympic Institute in Berlin; and General Walter von Reichenau, a high-ranking Nazi military official (and later, notorious war criminal), was elected to the IOC.[107]

The amateur commission also, for the first time in Olympic history, "condemned most strongly" the doping of athletes. Like other issues addressed by the commission, the nationalization of Olympic sport had brought the doping issue to the surface. Throughout the 1930s, authoritarian regimes had expended state funds to experiment with stimulants to enhance military and (to a lesser extent) sporting performance. The Italians had opened a state-sponsored sports medicine and training unit in Bologna that examined biomechanics, nutrition, and even the effects of tonics, stimulants, and hormones (substances the IOC would later consider doping).[108] The Germans also devoted state resources to the science of performance enhancement, which some believed included research on doping.[109] In fact, this merging line of scientific inquiry helped German scientist and Nazi party member Adolf Butenandt make major breakthroughs throughout the 1930s in synthesizing testosterone, for which he would earn the 1939 Nobel Prize in chemistry. Perceptions of clandestine government-funded doping programs, coupled with prevailing fears over the "moral" sanctity of amateur sport, heightened the IOC's interest in the topic.

Baillet-Latour presented the doping issue to the amateur commission. The IOC president, who had owned several racehorses and been president of the Jockey-Club Bruxelles, was likely first introduced to the issue of doping through his time in the horseracing world. The widespread practice of administering stimulants to horses as a way to fix races and control gambling odds, led Baillet-Latour to place doping within the context of amateurism.[110] "Amateur sport is meant to improve the soul and the body," he opined, "therefore no stone must be left unturned as long as the use of doping has not been stamped out. Doping ruins the health and very likely implies an early death."[111]

Under Baillet-Latour's direction, the IOC began collecting files and reports on doping in an attempt to better understand the subject.[112] The documentation underlined Baillet-Latour's health and ethical concerns about athletes using drugs or stimulants in sport and the ties to national sporting bodies. The perceived dangers of doping helped convince Brundage to draft antidoping language, even if the definition or the list of stimulants remained unclear. Somewhere between the 1937 IOC session in Warsaw and the 1938 session in Cairo, Brundage wrote out by hand the following statement: "The use of drugs or artificial stimulants of any kind cannot be too strongly denounced and anyone receiving or administering dope or artificial stimulants be excluded from participation in sport or the O.G. [Olympic Games]."[113] Despite the glaring omission of policies for testing and enforcement, the amateur commission agreed upon almost identical language in Cairo. The IOC's prohibitions against doping would form part of its Rule 26 under "Resolutions regarding the Amateur Status" in their next published charter in 1946.[114] This language would continue as part of Rule 26 until 1975, when it was transferred from an amateur eligibility rule to part of the IOC's new medical code with separate by-laws created by the IOC's Medical Commission.[115]

On other topics, the amateur commission outlawed Olympians using their fame to secure positions within journalism, film, and broadcasting. It also forbade athletes from receiving reimbursements for expenses other than those related to travel, board, and transportation. Brundage and his colleagues also reaffirmed its opposition to broken-time payments.[116] The IOC adopted the amateur commission's policy recommendations with little opposition. Therefore, the Cairo session represented (to that point) the IOC's most serious and far-reaching attempt to settle the issue of amateurism. With officials such as Baillet-Latour, Edström, and more recently Brundage within its leadership ranks, the IOC finally displayed the ideological conviction to assert a clear, defensible amateur agenda. It flexed its newfound bureaucratic confidence even further, when members in Cairo also voted to exclude the FIS-sponsored Alpine skiing contests "under any shape or form" from the 1940 Winter Olympic Games.[117]

The IOC's rulings in Cairo stood in philosophical and practical opposition to the beliefs of the founder of the modern Olympic Movement, the recently

Three of amateurism's most ardent advocates, (left to right) Henri Baillet-Latour, Avery Brundage, and Sigfrid Edström, each served as president of the IOC. Collectively these three shaped and defended amateurism from 1925 to 1972. (Courtesy of the International Olympic Committee)

deceased Pierre de Coubertin. Speaking before his 2 September 1937 death, the baron candidly revealed his true feelings on the subject of amateurism in an interview with the French publication *L'Auto*:

> Olympic amateurism is a stupid old question. And how often and how wrongly have people blamed me for the so-called hypocrisy of the Olympic sermon. Just read this famous Olympic sermon of which I am the proud and happy father. Where do you find that it demands from athletes appearing on the Olympic Stadion the absolute amateurism which, I am the first to recognize, is impossible? All I demand is loyalty to sport. Loyalty to sport, however, is not the monopoly of amateurs. I have known professionals and even circus professionals who showed a sporting spirit which the majority of amateurs could envy. It is this very sporting spirit which interests me and not the ridiculous concept which only enables millionaires to devote themselves to sport without doing violence to superseded dogmas. I am not the one who wanted that kind of amateurism. It was imposed by the International Federations.[118]

Coubertin discovered through decades of failed legislation, hypocrisy, and bureaucratic wrangling that, as a matter of motive, attitude, or spirit, amateurism defied regulation. With his life's work laid before him, Coubertin reflected somberly on the fact that his vision of amateurism as a moral, aesthetic, and spiritual ideal had been reduced to a complex web of prohibitive regulations that effectively served to marginalize working-class athletes from the Olympic arena.

In the months after the Cairo session, geopolitical convulsions ensured that the IOC's attempts to embolden amateurism—against the baron's last wishes—would be lost to the pages of history. The growing belligerence of an axis of authoritarian regimes brought the great powers into a devastating six-year conflict that would forever shape the political, economic, and sporting landscape. For the second time in the Olympic Movement's brief history, the winter and summer games (originally scheduled for Sapporo and Tokyo, Japan, in 1940) were canceled because of the outbreak of war. The IOC was later forced to scrap the proposed 1944 games when the global military conflict showed no signs of abating.

5 THE AMATEUR APOSTLE
AND THE COLD WAR GAMES

No figure played a more significant role in the history of Olympic amateurism than Avery Brundage. For more than four decades and across all layers of Olympic governance the American defended amateurism seemingly with religious conviction. His deeply conservative views and passionate defense of the amateur ideal set the tone for the IOC in the Cold War years, helping insulate the movement from the radical currents that were transforming postwar societies and global affairs.[1] Both in his lifetime and in the years since, portrayals of Brundage depict a Quixote-esque idealist providing the Olympic Movement's only firm line of defense against professional and commercial encroachments.[2] He was at times an "idealistic dreamer" and "out of touch with reality."[3] Other descriptions of Brundage invoked religious vocabulary. He was a "defender of the faith," he had the "fervor of a revivalist," a "humorless man carrying on a crusade for amateurism."[4] Yet, above all else, Brundage has been labeled as consistent and uncompromising. The orthodox view of Brundage as an unwavering apostle of amateurism overlooks the finer, more nuanced realities of his administration. Despite his anticommercial rhetoric and investigatory crusades, Brundage also appeased, compromised, and even spearheaded initiatives that broke with the Olympic Movement's amateur traditions.

A former pentathlete and veteran of the 1912 Stockholm Olympic Games, Brundage embraced the Olympic Movement as a secular religion, a shining light in an imperfect world soiled by corruption, commercialism, and gross socioeconomic inequalities. He possessed a level of idealism that far surpassed that of his ideological master, Pierre de Coubertin. Where the baron was charming, gregarious, philosophically flexible, and politically motivated, Brundage was dour, taciturn, and rigid. He was seemingly above compromise and immune to the seductions of modernity and self-interest.[5] Unlike the baron, he conceived of amateurism in a remarkably simplistic fashion: as an "inflexible, an absolute and universal thing."[6] It was a spiritual, metaphysical ideal, he exclaimed, a "moral law" that transcended national boundaries. In rhetoric and policy, Brundage refused, or, rather, chose not to accept amateurism's social, moral, economic, medical, and aesthetic dimensions, nor its numerous sporting applications and national and cultural interpretations. Revealing his intellectual limitations, he drew a simplistic play versus work, amateur–professional dichotomy. Amateur sport, he preached, was an autotelic endeavor—the reward resided purely in the doing. It was an avocation; a temporary, playful pursuit in which one must compete "solely for the love of the game" rather than as a full-time, serious vocation.[7] Brundage favored a clear-cut sociological distinction that emphasized both "spirit" (play as leisure) and "occupational category" (play without monetary reward). Amateur sport required "sacrifice" he demanded, a moral, physical, and financial commitment.[8] Athletes who required monetary compensation or those who elevated victory and a quest for records to the detriment of the play spirit fell short of this exalted amateur ideal.

From Olympic athlete to long-serving IOC president (1952–72), Brundage's bureaucratic footprint was deep and far-reaching. After a decade working within the framework of the U.S. Olympic Movement—beginning in 1928 as U.S. AAU president and then in 1932 as president of the United States Olympic Association (USOA)—he quickly ascended to the upper echelons of IOC governance. After his election to a seat on the IOC in 1936 and subsequent promotion onto the executive board in 1937, Brundage's organizational acumen and energy captured the attention of Sigfrid Edström. In Brundage, Edström discovered an intimate friend and trusted political ally. They shared an ideological commitment to the amateur ideal, crafting and enforcing Olympic policy, and schooling outsiders in the virtues of "sport for sport's sake." In his position as IOC vice president and later president, Edström personally guided the American's rise to bureaucratic power. During the first postwar meeting of the executive board in August 1945, Edström elevated Brundage to the rank of IOC vice president. After his own election to the office of IOC president the following year, Edström again played the role of benefactor by positioning Brundage as his "first" vice president and heir apparent. From the IOC's headquarters in Lausanne, or more frequently, from his home in southern California and office in Chicago, Brundage promulgated the Olympic ideals of fair play, good sportsmanship, and amateurism with a vigor and passion unmatched by any other personality in Olympic history. An avid reader of international newspapers, journals, and magazines, he possessed a remarkable ability to detect amateur violations, launch personal investigations, and occasionally, dispense sanctions.[9]

Unlike many of his colleagues on the IOC, the Michigan native did not hail from an aristocratic background. The son of a stonemason, Brundage was in the words of his biographer Allen Guttmann, a "self-made man in the Franklinian tradition."[10] Working his way successfully through a civil engineering degree at the University of Illinois, Brundage began a construction firm that, despite the calamity of the Wall Street crash, transformed him into a multimillionaire. He celebrated the virtues of laissez-faire capitalism, an economic system that allowed him to escape the handicaps of poverty through a blend of perseverance, hard work, and moral rectitude. Throughout his life, Brundage credited his athletic background with instilling the attributes needed to flourish in the capitalist U.S. society. He played by the rules, respected authority, and was beyond reproach—his marital infidelity notwithstanding. Brundage believed that the values he acquired through amateur sport also protected him against the political corruption and moral bankruptcy that blighted his home city of Chicago during the interwar years. Under Al Capone's rule, bootlegging, dishonest businessmen, and politicians on the take blackened the landscape. The 1919 "Black Sox" scandal revealed to Brundage that even Chicago's professional baseballers were not immune

Avery Brundage modeled his views of amateurism on himself. Here is a young Avery Brundage on the eve of the 1912 Olympic Games. (Courtesy of the University of Illinois Archives)

to the prevailing forces of deceit and financial self-interest. These formative experiences (of poverty and corruption) crystallized Brundage's attitudes toward amateurism. He imagined Coubertin's Olympic Movement as a shining contrast to the sordid underbelly of Chicago politics and business; a democratic arena where determined, dedicated, working-class amateur athletes (like his young self) could achieve Olympic honors. Through this romantic lens, Brundage celebrated the Olympics as the "greatest social force in the world."[11]

From the corrupt streets of Al Capone's Chicago to the palatial European halls of IOC meetings, Brundage spent his entire bureaucratic career molding the amateur ideal in his own image. Rejecting the strict social-class prohibitions of Victorian Britain, Brundagian amateurism emphasized fair play, impartial rules, moderation, and opportunity and achievement based on individual merit—it was not *who* played, but rather *how* you played. The Olympic amateur of Brundage's imagination was Brundage himself: a dedicated, all-around athlete who competed for the love of the game. In contrast to the gloss of Brundage's romantic idealism stood an ominous reality: an elite, highly specialized, state-subsidized Olympic amateur who competed in the pursuit of victory, for fame, for wealth, and for the bestowing of national and ideological prestige. It was this vision of an amateur that, despite Brundage's passionate but inconsistent efforts, came to dominate the postwar Olympic landscape.

NEW MOVEMENT, OLD PROBLEMS

The IOC remerged from the maelstrom of World War II disoriented and bitterly fragmented. Nazi belligerence undermined the pacifist spirit of Olympism, ground the wartime operations of the Olympic Movement to a halt, and forced the cancelation of both the 1940 and 1944 Olympic spectacles. Upon the 1942 death of Henri Baillet-Latour, Sigfrid Edström took over the reins as IOC president. Sweden's neutrality granted him the freedom to speak across both sides of the aisle and restore the Olympic Movement to a position of normality and relevance. Edström faced a daunting task. When the IOC reassembled at its first postwar session in Lausanne, the members found their ranks significantly depleted—of the members in attendance, half were new to the IOC. For delegates whose countries had been ravaged by German and Italian conquest and occupation, for former Nazis and Fascists to remain on the IOC was an intolerable outrage. Turning from bitter squabbles over war guilt, Edström also was forced to navigate postwar geopolitical considerations. Germany and Korea became divided into mutually hostile fragments, the Soviet Union sought to intensify its grip on Eastern Europe, and China convulsed into a civil war between communist and anticommunist factions. As Edström and the IOC voted to revive the winter and summer games in St. Moritz and London in 1948, internal and external political forces cast an ominous cloud over the Olympic Movement.[12]

In his new position as vice president, Brundage and the newly reconstituted IOC worked to survey and repair the damage wrought by another global war. Amid discussions over the dizzying array of new geopolitical configurations and the participation of enemy powers, the question of amateurism regularly appeared on the IOC's postwar agenda. Brundage chaired an ad-hoc amateur commission with the responsibility of reviving and reexamining the Olympic Movement's amateur code.[13] He viewed the cessation of war as an unprecedented opportunity to rebuild the Olympic Movement upon a "purely idealistic, non-materialistic, non-commercial, non-political foundation." Before him stood a chance to right historical wrongs, to renew the IOC's commitment to the amateur ideal. "Now is the time to eliminate abuses of all kinds" he told British IOC member Clarence Napier Bruce, Lord Aberdare, and encouraged his colleague "to eradicate sources of trouble, to add authority where it is needed, and to strengthen and add luster, to the movement."[14]

The revival of Olympic competition afforded Brundage with what he perceived as an opportunity to recast and strengthen the amateur ideal, but it also presented his opponents with a chance to advocate for change on more open, egalitarian terms. During a January 1946 international meeting of the Danish (Dansk Athletik-Forbund), Finnish (Suomen Urheiluliitto), Norwegian (Norges Fri-Idrettsforbund), and Swedish (Svenska Idrottsforbundet) sporting associations, representatives proposed a number of "minor adjustments" to the amateur code. Reclaiming their mantle as the liberalizing agents of world sport, the Scandinavian and Finnish officials called for a raise in the "maximum value of a prize" for an amateur contest from 10 to 15 pounds (or its equivalent in the national currency), as well as the sanctioning of broken-time payments to reimburse amateur athletes for time away from the workplace. Officials hoped that in reviving these prewar proposals, "the reputation of modern sport as one of the democratic movements of our time, shall not be jeopardised."[15] Fearing that Brundage's sponsored stance on amateurism would prevent its athletes from competing at the 1948 Summer Olympic Games in London, the Ligue Belge d'Athlétisme reiterated the call for legislative change. Endorsing broken-time payments as another step in fulfilling the universal mission of sport, the Belgian athletic body reasoned that it would be "profoundly immoral" to see an athlete of modest wealth unable to represent his nation "because his personal resources do not allow him this without compromising the budgetary balance of his house and his home."[16] Led by Swedish IOC member Bo Ekelund, this rebel band of European social democracies succeeded in placing the issue of indemnities on the IAAF's agenda for its 1947 annual congress.[17]

For Brundage, the European push to align amateur policy with the economic and social realities of the postwar world constituted heresy. Viewing amateurism as a philosophy akin to a global religion, Brundage believed that its central precepts were permanent, universal, and incapable of change. Amateurism was not the product of dramatic social and economic transformations in Victorian Britain, he argued, but a fixed "moral law" that traversed the ages. With a characteristic blend of historical inaccuracy, he pontificated that amateurism, "coming to us from antiquity, [has] contributed to and strengthened the noblest aspirations of great men of each generation."[18] From this perspective, Brundage viewed the passage of broken-time payment as "the entering wedge for professionalism."[19] Modifications, no matter how small, imperiled the "spirit" of amateurism. In a detailed article on the subject published in *World Sports*, he argued that the European proposals were "utterly foreign to the spirit of play, of fun and of diversion that makes it sport."[20] Unlike a growing number of his contemporaries, he dismissed democratic arguments in favor of broken-time. Brundage viewed the world from his personal perspective, through his own lived experiences. He was once a poor, hard-working athlete who made a personal and financial sacrifice to realize his Olympic ambitions; he failed to understand why others were not prepared to do the same. For these reasons, the broadening socioeconomic, gender, and racial disparities of Olympic amateur sport never truly resonated with him. He simply equated remuneration for lost time with greed and indolence. "I have known athletes who were too rich to compete in the Olympic Games (because they had too many responsibilities), I have never known one who was too poor to compete," he lectured.[21] In a series of correspondence with Edström, he vowed to defeat the European proposal, fearing that otherwise "the death knell will be sounded for the Olympic games."[22] The defense of amateurism was a zero-sum affair. "Better, no Olympic Games than any relaxation of the fundamental principles on which the whole Olympic structure is built," Brundage blustered.[23]

Through the intervention of Brundage and his allies, the IAAF successfully repelled Swedish-led advances. Members rejected the propositions to increase the value of cash prizes and to sanction the award of indemnities for lost time.[24] With the calls to democratize sport temporarily silenced, Brundage worked to protect the amateur ideal against a more serious threat: the growing commercial orientation of Olympic sport. Despite his own vast personal wealth, he viewed money as a gateway toward greed, corruption, and professionalism. He frequently evoked the "erroneous" example of the downfall and dissolution of the ancient Greek Olympic games as a warning to those who advocated change on populist grounds. "We all know what happened when the ancient games were commercialized. The same will happen again if we are not vigilant," he admonished."[25] Although Brundage's gloomy foreboding proved historically inaccurate—the Christian Roman Empire abolished the pagan Olympics of Greek antiquity on religious rather than commercial grounds—he dedicated his entire Olympic career to eliminating the lure of financial reward in all its many guises (e.g., commercial advertising, television and tax revenue, salaries for IOC members and athletes). "We must stand fast against the tide of materialism," Brundage intoned. "If we yield and open the door a crack, all will be lost."[26] In keeping with a strict anticommercial interpretation of the spirit of amateurism, Brundage expressed concern that the British Olympic Association's use of London's Wembley Stadium—a privately owned property—to stage the 1948 summer games would compromise Olympic principles.[27] Even in London, a bomb-shattered landscape whose inhabitants were still rationing food, clothing, and fuel, Brundage remained insistent "that no one makes any money from this enterprise."[28] His intensity was unrivaled.

The 1948 St. Moritz Winter Games further illustrated the fervor with which Brundage resisted the commercial forces threatening the postwar Olympic landscape. A jurisdictional clash between the U.S. AAU and the American Hockey Association (AHA) over the governance of Olympic ice hockey set the IOC vice president on an amateurism crusade.[29] The AHA, a rebel group established by team owners and rink operators, split from the AAU in 1937 in protest over its strict antiprofiteering regulations. Seeking to maximize revenue at the box office, the commercial vendors who ran the AHA and its affiliated teams endorsed the payment of leading U.S. ice-hockey players. When the liberal French-led Fédération Internationale de Hockey sur Glace (FIHG) recognized the AHA as the sole representative member from the United States, Brundage sprang to attention.[30] In accordance with the *Olympic Charter*, only national governing bodies recognized by their respective international federation could—with the exception of soccer—compete at the Olympic Games. Facing the prospect of a "business institution that has no place in amateur sport" representing the United States at the St. Moritz Games, Brundage pleaded with the Swiss Olympic organizers to disallow the AHA's entry.[31] For the Swiss, however, commercial considerations ran paramount. Eager to revive their tourist trade, the Swiss were focused on attracting the leading U.S. players, professional or otherwise. Gate receipts from hockey were the only way to fund the games, with the historically paltry audiences for other winter Olympic sports.

After months of overheated rhetoric and boycott threats, the IOC and the Swiss organizers brokered a solution: The "professional" AHA could compete in an unofficial capacity, and the AAU team could march in the Opening Ceremony. Bitterness over the episode, though, appeared to linger among Brundage and his fellow amateur enthusiasts. The appearance of an openly professional team demonstrated that economic concerns were slowly taking precedent over amateur ideals. In retaliation, the IOC suspended the renegade international federation from Olympic membership, thereby eliminating ice hockey from future Winter Olympics. The IOC would later reverse this decision after the FIHG agreed to conform to Olympic amateur rules.[32]

With the ice-hockey imbroglio temporarily settled, Brundage and the IOC turned their attention toward a source of persistent trouble: the Fédération Internationale de Ski (FIS) and its policy of sanctioning paid ski instruction. This common Scandinavian and European practice, which had been fueled by a booming post–World War II winter tourist industry, brought the world's leading Nordic and Alpine skiers in direct confrontation with the rules enshrined in the *Olympic Charter*.[33] Viewing any deviation of Olympic rules as a "disaster" for the amateur ideal, Brundage called upon Edström to expel FIS on the principle that "paid coaches and teachers are not and never were amateurs."[34] With Brundage fueling the ideological fire, the IOC Executive Board adopted a resolute stance, threatening FIS to either accept Olympic amateur regulations or else engender the cancelation of the Winter Olympic Games entirely.[35] After months of negotiation, FIS, not for the first time, eventually backed down. Its members voted to prohibit from Olympic competition those ski instructors exercising their profession after 1 August 1946 and later even agreed to align its statutes with IOC amateur rules.[36] The amateur ideal remained intact. The St. Moritz Olympics would go on. For Edström, however, the latest winter Olympic experience had been too much to bear. He again raised the question of whether "it is not best to drop [them] entirely. They are getting more and more professional."[37]

As the Olympic spectacle made its way from the unscathed neutrality of the Swiss Alps to the austerity of war-ravaged London, Brundage refocused his attentions on rewriting the IOC's amateur code. Whereas in the previous *Olympic Charter* one and a half pages had been devoted to amateur rules, the IOC's new definition appeared clearer and simpler:

> An amateur is one who participates and always has participated in sport solely for pleasure and for the physical, mental or social benefits he derives therefrom, and to whom participation in sport is nothing more than recreation without material gain of any kind direct or indirect and in accordance with the rules of the International Federation concerned.[38]

Soaked in Brundagian idealism, this five-line amateur definition replaced the three detailed conditions (related to professionalism, payment, and instruction) and definition that appeared in previous *Olympic Charters*.[39] Brundage hoped that this new formulation would empower the IOC by denying athletes and federations room to interpret Olympic rules in a more lenient, less scrupulous fashion. Some of his colleagues, however, took a different view. The Marquis Melchior de Polignac, a long-serving French member to the IOC, felt that Brundage's legislative efforts proved once and for all that the Olympic Movement "seems unable to solve the problem of amateurism." He proposed handing the reins of amateur governance back to the international sports federations so they can "shoulder the responsibility."[40] During the 1950 IOC session in Copenhagen, Norwegian members Olaf Christian Ditlev-Simonsen and Thomas Fearnley put forth a motion to this effect.[41]

Unlike a faction of his colleagues, Brundage sensed the inherent danger. Relinquishing authority over amateurism to the international sports federations—each boasting widely contradictory definitions of an amateur—would create organizational mayhem and inevitably open the floodgates to professionalism. In a prepared policy speech, "Stop, Look and Listen," Brundage waxed lyrical: "The tremendous development, unequalled in any other field, has been due to the fact that the Games, despite the materialism of the times, have been conducted in a highly idealistic manner for the welfare of humanity under the regulations laid down by the foreseenic [sic] Baron de Coubertin, and enforced all these years by the I.O.C." In his newly reelected post as vice president, Brundage called upon his colleagues to uphold the IOC's status as an "independent, impartial organization" and reaffirm its historical commitment to the amateur ideal.[42] In a strong show of support for Brundage, the Norwegian proposal suffered a heavy defeat at the ballot box in Copenhagen. The IOC maintained its authority over amateurism for another day. Yet the dangers of commercialism, broken-time payments, and professional ski instruction paled in significance to the threat posed to amateur sport by the emergence of the Soviet Union and its Communist satellites on the international stage.

DRAWING THE IRON CURTAIN

Before World War II, the Soviet Union had refused to take part in what they perceived as a "bourgeois invention," a misogynist, colonialist, and elitist movement that served to deflect workers from class struggles. The Olympic Games, the Communist youth newspaper *Komsomol Pravda* furiously railed, represented a tool of "imperialist propaganda" ensconced underneath "hypocritical phraseology about fidelity to the idea of brotherhood and friendship of the peoples in sport."[43] Emphasizing the Communist contempt for the Olympic idea of apolitical sport, Soviet leaders rejected the Olympic Movement, refused to affiliate with international sports federations, and boycotted—in most instances—direct competition with the West.[44] Sport was considered a subsidiary affair, subordinate to the intellectual, moral, and physical education of the Communist worker. Rejecting the quantified, record-driven sports of its Western rivals, the Soviets favored mass participatory (*Massovost'*) centralized state sport designed to promote national defense, social integration, health, hygiene, and nutrition.[45] Ironically, Communist beliefs in the moral and educative power of amateur sport and physical culture bore a close resemblance to the ideas of Pierre de Coubertin.[46] In fact, the Red Sport International (*Spartakiad*) of the 1930s perhaps afforded a truer application of the spirit of amateurism than the baron's socially and racially exclusive, patriarchal, and increasingly commercialized Olympic Games.[47]

The postwar geographical restructuring of the world's political and economic balance forced the Soviet Union cautiously out of diplomatic isolation and toward a dramatic shift in attitude toward participation in elite international sport. The binary separation of the world along an East–West axis—as precipitated by the emergence of the Communist world system, the formation of the North Atlantic Treaty Organization (NATO), and the implementation of the Marshall Plan—led Communist and capitalist rivals into an all-out cultural and ideological battle for the hearts and minds of the world. Aside from the United Nations (in which the Soviet Union served as a founding member), international sport provided the most public, symbolic forum for Cold War rivals seeking to affirm the superiority and vitality of their respective ways of life.[48] The Olympics offered great publicity potential, as forcefully illustrated by the Fascist and Nazi appropriation and politicization of the prewar Olympic spectacle. Therefore, Soviet leaders hastily jettisoned the Leninist model of mass collective physical culture in favor of individual, elitist, competitive sport.[49] Soviet athletes were transformed into nationalist proxies—or, more appropriately, ambassadors for socialism—tasked with the responsibility of bringing international glory to the Soviet Union over bourgeois states.

The integration of scruffy Communist revolutionaries into the realm of international sport provoked inevitable concern amongst the princes, counts, barons, generals, and wealthy businessmen that composed the IOC. These were the gatekeepers of the cultural propaganda battlefield of international sport.[50] Reflecting the antisocialist and anti-Bolshevik sentiments of their movement's founder, Pierre de Coubertin (as captured in his 1919 publication, *Le Dilemme*), Olympic officials viewed the Soviet emergence from isolation with keen suspicion.[51] "The situation is loaded with dynamite," Brundage worriedly observed. He cautioned Edström that "we must be very careful or the whole structure of amateur sport and the Olympic Games for which we have labored so many years to create will be wrecked and ruined."[52] Bridging the ideological East–West gulf appeared a considerable task, even for a movement philosophically (not practically) committed to the lofty principles of universalism. Although the postwar participation of preexisting Slavic, newly Communist nations such as Bulgaria, Czechoslovakia, Hungary, Poland, Romania, and Yugoslavia did not seem to trouble IOC leaders, the prospect of the Soviet Union joining the Olympic family proved particularly vexing. How could a predominately Eurocentric, elite organization suddenly open its doors to a nation, or more broadly defined, a world system, that opposed the very precepts upon which it rested? Soviet affiliation into the Olympic Movement would mark a victory for Coubertin's brand of idealistic internationalism but, as IOC officials debated, at what cost?

For Brundage and his colleagues on the IOC, the overtly politicized and professionalized nature of Soviet sport brought the Communist bloc into direct conflict with the Olympic Movement's apolitical amateur principles. Though reliant on media suspicion, vague reports, and the claims of Communist defectors to the West, the IOC gradually came to the consensus that sport in Stalinist Russia was an instrument of the state, directed by the Politburo in the pursuit of specific sociopolitical objectives.[53] Unable to compete with the West in the economic arena, the Soviets conceived of sport as a political platform for defeating their ideological opponents.[54] As a political institution, all Soviet sports facilities and clubs came under the absolute control of the state, which devised methods for discovering, nurturing, and harnessing sports talent.[55] Though evidence remained murky, IOC officials gleaned that Soviet athletes were state employees, remunerated generously in accordance with their ranking, qualifications, and attainment. "Amateurism is not at all understood," Edström inveighed anxiously.[56] "They are freed from their jobs, are well paid by the governments and receive—with their families—more and special food."[57] Brundage agreed. The IOC vice president cautioned that the Soviets "must not be admitted to international or Olympic competition unless we are positively certain that they are amateurs. Any other course will only invite disaster."[58] Brundage feared for the very sanctity of Olympic amateurism:

> We are endeavoring to keep the Olympic Games pure and undefiled, we are barring ski teachers, the Swedish Association has cleaned house and eliminated

its professional runners, and if we allow nationally subsidized Russian athletes, athletes who receive cash prizes, or other professionals to participate there will be a storm of righteous disapproval from all over the world.[59]

The philosophical paradoxes and contestations of Olympism were laid bare. Bestowing Olympic status to the Soviet Union and furthering the global reach of the Olympic Movement would violate the IOC's ideological commitment to amateurism and apoliticism. A powerful Communist presence on the IOC would further, from a crucial geopolitical perspective, undermine the West's historical domination of Olympic affairs. "Now, what shall we do?" a frustrated and perplexed Edström mused. "Our young athletes all over Europe are crazy to have the Russian athletes participate."[60]

Lofty idealism ultimately drove IOC policy on the Soviet issue. Illustrating what historian John Hoberman labels amoral universalism, the Olympic Movement played the "chameleon" by ignoring its codes and regulations in order to achieve global participation; Olympic universalism outweighed both an ideological opposition to Communism and fidelity to amateurism. Despite Brundage's vocal defense of the amateur ideal, the IOC followed the international federations' lead in opening a dialogue with the Soviets on the issue of Olympic membership. In a 25 November 1946 missive, Edström instructed Nikolai Romanov, chairman of the All-Union Soviet Sports Committee, that in order to compete at the forthcoming summer Olympic Games in London, "your country's sports organization must adhere" to the rules and amateur regulations of their respective international sports federations "and an Olympic committee must be formed in Moscow."[61] To Edström's dismay, his invitation went unanswered.[62] In an era of heightened xenophobia, as evidenced by the imprisonment, beating, and political purging of Soviet officials deemed to be working too closely with Westerners, Stalinist Russia proceeded cautiously in its postwar reentry into elite sport.[63] Under Stalin's regime, winning was absolutely necessary in order to justify participation in international competitions. If an athlete failed, the whole propaganda message was in danger. Poor performances were seen as damaging to the Soviet image.[64] The Politburo desired Olympic membership, but only at a stage when Soviet athletes posed a legitimate threat to the West and only on legislative terms deemed favorable to Moscow.

The Soviet leadership eventually played its hand. On 29 January 1947, in correspondence with Lord Burghley, Romanov formally applied for Soviet membership to the IAAF.[65] This request, seen as an inevitable move toward Olympic qualification, heightened the IOC's anxiety on the amateur issue.[66] Burghley traveled to Russia on an exploratory mission during which he educated Romanov in the "guiding principle" of amateurism: "a man should not make money out of his athletic accomplishments."[67] The Soviets reassured the IAAF president that the existing Soviet policy of remunerating athletes had been abolished and that they now fully understood and accepted Western rules on amateurism.[68] Despite the Soviet distaste for the kind of social, racial, and sexual privilege reflected in the IOC's amateur code, they had to play the game (at least, in appearance) by Western rules. Admittance to the international sporting arena depended on it. In a move that would typify Burghley's conciliatory attitude toward the Soviets, he promptly endorsed their application for full membership to the IAAF and even agreed to grant amnesty to Russian athletes who had previously received cash payments. By the end of 1947, the Soviets had rejoined the international sports federations of soccer, basketball, track and field, weightlifting, and wrestling. Their integration into international, competitive sport was almost complete.

THE RISE OF THE STATE AMATEUR

The Soviet Union ultimately failed to form a national Olympic committee in time for the 1948 London Games. Unable to guarantee a propaganda victory in the British capital, Romanov and his superiors in the Politburo bided their time. A Soviet emissary did attend the London Games, however, as part of a fact-finding mission charged with observing Western training techniques and customs.[69]

The anticipated Cold War Olympic struggle would soon be realized. After four years of discovery, training, and competition in international sport, the Soviets appeared ready to enter the Olympic stage. Edström announced the 23 April 1951 formation of a Soviet national Olympic committee and the receipt of a formal appeal for Olympic membership.[70] Fueled by an idealistic desire to spread Olympism to the Communist East, Edström placed the matter of Soviet membership on the IOC's agenda for its 1951 session in Vienna. "I am very glad . . . that we have this opportunity to have an arrangement with Russia," he enthused. "The satellite states will surely follow their example and then the Olympic movement all over the world will be united."[71] Not all IOC leaders greeted the prospect of Soviet membership with such enthusiasm. Brundage delivered an ominous forecast: "Not understanding fair play, good sportsmanship and amateurism, I am sure they [Soviets] will bring with them nothing but trouble."[72] For Brundage and others on the IOC, Soviet participation not only threatened the hallowed nature of amateurism, but it also opened up the Olympic Movement—a supposedly independent, nongovernmental organization—to direct state interference. In Soviet national Olympic committee president Konstantin Andrianov, a high-ranking Communist Party official and former head of the Moscow Sports Union, Brundage's worst fear was realized: an Olympic official contaminating the movement with socialist state interests. "Governmental interference for purposes of national aggrandizement cannot be tolerated," Brundage warned.[73] He cautioned further that the looming disintegration of the Olympic Movement into a Cold War political platform would undermine the IOC's ability to remain an impartial purveyor of friendly internationalism.[74]

The Communist bloc nations were certainly not alone in seeking to use the Olympics for advancing state interests. A post–World War II survey undertaken by the Belgian national Olympic committee revealed that only six national Olympic committees (of the forty that responded) were, in accordance with Olympic principles, truly independent, nongovernmental entities—thirteen received full governmental support, and the remaining twenty-one relied on partial state subsidies.[75] Latin America proved a notable hotspot for political entanglement. In a series of correspondences, Peruvian Alfredo Benavides warned his colleagues on the IOC that sports are suffering in Latin America "through the ominous, exaggerated intervention in them of the Governments, politicians and speculators."[76] The establishment of ministries of sport, which pulled national Olympic committees under their organizational umbrella, eroded the IOC's claim of political independence, and from Brundage's perspective, threatened the future of the Olympics as well as the formative regional Pan-American and Central American games that he had helped to establish.[77] The governmental takeover of Olympic governance appeared to be a global trend, which, Republic of China (Taiwan/Formosa) IOC member Gunsun Hoh argued, had spread as far east as Asia. With the Communist Party coup of mainland China likely fresh in his mind, Hoh observed that the postwar militarization of Asian governments has "fatally" pulled Olympic sport "under the direct supervision of the State which subsidises them."[78] The growing relationship between sport and the state spun Brundage and his colleagues into a panic. In a bid to save the Olympics from the clutches of governmental control, they hastily drew up plans to depoliticize the Olympic Movement through a program of Olympic education, as well as a careful screening and selection of future IOC members.[79]

As the first half-century of Olympic competition forcefully revealed, sport did not operate in a vacuum. It was pulled, directed, and shaped by the prevailing social and political currents of the time. The Cold War tensions enveloping the IOC session in Vienna dictated Olympic policymaking over the issue of Soviet membership. By 1951, the Soviet Union had detonated an atomic bomb, Mao Zedong's Communist Party had come to power in China, the NATO alliance was consolidated, Germany had been divided in two after the failure of the Berlin blockade, Eastern Europe had become part of the Soviet bloc, and the Korean War had begun. These events, argues historian Jenifer Parks, likely enhanced anxieties about war and peace and fueled romantic beliefs among IOC members that the Olympic Movement could serve as a symbolic vehicle for bridging Cold War differences and fostering international understanding.[80] Caught up in a wave of idealistic fervor, IOC members voted (thirty-one in favor, three abstentions) to admit the Soviet Union into the Olympic Movement. Members also elected Soviet national Olympic committee president Konstantin Andrianov to a seat on the IOC. A weary Brundage considered these decisions an inevitable conclusion. "If the application for recognition was denied," he later remarked, "it was apparent that there would be a noisy Communist outburst against the committee which would be charged with violating its own regulation against politics in sport."[81] He found consolation in the hope that over time, and through appropriate education, the Soviets might learn to conform to Olympic principles and elect to abandon the professional character of Communist sport.

The introduction of the Soviet Union would not denigrate, as Brundage feared, the "greatest social force in the world." The nationalism that Brundage and many of his colleagues on the IOC viewed as anathema to the movement actually heightened the global status and influence of the Olympic Games. The Communist and capitalist worlds would compete with savage intensity in the Olympic arena. The sight of Communist athletes challenging their ideological foes from the West provided the Olympics with a recipe for enormous public success. As historian Barbara Keys observes, the Cold War (East versus West) narrative boosted the Olympic spectacle in all three areas: "spectatorship and viewership, the size of the events and the athletic contingents, the financial footprint of the Games, and the levels of commercialism."[82] While Brundage waged a tireless campaign to remove the scent of Cold War nationalism from the Olympic arena—prohibiting Olympic medal tables and lobbying (albeit unsuccessfully) to replace national anthems with the Olympic hymn and a fanfare of trumpets—the games had been transformed into a relevant twentieth-century mass cultural spectacle.[83]

The 1952 Summer Olympic Games in Helsinki marked the first meeting between athletes from the rival Cold War states. After the Soviets decided to forgo the winter games in Oslo, the political propaganda stakes were raised to a feverish pitch. Reversing Coubertin's fabled proclamation, both sides of the East–West divide acknowledged that winning was more important than taking part. In Moscow, the Soviets were mobilizing for success on an unprecedented scale. In order to overcome Stalin's distaste for contact with the West, the Soviets left no stone unturned in their quest for Olympic glory. Internal memoranda reveal that in February 1952, Politburo member Mikhail Suslov authorized the ministries and departments to release all Olympic athletes from work and school with elevated pay for the six months leading up to the games. Under the close supervision of state medical personal and the Komitet gosudarstuvennoĭ bezopasnosti (KGB), the Sports Committee further authorized the use of experimental drugs on Soviet athletes less than two months before the opening of the Olympics.[84] Although the *Literaturnaya Gazeta* ferociously denied Western allegations of impropriety as "a foolish bit of slander," it became evident, even to the most myopic of Olympic officials, that the Soviets had paid scant regard to the IOC's antiprofiteering and antidoping regulations, as well as its prohibitions on training camps extending beyond two weeks.[85] The Soviets developed a highly specialized, scientific system designed to prepare its athletes physically and politically for their duty on the propaganda battlefield. These were not the playful amateurs of Brundage's imagination. On the contrary, all Soviet athletes earning the master of sport ranking or above (international class master of sport and merited master of sport) received sinecures via the armed forces (TsSKA, the Central Sport Club of the Army) or the state security services (the Dinamo Club), or they received payment for fictitious work. Many were state-supported full-time students (and would remain so throughout their entire athletic careers) and attended one of a network of forty-two elite performance sports boarding schools.[86] In rubber-stamping Soviet membership into the Olympic family, the IOC tacitly acknowledged and legitimized state amateurism. Unaware, perhaps, of the extent of the Soviet sport apparatus, Olympic officials knew, as internal correspondences testify, that the Communist athlete did not "play the game" as those in the West understood it.

The IOC proved not only complicit in the emergence of state-sanctioned professionalism but also powerless to curb its growth. Replicating the British amateur model of voluntarism, the IOC operated on the basis of personal endeavor, ingenuity, and private membership. Subsequently, it lacked the professional mechanisms to effectively regulate and enforce its own codes. Financially weak and administratively overburdened, the IOC failed to establish an investigatory committee to unmask unscrupulous Communist practices. The Soviet national Olympic committee, the Olympic Movement's primary line of defense against professionalism, followed state directives and swore its allegiances to Stalin. The international sports federations proved equally ineffectual, casting aside amateur considerations in an attempt to secure Soviet participation, expand its global visibility, and enhance ticket sales. The IOC was at the whim of Soviet authorities. Only Brundage's pathological paranoia offered any defense against state amateurism. He conducted his own personal investigations via a daily scouring of international newspaper headlines and regularly challenged Soviet IOC member Konstantin Andrianov, demanding "some definite supporting evidence which might offset this growing indignation against Communist methods which are alleged to be in violation of Olympic rules."[87] The Politburo's mastery of defiance and misdirection continually kept Brundage and his colleagues guessing. Soviet officials and the state-run media played a perfectly orchestrated game of silence, ignorance, and denial. "Calumniatory accusals of soviet sportsmen in 'professionalism,' by some representatives of foreign press," Andrianov decried, "do not contribute to the strengthening of friendly relations between the sportsmen of all countries and to the rising of the authority of the Olympic Movement."[88] The Soviets maintained that their athletes were amateurs in strict accordance with IOC regulations. Claims to the contrary were simply dismissed as inaccurate and politically motivated.

Brundage's crusade against state amateurism almost came at a personal cost, as Soviet Olympic officials engineered a Communist campaign to derail his 1952 IOC presidential bid; they voted (albeit unsuccessfully) en bloc for Brundage's primary opponent, Lord Burghley. The Soviets, masters of bureaucratic subterfuge, continually fought to recoil Brundage into the role of defendant, skillfully diverting accusations of professionalism into their own charges of Western hypocrisy. Capitalism, the Communists retorted, encouraged the prevalence of shamateur practices in bourgeois states. The U.S. collegiate scholarship system drew the ire of Soviet officials and commentators. *Fizkul'tura i sport* recounted how athletes in the United States were "bought for big money" through extravagant scholarships that served the interests of "big business."[89] "America has the most professionals of all," Andrianov agreed.[90] The Soviets found a keen political allay in the form of Burghley, a vocal apologist of the Communist sports system. The British IOC member regularly did the Soviets' bidding, warning Brundage that the commercial orientation of collegiate sport "makes the United States' representatives so vulnerable, when they talk about amateurism."[91] Brundage had been forced to retreat. He acknowledged the professional and commercial realities of U.S. collegiate sport, complaining that "it is scandalous that institutions of higher learning should permit such practices."[92] Though newcomers to the Olympics, the Soviets recognized that rival Western nations had long loosely interpreted and openly flouted the IOC's amateur standards. Professional structures and scientific practices bred Olympic champions. The Soviets were simply the first to subsume all aspects of Olympic affairs within the framework of the state.

The 15th summer Olympics in Helsinki marked the debut of the Soviet Union and its Eastern bloc satellites on the Olympic stage as Communist nations.

Illustrating the extent of Soviet preparations, a 295-person team of athletes arrived in the Finnish capital to contest all events in the Olympic program except field hockey—an unknown sport at the time in the Communist East. With Brundage and Edström looking on disapprovingly, the infamous Paavo Nurmi lit the Olympic cauldron to mark both the commencement of the games and the dawn of the Cold War era in Olympic history; ironically, Nurmi's past transgressions as a shamateur failed to muddy his reputation amongst his fellow countrymen. As fierce debates over the participation of the divided Germanies (West Germany and the GDR) and China (Peoples Republic of China and Taiwan/ Formosa) engulfed the IOC, the dueling globalization projects of capitalism and Communism symbolically squared off. The Soviet desire to translate Olympic gold medals into a propaganda victory was dealt a blow as their ideological foes narrowly topped the unofficial medal standings. Despite implementing scientific training methods and professional practices, the Soviets lacked the requisite experience and tradition long enjoyed by the United States. Defeat, however, failed to halt the Soviet propaganda machine. Reflecting the heightened political realities of post–World War II Olympic competition, *Pravda* misleadingly celebrated the victory of Soviet athletes. "On the number of points gained and in the number of prize-receiving places gained," the newspaper asserted, "the Soviet Union's sportsmen have taken first place."[93] Deliberately refusing to publish the final standings, *Sovetsky Sport* loudly trumpeted its nation's alleged success as proof of the superiority of Communism as an economic, social and political system:

> The victory of the Soviet sportsmen at the Olympics is a clear demonstration of our tremendous advance, of the development of our people and of an upsurge of talents such as is unthinkable in any capitalist country. . . . The Soviet land is proud of her sportsmen. Victory at the XV Olympics lays upon Soviet sportsmen the obligation of working still more persistently and steadfastly to perfect their sporting skill, to achieve new successes in sport to the glory of our great socialist Motherland.[94]

Win or lose, the introduction of the Soviet Union and its Communist allies irrevocably changed the Olympic Movement. The Olympic Games had fast become a politicized global spectacle, an evolution that further undermined the IOC's weak control of amateurism.

THE INCONSISTENT AMATEUR APOSTLE

The Soviet Union's entrance into the Olympic Movement coincided with broader Soviet efforts to consolidate its sphere of influence in Eastern Europe.[95] After Stalin's death in March 1953 of a cerebral hemorrhage, Nikita

Khrushchev's government sought to intensify Soviet political and ideological control over the region. During this period of de-Stalinization, Soviet administrators and party leaders in Moscow used Olympic sport to try to bind its Eastern bloc satellites to Soviet institutions and policies. Although the Communist world system never achieved full agreement on its policies and aims—despite the 1955 formation of the Warsaw Pact—Moscow succeeded in fostering a collective socialist identity through elite sport. Soviet envoys visited neighboring Communist countries intent on establishing Soviet-type administrative structures and scientific fitness programs, as well as promoting state amateurism through army and security forces clubs, elite boarding schools, and other sinecures.[96] Despite the Slavic desire to preserve their cultural identity, an integrated, Communist state–sport system emerged on a transnational scale to challenge the Eurocentric insularity and amateur policies of the IOC.

A coordinated Communist faction voting en bloc on key Olympic policy and propagating professional practices posed an unprecedented threat to the Olympic Movement. In his recently conferred position as IOC president, Brundage wrote a number of inquisitive letters to his colleagues Dr. Jerzy Loth (Poland) and General Vladimir Stoytchev (Bulgaria) in an attempt to establish the degree of Communist cooperation, state influence, and professionalism.[97] Both, predictably, were not very forthcoming. IOC member Loth vigorously downplayed the extent of Moscow's ideological and institutional control over Polish Olympic affairs but did concede "that the principles of amateur-ship are interpreted differently in the democratic countries, in which sport is protected by the state."[98] The mounting politicization of Olympic sport prompted Brundage to action. Under his direction, the IOC established Rule 25 of the *Olympic Charter* to ensure that "National Olympic Committees must be completely independent and autonomous and entirely removed from political, religious, and commercial influence."[99] In a thinly veiled attack on the emerging Communist bloc, Brundage maintained that the IOC needed protection from non-Western national Olympic committees being organized by outsiders (governmental officials) who are not properly educated in Olympic ideals. "This rule has not been drawn up for the well-advanced countries who are perfectly well aware of what is meant by the Olympic spirit," he stated.[100]

Despite the expanding orbit of Communist influence, Brundage's attitudes toward the Soviets and its Eastern-bloc satellites soothed considerably in the aftermath of the Helsinki Games. The right-wing radicalism (anti-Semitism and anti-Communism) that characterized his early administrative career gave way to a position of tolerance and, on the surface, even acceptance. In his new role as IOC president, he gradually became a far more sophisticated observer of the political climate. Brundage considered himself an impartial leader of a global movement, immune to patriotic and ideological allegiances. In truth, Brundage traded his ethics for his idealism. Like Edström before him, he sacrificed the amateur ideal to ensure the universal growth of the Olympic Movement. Brundage also grew to reconcile his abhorrence of state amateurism, finding an ideological common ground with the Communists through a shared disdain for commercialism. Unlike Western athletes, the Soviet Union and its satellites were divorced from the private sector and the athletic free market. Behind the anticapitalist barrier of the Iron Curtain, Communist athletes were effectively immune to the financial and exploitative lure of the Western television companies, manufacturers, and marketers eager to peddle images, brands, and goods stamped with an Olympic insignia.[101] The Communists bowed their allegiance to the state rather than the almighty dollar—a lesser of two evils in Brundage's philosophical playbook.

Brundage and the Communists became strange bedfellows. At the behest of Soviet authorities, he toured the Soviet Union in 1954, meeting with state officials, visiting athletic facilities, and attending the annual mass-orchestrated "All-Union Day of the Athlete." He chronicled his three-week adventure on the pages of the *Saturday Evening Post*, in which he offered a glowing eulogy to the "tremendous athletic development" of organized competitive sport behind the Iron Curtain. Amid the cordiality and state pageantry, Brundage sought to personally verify or disprove the accusations circulating within the Western media about state-sanctioned professionalism, extensive training camps, and clandestine doping programs. He recounted private meetings with both Romanov and Andrianov, the highest-ranking state sporting officials, in which all charges were "empathically denied." The loyal Communist Party bureaucrats disabused Western allegations, claiming that "the Soviet Union does not have or want professional athletes. In the past, cash prizes had been given for outstanding performances, but this practice has been discontinued. No special inducements or material rewards are given in Russia." Brundage appeared to have fallen victim to the Politburo's chicanery. He reassured his readers that "I saw nothing during my brief trip which would make me question [these] statements."[102] Western observers were incredulous.

During IOC sessions, at executive board meetings, or through written circular letters and media interviews, Brundage spent the remainder of his administrative career downplaying the political and professional realities of Communist sport. In an extensive interview with Swiss sport editors, Brundage created an international stir when he again dismissed accusations of Soviet professionalism. "Sportsmen are presumed to be honest," he avowed. "Since we have no police force we must trust the authorities in those [Communist] countries until we discover that they are not complying with the regulations."[103] A barrage of condemnation greeted Brundage's refusal to accept the increasingly stark realities of Soviet sport. The Zurich daily newspaper *Neue zürcher Zeitung*, scolded the IOC president for his insistence that the amateur ideal "is relatively well respected" in the East.[104] A contributor to the World Athletic Service took a far more critical perspective. Calculating that the average Soviet athlete spent 110 days (excluding training) in 1954 in direct competition, the author disparaged Brundage for his ignorance on the subject: "This strong position of the President of the IOC and highest representatives of amateur sport in the world, surprises those who know well the true conditions in Russia."[105] Throughout the remainder of Brundage's tenure, the IOC did little to effectively combat Communist state amateurism. In response to intense media pressure, letters of inquiry were occasionally sent to Moscow (yet rarely replied to), while discussions among IOC members on the controversial subject were regularly deferred to future meetings (and consequently never fully discussed).[106] Through experience, Brundage discovered that the Iron Curtain was impossible to penetrate and thus immune to IOC oversight. Brundage effectively granted the Soviet Union and its Eastern bloc satellites free reign to develop the Communist sport apparatus to a systematic, scientific level that both he and his contemporaries could never have imagined.

Unable and, perhaps, no longer willing to confront the Communists, Brundage channeled his administrative efforts into combating professional practices prevalent in the West. He tackled the low-hanging fruit, notably amateur violations in the form of surreptitious cash payments, padded expense accounts, valuable gifts, nominal employment, income derived directly from athletic fame, coach athletes, athletic scholarships, and broken-time payments.[107] He amassed a "thick dossier of articles and press cuttings" that chronicled Olympic amateur violations and from his home in southern California launched personal investigations, concluding, "Where there is so much smoke there must be fire."[108] He targeted two-time Olympic gold medalist Adhemar Ferreira da Silva, a Brazilian triple-jumper, for allegedly accepting a house for his mother, and the Comité Olímpico Argentino for awarding automobiles to its amateur footballers and a house to Olympic marathon champion Delfo Cabrera.[109] He also took aim at the USOA—which he formerly presided over—for permitting U.S. army personnel to compete as amateurs knowing that they had been released from their military duties to train full-time for the Olympics.[110] True to his humble origins, Brundage challenged the Fédération Équestre Internationale to revise its prohibitive rules and allow enlisted cavalrymen to ride as amateurs—under existing regulations only commissioned officers (gentlemen) were consider eligible. He also demanded that the international equestrian and shooting federations follow through on their earlier promises and discontinue awarding cash prizes to amateur competitors.[111]

Brundage's idealism in the face of mounting opposition was unending. He attempted to stem the heightened flood of amateurs rushing to parlay their Olympic success into professional careers. Women's figure skating drew Brundage's wrath. Following the prewar example set by Norwegian starlet Sonja Henie, Olympic female skaters cashed in their amateur statuses for the lure of Hollywood, commercial endorsements, prizes, and professional careers. When Canada's Barbara Ann Scott received a brand-new Buick convertible from the city of Ottawa to commemorate her victory at the 1947 World Championships, Brundage took action.[112] He proposed an amendment to the athletes' oath that, if passed, would force prospective Olympians to swear that they "are" and "intend to remain" amateurs for the remainder of their careers. This proposed insertion unleashed such a storm of protest that Brundage was forced to retain the original ruling for the both 1956 Cortina d'Ampezzo and Melbourne winter and summer Olympic Games.[113] Like his favorite literary hero Don Quixote, Brundage expended much of administrative efforts in the defense of amateurism "tilting at windmills."

Throughout the 1950s, opponents continued to level criticism at Brundage and the IOC for ignoring reality and clinging hypocritically to a long-outmoded ideal. Broken-time payments continued to garner the support of populist-minded European democracies. During the 1954 IOC session in Athens, Swiss IOC member Albert Mayer revived the call for indemnities to cover an athletes' time away from the workplace. He contended that the IOC's refusal to sanction broken-time had created a culture of "'SHAM Amateurism'" that, he argued, existed "on a scale which has assumed unbelievable proportion." Both the Swedish and Swiss national Olympic committees, Mayer revealed, openly sanctioned broken-time payments in direct violation of Olympic rules. He attacked Brundage and the IOC for tolerating these infractions without having the courage to penalize the offense. The IOC "takes note of these infringements to the Rules, fails to take any steps to stop them and goes on shutting its eyes. This attitude creates a feeling of hypocrisy against which I protest energetically," Mayer fumed.[114] Reimbursements on an open, controlled, and democratic foundation, he proposed, would eliminate the culture of dishonesty that dominated the Olympic landscape. Brundage stood firm. Viewing amateurism as a fixed, timeless philosophical ideal, he refused to countenance the possibility that amateur regulations needed to be reevaluated from time to time to enable the IOC to keep pace with changing socioeconomic conditions.[115] From his position of vast wealth and power, Brundage remained out of touch with reality. "The argument for easing the rule on the grounds that 'times have changed' is ridiculous on the face of it," he retorted, "since the change has been all for the better in that wages have increased and working hours have been lowered in all countries, thus making more leisure time for all."[116] Brundage's opponents remained steadfast. The call for the introduction of broken-time payments and other liberal initiatives would not be silenced.

6 THE GLOBAL GAMES AND THE INTRANSIGENT DICTATOR

In the aftermath of the 1956 Olympic Games in Melbourne, public and media sentiment in the West toward Olympic amateurism took a decidedly negative turn. Journalists, athletes, sport officials, and politicians raised their collective voices to proclaim "Halt this amateur sham."[1] The sight of Soviet state-sponsored athletes atop the medal podium in Melbourne prompted Western observers to press the IOC for drastic legislative reform. "There is a solution, as bold as the first Sputnik," announced former U.S. speed skating gold medalist Irving Jaffee. "Why not let pros, as well as amateurs, enter the Olympics?" he proposed. "No more our amateurs against their professionals. Instead a fair match among every nation's champions—paid or unpaid—in the best Olympic tradition."[2] From across North America to Europe, from former governor-general of Canada Earl Alexander to British winter sports enthusiast and administrator Sir Arnold Lunn, the call for open games to confront Soviet Olympic dominance received widespread backing.[3] Even *Sports Illustrated*, a keen chronicler of the Olympic spectacle, resigned itself to the fact that the forthcoming 1960 Olympics in Rome "will see the last amateur Olympics."[4] In the throes of the Cold War Olympic medal race, amateurism appeared an increasingly unenforceable, hypocritical, and inconvenient ideal. "Amateurism is grasping out its last few breaths in a world too intent on ultimate survival to care about the health of such trifles," a contributor to the *Amateur Athlete* opined. "[It] is either dead, dying or hibernating."[5]

As a diligent warden of amateurism, Avery Brundage kept apprised of the growing storm of Western discontent. Resolute in his belief that a vibrant and prosperous Olympic Movement rested upon the ideological foundations of amateurism, the IOC president strove to publicly challenge what he labeled as scurrilous and nationalistically motivated calls for reform. At the 1960 IOC session in San Francisco, he even proposed the creation of a literary prize to be awarded to the "journalist who writes the best article in favor of the defense and better understanding of amateurism and of Olympism." He believed that a strong media offensive would help to counter those critics championing the end, or at least a liberalization, of his cherished ideal. Who better to be the first recipient of this award, than Brundage himself? Led by French IOC vice president Armand Massard, Olympic officials voted to extend the inaugural prize to Brundage "on account of the unfailing devotion and courage he is displaying in the defense of amateurism."[6] In the face of systematic, state-sanctioned rule violations and subsequent calls for legislative change, the IOC acted like a trifling and self-congratulatory body moving increasingly out of step with both reality and popular opinion.

In truth, Brundage's dismissive attitude toward calls for reform belied a deeper, more nuanced understanding of the climate. His finger remained firmly on the pulse. His aristocratic rule, strength of character, and unwavering commitment to the Olympic Movement provided sufficient glue to keep the amateur ideal alive during the Cold War years. The radical shifts transforming the games, however, exposed the limitations and paradoxes of his own Olympic idealism. Brundage spoke of universal Olympic Games, free from political intervention and financial self-interests, conducted in accordance with amateur rules and regulations. The realities of Cold War politics, Third World decolonization, and a telecommunications and sports marketing revolution forced him to steer further away from his own ideals throughout the 1960s. Although he disavowed politics and professionalism, he continued to sanction the participation of Communist-bloc nations in keeping with the universal aspirations of the Olympics. And because he raged against commercialism, he denied the Olympic Movement the financial and bureaucratic capacity to promote Olympism around the world. While publicly proclaiming his adoration for the amateur ideal, his narrow and often selective metaphysical understanding of amateurism hindered the IOC's ability to craft more relevant, realistic, and enforceable legislation. Entering his second term as IOC president, Brundage's oscillating ideological blend of compromise and rigidity exposed the Olympic Movement to renewed charges of hypocrisy, inconsistency, elitism, and anachronism. Despite his own best intentions and indefatigable efforts, Brundage's policymaking ironically served to hasten the disintegration of Olympic principles and the amateur ideal.

BEHIND THE IRON CURTAIN

The success of Soviet athletes at the Melbourne Olympics revealed both the extent and potency of the Communist sport apparatus. After World War II, the Soviets had emerged from the international sporting wilderness to triumph over their more experienced capitalist rivals. While the Western media cried foul play, Brundage continued to dismiss stories of Soviet state-sponsored professionalism. Through his private actions rather than his public utterances, however, he recognized that the stories of Soviet rule violations contained an obvious grain of truth. His colleague and close confidante, the Canadian Sidney Dawes, reinforced this realization in a private correspondence. "Everyone knows," Dawes contended, "that the socialistic or communistic countries, employing as they do all their people, have a tremendous advantage in being able to give as much time for training as possible to their athletes."[7] Brundage continued to forward these accusations to Konstantin Andrianov for his appraisal. The Soviet IOC official pretended to be nonplussed. "There are simply no conditions for the existence of professionalism in Soviet sport," he retorted. Andrianov pointed to the shifting post-Stalinist social and political landscape, and the subsequent improvement in living standards, better wages, and lower working hours, as an explanation for the remarkable success of Soviet Olympic athletes. The stories of training camps, nominal state employment, and lavish monetary rewards are mere fabrications, Andrianov explained, generated by the Western media who "make it their thankless task to discredit Soviet athletes in the eyes of their readers."[8] Brundage remained mindful but unwilling to act. Short of expelling the Eastern European national Olympic committees from the Olympic Movement, his personal investigatory efforts appeared paltry. The pursuit of Olympic universalism, and the prestige, publicity, and commercial interest that an increasingly global Olympics generated, continued to trump pure and honest amateurism.

As long as the IOC turned a blind eye, Moscow continued to enjoy the freedom to bind its Warsaw Pact allies to Soviet institutions, administrative structures, and elite sport policies. The German Democratic Republic (GDR) of East Germany, perhaps more than the other Eastern bloc countries, best adapted the Communist model of systematic, state-run amateur sport.[9] Politically, ideologically, and, from August 1961, geographically walled off from its Federal Republic neighbor to the West, the Communist GDR embraced the Olympic Games as a tool for nationalistic propaganda. A February 1956 "paper of laws" decree revealed East Germany's political aspirations, as Communist

Party officials elevated elite sport as a direct affair of the state.[10] Manfred Ewald, chairman of the Soviet Zone Committee for Physical Culture, announced that all athletes, coaches, and sports leaders in the GDR were to be selected on the basis of their sporting and political acumen "so that the victories . . . strengthen the confidence and the might of our republic."[11] The GDR cultivated a sports system built on the age-old adage that sport and politics were inseparable spheres, that achievement in sport reflected the strength and vitality of the East German state.[12] As the *Leipziger Volkszeitung* explained with a characteristic blend of Communist Party blather, "Records in sport are not the private achievement of some odd fanatics, they are a struggle for a united, democratic and peace loving Germany."[13]

The GDR made its entry onto the Olympic stage at the 1956 winter Olympics in Cortina d'Ampezzo, albeit as part of a politically brokered team from both Germanies. Amid heated debates over the selection of competing national anthems, flags, and colors, the uninhibited idealist Brundage still found room to celebrate the unification of the divided Germanies as a triumph for "sport over politics."[14] The GDR took a drastically different perspective. Intent on achieving independent Olympic success, particularly over its ideological rivals to the West, the Communist Party–controlled Nationales Olympisches Komitee der Deutschen Demokratischen Republik (the East Germany national Olympic committee) pursued separate IOC recognition. Brundage, a close friend of Karl Ritter Von Halt and other West German Olympic officials, stifled the GDR's political agenda. He encouraged his colleagues on the IOC to rule in favor of a single team from both republics over a two-state solution, even as the construction of the Berlin Wall and the subsequent cessation of sporting contacts between the two Germanies hindered IOC appeals for mutual cooperation.[15]

It would be 1965 before the IOC finally approved the GDR's numerous appeals for Olympic independence—in the interim, the two Germanies continued to forge a "united" German team for both the 1960 and 1964 winter and summer Olympics. The long wait for Olympic recognition, however, failed to stymie East Germany's development of a Soviet-style, elite sports system. Ensconced behind the Iron Curtain, GDR scientists, Communist Party officials, and State Security Ministry (Stasi) enforcers enjoyed free rein to develop Olympic-caliber athletes via illicit systematic doping and enhancement programs,[16] cash-reward and subsidy schemes, and state-funded elite training schools.[17] Newspaper reports, as well as the revelations of defectors to the West told in vivid detail of the GDR's blatant violation of the IOC's amateur code. The West German tabloid *Das Bild* claimed to have uncovered the professional realities of sport in the Soviet-occupied zone.

Seemingly mirroring the cash-and-title reward system first introduced in the Soviet Union, *Das Bild* told of GDR athletes and coaches receiving lavish performance-driven cash benefits ranging from 3,500 DM to 7,000 DM for Olympic medal honors.[18] Hans-Joachim Neuling, an East German member of the combined German Olympic rowing team at the 1960 Olympic Games in Rome, provided the IOC with a detailed testimony of life as an Olympian in the GDR. Neuling, once designated a Champion of Sport by the East German government, recounted that he had received gratifications that contravened "appropriate amateur definitions." He continued openly:

> We continuously got compensations which were different according to our political and sports merits in addition to these win-premiums. They were executed in form of paid free-time, scholarships or lengthening of our college years. The money was paid down in cash by a representative of the German Federation for sports and gymnastics. He personally gave the money to us with duty of secrecy.[19]

Combining scientific research in medicine (a euphemism for doping and performance enhancement), sports equipment, and training methods with talent-identification schemes and centralized training camps, IOC Chancellor Otto Mayer warned Brundage that the GDR violated many of the IOC's rules by using "athletes for political propaganda and nothing else."[20]

The IOC's response to these mounting private and public allegations offered further proof of its bureaucratic ineptitude. Brundage, still weary from his earlier clashes with Soviet and Eastern-bloc officials, pursued the IOC's only line of investigation by writing accusatory letters to the East German national Olympic committee and its president, Heinz Schöbel.[21] "If the newspaper stories are true, of course all your athletes will be ineligible for Olympic . . . competition," he warned.[22] Replicating the Soviet model of silence, ignorance, and disavowal, the GDR Olympic authorities simply denounced the slanderous charges as "not in accordance with truth."[23] Without an operational investigatory committee on eligibility, Brundage and the IOC were again powerless. Throughout the 1960s and beyond, state amateurism remained the elephant in the room. For Western observers, the IOC president's inability to tackle Communist abuses further undermined his fidelity to the amateur ideal, as well as his avowed internationalism. The Swiss newspaper *Neue zürcher Zeitung* agreed, even going as far as to brand him "the red cap of the Olympian Brundage," a Communist sympathizer.[24] Non-Communist athletes, officials, and journalists grew to believe that the IOC's amateur rules served as a handicap favoring the state-sponsored athletes of the Communist East who achieved victory over their more "honest" capitalist opponents.[25]

Determined to finally silence the chorus of Western condemnation on the subject of state amateurism, Brundage convened a meeting between the executive board and the IOC members of Communist Europe. In a desperate plea, Brundage appealed to his colleagues "to obtain an official statement . . . in view of destroying the existing prevailing impression concerning the state amateurs."[26] In hindsight, his actions appear remarkably naïve. A signed declaration dismissing allegations of impropriety would have done little to stem the tide of suspicion emanating from across Western Europe and North America. What is more, the Olympic officials representing Communist Europe were high-level governmental bureaucrats, well versed in the art of political brinkmanship. Leading the Communist response, Soviet IOC member Aleksei Romanov turned the tables on Brundage by highlighting the prevalence of amateur infractions outside the Iron Curtain. Romanov challenged Brundage: Since "similar criticisms are also made of athletes belonging to other countries . . . do you intend to convene the members of the IOC of those countries?"[27] The IOC president had been outmaneuvered. He knew full well that the pursuit of *Citius, Altius, Fortius* and the lure of Olympic victory had long diminished the integrity of athletes, coaches, and officials on both sides of the Cold War divide. Western outrage met with Communist charges of hypocrisy. Not for the first time, Brundage had been forced to retreat.

The high political stakes of elite sport tempted an increasing number of non-Communist governments to transgress the noninterventionist spirit enshrined in Rule 25 of the *Olympic Charter*. Brundage led personal investigations during the 1960s into the encroachment of the governments of Argentina, Colombia, France, and Sweden in the administration of their respective national Olympic committees.[28] Behind the high-minded veil of indifference, Western governments increasingly craved Olympic victory, ironically moving toward the Communist model of state interference in order to guarantee success. Even the government of Brundage's homeland, the United States, intruded into Olympic affairs. Alarmed by the growing success of the Soviet sport system, U.S. politicians of both persuasions took to the floor of Congress to debate the subsidization of future Olympic teams. This proposal, a direct affront to the private voluntary model that had funded previous U.S. Olympic campaigns, attested to the political conditions of Cold War competition. Although the subsidization of U.S. Olympic athletes failed to win congressional approval, clandestine governmental programs began to seek ways in which to curb the rising Communist sport offensive. As historian Toby Rider has shown via declassified documents, propaganda experts planned targeted campaigns to expose the professional realities of

Communist sport. U.S. government officials calculated that the unmasking of the Communist state sport apparatus would force the IOC to finally take decisive action and negatively influence global opinion of the Soviet Union. Attempts to contrast the fair-minded U.S. amateur against the unscrupulous Soviet professional faced one major stumbling block, however: It did not mesh with reality.[29] International observers, including Brundage himself, had long recognized that U.S. Olympic athletes received indirect subsidies through college scholarships and privileged treatment, and U.S. military personal were regularly relieved of duty to prepare for Olympic competition.[30] Shamateurism transcended ideological affiliation, underlining the U.S. sportswriter Paul Gallico's famous dictum: "Amateurs—there ain't none."[31]

HERE COMES THE REVOLUTION!

As the Cold War raged on through reciprocal cultural offensives, rival Communist and capitalist powers continued to tarnish the frail sanctity of the IOC's amateur code with near impunity. Brundage, the inconsistent and toothless defender of amateurism, continued to fight the occasional good fight. When Olympic athletes were reported in print to be receiving illicit cash payments and extravagant prizes or using their names and images to endorse a commercial product, Brundage led personal investigations.[32] He continued to challenge the Fédération Équestre Internationale for persisting in its policy of awarding cash payments to amateur riders; he issued denunciations of the yachting and shooting federations for similar infractions.[33] The Union Cycliste Internationale also came under questioning for its decision to allow amateur riders to wear uniforms sporting the names of cycling manufacturers and commercial sponsors.[34] FIFA, the world governing body of soccer, provided Brundage with another serious headache. Buried under a mountain of press accounts of professional players posing as FIFA-certified Olympic amateurs in Melbourne (1956) and Rome (1960), Brundage passionately championed the elimination of soccer from the Olympic program entirely.[35] By the 1960s, Olympic sport had reached such a high level of performance and specialization that amateur athletes found it increasingly difficult to compete at the top level in addition to holding paid employment. Professionals and state-sponsored Communists flooded the Olympic landscape, transforming the Olympics into what the leading Canadian newspaper the *Globe and Mail* branded "a distasteful farce."[36]

Despite his anticommercial rhetoric and investigatory crusades, Brundage's legacy as an unwavering apostle of amateurism demands a revisionist interpretation. Previous scholarly attempts to draw a clear, consistent line across the length of his Olympic career ignore the finer, more nuanced realities of his administration. In truth, Brundage's ideological grasp and administrative defense of amateurism fluctuated selectively between the pillars of rose-tinted idealism and bureaucratic pragmatism. Self-preservation as well as the sustained growth of the Olympic Movement along ideologically compatible lines informed Brundage's attitude toward amateurism. The passionate stump speeches and romantic platitudes that one typically associates with his presidency remained, but behind the scenes he increasingly became a selective enforcer. As his tolerance of Communist state amateurism indicates, Brundage chose to fight only the battles he knew he could win, or, at the very least, the battles he knew would not jeopardize the universal mission of the Olympic Movement. With the benefit of hindsight, it could be argued that in the age of increased global commerce, as well as an emerging telecommunications revolution, amateurism was an ideal doomed to failure. However, Brundage could have placed amateurism on an alternative, more promising trajectory. Entering his second term as IOC president, his obstinate refusal to support policy reform, coupled with a fanatic desire to operate the IOC on the principles of voluntarism and anticommercialism, served only to hasten amateurism's post–World War II decline.

Albert Mayer, a Swiss representative to the IOC, sensed the inherent danger. Frustrated by the IOC's growing inability and apparent unwillingness to strictly enforce amateurism, Mayer, not for the first time, proposed a significant revision to Rule 26. In a treatise titled "Amateurism—Project No. 2," the Swiss IOC official outlined his vision for a more liberal, comprehensive, and enforceable amateur code. Mayer contended that on paper, the IOC's existing regulations were so prohibitive, arbitrary, and hypocritical that the average working-class athlete was forced to either stay at home, or alternatively, violate the rules in order to finance Olympic participation.[37] "The actual situation cannot go on any longer," he pleaded with Brundage.[38] Mayer assumed a progressive position, championing the sanctioning of reimbursements for broken time, a clothing and equipment indemnity, pocket money to cover daily expenses, and the award of nominal monetary gifts. He urged his colleagues on the IOC to tackle the real shamateurs, not the athlete receiving compensation for time away from the workplace, but those who sought to profit personally and significantly from their Olympic status. Mayer favored clear, fair, and descriptive rules; strong punishments; and an effective mechanism for enforcing new amateur standards. "The problem of amateurism must be provided with a better solution, a better basis of interpretation, and it should be given a more comprehensive definition in order to deal with the countless abuses which are now taking place and which could bring about the gradual death and disappearance of the Olympic ideal," he concluded.[39]

Mayer presented his proposal at the 1960 IOC session in Rome, calling upon his colleagues to approve the formation of an amateur committee to investigate his initiatives further. Brundage considered Mayer's proposal a capitulation. The intractable IOC president allowed his ideological convictions to cloud his better judgment. Again, he appealed to a misguided conception of amateurism as a fixed, transcendent ideal. He considered regulatory change, however small or well-intended, sacrilegious. Broken-time payments, expense allowances, or any other deviation from the "original" spirit of amateurism as allegedly forged by the ancient Greeks on the sacred plains of Olympia, threatened the very fabric of the Olympic Movement. "It would be a major disaster," he admonished.[40] A remarkably poor metaphysical and practical understanding of amateurism forced Brundage to misread the situation. Mayer sought to embolden and elevate rather than weaken or eliminate amateurism. This was not a "revolution," he assured him, but rather a serious and necessary mandate on the future governance and prosperity of Olympic amateurism.[41]

The majority of IOC members agreed with Mayer's assessment, voting to approve the creation of an amateur committee.[42] Chaired by Mayer, and composed of Mohammed Taher (Egypt), François Piétri (France), and Ivar Vind (Denmark), the amateur committee set out to revise Rule 26 on amateurism. Within Olympic circles, momentum in favor of legislative reform appeared to be growing. Bo Ekelund proposed a radical simplification of the rule altogether. The Swedish IOC member suggested defining the professional rather than the amateur, a move that would have permitted almost everything short of the pursuit of sport as a full-time vocation.[43] The Communists also waded into the fray. Bulgarian General Vladimir Stoytchev, the first Eastern European to serve on the IOC Executive Board, shared Ekelund's opinion that Rule 26 was too restrictive. Stoytchev tried to clear the legislative way for the open sanctioning of state subsidies, nominal employment, and extensive Olympic training camps by defining an amateur simply as "a man who has a profession."[44] Soviet IOC officials Andrianov and Romanov reiterated the Communist call for a loosening of amateurism. Rallying behind the banner of idealism and democracy, the Politburo spokesmen challenged Brundage to lift IOC restrictions against broken-time payments and other minor indemnities.[45]

After months of deliberation, the amateur committee pitched its own vision at the 1961 IOC session in Athens. In keeping with the spirit of Albert Mayer's "Project No. 2," the committee proposed the following definition:

> An amateur is one who participates and always has participated in sport without material gain.

To qualify as an amateur, it is necessary to comply with the following conditions:

a) Have a normal occupation destined to insure his present and future livelihood.
b) Never have received any payment for taking part in any sports competitions.
c) Comply with the rules of the International Federation concerned.
d) Comply with the official interpretation of this regulation.[46]

Under these stipulations, broken-time payments, traveling and living expenses, and clothing and equipment indemnities were openly permitted. Professional journalists, radio and television reporters, elementary-level physical educators and coaches, and athletic facility workers also would qualify for Olympic amateur status. Mayer stressed that prohibitions against competitors profiting commercially from their athletic fame, participating in training camps exceeding three weeks, and exploiting amateur sport as a steppingstone to a lucrative professional career would remain in place. The proposed reforms, which were deferred to the 1962 IOC session in Moscow for an official vote, marked a concerted attempt to evolve the spirit of amateurism into fairer, more relevant, and more enforceable legislation.

Brundage greeted the amateur committee's proposal with fierce disapproval. In the months leading up to the Moscow session, he worked through IOC circulars and a revised policy stump speech titled "Stop, Look and Listen," to ensure its demise at the ballot box. "There have been some mistakes, there has been some cheating," Brundage conceded, "but in our efforts to improve the Games let us not adopt measures we will soon regret. Above all we must not tamper with the Amateur Rule."[47] The IOC president and the amateur committee remained philosophically distant in their approach to best tackling growing commercial and professional abuses. When attempts to resolve the gulf between the two parties failed in a March 1962 meeting with the IOC Executive Board, Brundage adopted a more guileful approach.[48] Exploiting his presidential powers, he declared that a two-thirds majority would be required to approve any modifications to Rule 26. "As president, I would be remiss in my duties if I permitted a question so vital to the success of the Olympic Movement to be settled by a simple majority," he insisted.[49] Still, momentum among IOC members in favor of Mayer's proposed reforms appeared to be growing. In an effort to save face publicly, Brundage was forced to allow a watered-down passage on broken time wherein only competitors who could prove financial hardship for their dependents were eligible for remuneration.[50]

At the 1962 Moscow session, IOC members voted overwhelmingly to accept the amateur committee's amended proposal.[51] The new amateur eligibility rules, which appeared in the 1962 *Olympic Charter*, demonstrated that Olympic officials envisaged the need for honest reform.[52] Brundage took the defeat badly. He worked behind the scenes to undermine the payment of broken time at every turn, writing a short letter to the U.S. AAU pleading with his old colleagues to renounce the benefits offered by the new ruling. "If [you] would adopt a resolution to the effect that in a prosperous country like the United States of America there is so much pride when an athlete becomes a member of an Olympic team that dependents are always cared for privately and there is, therefore, no need of invoking a rule of this kind, the effect would be most salutary."[53] Once again, Brundage demonstrated that he was clearly out of touch with reality. Aside from a small cadre of wealthy, predominately Western athletes, most Olympians did not enjoy the privileged support of family members and generous benefactors. Through his elitist, rose-tinted lenses, the IOC president failed to fathom the idea that the majority of Olympic athletes were unable to carry the financial burden of time away from the workplace for training and competition without the benefits afforded through broken-time reimbursements. Despite his resolute opposition, Brundage watched as his colleagues empowered the national Olympic committees with the authority to directly compensate competitors suffering hardships a comparable amount for a period not exceeding one month.[54] After decades of debate, charting all the way back to FIFA and the 1928 Amsterdam Olympics, the dam had finally been breached. The IOC officially permitted broken-time payments.

Legislation was one thing; compliance with the law another. As Brundage publicly warned, the IOC's concession now exposed the Olympic Movement to even greater abuses at the hands of partisan, increasingly government-controlled and funded national Olympic committees. *Le Monde des Sports* articulated the IOC president's concern, predicting that "numerous federations" will now exploit the hardship clause as a "cocoon to pay their sports people out of their profession."[55] Brundage called for stronger enforcement and closer vigilance as an urgent necessity. He wrote a circular letter to the national Olympic committees requesting their cooperation in enforcing these new regulations: "It is hoped . . . that all NOCs [national Olympic committees] will be very cautious in applying this rule, which was designed to cover very rare instances only."[56] Even as late as the 1960s, the defense of Olympic amateurism rested solely on the basis of trust. The IOC trusted international federations to issue amateur certificates in good faith; they trusted competitors to sign these certificates and swear an Olympic oath pledging that they were amateurs in good standing; they also trusted national Olympic committees to countersign certificates and ensure that their representatives conformed to Olympic amateur regulations. Aside from paranoia-fueled investigations that Brundage was undertaking on his own, the IOC looked on naïvely, seemingly powerless to reverse the disintegration of the amateur ideal.

As the Cold War medal race gathered steam, the defense of amateurism required an organizational and jurisdictional restructuring of the entire Olympic Movement. The national Olympic committees and the international sports federations had long proven financially and bureaucratically incapable, and often philosophically unwilling, to enforce amateurism. The IOC, whose small Swiss headquarters boasted a remarkably meager staff of two part-time employees, also lacked the administrative capacity to effectively regulate and enforce its own amateur rules. Brundage and the Olympic Movement came to an unavoidable crossroads: either shamateurism would continue to prevail at the hands of partisan, administratively overburdened, financially ill-equipped governing bodies or, alternatively, the tripartite of Olympic partners could shed its anticommercial, voluntary cloaks and undergo professional organizational restructuring.

SELLING THE OLYMPIC RINGS?

From its establishment in 1894, the IOC operated on a very limited budget. Through the financial largesse of its principal founder, Baron Pierre de Coubertin, the organization teetered along the brink of insolvency throughout the early decades of the twentieth century. Operating on the basis of voluntarism, the IOC drew its financial income from annual membership fees and small profit-sharing contributions from host cities.[57] Under Brundage's reign, the IOC's financial situation remained precarious despite his own generosity in supporting Olympism. With an intensity and conviction unmatched by any of his predecessors, Brundage strove (at least in the early stages of his presidency) to resist the stain of money in every way, shape, and form.[58] He seized control of Olympic symbolism and even the word *Olympic*, famously battling both the Greek government and, earlier in his role as IOC vice president, the Helms Bakery of Los Angeles over trademark ownership. Brundage also launched a bitter fight during the 1960s with European and North American sports manufacturers such as Rossignol, Adidas, and Puma over their growing exploitation and peddling of Olympic insignia.[59]

Fueled by his amateur convictions, Brundage saw it as his duty to distance the Olympic Movement from the appearance of financial profitability and excess. When IAAF president and IOC vice president the Marquess of Exeter (formerly Lord Burghley) proposed the introduction of a 5 percent tax on ticket sales to help facilitate the expanding activities of the Olympic Movement, Brundage rejected the initiative.[60] At the 1959 IOC session in Munich, two years after his first proposal, Exeter championed the introduction of a lesser 2.5 percent tax, warning Brundage that failure to support the scheme might force the cash-strapped international sports federations to establish their own world championships to rival the Olympic Games.[61] Brundage outlined his opposition in an interview with the *Chicago Daily Sun-Times*. "No one is permitted to profit from the Olympic Games," he intoned. "The games rest on this splendid and solid foundation and all are determined that neither individuals, organizations or nations shall be permitted to profit from them politically or commercially."[62] The IOC was not exempt from these anti-profiteering restrictions. Brundage demanded that his beloved IOC continue to function on the basis of gratuitous, voluntary service, even at the cost of organizational efficiency and a globally and demographically representative membership base.

A post–World War II telecommunications revolution presented the biggest threat to Brundage's anticommercialism. Although Olympic images had long been broadcast throughout Europe and North America via cinematic newsreels, the television provided the technological catalyst for the globalization and full-scale marketing of the Olympic Games. As interest in the Cold War Olympic spectacle continued to heighten, rapacious television and marketing executives vied to obtain live broadcasting rights. The lure of television revenue presented new possibilities for an IOC hamstrung by a shoestring operational budget. Unlike his presidential rival, the Marquess of Exeter, Brundage remained vigilant about merging Olympism with the sordid worlds of television and corporate marketing. Although keen to avoid commercial entanglements, Brundage also failed to envision the telegenic or financial viability of the games.[63] The quality and size of early television models likely fueled his hesitation. When the IOC first addressed the issue of television rights at its 1956 annual session in Cortina d'Ampezzo, Brundage implored his assembled colleagues to tread cautiously. "We in the IOC have done well without TV for 60 years and will do so certainly for the next 60 years too," he counseled.[64] Brundage feared that live television broadcasts of the games would hurt spectatorship and open up a financial Pandora's box that would shake the organizational foundations and distort the philosophy and amateur image of the Olympic Movement. But he could not have it both ways. The growing gigantism of the Olympic Games contributed to an explosion in the IOC's administrative costs. The Olympic Movement had to generate revenue in order to sustain itself and fulfill its administrative responsibilities. The defense of amateurism depended upon it.

Brundagian amateurism proved a paradoxical, self-defeating philosophy. His fierce commitment to the anticommercial tenets of Victorian amateurism ensured that the IOC lacked the financial resources and administrative capabilities to effectively regulate and enforce its own code. Brundage's philosophical romanticism (or, rather, stubbornness) stifled practical application and enforcement. Demonstrating both his intellectual limitations and ideological convictions, he could only perceive of commercialism, whether in the form of ticket sale taxes, television revenue, or corporate sponsorship, as antithetical to Olympic amateur principles. From a more enlightened position, Olympic commercialism could have been embraced as amateurism's savior. By allowing the Olympic Movement to enter the world of commerce in a measured and tactful manner, Brundage would have granted the IOC the financial resources to enforce and uphold his cherished ideal. Like the U.S. National Collegiate Athletic Association, which has maintained a rigorous, albeit ethically suspect and perhaps ineffectual, defense of amateurism into the twenty-first century by exploiting commercial opportunities, the IOC would have been empowered to play a far greater administrative role. Based in Lausanne, a small army of professional bureaucrats with appropriate training, expertise, and resources could have bolstered the voluntary, administrative efforts of IOC officials. Resources would have been available to help ensure a level playing field across broad social classifications such as class, gender, and nationality that traditionally drove inequality and lured aspiring athletes to professional practices. The IOC also could have established an active and engaged eligibility committee responsible for verifying and countersigning amateur certificates, investigating stories of impropriety, and dispensing requisite punishments. It could have used the commercial windfall of the Olympic Games to coerce national Olympic committees and international sports federations into strictly enforcing amateur regulations for fear of financial retribution in the form of withholding television revenues and other monetary funds. The stark hypocrisy of preventing sportsmen and sportswomen from personally capitalizing on their sporting fame would have remained as prohibitive, exploitative, and troublesome as ever. But unscrupulous competitors, officials, and governments, on both sides of the Iron Curtain, might have finally met a worthy match.

Instead, Brundage's presidency was guided by fear rather than possibility, by ideological rigidity rather than organizational creativity. Brundage defended his belief that the success of the Olympic Movement rested on its ideological convictions rather than its financial prosperity and bureaucratic reach. "We have no guns, we have no money, as I have said many times; we have nothing but the strength of an idea. And, we better preserve it," he regularly reminded his colleagues.[65] Throughout the remainder of his tenure, Brundage fought to preserve the private, Eurocentric, and voluntary structure of the IOC, even as the Olympic Movement slowly embraced the emerging financial riches of televised games. He blocked numerous Soviet attempts to undertake a major reorganization of the IOC by expanding both revenue streams and membership opportunities on anticommercial and apolitical grounds.[66] He later displayed a similar aversion to a proposal put forward by IOC Secretary General Johann Westerhoff, who took the view that a larger headquarters, a larger staff, and a far greater income was required to cope with the expanding demands of running the Olympic Movement.[67] Under Brundage, the IOC remained small, ideologically contained, administratively overburdened, and incompetent. It was incapable of either promoting Olympism around the world or enforcing its own amateur rules. Within the Olympic stadiums, arenas, and pools, the consequences of Brundage's administrative policies were evident. Money flowed, professionalism flourished, and hypocrisy continued to reign.

The organizational limitations and inefficiency of the IOC grew even more apparent during the 1960s as the Olympic Movement underwent transformative growth. The debilitated post–World War II economies and industrial capacities of European powers sparked a period of rapid decolonization throughout Africa and Asia. Impoverished and unindustrialized Third World nations emerged from behind the shackles of colonial oppression to assert their claim for self-determination. In sub-Saharan Africa alone, thirty new countries achieved statehood in the years between Ghana's independence from Britain in 1957 and Lesotho and Botswana's independence in 1966.[68] These incipient Third World nations were eager to participate in the Olympic Games and to reap the symbolic and legitimizing benefits afforded by membership in the world's highest "cultural club."[69] The emergence of a power bloc composed of newly liberated states from Africa and Asia threatened to transform the IOC from a voluntary Eurocentric gentleman's club into a modern, egalitarian international body who values, practices, and philosophies were truly representative of its global membership.

AMATEURISM AND THE THIRD WORLD

From its very inception in the late nineteenth century, the modern Olympic Movement extolled the virtues of multi-racialism and universalism. The Olympics, in Coubertin's vision, would be open to "all games, all nations." As the next six decades of Olympic competition revealed, however, the baron's idealistic internationalism could not accommodate a multiracial agenda. Decades of self-recruitment and a right-wing, aristocratic composition ensured that IOC members displayed a strong racial paternalism rooted in Darwinian, color-coded thinking about race.[70] Through this hierarchal, paternalistic lens, Coubertin and his successors to the IOC presidency assumed that colonial and indigenous populations lacked the psychological and social attributes, not to mention the developed sporting infrastructure, needed to play the game.[71] The IOC's noninterventionist stance on the issue of apartheid in South African and Rhodesian sport during the postwar years illuminates its empty multiracial rhetoric.[72] Non-Western nations were originally excluded, and later, marginalized from Olympic participation ensuring decades of European and North American sporting and bureaucratic dominance.

The rising post–World War II forces of decolonization, Third World solidarity, and anticolonialism demanded that the Olympic Movement finally reevaluate its longstanding exclusionary Eurocentric policies. Brundage looked upon the emergence of a liberated Third World with a customary grain of optimism and keen suspicion.[73] An expanding, representative global membership base fulfilled the universal ambitions of Olympism; Brundage, however, remained fearful of the breakneck speeds with which African and Asian nations were emerging. He wished to chart these uncertain geopolitical waters carefully, urging his colleagues to undertake a close surveillance of the situation before extending Olympic membership.[74] He revealed his own racial paternalist thinking on the subject, demanding that before membership could be bestowed on the Third World, African and Asian nations had to be educated and enlightened in the "idealistic principles of the Olympic Movement."[75] Brundage calculated that the introduction of non-Western Olympic governing bodies, officials, and competitors bred in a school of sportsmanship far removed from the chivalric, muscular Christian virtues of Anglo-Saxon moral superiority and amateurism would radically alter the philosophical tenets of Olympism. He expressed his trepidation during a February 1963 meeting with the IOC Executive Board, at which he advised his colleagues "to avoid granting recognition to committees representing very small countries which only possess a very vague notion of sport matters and of what Olympism stands for."[76] Herein lay the crux of Brundage's discomfort. Postcolonialism threatened the ideological and hegemonic stranglehold that Western nations had long held over elite international sport. A deluge of Third World nations flooding the Olympic Movement threatened to democratize the IOC. Brundage feared that a larger, more representative body would inevitably take aim at amateurism, repealing its most sacrosanct tenets in order to facilitate the participation of underprivileged and unrepresented African and Asian athletes.

Postcolonial Africa and Asia represented a sporting tabula rasa. The oppressive, impoverished, and unindustrialized realities of the Third World negated both the development of professional sporting structures and the intrusion of commercial influences in these regions. Kenyan IOC member Reginald Alexander later confirmed this reality after an extensive survey of conditions in Africa. "We are satisfied that, at the moment, there is little evidence in Africa of professionalism in sport," he declared. Alexander issued a note of concern, however, warning his colleagues that "great vigilance on this subject will be necessary" as Third World nations become wealthier and their respective governments assert more influence over Olympic affairs.[77] Brundage remained anxious. He believed that the unknown political and ideological orientations of non-aligned African and Asian nations posed a grave threat to the Olympic Movement. Brundage particularly feared the encroachment of Communism and the philosophical and organizational challenges that it would inevitably pose. Citing the example of Soviet political maneuvering within the United Nations, he envisioned a power bloc of Eastern European and Third World nations asserting a Communist agenda within the IOC, eradicating amateurism, and upsetting the traditional balance of power.[78] The image of a governmentally controlled IOC, espousing Communist ideals and state-funded professional sporting practices, drove Brundage to despair.

Illustrating his administrative rigidity, Brundage failed to effectively address these concerns. When French IOC member Comte Jean de Beaumont proposed the creation of the Committee for International Olympic Aid (CIOA) [later Olympic Solidarity] as an educational and financial framework through which to disseminate a Western, Eurocentric model of knowledge on Olympic values to the peoples of the Third World, Brundage greeted the notion with skepticism.[79] He argued that the IOC lacked the financial and administrative resources to support such a broad undertaking, an ironic consequence of his own strict anticommercialism.[80] Privately, he believed that the CIOA would become a choice target for Soviet and Eastern bloc Olympic officials seeking to promulgate Communist ideology.[81] Although educational support eventually came in the form of the IOC's sponsorship of regional games in Africa, Asia, Central America, and the Mediterranean, Brundage's philosophical conservatism again forced the IOC to forgo a momentous opportunity to embolden amateurism. By loosening his anti-commercial restraints, Brundage would have endowed the IOC with the financial flexibility and administrative capacity to disseminate and assert the ideologies of amateurism and Olympism throughout the Third World.

The IOC's largely noncommittal attitude toward the Third World occurred against the backdrop of a broader mobilization of nonaligned states. Soaked in the spirit of the 1955 Asian-African Conference held in Bandung, Indonesia, Third World states formulated a series of international organizational alliances such as the G77, the Arab League, and the Organization of African Unity to confront continued Western hegemony and the slow pace of decolonization.[82] The solidarity declared at Bandung inspired the establishment of other Third World movements in the sporting realm, notably the Supreme Council for Sport in Africa (SCSA) and the Games of the New Emerging Forces (GANEFO). These organizations sought to extend their influence throughout the newly emancipated Third World by condemning the allegedly hypocritical, imperialist, and undemocratic structure of the Olympic Movement. While the SCSA rallied behind the antiapartheid cause in South African and Rhodesian sport, the GANEFO arose as a hegemonic rival of the Olympic Games.[83]

Fortune ultimately favored the IOC. The short-lived success of the GANEFO—following Indonesian president Sukarno's fall from political power, the advent of the Chinese Cultural Revolution, and a lack of financial resources—ensured that the IOC was left unopposed to gain access to and control of African and Asian sport.[84] Beginning with the entrance of Nigeria at the 1952 Helsinki Olympics, nineteen African and eighteen Asian national Olympic committees received IOC accreditation in the years leading up to the 1964 Tokyo Olympics. The integration of Third World nations into Western imperial sporting structures reproduced the old colonial power dynamics. The IOC imposed a policy of cultural assimilation rather than reconciliation. Though portrayed as a global phenomenon, the Olympic Movement continued to privilege Western, capitalistic ideologies. Brundage and the IOC never entertained the idea of incorporating indigenous African and Asian sporting and movement practices into the Olympic program. Anglo-Saxon sport, conducted in accordance with prohibitive amateur rules and regulations, continued to prevail. Even when allowed to participate under highly circumscribed conditions in Western-style sports and venues, Third World nations were rarely allowed a meaningful voice in the governance of the Olympic Movement. By 1960, IOC membership continued to be overrepresented by wealthy white Westerners—thirty-eight of sixty-five members hailed from Europe and North America.[85] Integration into the Olympic Movement represented a new form of colonialism, whereby former colonized nations participated in Western Olympic sports, in accordance with Western values and systems of governance. Thus, Olympic participation forced emerging Third World nations to assimilate themselves, often quite literally, on foreign fields of play. Amateurism, the philosophical invention of Victorian Britain, continued to serve—on paper at least—as the ideological and regulatory framework governing the Olympic Games.

PROFESSIONALISM, MONEY, AND INTERNAL STRIFE

The steady transformation of the Olympic Games into a global, multiracial sporting festival during the 1960s only served to whet the appetites of television executives and corporate marketers eager to broadcast live Olympic images. The Squaw Valley and Rome Organizing Committees dispelled Brundage's initial doubts about the financial viability of the Olympics after successfully brokering the sale of television rights to the 1960 winter and summer Olympics. Rome, for its part, offered the IOC 5 percent of its relatively nominal television revenues. Although the Olympic Movement continued to operate on the brink of bankruptcy, with the IOC reporting annual financial deficits in the years 1967–71, the stage had been set for increasing the commercialization and commodification of the Olympics.[86]

Brundage long warned that money fostered conflict, bold ambition, and financial self-interest among amateur organizations. His intuition proved correct. As the Olympic Movement grew in size, complexity, and wealth, interorganizational disagreements emerged between the three Olympic partners over both the distribution of television revenues and the assertion of bureaucratic power. The international sports federations, led by Ireland's J. Francis "Bunny" Ahearne of the Fédération Internationale de Hockey sur Glace, demanded a one-third share of the sale of future Olympic television rights. When the advent of satellite technology and fierce competition between rival U.S., and to a far lesser extent Australian and Canadian, television networks pushed the contracted sums even higher, the national Olympic committees emerged alongside Ahearne and the international sports federations to demand their own share of the growing Olympic riches.[87] A bureaucratic power struggle ensued. Eager to diffuse interorganizational frictions, Brundage helped broker the "Rome Formula," which mandated an equal 11.1 percent division of television revenue between the three parties—the Olympic Games Organizing Committees would receive the remaining 66.7 percent share. Still, the division of what remained at the time paltry sums failed to satiate all parties. Clamoring for a greater role in Olympic administration and decision making, the national Olympic committees and international sports federations mobilized to form their own representative general assemblies as a lobbying platform against Brundage and the IOC.[88]

The rebellion of the national Olympic committees and international sports federations reached maturity in 1965 and 1967, respectively, with the establishment of the Permanent General Assembly of National Olympic Committees (PGA-NOC) and the General Assembly of International Federations.[89] The formation of these organizations threatened Brundage's authoritarian hold over Olympic affairs. Boasting strong Communist and Third World backing, the assemblies challenged the insularity of the IOC by articulating a singular and democratic voice in how the Olympic Movement should be administered and financed. Amateurism, the philosophical ideal of Brundage and his fellow Eurocentric powerbrokers on the IOC, inevitably came under attack. When the PGA-NOC first assembled in Rome during autumn 1965, it demanded that the IOC cede full responsibility back to the international sports federations to govern and enforce amateurism in their respective Olympic sports. Revealing the democratic sentiment of Communist and nonaligned national Olympic committees, the delegates called for a "new general formula, to be specified separately by each International Federation."[90]

The recalcitrant Brundage worked to undermine the general assemblies and their revolutionary agendas at every turn. Through decades of administrative experience, he learned firsthand that the international sports federations maintained widely diverse and increasingly liberal definitions of an amateur. Under the leadership of Australian IOC member Hugh Weir, Brundage formed a new amateur commission to examine and effectively counter the proposals put forward by the representatives of the PGA-NOC.[91] In a preliminary report on the subject, Weir reaffirmed the IOC's desire to continue overseeing amateur enforcement. He proposed an entirely different approach to the defense of amateurism: a code of eligibility enumerating a series of infringements "which will definitely render a competitor *ineligible* to take part."[92] Brundage backed the initiative, arguing that "unless we have our own rule spelled out precisely and in detail, specifying who is eligible to compete in the Olympic Games and who is not, there will be confusion much of the time."[93] Mindful that the defense of Olympic amateurism rested on interorganizational cooperation, Brundage entrusted the amateur commission with brokering a compromise and achieving conformity with the international sports federations in the formulation of a new code.[94]

While the amateur commission worked to revamp the IOC's amateur policies for the second time in less than a decade, professionalism continued to flood the Olympic arena. In an interview with the German newspaper *Die Welt*, Otto Mayer offered a stark and honest assessment of the growing plight of Olympic amateurism. The former IOC chancellor proclaimed that "Amateurism . . . no longer exists in the world." "Where can you still find amateurs at the present time?" he asked. "In field hockey, perhaps, and in certain of the least important sports. But except for those, wherever you look, there are professionals."[95] A survey of the Olympic landscape throughout the 1960s supported Mayer's crestfallen tone. In soccer and cycling, the scourge of professionalism appeared so great that Brundage requested that FIFA and the Union Cycliste Internationale reconstitute themselves to allow for the creation of separate amateur and professional governing bodies.[96] Elsewhere, the payment of cash prizes to amateurs in the shooting, yachting, and equestrian events persisted despite the IOC's growing frustration. The winter games, the overtly commercialized awkward stepsister of the summer festival, also continued to operate as a thorn in Brundage's side. Stirred by reports of West German figure skaters Marika Kilius and Hans-Jürgen Bäumler using the Olympics as a steppingstone to lucrative professional careers, as well as the untold number of alpine skiers who were the recipients of commercial sponsorship deals, paid employment, and under-the-table cash rewards at the 1964 Innsbruck Games, Brundage revived calls for the cancelation of the winter games altogether.[97] "The situation is worsening; the dispersion of competitions and the professionalism raging in several sports are difficulties which must not be ignored and should make us reflect. We ought to make our rules respected or stop organizing the Winter Games," he fumed.[98]

Throughout the remainder of the decade, Brundage's threats continued to ring hollow. The IOC's authority was increasingly mocked, athletes were corrupted by the lure of financial riches, money flowed, governments encroached, hypocrisy flourished, and the Olympic Games gradually transformed itself into a branch of commercial entertainment. The decline and fall of amateurism carried an air of inevitability. Cold War *realpolitik*, rising global commerce, interorganizational friction, and the advent of television converged to deliver debilitating blows to the amateur ideal. Still, Brundage had the opportunity to position Olympic amateurism on a more favorable and defensible footing. By lifting the hermetic seals to the IOC's financial coffers, undertaking professional and jurisdictional restructuring, and adopting an uncompromising stance toward known violators, he might have given amateurism a greater chance of survival. Instead, as the Olympic Movement headed to Grenoble and Mexico City to celebrate the 1968 winter and summer editions of the games, Brundage's lack of administrative foresight inadvertently pushed amateurism further down the path toward dissolution and decline.

7 SELLING OUT THE AMATEUR IDEAL

The 1968 winter and summer Olympics marked the beginning of the end of amateurism. As the games traversed the mountainous alpine resort of Grenoble and the high plateau of Mexico City, centrifugal forces converged to further expose the hypocritical realities and philosophical incompatibility of the amateur ideal in an age of televised, high-performance sport.[1] With hindsight, signs of its demise could be seen to have long loomed large on the Olympic horizon. The transformation of the Olympics into a platform for Cold War propaganda and the commercialization of an increasingly global spectacle undermined Avery Brundage's lofty insistence that the Olympics promoted clean, honest amateur sport. Or perhaps the opportunistic Baron Pierre de Coubertin sealed amateurism's fate from the start by inserting the Anglophone ideal of "sport for sport's sake" in a movement devoted to *Citius, Altius, Fortius* and by establishing participation on the basis of national representation.

Among the many causes of its unraveling, amateurism endured a marked decline during the late 1960s and 1970s. Soaked in the countercultural spirit of the era, movements around the world challenged social norms and social order, often through radical and subversive efforts. Western nations such as France, Great Britain, the United States, and West Germany took leftward political turns and sought progressive social reforms. The sustained push for civil rights along racial, gender, and social lines, as illuminated by the dissonant tones of "We Shall Overcome," Janis Joplin, and the Black Panthers' "Free Huey" movement, powerfully exposed the system of inequality in capitalist societies.[2] Amateur sport was not immune to emerging cultural movements that challenged exploitation and threatened the status quo.[3] Hair gradually lengthened as athletes questioned the authority of coaches and administrators. The Olympic gold medalist Cassius Clay changed his name to Muhammad Ali, defied the Vietnam draft, and angrily decried police brutality and racial injustice. The sociologist Harry Edwards founded the Olympic Project for Human Rights in 1967, which also protested racial discrimination in both sport and society at large.[4] Even sportswomen mobilized in their push for greater inclusion and pay equity, particularly as television and commercial marketing transformed elite sport into lucrative commodities.[5] Athletes attempted to break free from the shackles of conformity and raise their collective voices (and fists) in the name of equality and fairness.[6] In this era of cultural dissent, the amateur system of unpaid labor, which privileged octogenarian, patriarchal sporting administrators and greedy promoters, became a choice target for rebellion and reform.

The IOC suddenly found itself caught between the pillars of tradition and modernity. Under the leadership of its aging president, Avery Brundage, it struggled to keep pace with the shifting sporting landscape. Sparked by a satellite communications revolution, revitalized mass production, and secure global trade, sport, and especially sporting goods, became important commodities. Adidas and Puma rivaled for control of sports shoes. Ski manufacturers battled for shares of the exploding leisure ski market. U.S. television networks vied for Olympic broadcasting rights. Even nonsport companies devised more elaborate ways to use Olympic athletes to sell their products in a global marketplace. The result was both overt and covert sponsorship deals for amateur athletes and sporting organizations. From FIFA to the feet of athletes, everything suddenly had a price. As Brundage entered his last term as IOC president, the influx of global commercialism and the rise of television and mass media plunged Olympic amateurism into a moribund state.

TELEVISING THE OLYMPIC SPECTACLE

Brundage began 1968 facing reelection. His detractors, mounting in number and confidence, planned an electoral coup. Their preferred candidate, French IOC member Jean de Beaumont, proved unable to unseat the eighty-one-year-old Brundage. His reelection, however, did little to reassert his waning authority.[7] Critics continued to accuse the American of monopolistic rule, high-handedness, and a stubborn resistance to democratic change. The national Olympic committees and international sports federations voiced their growing opposition through the General Assemblies. Italian Giulio Onesti, the driving force in the creation of the Permanent General Assembly of National Olympic Committees (PGA-NOC) and a constant thorn in Brundage's side, revived calls for the democratization of the Olympic Movement along more socially equitable and geographically representative lines.[8] The Italian personally toured sub-Saharan Africa, visiting athletic facilities and meeting with local sporting administrators in Kenya, Ivory Coast, and Nigeria, in an effort to expose the inequity that prevailed under Brundage's leadership.[9]

Onesti and the PGA-NOC also championed the formulation of a more progressive stance on amateurism in line with prevailing social and economic conditions. In keeping with his democratic agenda, Onesti even proposed enfranchising the athlete to help shape the future direction of amateur eligibility.[10] Such revolutionary ideas were anathema to Brundage. He retreated to a familiar (and convenient) defensive posture. Amateurism was a fixed, timeless ideal incapable of change, he insisted. The calls for reform resonating both within and outside the Olympic Movement would not be silenced. Pressure continued to mount. With the work of the IOC amateur commission grinding to halt after the death of chairman Hugh Weir's son, Brundage was forced to concede some ground.[11] At the 1968 IOC Annual Session in Mexico City, he tasked the Romanian IOC member Alexandru Şiperco to lead a Joint Commission that included representatives from various national Olympic committees and international federations to help draft new eligibility rules.[12] The issue of amateur eligibility became even more pronounced during the late 1960s as the Olympic Movement opened itself up to a far greater degree of commercialization through the proliferation of television and the increasing refinement of satellite technology.

As a mass-communicative medium, the television fueled an exploding global interest in elite sport. It convened the essential elements of sporting competition. It provided intimacy and image, detail and analysis. With live broadcasts becoming available in color, the television represented the most important advertising medium for a burgeoning sports industry.[13] Corporations and marketing agencies embraced televised sport as a platform for showcasing their range of products to both national and global audiences. The price of broadcast rights soon soared as U.S. television and cinema newsreel networks vied to secure these valuable sporting images.[14] The Olympic Games, the world's largest multisporting event, reaped the benefits of escalating payments for television rights. After securing modest profits from the 1960 and 1964 Olympiads, the Mexico City Olympic Organizing Committee brokered a $4.5 million deal with the American Broadcasting Company (ABC) for rights to the 1968 Olympics. Even though the European Broadcasting Union's monopoly over the European market kept Olympic broadcasting prices down, international television sales totaled a staggering $9.75 million, a sixfold increase over the Tokyo Olympics. Spiraling technical and production costs, coupled with higher advertising demand, drove television fees in

1972 to previously unimagined levels: ABC paid \$13.5 million for the rights to the Munich Olympics, while its competitor, the National Broadcasting Company (NBC), paid roughly \$6.4 million for the Sapporo Olympics.[15]

Inevitably, the question of television rights became the source of sustained debate within the Olympic Movement. The tripartite Olympic partners—the IOC, national Olympic committees, and international sports federations—entered into protracted technical and legal discussions and negotiations over the distribution of revenues. The exorbitant costs of staging the Olympics also led Olympic Organizing Committees to demand a larger share of the profits through a more favorable readjustment of the Rome Formula, the profit-sharing agreement drafted in 1966. (See chapter 6.) Despite his strong initial fears about the impact and appearance that a relationship with the television industry might have on an amateur organization, Brundage presided over a philosophical shift in the Olympic Movement's attitudes toward money. In fact, his third term in office marked the initial evolution of the IOC into a commercially driven corporate entity. Brundage supported the establishment of a finance commission to advance the financial interests of the Olympic Movement and even began demanding that the IOC assume a greater role in future television negotiations.[16] His gloomy forewarnings of the dangers of commercialism contradicted the Olympic Movement's mounting fiscal attitudes and financial procedures.

With Brundage at the helm the Olympic Games gradually transformed into a branch of commercial entertainment. The development of new athletic technology and commercial television seduced Brundage and the Olympic Movement into a dance with the devil. As television revenues rose, corporations and advertisers sought creative ways to capitalize on and commodify the Olympic spectacle. Money saturated Olympic arenas, stadiums, and pools. Athletes became running and jumping billboards as marketing agencies sought Olympians to endorse their products; *Citius, Altius, Fortius* draped in nationalism and patriotic fervor exuded commercial appeal. Brundage and the IOC were caught in an ideological and logistical bind: A concentrated campaign against the growing flood of amateur infractions would jeopardize the profitability and viability of the Olympic spectacle. Elite athletes, pure or otherwise, sold television. The IOC could not turn back. The gigantism of the Olympics, as well as the exploding administrative costs of the IOC, necessitated that television and commerce became vital partners in the Olympic Movement.

The shifting philosophical and financial direction of the Olympic Movement further exposed the exploitative and hypocritical realities of amateurism. Fierce U.S. television negotiations and unrestrained commercialization revealed to sportsmen and sportswomen exactly how many millions of dollars their unpaid athletic performance was worth and who stood to profit from their labor.[17] The façade of "pure" amateurism came crashing down, especially as the dollar amounts were featured prominently in the news media. Amateur athletes sensed this hypocrisy. They demanded a slice of the growing pie. As one Olympian explained, "Why should I sit around like a hermit when everybody else is making money out of these people? If I can give them publicity, they ought to pay me for it."[18] Echoing the rising sentiment of the 1960s, journalist John Underwood, a contributor for the popular U.S. magazine *Sports Illustrated*, presciently acknowledged the double standard. "Excluding the fan, the athlete is, ideally, the only unpaid part in a stadium of promoters, ticket takers, hot-dog vendors, sportswriters, and TV crews," he observed.[19] The commercial orientation of the Olympic Movement weakened Brundage's demands for absolute amateur purity. The Olympic Games entered into an era of startling hypocrisy: The IOC and its network partners and corporate advertisers harvested the financial riches of televised competition but ordered the athletes—the elite performers who made the Olympics an attractive commodity—to refrain from profiting in any capacity from their sporting abilities.

By the late 1960s and 1970s, the Olympic athlete defected from the one-sided arrangement imposed by amateur eligibility restrictions. Increasing television revenues and corporate advertisements fueled demand among promoters for marquee-worthy athletes who could draw in hordes of paying spectators. Across Europe and North America, promoters lured talented amateurs to their televised track meets, alpine ski races, and swimming galas with the promise of under-the-table appearance fees, performance-based bonuses, and first-class airfare and luxury accommodations.[20] The German newspaper *Die Zeit* revealed that the Kenyan runner Mike Boit received $20,000 from promoters in Zurich for finishing the 800 meters at a world record clip.[21] Amateur track meets in Athens, Berlin, London, New York, Oslo, Rome, and Stuttgart awarded similar lucrative prizes to record-breaking performers. Sagacious promoters even paid athletes not to appear at rival events.[22] Amateur athletes became increasingly comfortable justifying their shamateur lifestyles. "The athlete sees himself as being cheated so he cheats," John Underwood explained.[23] West German 400-meter runner Horst-Rüdiger Schlöske agreed with this justification. "If an athlete can get money, he should take it. And almost all Europeans do."[24] In a sporting world where advanced technical training and costly technology bred Olympic champions, few amateurs remained.

The 1968 Mexico City Olympics forcefully revealed the impact that television money, corporate ambition, and commercial considerations had on the Olympic Movement. The growing materialization of televised sport beamed straight from the Olympic venues to the living room—*with short breaks for a message from the corporate sponsors*—marked an unprecedented force pulling against the sacrosanct ethos of amateurism. Rival German shoe manufacturing giants Puma and Adidas were among the first to recognize the importance of televised Olympic sport for enhancing their brand recognition in an increasingly global marketplace. With the emergence of new Japanese competitors Mizuno and Tiger, Puma and Adidas embraced the feet of Olympic athletes as an inexpensive vehicle to promote their products. Telecast images of athletes running and jumping to Olympic glory in their shoes afforded incontrovertible proof of their product's supremacy.[25] The elite amateur athlete became a much sought after commodity. Rival sporting goods manufacturers engaged in a lucrative and highly competitive bidding war for the feet of Olympic champions, a war that would reach its zenith in the high altitudes of Mexico City.

THE SHOE WARS

In 1948, an acrimonious falling-out between Adolf "Adi" Dassler and his brother Rudolf precipitated the division of their Gebrüder Dassler shoe company into two rival factions, Adidas and Puma. In the succeeding decades, the two rival German shoe companies ruled over Olympic sport, making shoes for nearly every event on the Olympic program—alas, neither company ever figured out how to develop a shoe for swimming. Their success only intensified their fraternal rivalry. Espionage and sabotage became staples of their corporate marketing campaigns. The opening salvo in this sneaker war came when the Adidas patriarch, Adi Dassler, sent his twenty-year-old son, Horst, to the 1956 Melbourne Olympic Games. Horst had both vision and charisma. He negotiated with Frank Hartley, the owner of the Melbourne Sports Depot, to hand out free Adidas track spikes to all Olympic track and field athletes. Though endorsements clearly violated IOC amateur rules, Horst calculated that track spikes qualified as technical assistance. The voluntary nature of the program kept enough distance between the athletes and the shoe company that Brundage and the IOC did not take notice.[26] The live and rebroadcast images from the Melbourne Olympics were transmitted to viewers around the world. The sight of Olympic champions such as Ireland's 1500-meter gold-medalist Ron Delaney and Polish long-jump champion Elżbieta Krzesińska on the victory platform with the Adidas logo emblazoned on their shoes proved to be an ingenious marketing ploy. American Bobby Morrow's three gold medal victories in the sprints even landed him and his Adidas shoes on the front cover of *Life*, a popular general-interest magazine in the United

States.[27] Recalling the photograph, Chris Severn, one of Adidas's U.S. sales representatives, explained that "there he [Bobby Morrow] was on the cover of *Life* magazine with his three-striped spikes. It caused quite a stir, and all of a sudden retailers became interested."[28]

The convergence of media and the Olympic Games escalated the rivalry between Adidas and Puma, in which both embarked on a pitched battle for the hearts and feet of the athletes. Since their brands' logos—the three stripes for Adidas, the single sweeping stripe for Puma—remained visible when captured in photographs or on television, both companies believed it was essential that their shoes grace the feet of the world's elite athletes. But free shoes would not be enough! Puma set the standard by paying professional football players to switch allegiances from their rival Adidas. At the 1960 Rome Olympics, Puma paid Armin Hary, the West German Olympic champion and world record holder in the 100 meters to run in their latest spikes.[29] The ever-increasing number of Olympians defecting to Puma forced its rival Adidas to also begin paying athletes. As Horst Dassler, chief executive at Adidas, confirmed: "When we could see people, very important medal prospects, who used to wear Adidas, now in the brand name Puma's, it was hard to sit back and let this happen. So the bargaining began."[30] Olympic "amateurs" guilefully mastered the art of negotiation. One track star played the manufacturing giants against each other to such an extent that the highest bidder, Puma, sent both him and his wife to Acapulco for a vacation after the Olympics.[31] Adidas signed exclusive contracts with the Mexican government and the Mexico City Olympic Organizing Committee securing sole access to the Olympic Village and preventing Puma from importing shoes into the country. Still, Puma devised ways to circumvent these barriers.[32] A corporate battle ensued. Monetary payments, ranging in scale between $500 and $1,000, were placed in the shoes and spikes of Olympic athletes as part of a bidding war that violated Olympic amateur rules that expressively forbade athletes to profit from their talents and images.[33]

The corporate takeover of the Mexico City Olympics drew the attention of Brundage, who struggled to understand the extent of corporate subterfuge. His desk became submerged with correspondence between the Mexico City Organizing Committee and representatives from Puma and Adidas.[34] A perusal of the documentation Brundage gathered suggests that Puma fired the opening shot by attempting to buy as many of the U.S. track-and-field athletes as possible during their Olympic training camp in Lake Tahoe, California.[35] Puma and Adidas aggressively targeted athletes from the United States—the largest consumer of an exploding global shoe market. The prospect of U.S. Olympians clinching gold in their respective footwear before the eyes of the world represented an unprecedented marketing opportunity. *Sports Illus-trated* calculated that had the IOC intervened and issued suspensions, the U.S. track-and-field team would have returned home without any medals.[36] In fact, one of the most widely seen protests at the 1968 Olympic Games revealed the direct influence of the shoe wars. When Tommie Smith and John Carlos raised their black gloves as a symbol of defiance, Smith, though barefooted, placed his Puma shoes on the medal podium next to him. Smith recalled "I had taken them [the Puma shoes] off, of course, as part of my silent protest. But it was important for me to have them on the stand, because they helped me get there during the race and long before."[37] Smith was referring to the financial support Puma provided that sustained his wife and daughter while he trained in the months leading up to the Mexico City Olympics. For Smith, intentionally carrying his Puma spikes onto the victory stand was not only a tangible act of defiance against the governing bodies but an illustration of the hypocrisy of the amateur rules.

Newspaper headlines exposed to the public the degree to which corporate dollars infiltrated the Mexico City Olympics. The *Tribune de Lausanne*

Puma and Adidas had sought the coveted space on the feet of amateur athletes as a way to market their brands. As can be seen here in the 1968 Mexico City Olympics, while the members of the United States and Italian team celebrate after the 110 meter hurdles, Adidas and Puma are not only easily seen but the only brands featured on these Olympic medalists. (Courtesy of the International Olympic Committee)

claimed that more than two hundred athletes had received money from the German shoe manufacturers.[38] The *Los Angeles Times* estimates were higher, citing that "virtually every country in the Olympics are [*sic*] guilty of violations in the equipment scandal."[39] Even Olympic officials were complicit in the affair, the *New York Times* revealed, as the moneyed aristocrats and wealthy businessmen proved susceptible to free sneakers and complimentary gym bags.[40] Determined to establish the truth, the United States Olympic Committee (USOC) in conjunction with the U.S. AAU launched a full-scale investigation.[41] The USOC's final report revealed that a significant portion of the U.S. team were in receipt of either checks drawn from West German banks or U.S. dollar bills marked with consecutive serial numbers.[42] Puma and Adidas, however, refused to cooperate with the governing bodies,[43] leaving AAU secretary-treasurer Daniel Ferris to remark frustratingly: "We cannot afford to go off half-cocked. We must have concrete evidence which will stand up in a court of law."[44] Adidas and Puma had spread the cash and shoes so far and wide (likely including handouts to Olympic officials) that no single athlete could be dismissed lest the IOC wished to take them all down. Consequently, no U.S. athletes lost medals or received a sanction since

The 1968 shoe scandal after the Mexico City Games illustrated the willingness of manufacturers to pay athletes in violation of Olympic amateur rules. Adidas and Puma engaged in a heated battle to spread their brands throughout the Olympic Village. Here a member of Great Britain's Olympic team sports her new Adidas shoes and bag (tag still attached). (Courtesy of the International Olympic Committee)

the investigation failed to uncover evidence linking payments to specific individuals.

That is not to say that Brundage did not have proof such payments had occurred. He received full disclosure from one of the few individuals who understood the extent of the corruption: Horst Dassler. In an interview with *Sports Illustrated,* the heir to the Adidas fortune recounted that "when the games were over, I went to see Mr. Brundage in Mexico City. I said 'Athletes have been paid,' . . . I did not tell him any names. I just excused myself and said, 'Things happened that should not have happened, but we would have lost nearly the whole American team, and instead of 85% of the medal winners we would have had 30%.'"[45] Dassler's confession to Brundage was not motivated by repentance for his sins, but rather represented the only way to rein in the outlandish spending that neither Adidas nor Puma could sustain. Along with an untold number of free shoes, clothes, and goods, both companies spent roughly $300,000 during the 1968 Olympic Games.[46] The two shoe companies emerged from Mexico City with roughly the same percentage of medals that they had garnered at the 1960 Rome and 1964 Tokyo Olympics. Their race to gain a larger market share had enriched the athletes but not necessarily the rival companies. Dassler hoped that by blowing the whistle on the scandal, he could enlist the IOC's help to slow down the escalating spending.

In the wake of the 1968 shoe scandal, the IAAF explored reforms to stem the flow of corporate dollars reaching the pockets of amateur athletes. A "white shoe" proposal generated considerable discussion. This initiative would require all amateur track athletes to compete in all white shoes with no identifiable commercial logos.[47] Although Puma appeared on board, it was clear that the scheme would neither stop the flow of money nor squelch commercialism.[48] After all, the rival companies could still advertise how their shoe had been on the feet of victorious athletes. At its 1970 annual congress, the IAAF proposed an alternative solution: permit the national sports federations to sign commercial contracts with the manufacturer rather than the individual athletes. For the IAAF, the issue was apparently not the infiltration of commercial dollars sullying the sacred realm of amateur sport, but rather who stood to profit from the frantic drive for corporate global sales.[49] Herein lay the inconvenient truth that stimulated the decline and fall of Olympic amateurism. Governing bodies of amateur sport packaged and sold amateur virtue to the public while privately cultivating corporate relationships and signing lucrative commercial endorsements.

Adidas, Puma, and their growing list of sport manufacturing rivals such as Dunlop, Head, and Nike, turned their attentions from the athletes to the federations, influencing them with cash or financing and supporting their championship events. In the years after the Mexico City Olympics, Dassler and his Adidas shoe company acquired valuable contracts, becoming the official supplier to the sports federations of the Soviet Union, East Germany, and much of the Third World. Under the aegis of his International Sports and Leisure marketing agency, as well as his connections with public relations firm West Nally, Dassler would later use his repertoire of corporate chicanery and commercial influence to dominate the world of amateur and professional sport.[50] The Mexico City Olympics marked the beginning of an era in which some amateur governing of bodies freely scarified all pretence and openly reaped the riches of televised, commercialized sport. The federations' coffers filled with the money earned off the backs and feet of unpaid labor made possible through the ongoing use of amateurism as a criterion for eligibility to the Olympic Games.

"OLYMPIC GAMES IN DANGER"

The fusion of commercialism, television, and corporate influence had earlier converged to greater effect at the 1968 Winter Olympics in Grenoble. Here in the foothills of the French Alps, Brundage watched on in despair as Alpine racers made a small fortune from their amateur statuses, advertising the latest Kneissl or Rossignol ski equipment and appearing in advertisements for winter tourist destinations.[51] Brundage railed against France's Jean-Claude Killy and Austria's Karl Schranz, brandishing the Alpine skiers as "living advertisements" who subjected themselves to the whim of the ski and clothing manufacturers that paid their exorbitant salaries. "Practically all of the participants in the 'Alpine Circus' today are paid more or less openly," he charged.[52] Financed by Charles de Gaulle's French government at an estimated cost of $240 million, the Grenoble Olympics symbolized everything that Brundage resented about the televised age of Olympic sport. He gathered a mass of global newspaper headlines that condemned the Gallic blend of crass commercialism, nationalism, and semiprofessionalism. "Ski Payoffs May Doom Olympics," "Winter Games Should Be Discontinued," "Le Semi-Professionalisme des Skieurs," "Lets Ditch the Olympics," "Most Olympians Are Professionals," the media headlines howled. For Brundage, the Grenoble Olympics represented the last straw. "Alpine skiing does not belong in the Olympic Games!" he thundered.[53]

Alpine skiing's close ties to tourism and ski manufacturing exposed its athletes to greater commercial influence and manipulation. For decades, Alpine skiers had been tempted to accept endorsement deals and monetary payments from ski and winter apparel manufacturers eager to paint or sow their emblems onto equipment or clothing. These trends grew even more pronounced in the decades after World War II, when television transformed winter sports into big business.[54] Tourism and equipment sales to affluent North Americans and Europeans increased the marketability and commercial appeal of famous Olympic ski racers. As one news article explained in 1964, "At a time when the number of skiers is increasing from year to year all over the world, ski manufacturers have to publicize their products by having them win top honors. It's big business."[55] Media reports illustrated the growing infestation of commercial dollars into winter sport. Stories circulated providing detailed descriptions of negotiated contracts between Olympic skiers and corporate sponsors, with top amateur ski racers receiving more than a million French francs ($2,000 USD) per month, a handsome wage in this period.[56]

Brundage had sensed the inherent danger. To prevent athletes from marketing skis to televised global audiences during the 1968 Grenoble Olympics, the IOC had sought to blot out any brand or trademarks on skiers' equipment. It pressured the Fédération Internationale de Ski (FIS) to work with the ski manufacturers and to implement the necessary changes. The commercially orientated FIS remained unconvinced that such an action was possible. FIS president and Swiss IOC member Marc Holder did agree, however, to ensure that the skiers would have their equipment taken away from them after the competition before they could appear in front of the hordes of television cameras and photographers.[57] This failed to stymie the more industrious and cunning. When Jean-Claude Killy stormed to one of his three gold medals in Grenoble, he had his girlfriend hold a spare pair of his skis and gloves near the finish line so that when he received his celebratory hug, his sponsor's trademark remained firmly on display for all the media to capture.[58] In truth, Killy represented the head of the snake. In a conversation captured in *Time* magazine, Brundage accosted Colonel Marceau Crespin, France's director of sports, and asked, "I hear that half the skiers on the French team don't live up to our definition of amateurism. Is that true?" Replied Crespin, "You have been misinformed, Monsieur. No one on the French ski team lives up to your definition."[59] The gilt had been firmly and publicly knocked off Brundage's cherished amateur ideal. Bitter and distraught, he refused to attend the Alpine ski events in Grenoble and distribute Olympic medals.[60] "This poisonous cancer must be eliminated without further delay," he fumed.[61]

From Brundage's perspective, the growing commercialism of the Olympics undermined the integrity and viability of the Olympic Movement in the eyes of the public. The IOC's image had taken a bruising. Tense internal fights over television revenues and rampant violations of amateur rules, cast against a turbulent political environment marred by debates over South African and Rhodesian apartheid, the mass shooting of unarmed student protesters in Mexico City, and the infamous black power salute, drove Brundage to despair.[62] He took to the floor at the 1970 IOC Annual Session in Amsterdam, to admonish his colleagues that the Olympic Games "are in trouble, in serious trouble."[63] In a rambling polemic, Brundage touched upon nearly every issue facing the IOC, including the size of the Olympic program, the inclusion of heavily commercialized team sports, and egregious violations of the amateur ideal. He interpreted the city of Zurich's referendum, in which the citizens had voted by a 3½ to 1 margin against bidding for the 1976 Winter Olympic Games, as evidence of growing public disenfranchisement with the IOC's direction. He pinned the problem squarely on amateur eligibility. Conditions "are steadily getting worse and in Alpine skiing today are evidently out of hand," Brundage warned. "The patience of the public is exhausted, the people have spoken; they will not support a fraud!"[64] The irony of his own words was obviously lost on Brundage. The IOC sought and cultivated a relationship with television and commerce. The huge capital gains generated by televised Olympic spectacles were now available for all to enjoy—the IOC, the federations, the national Olympic committees, the state, the industry, even the amateur athlete. Amateurism was floundering under the conditions of Brundage's and the IOC's own making.

Factions within the Olympic Movement were quick to recognize the hypocrisy. Under the chairmanship of Alexandru Şiperco, the Joint Commission on Eligibility proposed amateur reforms that would push the needle toward liberalization. The Romanian IOC member acknowledged that "changes have occurred in the past few decades in social life and in the conditions for practicing the sport of high-performance." Thus, he advocated the adoption of "some new interpretations of the rule of eligibility for the Olympic Games."[65] Şiperco outlined his commission's proposed reform of Rule 26 during an October 1969 meeting in Dubrovnik, championing the replacement of the concept of "amateur" with that of "Olympic athlete," as well as the introduction of an insurance scheme for injured athletes. He also called for the IOC to draw a distinction between social assistance (i.e., living, training, and travel support) and deliberate exploitation (i.e., profiteering) when shaping amateur regulations.[66] Composed of IOC members from Lebanon, Nigeria, Peru, Romania, and Yugoslavia, as well as representatives of the national Olympic committees of Belgium, Canada, Greece, Ireland, Luxembourg, and Norway, the Joint Commission on Eligibility's proposed reforms captured the shifting ideological tenor of the Olympic Movement.

Brundage greeted Şiperco's proposal with characteristic disdain. He used all his administrative acumen to ensure that such liberal initiatives never reached the ballot box. Brundage adopted stall-and-delay tactics, sending Şiperco's report first to the national Olympic committees and then to the international sports federations for review.[67] He sought to broaden the democratic process further, calling upon fellow amateur ideologue Hugh Weir and the Standing Eligibility Commission (formerly amateur committee) to interrogate and critique Şiperco's report. The report "is loaded with dynamite and I hope our colleagues recognize this fact," Brundage charged.[68] Even during the final stages of his presidency, Brundage refused to countenance the idea of reform. He worked secretively behind the scenes, reconfiguring the composition of the Standing Eligibility Commission to ensure a more conservative reviewing authority. Brundage appointed New Zealander Cecil "Lance" Cross and West German Georg von Opel to join the fight against Şiperco's "radical changes."[69]

After being filtered through a number of levels of bureaucratic review, Şiperco's proposed reforms had eventually become stripped of their substance.[70] The new amateur text, which came into force on 5 April 1971, after an IOC postal vote, appeared in the revised *Olympic Charter* that same year.[71] None of Şiperco's reforms was included. In fact, the IOC produced a strict eligibility code that enumerated a number of key problems, notably advertising, training camps, broken-time payments, monetary prizes, scholastic aid, professional instruction, and state amateurism, that had long plagued the Olympic Movement.[72] Rather than dissolving the Olympic Movement's highly profitable relationship with television, commerce, and the state—the very axis that heightened professionalism within the Olympic arena—Brundage and his colleagues pursued stricter regulation and enforcement of the amateur code. For an organization shedding all appearances of organizational amateur purity, the IOC's actions smacked of hypocrisy and temerity. Brundage reveled in delight. He confided to Hugh Weir that the eligibility code "turned out better than I expected."[73] His amateur crusade would wage on.

In the next few months, the IOC president worked to establish a permanent Eligibility Committee to police the new rule changes. For the first time in modern Olympic history, Brundage empowered (at least in theory) the IOC to protect the Olympics against amateur infractions. The fox was no longer left alone to guard the hen house. "We have left it entirely to the National Federations and NOCs . . . and the results are what could be expected with such an agreement," he exclaimed.[74] Who better to lead this new committee than Brundage's own trusted lieutenant, Hugh Weir, a self-professed "tough

old realist with perhaps old fashioned ideas."[75] In truth, voluntary membership on the Eligibility Committee curtailed its effectiveness. Weir was quick
to recognize this inherent limitation. He lobbied Brundage to subsidize travel
costs so that committee members could "meet conveniently as and when
required to discuss and examine questions of eligibility should they arise."[76]
In keeping with his amateur convictions, Brundage refused the request. It
took him nearly two decades to create an "investigatory and enforcement"
committee, only then to deprive it of the necessary funding and flexibility to
ensure its effectiveness. His parsimony helped fuel the decline of the amateur
ideal. Once again, Brundage demonstrated that his version of amateurism
was both paradoxical and self-defeating.

When the Eligibility Committee met in Luxembourg for the first time in
September 1971, Weir articulated president Brundage's first order of business:
to establish "one or two cases of infringement of rules to be severely punished
as an example to others."[77] With his retirement fast approaching, Brundage
decided to make a philosophical last stand. He vowed to defend a vision of
amateurism that seemed increasingly incompatible with prevailing social,
economic, and competitive realities. Alpine skiing and, more specifically,
one of its most famous stars, Austrian Karl Schranz, appeared at the top of
Brundage's wish list.[78]

ENTER KARL SCHRANZ

Sapporo, the capital city of the Japanese island of Hokkaido, played host to
the 1972 Winter Olympics. The Sapporo Olympics etched their way into the
annuls of Olympic history thanks in large part to the disqualification of Karl
Schranz.[79] The Austrian, a veteran of the Grenoble Olympics and winner
of three of the first four World Cup downhill races during the 1972 season,
emerged as a favorite to clinch Olympic gold in Sapporo. Despite his run
of success, Schranz was hardly the most talented in Alpine skiing. Yet his
celebrity through his string of endorsements had outpaced his celebrity on
the slopes. His commercial appeal drew the attention of Brundage. In his
speech at the 1970 IOC session in Amsterdam, he identified Schranz as being
a leading violator of Olympic eligibility rules. He scolded the Austrian for
"conspicuously wearing the uniform and using the marked skis of the firm in
whose employment he has been for many years." He estimated that Schranz
derived an annual income of $50,000–60,000 per year from his shamateur
exploits.[80] Brundage had found his mark.

The Schranz affair marked the apotheosis of Brundage's career-long administrative battle against shamateurism. The Austrian's disqualification

Karl Schranz, seen here playing a relaxing game of soccer in the snow at the 1972 Sapporo Olympic Village, was always a larger-than-life figure. Shortly after this photograph, the IOC took the unprecedented step of removing Schranz from the Olympic Games for violating the amateur eligibility code. Schranz returned to a hero's welcome in his native Austria while the hypocritical move generated negative press for Brundage and the IOC. (Courtesy of the International Olympic Committee)

represented a deliberate gambit on behalf of Brundage to publicly condemn Alpine skiing and the commercialized, professional culture that the sport had long fostered. The seeds of his discontent were sown in Grenoble. During an IOC Executive Board meeting after the 1968 Olympics, he lectured FIS for "permitting contestants to advertise ski resorts, skis and ski equipment and to be paid directly instead of under the table." Brundage threatened that unless serious reforms were forthcoming, Alpine skiing would be stripped of its place on the Olympic program.[81]

In the years leading up to the Sapporo Olympics, FIS did reform its eligibility rules but not in the direction that Brundage had demanded. Under its revised amateur code, FIS permitted sponsors seeking to use an athlete's image and endorsement to negotiate contracts directly with national ski federations. By funneling the money through the federations, rather than directly into the pockets of the athletes, FIS contended—rather sanctimoniously—that it could best protect an athlete's Olympic eligibility and tamp down the commercial forces that had overrun winter sport. The revisions specified that all monies received would be used to support an athlete's training and travel costs.[82] FIS president Marc Holder proffered the defense that "such a use is compatible with Olympic eligibility rules, as long as the athlete is not acquiring personal gain."[83] Brundage disagreed. He branded FIS revisions as "commercial exploitation," an ostensible move on behalf of the federation to harness their athletes' entrepreneurial spirit for their own gain. "Instead of trying to stop the scandalous abuses which have been apparent in Alpine skiing for the last twenty years," he wrote to the IOC Executive Board, "the FIS has opened the gates and all participants in the 'circus' are more-or-less openly being paid."[84] Brundage continued along his warpath. He challenged his colleagues on the IOC to decide whether we are "going to permit Olympic competitors to be exploited in such a cheap, crass and undignified manner?"[85]

Reports of widespread amateur rule violations only heightened Brundage's anxiety. The IOC Eligibility Committee investigated German alpine skiers Rosi Mittermaier, Max Rieger, and Hansjörg Schlager for using their names for advertising purposes.[86] L'Équipe cast an accusatory barb at French slalom racer Françoise Macchi for advertising the energy drink Banania.[87] French skier Annie Famose faced suspension for signing a commercial arrangement to provide paid correspondence during the Olympics.[88] The Austrian newspaper the Kurier revealed that Swiss downhill star and reigning world champion Bernhard Russi violated Olympic eligibility standards by appearing in advertisements for the Swiss insurance company Zurich Financial Services.[89] These accusations frequently followed the same narrative: the press made accusations of payments, the Eligibility Committee deferred the matter to the relevant national Olympic committee, an investigation ensued, the athlete in question asserted that his or her image had been used without their permission, a lack of evidence materialized (in part because of off-the-book payments), and then the charges were dropped.[90] The clear hypocrisy led Jean de Beaumont to resign in protest as president of the French Olympic Committee after its executive board voted to classify all French skiers as amateur despite the admitted violations of the IOC's eligibility rule.[91]

By the eve of the 1972 Sapporo Olympics, it remained unclear whether Alpine skiing would even be included in the Olympic program. Brundage wrote to the national Olympic committees, admonishing them not to certify any skiers who would be declared ineligible under IOC eligibility rules.[92] Privately, he calculated that if this warning were heeded, "few if any of the prominent skiers [would be] eligible."[93] The potential loss of Alpine skiing, the most popular spectacle in the Winter Olympics, alarmed the Sapporo Organizing Committee, who dispatched Royal Prince Takeda to Sydney to speak directly with Hugh Weir. After securing a record $6.4 million television contract with NBC for exclusive broadcasting rights to the Olympics, the Sapporo organizers were rightfully worried about looming financial losses should the IOC decide to exclude Alpine skiing from the program.[94] After his meeting with the Japanese delegation, Weir wrote to Brundage warning that the Sapporo organizers were adamant that any drastic actions would be unacceptable.[95] In order to preserve the credibility of Olympic amateurism, Brundage recognized that he needed to take harsh measures. Yet he also acknowledged that strict application of the rule jeopardized the future of the Olympics, since future hosts would look warily on Sapporo's plight, and also compromised the multimillion dollar television contracts that financed Olympic operations, as sponsors would be hesitant to invest in an event that could not provide marquee-worthy athletes.[96] He was forced to tread carefully. Since his grander desire to jettison Alpine skiing from the Olympics proved financially intolerable, Brundage pursued an alternative course of action. He selected one ski racer, Karl Schranz, as a *cause célèbre*.[97]

When *Le Tribune de Lausanne* published a photograph of Schranz and his Austrian compatriot Henri Messner holding skis emblazoned with a manufacturing logo in large lettering, Brundage leaped to attention.[98] In accordance with IOC protocol, the Eligibility Committee requested that the Austrian Olympic Committee investigate.[99] In an official deposition, Schranz claimed that the picture in question was taken by an unknown photographer after the Val d'Isère men's downhill event and that he never intended to advertise his skis. Messner maintained a similar defense.[100] The ski manufacturer, Kneissel, who had employed Schranz in their factory since 1956, lent its voice to the investigation, insisting that the writing on the skis conformed to FIS's thirty-millimeter height limit.[101] Apparently satisfied, the Austrian national Olympic committee found no evidence of wrongdoing and promptly named Schranz to its Olympic team.[102] Brundage was unfazed. Even though Schranz had not done anything particularly egregious, the Eligibility Commission recommended that he be declared ineligible for the 1972 Sapporo Olympics for "the manner in which he has permitted the use of his name and picture in commercial advertising in recent years."[103] Schranz's teammate, Messner, avoided any charges.

When Weir presented his committee's recommendation to the IOC Executive Board, confusion reigned. Some officials were still unclear about what Schranz had even done wrong. When the Dutch IOC member Herman van Karnebeek pushed for "air-tight proof for Schranz's disqualification," Brundage retorted that "they had plenty but even if they had not, he could be disqualified under paragraph 1 of rule 26, 'A competitor must observe the traditional Olympic spirit and ethic.'" Brundage's equivocating response revealed his true motive. He had decided to make an example out of the Austrian even before he had found a smoking gun. Perhaps somewhat bewildered, the executive board agreed to have the IOC vote on the recommendation during its Seventy-Second Session in Sapporo.[104] By going after

Schranz, Brundage again chased the low-hanging fruit: not the Communist bloc and their systematic, increasingly scientized state-run sport programs, but an individual skier who allegedly committed a minor infraction or violated some nebulous, unwritten Olympic "spirit" and "ethic." He sought an easy win that reasserted his seriousness about amateurism and fortified his legacy as a champion of the amateur ideal, while potentially scaring a few financially motivated athletes into compliance.

Brundage brought the question of Schranz's eligibility to the floor on the opening day of the 1972 Sapporo Annual Session. A considerable faction of IOC members, however, appeared reluctant to take such severe action. Jan Staubo of Norway, Maurice Herzog of France, Marc Hodler of Switzerland, and Gabriel Gemayel of Lebanon thought it wrong to vilify one individual. Ireland's Michael Morris, Lord Killanin, and Mohamed Mzali of Tunisia both feared that action directly against Schranz would turn him into a martyr and a hero.[105] In the interests of transparency and due process, Sven Thofelt of Sweden and Rudolf Nemetschke of Austria demanded that Schranz be given a trial. Brundage flatly refused, arguing that it was the IOC's decision alone to accept or reject the Eligibility Commission's recommendation.[106] In truth, a trial would have eroded Brundage's power by granting the skier a stage to publicly defend himself while potentially revealing the sheer extent of shamateurism within winter sport.[107] Brundage pushed for a definitive vote. When the secret ballots were tallied, members voted twenty-eight to fourteen in favor of the Eligibility Commission's recommendation to declare Schranz ineligible to take part in the Sapporo Olympics.[108]

News of Schranz's disqualification reverberated across the globe. He returned home a martyr. The *Oberösterreichische Nachrichten* reported that 100,000 Austrians greeted Schranz upon his return, proudly proclaiming him a national hero.[109] His fame increased dramatically. The Austrian Council of Ministers even awarded him the Order of Merit for Sports.[110] Since Schranz no longer had to worry about preserving his amateur status, he freely capitalized on his newfound notoriety. He left amateur ski racing and joined Jean-Claude Killy in the fledgling professional ski circuit.[111]

In contrast, Brundage faced a public backlash. He was portrayed as a "senile old fool," stubbornly defending an unrealistic, moribund ideal.[112] In an interview with the Japanese newspaper *Mainichi Shimbun*, he exposed himself further to public reviling when he expressed the opinion that no skiers at the 1972 Olympics qualified as amateurs. "We could not disqualify all of them and ruin the Games over which our Japanese friends had spent so much time and money," he reasoned.[113] His critics in the press latched onto this tin-eared gaff; equivocating on his hard-lined stand on amateurism and permitting scores of athletes who had violated the IOC's eligibility code made him appear enormously hypocritical.[114] His flagging credibility suffered a significant blow.

A NEW HORIZON

The 1972 Olympic Games in Munich represented Brundage's final act as IOC president. His legacy is both rich and complex. Under his stewardship, the Olympics took on greater levels of visibility and importance. He helped fulfill the universal mission of the Olympic Movement, transforming the Olympics into the largest multisporting phenomenon of the modern era. At the time of his departure, the IOC boasted a vast organizational network of 130 national Olympic committees (the majority of which were recognized under his presidency), as well as twenty periodical international or regional Olympics.[115] He was devoted to Olympism, an exceptional organizer who possessed an abundance of energy. The vast archival holdings at the University of Illinois that bear his name are a testament to these qualities.

Among his many attributes, both good and bad, Brundage is perhaps best remembered as an unwavering apostle of amateurism who singlehandedly defended his beloved ideal against the rapacious currents of nationalism, commercialism, and professionalism. This convenient image of Brundage as the "irascible high priest of amateurism," as he was dubbed in 1948 by *Life* magazine, obscures his true legacy.[116] Upon reflection, a new picture of an ideologically flexible Brundage emerges. He freely compromised his principles for the perceived universal, organizational, and financial growth and benefit of the Olympic Movement. His tolerance of Communist state-sponsored sport, alongside his willingness to bow to the emerging power of television, illustrates that he was not a romantic idealist tilting at windmills but rather an astute pragmatist. He was inconsistent, selective, naïve, and occasionally cowardly. Brundage's antidemocratic administrative style, fiscal conservatism, reliance on unpaid voluntarism, and inability (or, perhaps, refusal) to accept shifting social, economic, and sporting conditions ironically served to *hasten* the disintegration of Olympic amateurism.

In many ways, the 1972 Munich Olympics marked the culmination of Brundage's failure to stem the flow of professionalism, commercialism, and politics into the Olympic arena. He watched on as athletes walked freely around the Munich Olympic Village in Adidas paraphernalia bearing a special logo for the Olympics, the trefoil that featured three leaves with three lines running through the bottom. The U.S. swimmer Mark Spitz, a record-setting seven-time gold medalist, brazenly carried a pair of Adidas Gazelles during his last trip to the podium (Adidas finally discovered an inroad into swimming), and happily waved the shoes toward the German crowd as well as the millions of global viewers and consumers.[117] The Munich Olympics, and perhaps Brundage's entire presidency, is best remembered for the tragic events of 5 September 1972, when armed Palestinian terrorists assassinated nine members of the Israeli Olympic delegation. The horrifying scenes, transmitted across the globe, cast a sullen pall over the Olympic arena and rightfully relegated amateurism to a footnote.[118] While Brundage rushed to ensure the public that the games would go on, his presidency would not.

The Olympic Movement entered a new phase. Long-serving Irish IOC member Michael Morris, Lord Killanin, assumed the IOC presidency, only the sixth chief executive in the organization's history. Killanin, a liberal by reputation, brought a far gentler, more diplomatic approach to governance than his predecessor. The former World War II correspondent, respected journalist, and sports administrator was not a great reformer or passionate ideologue, but rather a calming influence that helped to guide the Olympic Movement through the turbulent waters of the 1970s. He had no time for ideological concerns. Killanin sought collaboration and consensus, demonstrated intellectual flexibility, and embraced the commercial realities of modern sport with optimism rather than fear. Unlike Brundage, he acknowledged the modern social and economic conditions of amateur sport. He accepted the broad metaphysical dimension of amateurism, recognizing that it was a malleable concept that varied relative to each sport, locality, and social class.

Under Killanin's leadership, the IOC worked to address the troubled issue of amateur eligibility. The 1973 Olympic Congress, in Varna, Bulgaria, set the stage for a debate on its future direction. The Varna Congress, a mass gathering of the Olympic tripartite powers, was the first of its kind since 1930, when officials met in Berlin to debate the issue of FIFA and broken-time payments.[119] Killanin and his colleagues faced a sizable task. Many felt Olympic amateurism needed to be reformed. Yet, like Swiss IOC member Albert Mayer before them, they simply sought practical reforms that would update eligibility Rule 26 to reflect the contemporary realities of elite sport and avoid much of the hypocrisy. Even the most ardent of amateur supporters resigned themselves to change. The U.S. AAU, long a bastion of Brundagian amateurism, passed a resolution in December 1972 to ask the USOC to liberalize its definition of an amateur so that "amateur athletes would be permitted to endorse products, author books and be employed as coaches," as well as permitting "a professional athlete in one sport to compete as an amateur in another."[120] After a lengthy debate, the USOC adopted these recommendations in order to, as its president Philip Krumm stated, "reflect changes in amateur sports competition."[121]

In his opening address at the Olympic Congress in Varna, Lord Killanin signaled his openness to reforming Rule 26 along moderate and controlled lines: "We do not want paid performers but also we wish to have equal opportunity as far as it is possible, throughout the world, for the training of competitors."[122] Killanin's remarks were not, at least in his mind, the opening wedge of professionalism. Rather, he favored inclusive, practical reforms to combat widespread eligibility violations and to restore the Olympic Movement to a position of legitimacy. Thomas Keller, president of the Fédération Internationale des Sociétés d'Aviron (rowing) agreed. Speaking on behalf of the international sports federations, Keller laid bare the real issue facing Eligibility Rules: "Everyone interested in sports knows that entries for the Olympic Games have largely become an open exhibition of lying," he admitted. "The International Olympic Committee attempts to support the fiction of amateur games with the help of 'Rule 26,' although it is fully aware that most National Olympic Committees and Sports Federations are primarily concerned to ensure that these conditions are circumvented as discreetly as possible, in order to be able to nominate their best athletes for the Games."[123] Keller called for new "rules governing amateur status which take reasonable account of the situation in their respective sports and to see that they are adapted to changing conditions with the passing of time."[124] How best to do that would dominate the conversation for the rest of the congress.

The Varna Congress failed to produce much consensus. At the very least, the congress attendees did agree upon a common goal: the retention of some spectrum of amateurism while pursuing reforms to modernize the IOC's eligibility rules in a way that did not appear to sell out the Olympic Movement or compromise its core values.[125] Over the coming months, Killanin pursued the subject of amateur reform. He sent a circular letter presenting his colleagues with two different positions that the IOC could take. The first presented a revised draft of Rule 26 prepared by Hugh Weir and the Eligibility Committee, the most ardent stalwarts in the defense of amateurism. Their proposal redoubled the IOC's dedication to amateurism, stripped the international federations of most of their autonomy over eligibility, and sought to stem the flow of money and endorsements that increasingly washed over Olympic athletes.[126] Killanin presented a second position: a new eligibility code crafted by the majority of international federations that read, "A competitor to take part in the Olympic Games must be eligible in accordance with the rules and regulations of his International Federation, as approved by the I.O.C. He shall be eligible provided he has not derived any personal profit from competing in his sport."[127] Killanin implored his fellow IOC members in the letter to "treat this as urgent" and send their comments on which option the Olympic Movement should pursue.[128]

After months of heated discussion, the IOC made what it thought to be a series of small revisions to Rule 26 at its 1974 Annual Session in Vienna. They dropped the language requiring that athletes "be engaged in a basic occupation to provide for his present and future" and also lifted the limits on days that an athlete could devote to training. These revisions marked a significant ideological evolution. Until then, the IOC maintained what had long become pretense: Olympic athletes should pursue sport only as an after-hours avocation. Now they were free to pursue *Citius, Altius, Fortius* with single-minded devotion. At the same time, the IOC also expanded broken-time payments. No longer were the indemnities restricted to "deserving cases" or limited to participation in the Olympic Games. All athletes became eligible for broken-time compensation and it could cover the time "in preparation for" as well for participation in the Olympics or other international competitions. These changes essentially meant that all athletes could train and compete as much as they wanted and receive compensation for that training and competition.[129] Finally, and in what might even appear to be a symbolic token, the IOC permitted the international sports federations to draft their own amateur eligibility bylaws, on condition that they receive approval from Lausanne.[130]

These decisions seemed mostly innocuous to those in the room, though they would ultimately lead to the IOC removing amateurism entirely from its eligibility rules. The IOC simply brought above board the practices that had already become commonplace. They wanted to stem the ridicule, condemnation, and charges of hypocrisy. Liberal reforms, no matter how democratic and well intentioned, would not represent a magical elixir. The nationalistic, political, and competitive desire for Olympic gold knew no boundaries; the commercialization of the Olympic spectacle would not be satiated.

8 THE ULTIMATE MOVE

The progressive reforms passed at the 1974 International Olympic Committee (IOC) session in Vienna temporarily calmed the tempest around amateurism. In this environment, the IOC's Eligibility Commission languished. The removal of Alpine skier Karl Schranz from the 1972 Sapporo Olympics had backfired on the newly formed committee as the press continued to hold up the Austrian's removal as evidence of the IOC's unrelenting hypocrisy on amateurism.[1] The Eligibility Commission suffered a serious setback after the death of its inaugural chairman, Hugh Weir, in 1975. The IOC Executive Board appointed Ivar Vind as a replacement[2] and assigned the fifty-five-year-old Dane the task of ensuring that the eligibility bylaws of all international federations' conformed with the IOC's own rules.[3] Again, circumstance plunged the commission into disarray. Vind's untimely death on 11 February 1977, prompted the executive board to suspend the commission's operations and ensure that no changes were made to Rule 26 until after the 1980 Moscow Olympics.[4] The Eligibility Commission would remain dormant until 1978, when Willi Daume was appointed as its new chairman.[5] During his tenure, the prominent West German Olympic official and chief architect of the 1972 Munich Olympics oversaw the final major unraveling of the IOC's eligibility code.[6]

Daume quickly left his mark on his new position. In his first report as chair of the Eligibility Commission in 1980, he spelled out to his colleagues some inconvenient truths: that neither the ancient Greeks nor Baron Pierre de Coubertin were the purported champions of amateurism, and that the financially orientated IOC can no longer invoke amateurism without appearing grossly hypocritical. With a customary grain of candor, Daume lectured his fellow IOC members:

Thanks to sport, manufacturers of sport clothing, sport shoes, skis and other sports articles, builders, the tourist industry and mass media, all make turnovers totaling several billion dollars and profits that can also be counted in the billions. Even the guardians of the Olympic idea—that is to say the IOC—are no exception. We are all mixed up with big business. We bargain with the world's television companies for licenses of fees worth several million dollars for the right to televise the Games. . . . It is only the athletes that have to make sacrifices and show proof of asceticism, put up with so much and place their personal interests, their studies or their professional training in the background, for they must be at the top of their form when the Olympic Games or other international competitions take place, and officials, coaches, governments, the press and TV viewers all expect it of them, while the idea we have had of them up till now required that they should derive no material profit from sport.[7]

Calling this situation an "exploitation of top human performances," Daume demanded that the question of whether amateur status constitutes a criterion for Olympic recognition should be examined as a matter of urgency.[8]

Daume's concern came from the rapidly changing state of amateur sport. Though not completely foreign to their predecessors, the seriousness with which elite athletes in the 1970s and 1980s approached their craft increased at an exponential clip. Athletes, coaches, and governmental officials flocked to sport science as a tool for improving performances and boosting national and ideological prestige. The latest in technological, physiological, and pharmacological innovations found their way—often through state funding—onto the training grounds and into the locker rooms. These applications of science to amateur sport ranged from minor violations of the traditional but unwritten amateur ethos to clear violations of the antidoping rule enshrined in the IOC's eligibility code. In this highly scientized, openly politicized climate, few amateurs remained.

The lines between amateurism and professionalism blurred further as professional sport grew in popularity during the late twentieth century. An expanding global media apparatus, in concert with avaricious corporations and shrewd marketing agencies, transformed professional athletes into global sporting icons. The Olympic Movement faced higher competition. Although the fusion of nationalism and *Citius, Altius, Fortius* made the Olympic Games an attractive commodity, the IOC's eligibility code—and the forced prohibition of some of the world's leading athletes—dampened the spectacle. Public condemnations and accusations of hypocrisy damaged the Olympic brand. With multimillion dollar television broadcasting deals at stake, Olympic officials displayed an unwillingness to make the necessary sacrifices to preserve amateurism. Financial and commercial considerations were paramount.

Amateurism subsided. Professional sport slowly entered the Olympic Movement at the precise moment that it best served the commercial and financial interests of the powerbrokers of elite, international sport.

THE SCIENCE OF AMATEUR SPORT

From its institutional seedbed in Victorian Britain, amateurism long dictated *who* could play and also *how* they played. This class-bound, overly romantic expression of moral and aesthetic refinement prohibited athletes from applying their scientific acumen toward achieving athletic success.[9] However, modern sport, of which the Olympic Games were clearly a product, had embraced post-enlightenment rationalization and quantification.[10] The Olympic Movement, which its ideological blend of amateur restraint and *Citius, Altius, Fortius*, set these irreconcilable ideals on a collision course as "Higher, Faster, Stronger" implied sporting specialization and scientific application.

Fin-de-siècle scientists first turned to modern sports such as cycling and track and field as a laboratory for understanding human performance and exploring human endurance capabilities.[11] By the 1920s, sport science and sport medicine had established themselves as viable fields deriving from their military application during World War I.[12] The human physiology laboratories of U.S. universities such as Harvard, Yale, and the University of Chicago helped to further legitimize scientific investigations into sport and human performance.[13] After World War II, sport science witnessed an explosion of research on endurance capacity, training adaption, VO2 max testing, work economy, and muscle velocity that had begun in the military research.[14] The altitude concerns presented by the 1968 Mexico City Olympics marked the further application of World War II science to sporting questions.[15] Scientists in this era also explored whether pharmacological substances such as anabolic steroids, blood transfusions, and amphetamines could boost sporting performances.[16] By the mid-1970s, the field of sport science, including exercise physiology, biomechanics, pharmacology, and even psychology, became essential for elite athletes seeking Olympic-level standards of performance.[17]

This application of science to sport occurred amid the growing political importance of sport in Cold War cultural diplomacy. The rise in the commercial value of sports, as well as their perceived social and political importance, amplified the resources provided to elite amateur athletes.[18] The capitalist and Communist worlds continued to fight with savage intensity for sporting and Olympic dominance during the 1970s and 1980s. Athletes on both sides of the East–West divide enjoyed the benefits of specialized sport scientists, high-quality training facilities, and better coaching.[19] Political leaders increased the state allocation of resources to the science of high performance sport with the hope that their nation's Olympic success would play well to audiences both at home and abroad.[20]

The intimate connection between sport and state—a relationship stringently proscribed within Rule 25 of the *Olympic Charter*—translated into a new era for boosting human performance. In this regard, the Soviet Union and its Communist satellites pioneered the way. Lavish state support extended beyond specialized coaching and training facilities to state-funded research on oral creatine to enhance muscle function and blood transfusions to boost aerobic endurance for its athletes.[21] In the Communist German Democratic Republic (GDR) of East Germany, politicians diverted enormous amounts of state money and infrastructure toward the scientific identification of talent, development of youth into elite athletes, training of coaches, and optimized training routines for athletes.[22] From 1970 to 1980, the government expenditure for the German Gymnastics and Sports Foundation (DTSB), the GDR's state-organized sport governing body, ballooned from 40 million GDR marks to more than 700 million GDR marks.[23] This provided funding for the German University for Physical Education and the Research Institute for Physical Culture and Sport, both of which made vital scientific contributions to the success of GDR athletes.[24] It also provided for State Plan 14.25, the GDR's state-sponsored doping program initiated by Manfred Ewald, the minister of sport from 1961 to 1988, and physician Manfred Höppner.[25]

The United States, which boasted a long tradition of mixing science and sport through its colleges and universities, parlayed Cold War sports nationalism into increases in investment in sport science.[26] The 1976 Montreal Olympics proved a low point for U.S. sporting success, and many in the West traced the nadir's cause to a growing failure to keep pace with Soviet-bloc sport science.[27] Citing concerns that "Eastern European countries had developed sophisticated sports medicine programs," the United States Olympic Committee (USOC) created a panel of experts to explore "nutritional, pharmacological and advanced medical approaches to training."[28] U.S. vice president Gerald Ford acknowledged the growing political currency of Olympic victories in a 1974 interview with *Sports Illustrated*. "It is not enough to just compete," Ford opined. "Winning is very important. Maybe more important than ever."[29] In the throes of the Cold War, the success of the Communist sports system captured the attention of U.S. policymakers. After decades of nonintervention, the U.S. government directly breached the apolitical arena of amateur sport. The 1978 passage of the Amateur Sports Act, which made the U.S. federal government a partner in an Olympic sport system, illustrated the prioritization of elite performance for the purposes of international prestige.[30]

The United States also pursued private ventures outside the orbit of governmental influence. Nike's "Athletics West," whose name was both a geographic (located in Oregon) and political (as opposed to Eastern bloc athletes) statement, provided resources for postcollegiate U.S. athletes.[31] In an arrangement that in their own words "undoubtedly broke amateur rules," Athletics West provided athletes with training facilities, living quarters, and monthly stipends, as well as access to coaches, massage therapists, exercise physiologists, sport psychologists, and even illicit anabolic steroids, corticosteroids, and blood transfusions.[32]

Athletics West was hardly alone in employing pharmacological substances to boost performances. Around the world, increasing financial resources and access to scientific knowledge created microclimates where doping, including anabolic steroids, amphetamines, and blood transfusions unsurprisingly flourished. Athletes of all Cold War political persuasions enjoyed various degrees of systematic, state-supported doping.[33] The GDR used its state-controlled laboratories to develop "sustaining means"—an official euphemism for doping substances—which transformed the small Communist nation into a sporting powerhouse.[34] From 1974 to 1988 the clandestine East German doping program, which was organized by the GDR's Ministry of State Security, provided oral Turinabol to an estimated 10,000 athletes.[35] Its ideological and geographical rival, West Germany, also employed a state-sponsored doping program—with the help of the United States—for its research into anabolic steroids for weightlifting athletes.[36]

The United States supported doping in both official and unofficial capacities. Some U.S. athletes privately secured anabolic steroids in sports such as weightlifting, swimming, and track and field. At other points, doping originated from more official sources. After the 1976 Montreal Olympics, the USOC's panel on the scientific and medical aspects of sport explored "areas considered taboo," which included "extensive research into the effects of anabolic steroids and blood-doping on performance."[37] Coaching staff also played a significant role in enhancing U.S. chances of success: Such was the case with the U.S. cycling team. At the 1984 Los Angeles Olympics, USOC staff member Ed Burke provided blood transfusions to his cyclists in the hopes of securing victories on home soil.[38] Cold War–era science pushed amateur sport to dangerous, dehumanizing levels, fueling cries for athletes' health and well-being.

In the midst of widespread abuses, the IOC separated its antidoping language from the eligibility code (Rule 26), where it had resided as a bylaw since its creation in 1938. The IOC created an Anti-Doping Commission in 1961 (which became the Medical Commission in 1968), and Olympic officials discovered that the lengthy list of prohibited substances, testing, and bans for violating antidoping rules should be an independent rule in the *Olympic Charter*.[39] In 1975, the first edition of the *Olympic Charter* after the Varna congress, the IOC introduced Rule 27 as its new antidoping rule and vested its Medical Commission rather than its Eligibility Commission with its enforcement.[40] By 1988, the IOC's Medical Commission had established itself as a leading authority in antidoping with a growing budget and increasingly sophisticated laboratory techniques to detect prohibited substances.[41] Canadian sprinter Ben Johnson would make international headlines when he tested positive for anabolic steroids after winning the 100 meters at the 1988 Seoul Olympic Games. By this time, however, few within the IOC or the general public likely recalled the lineage between the IOC's growing antidoping program and its waning amateur code.

THE SHIFTING POLITICS OF OLYMPIC ELIGIBILITY

The sophisticated doping infrastructures of both the athletes and the antidoping authorities attested to what many in this era had already accepted: Olympic sport had taken a decidedly unamateur approach to performance. Olympic sport was *high performance* sport; its athletes, coaches, and national Olympic committees became results-oriented, technologically innovative, and obsessive about winning.[42] The IOC's revised eligibility code struggled with this modern reality. Evidently, the culture of high performance sport had shifted its expectations for the amateur athlete. The public and the IOC had welcomed an era of excellence made possible through sport science. Though there was no longer any pretense about needing a vocation, athletes sought technical support from nutritionists, exercise physiologists, and professional coaches, as well as technical innovations in clothing and equipment. This required the cooperation—and at times collusion—of national Olympic committees and national and international federations. At the 1981 Olympic Congress in Baden-Baden, John Holt, the secretary general for the International Amateur Athletic Federation (IAAF), calculated that "providing the top athlete of today with the assistance he or she needs in order to attain and maintain the high standards we call for" meant not only thirty hours of training a week but also "compensation for the fact that their vocation or their studies are being interrupted."[43] The call for more comprehensive eligibility reforms had been sounded. Willi Daume, speaking as chair of the IOC Eligibility Commission, also championed the creation of a more liberal eligibility code. "If the contemporary athlete necessarily needs 1,600 hours a year training," Daume argued, "then the Olympic Movement, which expects athletes to pursue excellence, should not discriminate against or exploit the full-time athlete because of that excellence."[44] Reform loomed on the horizon.

For the Soviet Union, long a vocal proponent of democratizing IOC administrative practices and bringing Olympic sport to the underrepresented Third World, the prospect of liberalizing the eligibility code posed a serious threat to Communist state interests. In a departure from its previous ideological position, the Soviet Union and its satellites began advocating for stricter and more conservative eligibility rules that aligned with traditional amateur policies. For a nation devoted to ending the bourgeoisie's oppression of the worker, their sudden defense of an elitist amateur ideology appears counterintuitive. In truth, the Soviet's reversal stemmed from the success of their state-sponsored sporting infrastructure. Under the leadership of General Secretary Leonid Brezhnev, the Soviet Union had entered the "golden age of the Soviet system."[45] This was certainly true in Olympic sport, in which the Soviet Union had grown into a formidable athletic powerhouse. With the Kremlin employing amateur athletes as de facto professionals via its educational institutions and military service networks, Soviet athletes dominated the 1972, 1976, and 1980 Olympiads—the nation topped every Olympic medal count for both the summer and winter games in that period. Although the exorbitant degree of state support for Soviet athletes continued to draw concerns from within international sporting circles, the IOC launched no formal investigation and dispensed no requisite punishment.

Having found a system that worked to its advantage, the Soviet Union naturally feared changes to the status quo. Daume's public utterances on the subject of liberalizing the IOC's eligibility code threatened to diminish the Soviet Union's advantage over its capitalist rivals. Suddenly, Western nations could legitimately subsidize their athletes in a manner similar to the Communist system. To maintain their advantage, the Communist bloc in the IOC began to stymie any proposed reforms to Rule 26 on amateurism. IOC member Konstantin Andrianov strongly rejected the prospect of an "open" Olympics, branding the idea as "totally unacceptable."[46] In a stark ironic twist, the Communists joined a dwindling troupe of IOC members in attempting to uphold the traditional precepts of amateurism. No professionals, "whether open or hidden, should be allowed in the Olympic Games," Andrianov insisted.[47] The irony of the Communist reversal was not lost on IOC president Michael Morris, Lord Killanin, who noted wryly that existing eligibility arrangements benefited Eastern European countries where "there were no professional athletes but state athletes."[48] In an apt analogy, the U.S. AAU president Jack Kelly Jr. compared this marriage of convenience between Communists and Brundagian amateur ideologues to "the same unholy alliance you find when the bootleggers and the clergy combine their votes to maintain prohibition."[49] To the detriment of his homeland, Kelly explained, "The Russians who want to maintain their own form of amateurism . . . [are] aligning themselves with the old-line members of the U.S. and the International Olympic Committee."[50]

While the Soviets retreated to a position of conservatism, its ideological foes to the West began stimulating calls for amateur reform. Reflecting the shifting politics of Olympic amateurism, the United States sought to erode the advantages long enjoyed by the Communists by loosening the IOC's eligibility requirements, and, more ironically, by cultivating a state–sport relationship long perfected behind the Iron Curtain. U.S. officials came to the realization that its reliance on collegiate amateur athletes supported through scholarships—a frequent controversy for many at the IOC—no longer kept U.S. athletes out in front. Olympic medal tables made uncomfortable reading: At the 1976 Montreal Olympics the U.S. finished behind its Communist rivals, the Soviet Union, and the GDR. Alarmed by the nation's waning sporting prowess, the U.S. government stepped into the fray. In 1975, Gerald Ford established the President's Commission on Olympic Sport to "determine what factors impede or tend to impede or prevent the United States from fielding its best amateur athletes for participation in Olympic Games."[51] Testimony to the commission revealed that amateurism retained little popularity. "The ideal of amateurism . . . (is) an anachronism borne [sic] of a day when international competition on any advanced level was a luxury of a limited, aristocratic class of independent economic means," Ellie Daniel, a two-time Olympic swimmer, testified.[52] *The Presidential Report* concluded that the U.S. adherence to stricter amateur rules diminished the nation's chances of Olympic victory. Consequently, the report urged the United States to not only adopt "the most liberal permitted interpretations" of Olympic eligibility but also "work toward further liberalization of international codes as appropriate."[53] The public's growing disenchantment with amateurism aligned with a comparable lack of state support prompted the 1978 passage of the Amateur Sports Act.[54]

Other Western nations followed the growing U.S. tilt toward state intervention. A string of underwhelming performances in international and Olympic competitions prompted the British to reconsider their historic commitment to the high ideals of amateurism and noninterventionism. English Football Association secretary Stanley Rous captured this sentiment, lamenting the reality that "our more purist view of amateurism handicapped performance by giving us a more limited selection than some [Communist] countries with more elastic concepts."[55] After the publication of the Birmingham University report *Britain in the World of Sport* in 1956 and the subsequent establishment of Sir John Wolfenden's Committee of Inquiry into British Sport, the government heeded the calls for direct state intervention. In 1964, Harold Wilson's Labour Government appointed Dennis Howell as Britain's inaugural Minister for Sport. The bonds between sport and the state deepened after the 1971 establishment of the Sports Council, a quasi-autonomous organization formed to advance British sporting interests.[56] In Canada, Prime Minister Pierre Trudeau's federal government expanded the parameters of the Fitness and Amateur Sport Act (1961) to form the Task Force on Sport in 1968 aimed at identifying strategies to promote high-performance sport.[57] The Australians followed suit. Lackluster results fueled a government inquiry and the publication of the twin Coles reports, which helped the Australian government establish (and generously subsidize) the Australian Institute for Sport in 1981.[58]

The Olympic successes of the GDR prompted the Federal Republic (West Germany) to also bridge the sport–state divide during the 1970s. After years of resisting governmental intervention, Daume and his colleagues sought state funds to enable the nation to compete successfully against its Communist rival to the east. In preparation for the 1972 Munich Olympics, the federal government invested DM 23.5 million in an attempt to provide a West German victory on home soil. The levels of governmental intervention continued to rise as the pursuit of Olympic medals became a matter of national and ideological prestige. The twin establishment of the Bundesausschuss zur Förderung des Leistungssports (Federal Committee for Competitive Sports) and the Deutsche Sportkonferenz (German Sport Conference) illustrated to even the most naïve and romantic observer the rampant politicization of Olympic sport.[59]

Despite vocal opposition from behind the Iron Curtain, calls for further amateur reforms gained momentum. Such sentiment certainly received a sympathetic audience from Eligibility Commission chairman Daume. Along with the Marquess of Exeter, Jean de Beaumont, and Canadian Richard "Dick" Pound, Daume is perhaps one of the most influential members of the IOC never to serve as its president. The West German Olympic official first expressed his progressive views on amateurism during the 1972 IOC session in Munich. Speaking in his position as the chair of the Munich Olympic Organizing Committee, Daume implored his colleagues to reform amateurism in "a new, perhaps unexpected, direction" on the grounds that eligibility rules forced athletes "onto a path of untruth and destroys the belief in the entire Olympic movement."[60] Daume's words, delivered prior to the IOC's vote to elect Brundage's successor, surely caused the abdicating octogenarian to ponder another term.

PROFESSIONAL RIVALS

Although Lord Killanin failed to express a clear progressive stance on amateurism, his decision to appoint Daume in 1978 to the chairmanship of the
Eligibility Commission is revealing.[61] Killanin likely understood, even if it
was not exactly his immediate desire, that Daume's appointment would usher
in major reforms to amateurism. At the 1980 IOC session in Lake Placid,
New York, however, he quickly signaled that intent. Daume recommended
that the IOC "find some way of enabling top competitive athletes to receive
some form of compensation—in addition to the compensation for loss of
earning—for the many hard sacrifices they have to make and the negative
repercussions affecting their future professional careers."[62] His progressive
views reflected the growing general acceptance that paying athletes did not
constitute a morally objectionable practice. Long dismissed as a disreputable
distraction for the working classes, professional sports steadily became an ac-
ceptable interest and increasingly popular in both Europe and North America
after World War II. By the 1970s and 1980s, professional sports exploded into
a golden age of sporting excess. Professional athletes were sexy, exciting,
and larger than life. These disco-fueled oversized personas stood in stark
contrast to the politics, boycotts, and hypocrisy that engulfed the Olympic
Movement throughout this era.

In the United States, televised coverage of sports brought professional
athletes into the homes of nearly every U.S. citizen every week, if not daily,
via Turner Broadcasting System, cable sports broadcaster ESPN, and major
television broadcasters.[63] Satellite technology, greater television coverage,
and commercial marketing helped to further popularize the tripartite organizations of mainstream U.S. sports: Major League Baseball, the National
Football League, and the National Basketball Association.[64] The Open era
of tennis, which allowed amateurs and professionals to compete together in
Grand Slam tournaments, stimulated widespread interest in a game traditionally reserved for the upper classes. The Swedish legend Björn Borg began
his run of eleven Grand Slam titles in 1974. Romanian Ilie Năstase brought
verve and flair to European tennis, and Arthur Ashe, Jimmy Connors, and
John McEnroe ushered in professional tennis's increasing popularity with
U.S. viewers. The American Billie Jean King and the young Czech prodigy
Martina Navrátilová animated the women's game.[65]

The growing popularity of professional sports posed a significant challenge
to the Olympic Movement. Unrestrained by amateur eligibility requirements,
professional sporting ventures held the upper hand in convincing the world's
leading sportsmen and sportswomen to parlay their amateur sporting ce-

lebrity into lucrative financial rewards. The IOC watched on as a number of traditional Olympic sports developed rival professional circuits. The establishment of the International Track Association after the 1972 Munich Olympics provided fans with professional track and field events.[66] Fueled by corporate sponsorship money from the world's leading sporting goods manufacturer, Nike, the Association of Road Running Athletes emerged in 1980, bringing a generation of elite track athletes to international television audiences. Alpine skiing also launched a rival professional circuit. With the help of American Bob Beattie and the ignominious Olympic stars of the 1968 Grenoble Olympics, Karl Schranz and Jean-Claude Killy, professional ski racing presented the IOC with further reasons to doubt amateurism's hegemony in popular culture.[67]

The popularization of professional sport exposed many Olympic officials to paid athletes, who by this point looked very similar to the highly trained, highly specialized elite amateurs gracing Olympic podiums. Being labeled a professional no longer held the same stigma as it once had. In a signal of changing attitudes, the Marquess of Exeter, a consummate British aristocrat, commented at the 1980 IOC session that "professional sport was a perfectly reasonable way of earning a living."[68] Still, nearly every member of the IOC believed that Olympic sport represented moral and cultural values that professional leagues and circuits lacked. This explains, in part, why Daume and his colleagues objected to professionals competing at the Olympics. Instead, he favored the passage of liberal reforms that would help to keep the Olympics culturally relevant and commercially viable, while retaining a semblance of amateurism. His calls for reform would soon receive substantial support from Lord Killanin's successor to the IOC presidency, Juan Antonio Samaranch.

THE "SAMARANCH REVOLUTION"[69]

Swaddled by political and economic controversies, Lord Killanin's short tenure as IOC president marked a nadir in the Olympic Movement. The rising politics of Third World nationalism and a unified protest against South African and Rhodesian apartheid precipitated a mass African and Caribbean boycott of the 1976 Montreal Olympics.[70] Amid political turmoil and a diminished roster of participant nations, the Montreal Olympics recorded substantial financial losses. Cold War nationalism, long a key ingredient in the post–World War II growth and popularity of the Olympics, also took a decidedly deleterious turn. The Soviet invasion of Afghanistan led the United States to abstain from the 1980 Moscow Olympics in protest against Communist expansionism.[71] Lord Killanin looked on distraught as a second African-led boycott led to the fewest nations (80) in an Olympic meet since Tokyo in 1956. The Olympics lost their luster. The exorbitant costs of staging the games, aligned with the mounting politicization of Olympic competition, dissuaded global cultural capitals from hosting future Olympic spectacles. When the fires of revolution forced Tehran to withdraw from the race to host the 1984 Olympics, the city of Los Angeles was left unopposed to stage the games.[72]

The IOC sought a leader who could place the Olympic Movement on a more positive trajectory. At the 1980 IOC Annual Session in Moscow, members elected Samaranch with an overwhelming majority on the first ballot.[73] Throughout his presidency, the Spaniard worked to secure the financial prosperity of the Olympic Movement. He oversaw the unmistakable transformation of the IOC into a full-fledged corporate entity. Eager to elevate the Olympics above the growing cluster of professional rivals, he brokered—with the aid of his close colleague, Dick Pound—record-breaking television deals, revamped its commercial sponsorship arrangements, and eroded many of the remaining vestiges of Olympic amateurism. Samaranch's presidency, though marred by bribery, bidding scandals, and a culture of corruption, catapulted the Olympics safely from the brink of obscurity.[74]

The election of a commercially driven, progressive reformer illustrated the IOC's shifting demographics. At the time of Samaranch's election, thirty-one of the eighty-four voting members had joined the IOC after Brundage had retired.[75] Considering that Killanin's election in 1972 had occurred with seventy-nine of the eighty-four members appointed under Brundage's tenure, the generational turnover helped bring in a more globally representative cohort of members more open to embracing a philosophical shift on Olympic eligibility.[76] The Eurocentric power structure that sustained and legitimized the amateur ethos for more than eight decades was eroding, and its aristocratic sensibilities were eroding even more rapidly.[77]

With Samaranch at the helm, the IOC advanced discussions on revisions to Rule 26. During a February 1981 meeting of the IOC Executive Board in Los Angeles, Samaranch revealed his expressed intent "to make this rule more liberal." Under the proposed formulations, the IOC would remove existing antiprofiteering restrictions. Such a significant liberalization of the eligibility code met with dissent. Belgian Prince Alexandre de Mérode articulated his opposition to the proposed reforms: "While the former rule had been too extreme in one way," Merode argued, "the new text was too extreme in the opposite sense." He also voiced his concerns that the transition to an open Olympics would ensure that "the Olympic Spirit would be lost."[78] Reinforcing Communist contempt for liberal reforms, Romanian Alexandru Şiperco expressed the fear that "athletes could in the future receive unlimited sums of revenue from commercial contracts." The Soviet Union's Vitaly Smirnov cautioned that the rule would allow unrestrained professionalism into the Olympics. Amid a chorus of opposition, Samaranch tabled the issue for later discussion.[79]

The 1981 Olympic Congress, held in the Bavarian spa town of Baden-Baden, Germany, provided Samaranch with a broader platform upon which to articulate his vision for a "moderate evolution" of the eligibility code.[80] The Olympic tripartite powers expressed a growing appetite for reform. The 1981 congress revealed the complex terrain that international and national federations were being forced to traverse: how to retain their amateur traditions while becoming a popular, commercially viable, telegenic sport. Although the federations sought a significantly more liberal eligibility code than the IOC membership appeared ready to grant, they did agree "that there was no place in the Olympic Games for 'professionals' or 'open' competition."[81] Their recalcitrance on the issue of professionals can either be read as a continued fealty to amateurism, or, perhaps, more cynically, as a way in which to preserve a system of free labor that best served their own financial self-interests. With the needle tilting toward the retention of some form of amateurism, Daume and the Eligibility Commission proposed leaving Rule 26 completely unchanged for the time being. Nevertheless, they revived an initiative passed at the 1974 IOC session in Vienna to grant international sports federations license to craft their own eligibility codes on the strict condition that they receive approval from Lausanne.[82]

THE THREE HOLDOUTS

By the 1983 IOC Annual Session in New Delhi, all but three international federations had submitted approvable eligibility rules. With the variety of technical issues and organizational and participatory exigencies unique to each sport, the IOC was forced into making some concessions. The IAAF attracted scrutiny for its proposed Athletes Trust Fund, a progressive concept whereby amateur athletes could deposit prize winnings and earnings into a secure trust account and then either withdraw funds to cover training and travel expenses or, as would become the popular trend, bank significant amounts of prize money that they would then be free to enjoy at the end of their amateur careers.[83] Despite expressing uneasiness over an initiative that occupied a philosophical gray area, Samaranch and the IOC approved the IAAF's eligibility rules.[84]

The IOC's focus turned to discussions over the eligibility codes of three sports that had long challenged the amateur traditions of the Olympic Movement: soccer, ice hockey, and the demonstration sport of tennis.[85] FIFA, the powerful governing body of the world's most popular sport, predictably refused to conform to the IOC's eligibility requirements. As it had done in Amsterdam (1928) over the broken-time issue, and again in Berlin (1936) by requesting to bypass the *Olympic Charter* by granting national football federations authority to define amateur eligibility, FIFA asserted its own organizational agenda. Led by its president João Havelange, FIFA insisted on retaining its geographic eligibility rule, which barred European and South American players who participated in the World Cup from also representing their nations in Olympic qualifying and tournament games.[86] This rule was ostensibly an effort by FIFA to prevent professionals from competing as amateurs, but the ruse fooled few IOC members about its real intent. In reality, the rule sought to protect the primacy of the FIFA World Cup by ensuring that the world's most recognizable stars pulled on national jerseys only in its own marquee event.

FIFA's bureaucratic maneuvering upset IOC officials. At a January 1979 meeting of the IOC Executive Board, members invited Havelange and FIFA secretary general Helmut Käser to discuss the issue. Behind closed doors, the IOC Executive Board expressed the objection that FIFA's geographic eligibility rule contravened the universal mission embedded within the *Olympic Charter*. In truth, a disingenuous intent lay behind the executive board's objections. Daume depicted FIFA's move as a significant power play that eroded the IOC's authority and relegated the Olympic soccer tournament to a position of far lesser relevance. "If the IOC fails to adopt a strong position in the present case," he warned, it would mark "the beginning of the end of the IOC's jurisdiction over the Olympic Games."[87] Though couched in fidelity toward the Olympic ideals of amateurism and universalism, Daume wanted to preserve the preeminence of the Olympic Games and the IOC's authority in dictating terms to all international sports federations.

Presiding as it did over the world's most successful and financially lucrative single-sport tournament, FIFA balked at the IOC's demands. Havelange and Käser reminded Olympic officials that a failure to approve FIFA's eligibility rules would result in the removal of the Olympic soccer tournament and the loss of millions of dollars in commercial and television revenue. Käser referred to the Olympic Movement's estimated $1 million loss after the withdrawal of Ghana, Zambia, and Nigeria from the 1976 Olympic soccer tournament and the subsequent forced cancelation of many matches. He inveighed against the demand, noting that the loss of an entire soccer tournament would prove financially disastrous for a movement still reeling from the economic calamity of Montreal. The IOC's bargaining power was further diminished by the reticence among Olympic host cities to stage the games without the promised financial rewards of Olympic soccer. Executive board member and president of the Moscow Olympic Organizing Committee Vitaly Smirnov feared that the absence of soccer would strike a disastrous blow for Moscow and, perhaps more fatally, would likely deter the dwindling numbers of interested parties in submitting bids to host further Olympic Games. Inevitably, the IOC capitulated. Olympic officials accepted FIFA's eligibility rules in time for the 1980 Moscow Olympics despite their objections.[88]

Interorganizational tensions continued to mount. After the Moscow Olympics, FIFA had begun pushing for a new rule capping the age of Olympic eligibility at twenty-three while removing the professional–amateur distinction entirely. At the 1981 Baden-Baden Olympic Congress, Harry Cavan, the vice president of FIFA, explained this move was to ensure that "the FIFA world championship will remain as the highest football competition in the world."[89] From the IOC's perspective, Cavan's potential eligibility revisions threatened to strip the Olympic soccer tournament of all significance. Fearing the Olympic Games would be demoted to the status of a "Junior championship," the IOC expressed a willingness to allow FIFA to retain the previous (but objectionable) geographical regulations in their eligibility code for the 1984 Los Angeles Olympics and again for the 1988 Olympics.[90] After months of further negotiation, both parties issued a joint declaration that professionals would not appear at the 1984 Olympic soccer tournament.[91] This compromise ensured FIFA's World Cup remained the preeminent soccer event by keeping its most talented European and South American stars away from the Olympics. The IOC, on the other hand, balanced its fear of becoming an inferior spectacle with its desire to retain the popular and highly profitable soccer tournament on the Olympic program. The *Los Angeles Times* revealed that the compromise proved to be a mere smokescreen in that FIFA, with the tacit approval of Daume and Samaranch, openly sent teams of professional footballers to the 1984 Olympic Games.[92] The IOC's relaxation of its eligibility code and the silent influx of professional soccer players in Los Angeles reflected the growing pressures of television revenue—ABC agreed to pay a record-breaking $100 million for the rights to the 1984 Olympics, plus a further $150 million in technical costs.[93]

Though not nearly as popular as profitable as soccer, ice hockey posed a second eligibility issue for the IOC. Ice hockey had appeared consistently on the Olympic program since the Winter Olympics inception in 1924 and had grown in popularity to become a centerpiece of the quadrennial winter festival.[94] Disagreements on the subject of amateur eligibility between the Fédération Internationale de Hockey sur Glace (FIHG) and the IOC traced back to the 1948 Winter Olympics in St. Moritz. The influence of commercial

rink operators as well as the sport's longstanding tradition of mixing professional and amateur hockey players drew the ire of Brundage and many of his
Olympic colleagues. Suspicions heightened when the FIHG sought approval
for its revised eligibility code. Dissension emerged over two central issues.
First, the FIHG voted to grant Olympic status to all players except those who
held a professional contract with either of the two major professional leagues
in North America: the National Hockey League and the American Hockey
League. As Daume and the Eligibility Commission soon realized, this revision failed to preclude the untold number of European-based players who
were contracted to smaller, but increasingly lucrative, professional leagues
in Europe. In further opposition to Olympic eligibility standards, the FIHG
also insisted on bestowing Olympic status to "reamateurized" players, former
professionals who now plied their trade on the amateur circuit.

With ABC signing a $91.5 million contract for U.S. broadcasting rights to
the 1984 Sarajevo winter Olympics, the IOC, in conjunction with the Sarajevo
Olympic organizers, came under intense pressure to provide a superior product.[95] Thus, the participation of ice hockey, the Winter Olympics' most visible
and profitable sport, became an urgent priority. Again, the IOC demonstrated
willingness to compromise on the issue of eligibility. The FIHG agreed to remove its clause granting eligibility to former professionals on the condition
that the IOC overlook the participation of state-sponsored Communists and
European-based professionals at the Sarajevo Olympics.[96] Once again, Olympic
eligibility gave way to matters of financial and organizational expediency.

The International Tennis Federation (ITF) provided the last eligibility
issue for Daume and his commission to resolve on the eve of the Los Angeles Olympics. Tennis had previously left the Olympic Movement after the
1924 Paris Olympics when the ITF (formerly the International Lawn Tennis
Federation) refused to conform to the IOC's amateur eligibility conditions.
The sport remained entirely absent from the Olympic Movement until it
made a brief reappearance as a demonstration sport at the 1968 Mexico City
Olympics. In this time, tennis had developed from a country club sport into
a highly popular form of mass recreation with a viable professional circuit.[97]
In the United States, which had become the IOC's largest television market,
tennis had rapidly expanded from 5.5 million players in 1960 to 20 million
players by 1976. In that same period, sales of rackets and balls had doubled.[98]
With Wimbledon and its host of Open tournaments around the world, the
ITF already had a successful brand that reached an international audience
despite its absence from the Olympic Games. With its soaring popularity, the
ITF approached the IOC in 1979 about returning to the Olympic fold.[99] The

sport's highly commercialized professional circuits for both men and women proved very alluring for Samaranch, who issued orders to usher tennis back into the Olympics in time for the Los Angeles Games.[100]

Despite concerns over the games' growing size, the IOC granted approval for tennis to reappear as a demonstration event for the 1984 Olympics and even targeted the 1988 Olympics for its full debut.[101] The issue of eligibility ensured that the Olympic reentry of tennis proved difficult. Unlike FIFA who wished to restrict its star players to its own World Cup event, the ITF insisted that its leading professionals be eligible for the Olympic Games. If permitted, the ITF's request would mark the first time the IOC approved—at least officially—a federation sending professional athletes to the Olympic Games. Again, the IOC sought a compromise. The Eligibility Commission permitted the appearance of professionals on the condition that the ITF limited participation to players under the age of twenty. Despite the executive board's admonitions about the dangerous precedent of having a demonstration sport with open professionals, tennis reappeared on the Olympic program in Los Angeles.[102] The fact that the professional tennis players would not receive medals, because of their sport's demonstration status, seemed to placate the IOC's concerns.

The Eligibility Commission's concessions with the international sports federations of soccer, ice hockey, and tennis, pushed the IOC further toward an open Olympics. Writing on the eve of the 1984 Los Angeles Olympics, *New York Times* sports columnist Frank Litsky presaged the decline and fall of amateurism on the grounds that "hardly anyone cares" how many athletes are really amateurs.[103] A steady stream of calls for professional athletes in the Olympics flooded the news media. Bruce Furniss, a two-time U.S. gold medalist in swimming, commented that "it's ridiculous to bar professional athletes from the Olympic Games."[104] "All major sports," argued the London *Economist,* "will have to become honestly professional or else fall further and further into communist hands."[105] F. Don Miller, executive director of the USOC, also broke ranks with amateur orthodoxy, predicting that the Olympic Games "are gradually moving toward that time" when they will be completely open.[106]

The shifting mood away from amateurism also received currency within academia. The 1984 publication of classicist David C. Young's book *The Olympic Myth of Greek Amateur Athletics* discredited the notion that the ancient Olympians of classical Greek antiquity were amateurs in the British tradition. In a revisionist history, Young revealed that the ancient Greeks lacked both the ideology and vocabulary of amateurism. They were fiercely competitive, well trained, and lavishly remunerated professionals. Greek amateurism was a myth, consciously propagated by Coubertin and his successors in order to lay the intellectual and cultural foundations for the revival and success of their modern Olympic project. Young's demythologizing of amateurism and his exposure of a generation of flawed scholarship led by classicists E. N. Gardner and H. W. Pleket eroded the IOC's historical justification for preserving the ideology. Avery Brundage's insistence that amateurism was a fixed, timeless ideal incapable of change was proven misguided, as was his (and others') belief that that professionalism and commercialism precipitated the decline and fall of the ancient Greek games.[107] The IOC was no longer bound to an ideological anchor. It was liberated from the fear that money would again doom the Olympics to failure. As the 1984 Summer Olympics headed to Los Angeles, the Olympic Movement took further steps to dispense with at least one invented tradition by harnessing the ancient Greek fusion of professionalism, commerce, and elite performance.

THE FADING HUES OF AMATEURISM

The 1984 Los Angeles Olympics came at precisely the moment when the staging of the games generated controversy, condemnation, and harmful legacies. The fear of debt, infrastructural white elephants and urban blight, political boycotts, and terrorist attacks had grown so strong that global metropolitan cities abstained from even bidding on the Olympic spectacle. The Olympics stared over the precipice of disaster; the Munich, Montreal, and Moscow Olympics had elevated concerns about the relevance, viability, and necessity of future Olympic competition.

The city of Los Angeles, the capital of the world's popular culture industry, arose to redesign and revitalize the Olympic Movement and reenergize the Olympics at a crucial time. Despite a Soviet-led Communist boycott, the 1984 Olympics proved a smashing success, recording an unprecedented $232.5 million surplus. Led by the dynamic and sagacious Peter Ueberroth, the games set new standards in Olympic commercialism, boasting record-breaking television contracts and corporate sponsorship deals. Ueberroth's cleverly negotiated licensing deals with a limited number of sponsors granted companies such as Coca-Cola, McDonald's, and IBM exclusive rights as official Olympic sponsors.[108] Samaranch would subsequently embrace this model for commercializing the Olympic Games with the "Olympic Partner (TOP) Programme."[109] Millions of spectators attended. Billions more watched on television. Carl Lewis, Mary Lou Retton, Mary Decker Slaney, and Steffi Graf emerged as household names. Their faces beamed on billboard advertisements for Kodak and Nike around Los Angeles, something the IOC's previous versions of the eligibility code had sought to prevent.[110]

Steffi Graf enjoys her time on the top step of the 1984 Olympic Games women's singles tennis exhibition event. Already a professional since 1982, the fifteen-year-old Graf was part of the first wave of professionals to openly participate in the Olympic Games. By 1988, the IOC admitted tennis as a full Olympic sport understanding that professionals would participate. (Courtesy of the LA84 Foundation)

The 1984 Winter and Summer Olympics proved that the Olympic Movement remained popular despite the covert and overt participation of soccer, ice hockey, and tennis professionals.[111] With its financial coffers overflowing from record-breaking television contracts and commercial branding, the IOC took further steps to reform Rule 26 but still not in the direction of permitting professionals. At the 1985 IOC Annual Session in Berlin, Daume argued for unspecified "modernizing" of the eligibility code but stressed that an "'open' Olympics had to be avoided at all costs." His colleagues supported this sentiment. Masaji Kiyokawa of Japan opined, "There was no place in the Olympic Games for professionals," while Bashir Mohamed Attabrabulsi of Libya sought to have "all professionals barred without exception."[112] The reticence of the IOC at that point to throw open the doors to widespread professionalism undermines the widespread belief that the Olympic Movement discarded amateur eligibility requirements immediately after the retirement of Brundage in 1972. Tradition—invented or otherwise—proved difficult to jettison.

While the IOC debated potential reforms, the international sports federations of soccer, ice hockey, and tennis continued advocating for eligibility

rules that would permit sending professionals to the 1988 Olympic Games in
Seoul. FIFA formulated the idea of an "Olympic class" of players that, while
making no distinction between a professional and amateur, did set an age
limit of twenty-three for Olympic eligibility. The FIHG proposed replacing
its rule permitting European-based professionals with a cap limiting participation to Olympic hockey players under the age of twenty-one. Because the
FIHG refused to certify a professional contract until a player reached that
age, its revised eligibility code would ensure that all Olympic hockey players
were too young to have become professional. For those within the IOC who
wished to preserve amateurism, the ITF presented the most direct problem.
After the success of tennis in Los Angeles, the federation refused to consider
an Olympic tournament with anything less than their best players. This meant
no age cap or restriction on professionals.[113] The ITF promised in return to
ensure that the Olympic tournament would offer no prize money nor would
the relevant national federations and national Olympic committees reward
players financially for their participation.[114] The Olympic Movement faced the
prospect of major reform. In the case of both soccer and tennis, approving
eligibility rules meant officially permitting professionals into the Olympics.
In the cases of soccer and ice hockey, the proposed revisions would effectively demote the Olympic tournament for each sport to the level of junior
championships, inferior to the FIFA World Cup and the North American
professional hockey leagues.

The demand for eligibility reform forced the IOC to consider whether
preserving amateurism was worth relegating the Olympic Games to an inferior status. This debate would play out at the 1986 IOC Annual Session in
Lausanne. Dick Pound trumpeted the push for an open Olympics, observing
that "evolutionary and revolutionary social changes had taken place over the
past hundred years which had been unthinkable in the 1890s." He argued that
the Olympic Movement should reorient its thinking since "professionals had
proved themselves as capable of observing the Olympic spirit and fair play as
anyone." Pound's colleagues, particularly those from behind the Iron Curtain,
proved far less accommodating.[115] Although Samaranch and Daume were able
to convince FIFA and the FIHG to table their proposed reforms until after
the 1988 Olympics, the ITF remained steadfast in sending their best players
to Seoul. Viewing an open Olympic tennis tournament as an "experiment,"
the Eligibility Commission "strongly and unanimously" supported the request.[116] Revealing the IOC's financial and commercial motivation, Daume
explained that an "Olympic tennis tournament would attract all young target
groups worldwide and at the same time would be of great advantage in view
of the IOC's economic activities." Daume did insist upon some restrictions:

professional tennis players would be forced to adhere to Rule 26 and cancel any contracts with agents or sponsors during the Olympic Games.[117] He calculated that this stipulation would bring tennis closer to Olympic ideals by removing the scent of greedy agents and unsavory commercialism.

The question of a professional Olympic tennis tournament appeared as the key issue on the agenda at the 1987 IOC Annual Session in Istanbul. It was clear to all members that despite Daume's insistence that professional tennis was an experiment, the vote would mark a historic moment in Olympic history. Austrian IOC member Phillipp von Schoeller captured the gravity of the situation, noting that perhaps "for the first time the IOC is legalizing the breach of the amateur status." Calling this vote the "ultimate move," von Schoeller predicted that the IOC would not be able to reverse a vote to approve professionals.[118] He was correct. The Olympic Movement took a major step toward removing the shackle of amateur eligibility by electing to permit professional tennis players at the 1988 Seoul Olympics on an experimental basis. IOC member Anita DeFrantz, among others, celebrated the move on the grounds that the Olympic Games were for the best players in the world, professional or otherwise.[119]

Although the IOC's Rule 26 still technically prohibited professionals, many of the world's major tennis players in 1988 attended the Olympic tennis tournament. On the women's side, Steffi Graf and Gabriella Sabatini, two stars of the late 1980s professional tennis circuit, played in the finals, and on the men's side three of the four singles medalists ranked among the world's top twenty players. The tennis stars also positively affected the Olympic Games, as newspaper reports from Seoul depicted the professionals happily residing in the Olympic village and enjoying the chance to play for their country rather than a paycheck.[120]

Before the Seoul Olympics closed, however, an unexpected scandal erupted over an amateur transgression. Canadian sprinter Ben Johnson tested positive for anabolic steroids after his world record victory in the 100 meters. With the positive test, the IOC stripped Johnson of his gold medal and awarded it to the second-place finisher, the American Carl Lewis. Johnson's punishment marked the first time the IOC and its Medical Commission had stripped a preeminent athlete of a medal during the Olympic Games for violating its antidoping rules.[121] In an Olympics featuring tennis professionals, an insertion in the IOC's old amateur code ironically took center stage to excommunicate a fallen athlete.

The juxtaposition of Johnson with professional tennis illustrates how the Olympic Movement had both compromised on its amateur code and preserved elements of its old moral code. Including tennis professionals at the

Seoul Olympics demonstrated the IOC's commitment to making the games a premier sporting event at the expense of its amateur traditions. What the IOC did not want, however, were athletes who violated the notion of sport as a healthy, character-building, and moral enterprise. Athletes using anabolic steroids did not fit that image or brand of Olympic sport. The twin desires for primacy and purity would drive the IOC to allow the international federations on the eve of the 1992 Barcelona Olympics to draft eligibility codes that permitted professionals while increasing their own antidoping efforts designed to preserve a pure vision of Olympic sport.

EPILOGUE

As the 1992 Barcelona Olympic Games drew to a close, Juan Antonio Sama-ranch, the president of the International Olympic Committee (IOC), declared that "the most important aspect of the Games has been the resounding suc-cess of the basketball tournament, as we've witnessed the best basketball in the world. The Palau d'Esports de Badalona has become the mecca of this sport."[1] With that, a watershed moment in the Olympic Games received its verdict from the Olympic Movement's highest court: the professionals were here to stay. The decision by the Fédération Internationale de Basketball (FIBA) to permit professionals to participate in the 1992 Olympic basketball tournament had resulted in the United States assembling its "Dream Team" of professional players from the National Basketball Association.[2] These were the greatest players that the U.S. basketball league had to offer; almost all had multimillion dollar professional contracts, lucrative commercial endorse-ments, and a few, like Michael Jordan, Magic Johnson, and Larry Bird, had attained the status of global celebrity icons.

For nearly a century, the fear among IOC officials had been that sending such stars to the Olympic Games would do significant harm to the Olympic Movement. Driven by financial greed, bold ambition, and a slavish devotion to sporting perfection, the professionals would allegedly tarnish the Olympic spirit of peace, fair play, and mutual cooperation. Accustomed to a life of luxury, how would these athletes even fit in with the humble accommoda-tions of the Olympic Village? many wondered on the eve of the Barcelona Olympics. Would their star power overshadow athletes in smaller sports or even the Olympic Games themselves? Could they embrace the Olympic spirit?

These concerns quickly subsided as the Dream Team captured the world's attention. Security concerns had driven the team to eschew the Olympic Village in favor of a luxury hotel. Mobbed by visiting fans of every nationality, U.S. professional basketballers had proven themselves consummate ambassadors. Only Charles Barkley's unnecessary flagrant foul (an elbow to Angola's Herlander Coimbra) provided detractors with reason to doubt whether the professionals belonged in the Olympic Games. Instead, stories of the oversized Barkley walking through Barcelona's touristy La Rambla, where he obliged fans with autographs and pictures, quickly endeared him to the public. Even the lopsidedness of the Dream Team's games—the closest being the gold medal final against Croatia, won 117–85—failed to dissuade IOC officials or the public. Professional athletes, it turned out, had not ruined the Olympic Games and by all verdicts appeared destined to stay.[3]

Professional basketball players had come into the Olympic Games through a remarkably fast turn of events, particularly considering the controversial appearance of tennis professionals at the 1988 Seoul Games. Sensing the potential for commercial and participatory growth, FIBA pushed the issue. At the 1989 IOC Annual Session in San Juan, Puerto Rico, Samaranch recommended that the IOC accept FIBA's decision for an "open" tournament because of their mutual desire that "participation of the best players" regardless of professional or amateur status would improve Olympic basketball. The motion passed with almost unanimous approval.[4] The IOC soon took another step toward an open Olympics by revising its eligibility code in the 1991 *Olympic Charter*.[5] This code, for the first time, entirely dropped amateurism's financial constraints from the *Olympic Charter*. No longer did Olympic eligibility hinge on an athlete not being a professional or not profiting from sport. Moreover, the *Olympic Charter* no longer used the appellations "amateur" and "professional" to describe Olympians. The only requirements were that athletes be in good standing with their respective national Olympic committee and national sports federation, respect the spirit of fair play and nonviolence, follow the antidoping rules, and avoid advertising during the Olympic Games.[6]

REMOVING AMATEURISM FROM THE OLYMPIC CHARTER

For an ideology ensconced in the fabric of the Olympic Games, the shift in the IOC's members from their 1988 position of "no open professionals" (excepting tennis) to the 1992 "Welcome Dream Team!" happened quickly. The process to arrive at an open Olympics, however, had been set in motion more than a decade previously with Samaranch's desire to liberalize the eligibility code. With the major pieces of the historical narrative in place, it is worth considering the process whereby Samaranch and the IOC unwound amateurism as its eligibility rule.

The IOC relied heavily on its *Olympic Charter* to define amateurism and stipulate what counted as a violation. Thus, the charter's Rule 26 became the central place where changes to amateurism played out, especially throughout the second half of the twentieth century.[7] Though debates within executive board meetings and IOC sessions reveal only individual attitudes, the changes to language in the charter reflect how the organization applied, and later gradually removed, amateurism as a condition of eligibility. An important, but misunderstood, shift occurred between the 1966 and 1967 editions of the *Olympic Charter*, when the title of the rule went from being "Definition of an Amateur" to "Eligibility." Yet the move away from the word *amateur* did not occur because the IOC wished to diminish the ideology. Just the opposite, in fact, is true. As Hugh Weir, the architect of this shift, explained: "The most effective method to ensure that the Olympic Games are confined to *amateurs* only will be to establish a code enumerating those infringements which will definitely render a competitor *ineligible* to take part in the Olympic Games."[8] Thus, the initial shift to eligibility did not correspond to a reduction in the IOC's commitment to amateurism.

It is also not correct to date amateurism's endpoint to any of the subsequent changes to the eligibility code in the *Olympic Charter* that occurred throughout the 1970s, though such dates are popularly cited. Although the liberalizing of the eligibility code at the 1974 IOC session in Vienna removed many tenets of amateurism, a considerable faction within the Olympic Movement and beyond still considered amateurism an important and relevant ideology. Even in 1980, as Willi Daume argued to permit athletes to receive compensation for more than lost wages, he claimed that "amateurism, even though the word was being avoided, remained a fundamental principle of the Olympic Movement."[9] Samaranch expressed a similar sentiment, observing "that many members still speak of 'amateurism'" while referring to the eligibility code.[10]

Such was the complicated relationship between the IOC and amateurism during this period of gradual liberalization. At the 1981 Baden-Baden Congress, speakers continued linking amateurism to the IOC's eligibility code. Robert Helmick, secretary general of the Fédération Internationale de Natation, reasoned, "Amateurism is tied to the word eligibility—who is eligible." Primo Nebiolo, president of the International Amateur Athletic Federation (IAAF), also appeared to conflate the two by advocating for a modern eligibility code while "preserving the valuable principle of amateurism which we have always kept."[11] After the Baden-Baden Congress, and with the subsequent removal of most references to "amateur" sport in the *Olympic Charter*, the IOC continued to believe that the Olympic Games remained amateur. The specific barring of professionals and the frequent appeals to amateur sport voiced during executive board meetings and IOC sessions throughout the 1980s reveals that the ideology of amateurism still exerted influence over Olympic affairs. In fact, when Daume argued in favor of an open tennis tournament at the 1988 Olympic Games, he stressed that sending professionals was an experiment and not meant to erode amateurism.

In hindsight, however, we can see that the decision to sanction professional tennis players marked the point of no return. The executioner's blow fell swiftly and cleanly after the Seoul Games. In 1990, with tennis having set a successful precedent, Daume led a massive revision of the *Olympic Charter* that not only deleted every reference to both amateurs and professionals but ensured that professional athletes could, at the decision of their international federation, participate in the Olympic Games. This revised eligibility code published in the 1991 *Olympic Charter*, now Rule 45 instead of Rule 26 (perhaps illustrating its diminished importance) marked the end of amateurism as a requirement for an athlete's Olympic eligibility.[12] The Eligibility Commission continued on, though it mostly addressed issues related to nationality, as the dissolution of the Soviet Union presented a number of geopolitical logistical issues.[13] In the coming years, most international sports federations approved eligibility rules that permitted athletes to pursue sport as a full-time, paid vocation.

Two major personages shake hands after the 1991 decision to remove the last vestiges of amateurism from the IOC eligibility code. IOC president Juan Antonio Samaranch (left) and IOC Eligibility Commission chairman Willi Daume (right) had both made moves to end amateurism in the decade leading up to this decision. (Courtesy of the International Olympic Committee)

THE GHOST OF AMATEURISM

Without amateurism codified in the *Olympic Charter*, one might assume that the ideology no longer holds sway in the Olympic Movement. After all, in the years after the Barcelona Games the IOC morphed into a full-blown commercial entity. Even the games themselves represent a corporate brand, capable of cross-platform promotions. As the glossy *Marketing Report* for the 2012 Olympic Games proudly proclaims, "As well as being hailed as a sporting success, the London . . . Games were also an unparalleled marketing triumph, with record television viewing figures around the world, more tickets sold than the three previous summer Games, a highly successful merchandise programme and an exciting array of sponsor activations."[14] For the Olympic Movement to tout its marketing prowess confirms what Avery Brundage and many within the IOC feared might happen if amateurism was abolished. Each Olympic Games seamlessly passes its star athletes through to its corporate sponsors so that the lines blur between the end of a sporting event and the start of a commercial enterprise. Snowboarders sell Big Macs and decathletes dance with the stars on prime-time television. Corporations line their pockets and, for as long as each athlete can remain in the public imagination, collude to use the athlete's Olympic success so both parties can cash in on their celebrity.

Despite this heavy dose of commercialism, the Olympic brand remains as popular as ever. The 2012 London Olympic Games reached an estimated 4.8 billion television viewers around the world, a half billion more than the 2008 Beijing Olympic Games.[15] The Olympic Games' growth is due in large part to the public's positive feelings associated with the sporting organization.[16] Such lasting popularity, we suspect, is due in large part to the Olympic Movement's insistence that the sporting event is about more than elite sport. To project this image, the IOC has carefully woven elements of amateurism's ethos into the multisporting spectacle.[17] This gives both the public and the athletes an impression, one both familiar and distant, so that even if they cannot quite articulate why, they sense that the Olympics have a higher calling, one that places sport on a moral plane, one that requires sacrifice and dedication, and which elevates the Olympics, much as they did in antiquity, to something that transcends ordinary life.

The Olympic Movement manages to project such an impression, however precariously balanced against its commercial ambitions, through continuing its use of the amateur ideal. Even though the IOC removed amateurism from the *Olympic Charter*, it continues to occupy an important, albeit circumscribed, role within the Olympic Movement. The IOC skillfully preserved the ideology's humanistic moral imperative of fair play and proper conduct, as well as its image of sport as healthy and free from doping. In the 1991 *Olympic Charter*, and in its numerous iterations since, the IOC requires athletes to "respect the spirit of fair-play and non-violence." It even appeals to the anticommercial tenets of amateurism by insisting that Olympic athletes omit advertising on their person during the Olympic fortnight—cynics might rightly claim, however, that this last rule simply benefits the Olympic Movement and its exclusive Olympic Partner (TOP) Programme sponsors.[18] The ethical and anticommercial properties of amateurism are evidenced further via the IOC's ongoing prohibitions against athletes using their image for advertising during the Olympic Games, or receiving payment for Olympic participation. Admittedly, this form of amateurism applies only during the Olympic fortnight as opposed to the unwavering adherence to the amateur ideal previously expected of Olympic athletes. The sole exception to this fortnight amateurism is the antidoping rule, which has remained a permanent fixture and now is constantly monitored through in-competition and out-of-competition testing. In 1999 the IOC sponsored the quasi-independent World Anti-Doping Agency, which receives half its funding from the IOC and oversees antidoping for all international federations in the Olympic Movement.[19]

Even beyond the eligibility rules of the *Olympic Charter*, the Olympics themselves use quasi-religious images (the dove, the eternal flame), oaths, and pageantry to elevate the sporting spectacle from simply pure competition. Although the IOC's fierce determination to ensure that the Olympic Games housed the most elite sporting events precipitated the removal of amateur eligibility rules, the spirit of amateurism lives on. Where the Olympic Movement once espoused amateurism as its ideological foundation, there is now a growing reference to Olympism—a humanistic and educational ideology developed by Pierre de Coubertin and seeped in the moral and aesthetic elements of amateurism. Though Coubertin spoke and wrote about Olympism, it became institutionalized only after the French aristocrat had passed away in 1937. Yet as the culture of elite sport increasingly made amateurism appear anachronistic, Olympism served as a useful substitute for the ideology's moral rigor. Today, Olympism blends the twenty-first-century demand for elite sport, with multiculturalism, inoffensive moral dictates such as fair play and healthy competition, and a subtle dose of antiquity thrown into the mix.[20] Carrying forward these values has allowed Olympism to serve as a useful substitute for amateurism, and it is hard not to notice the obvious parallels between the Olympic Movement's traditional ideology of amateurism and its current "diet" version of Olympism—same great taste, fewer inconveniences.

Today, the Olympic Games presents itself to be a purer, more wholesome, more traditional version of sport than the more common, rival product displayed on television. Even though it is often the same international sports federations, the same cast of athletes, and the same television networks broadcasting the event, the Olympic Games continues to use its historical legacy, built in large part on the ideology of amateurism, to separate itself from the ordinary professional matches and world championships. The final product provides the public with record performances, competitive drama, and superhuman feats all set against the backdrop of nostalgia and an apparent authenticity that audiences crave. This duality, of being anticommercial while embracing commercialism, of being anticorporate while serving corporate interests, of being healthy while requiring athletes to push bodies to the point of injury, illustrates how amateurism's cultural currency still shapes the public imagination toward Olympic sport. Even though few in the Olympics' global television audience long to see amateur sport, they still want to imagine their athletes as being bound to sport's higher calling.

Despite amateurism's enduring, albeit subtle, presence, it presents an inconvenient history. Look too closely and the history of amateurism shows the Olympic Movement as elitist, hypocritical, and exclusive. After all, Olympic officials promulgated amateurism's moral benefits while limiting participation to those who could afford its vow of poverty. Later, after sport had democratized to include working-class athletes from a wider circle of participant nations, amateurism ensured that the IOC could funnel the flood of television money into its private coffers while mandating the athlete not receive a cut. Those athletes who dared to divert from the IOC or its kin any of the streams of excess their sporting exploits helped produce found themselves cut off entirely from their sport, exiled to the desert with no recourse. Moreover, with the flood of professionals, the IOC's enforcement of amateurism appears even more draconian and pointless. "To ban an athlete because he or she endorsed a running shoe?" the next generation asks.

REIMAGINING OLYMPIC AMATEURISM

Contemporary concerns over amateurism's unpleasant history help explain the process of how and why amateur athletes, and in particular those publicly martyred for violating amateur regulations, have been recast in the modern era. The IOC's treatment of Jim Thorpe, Paavo Nurmi, and Karl Schranz, as well as the unknown number of athletes that various national Olympic committees and federations barred from the Olympic Games, appears with each passing generation overly harsh and exploitative, if not hypocritical bullying. Such sentiments have been largely ameliorated by the IOC's public treatment and rehabilitation of these infamous former Olympians, especially in the years since the Baden-Baden Congress liberalized amateurism in the eligibility code.

The IOC's appropriation and celebration of Jim Thorpe in recent years illustrates the manner in which the powerbrokers of international sport have striven to rewrite history for their own organizational and commercial benefit. The IOC's revocation of Thorpe's two Olympic gold medals after the 1912 Stockholm Games for accepting a nominal fee to play semiprofessional baseball remains one of the most morally and racially egregious chapters in the history of the Olympic Movement. Although the movement to posthumously restore Thorpe's Amateur Athletic Union amateur status and return his Olympic gold medals began outside the purview of the Olympic Movement, the IOC pledged its unwavering support for the cause. The commercially orientated and media-savvy Samaranch sensed that tales of the IOC's punitive treatment of a defenseless Thorpe represented a public-relations embarrassment for an organization that proudly proclaims the virtues of fair play and inclusion. Thus, on October 3, 1982, the IOC Executive Board unanimously passed a resolution to give Thorpe back his honors. In a special ceremony in Los Angeles, Samaranch presented reproductions of Thorpe's decathlon and pentathlon gold medals to his children.[21] With that, the IOC rewrote a particularly unsavory episode in its history. Thorpe is now remembered as one of the greatest Olympians of all time rather than the first victim of harsh and outdated amateur regulations.

Like Thorpe, Finland's Paavo Nurmi also has received a public rehabilitation. The IAAF, in close collaboration with the IOC, banned Nurmi on the eve of the 1932 Los Angeles Games for violating its antiprofiteering amateur regulations. Long reviled by the amateur sporting community (outside Finland), Nurmi's legacy has recently taken on a new luster. At the IOC's Olympic Museum in Lausanne, Switzerland, visitors' cross paths with a copy of the Wäinö Aaltonen's bronze sculpture of the Flying Finn. Depicted in the nude, the muscular Nurmi, caught in full stride, invokes the purity of the modern Olympic Movement as well as its tenuous links to classical antiquity. Ironically, no mention is made at the statue of Nurmi's past transgressions or his removal from the Los Angeles Games. The former villain of the Olympic Movement has been recast in recent decades as a symbol of the Olympic ideal, the personification of *Citius, Altius, Fortius*.[22] Nurmi's legacy continues to grow. In 1996, *Time Magazine* named Nurmi the greatest Olympian of all time, and in 2012 the IAAF named Nurmi among the first twelve athletes inducted into its Hall of Fame.[23]

A reproduction of Wäinö Aaltonen's 1925 Paavo Nurmi statue now adorns the IOC's museum in Lausanne, Switzerland. Nurmi, perhaps the most notorious shamateur, had been suspended for life by the International Amateur Athletic Federation on the eve of the 1932 Olympics. The prominence of this once-disgraced athlete illustrates how the legacy of amateurism has been rewritten in the postamateurism era. (Courtesy of the International Olympic Committee)

Karl Schranz has received a similar treatment. In 1988, the IOC Executive Board officially reinstated the former Austrian skier and awarded him a *post factum* "participant" medal for the 1972 Olympic Games for having "offered his collaboration for the strengthening of the Olympic Movement."[24] Reflecting upon the medal ceremony in his memoirs years later, Schranz revealed that Samaranch "admitted in his presentation the error and explained that I was responsible for the fact that today in most kinds of sport, the best [athletes] are at the start of the Olympic Games."[25] The fact that a standing IOC president publicly acknowledged wrongdoing on behalf of his organization, and more important, heralded Schranz—the "poisonous cancer" that Avery Brundage and his colleagues excluded from the Sapporo Games—as a champion of the Olympic ideal, perfectly illustrates the extent to which the IOC has sought to rewrite its own history by purging any evidence of foul play and bureaucratic heavy-handedness.

The reconstruction of these athletes in the popular imagination has served to benefit the Olympic Movement. Much like the embracing and memorializing of African American civil-rights leaders in the post–civil-rights era, such commemorations help place all parties on the right side of history. No doubt, for Thorpe and Schranz this case is easier to make in that both athletes were unfairly martyred outside the rules. For Nurmi, however, the picture is more complicated, for he extorted payments that violated amateur rules. Yet the permanent excommunication of a great athlete like Nurmi for a rule that no longer exists becomes harder to justify, especially because amateurism appears increasingly anachronistic and inconsistent to modern audiences. For that reason, it is easier for the IOC to relegate these transgressions to minor footnotes in the athletes' storied careers while appropriating the athletes' refurbished legacy.

At the same time, these revisions also have helped the mythology of amateurism reemerge amid the twenty-first century cultural nostalgia for authenticity. Amateurism has become a wholesome ideology without any clear victims—a better, purer, inclusive version of sport uncorrupted by greed. To a generation steeped in irony as a defense against cultural pastiche, the sentimentality of sport stripped from commercial packaging appeals to a public looking for unscripted sincerity. This affection for the past, however, would be diminished by harsh reminders of amateurism's complicated history. So it is much easier to forgive past sins and repackage amateurism into an ideology that simply could not survive in modernity's commercialized climate. Yet to chalk up amateurism's decline and fall to inevitability is to miss the many contingent points along the way. That it even entered the nascent Olympic Movement was an act of shrewd pragmatism, as well as a product of British cultural hegemony. That amateurism persisted for more than eight decades owed much to its ability to reinvent itself—a chameleon equally at home supporting democratic, Fascist, and Communist political ideologies and propaganda. Its fall came about only because it no longer proved convenient to those charged with enforcing it. Still, such points cannot obscure the power and force amateurism wielded and continues to wield over sport. As an ideology, it captured people's imaginations without their ever having had to fully understand it. It had the feeling of certainty while defying definition. It was an ethos enforced through law. Even today, its spirit still sanctifies the ambulatory Olympic stadium to help elevate sport above the profane, though one can find few apostles. Perhaps the following captures the essence of amateurism's complicated legacy: that it was always equal parts ideology, mythology, and nostalgia.

NOTES

Introduction

1. For an introductory history of the Olympic Movement, see Allen Guttmann, *The Olympics: A History of the Modern Games*, 2nd ed. (Champaign: University of Illinois Press, 2002).

2. Robert K. Barney, Stephen R. Wenn, and Scott G. Martyn, *Selling the Five Rings: The International Olympic Committee and the Rise of Olympic Commercialism*, rev. ed. (Salt Lake City: University of Utah Press, 2004).

3. Christopher R. Hill, *Olympic Politics* (Manchester, U.K.: University of Manchester Press, 1992); Alfred E. Senn, *Power, Politics, and the Olympic Games: A History of the Brokers, Events, and Controversies That Shaped the Games* (Champaign, IL: Human Kinetics, 1999); Richard Espy, *The Politics of the Olympic Games* (Berkeley: University of California Press, 1979).

4. Dikaia Chatziefstathiou and Ian Henry, *Discourses of Olympism: From Sorbonne 1894 to London 2012* (Basingstoke, U.K.: Palgrave Macmillan, 2012).

5. Stephen Wenn, Robert K. Barney, and Scott G. Martyn, *Tarnished Rings: The International Olympic Committee and the Salt Lake City Bid Scandal* (Syracuse, NY: Syracuse University Press, 2011); Helen Lenskyj, *Gender Politics and the Olympic Industry* (Basingstoke, U.K.: Palgrave Macmillan, 2013); Gyozo Molnar and Alan Bairner, *The Politics of the Olympics: A Survey* (London: Routledge, 2010); Dave Zirin, *Brazil's Dance with the Devil: The World Cup, the Olympics, and the Fight for Democracy* (Chicago, IL: Haymarket Books, 2014).

6. Christopher A. Shaw, *Five Ring Circus: Myths and Realities of the Olympic Games* (Gabriola Island, BC: New Society, 2008); Andrew Jennings, *The New Lord of the Rings: Olympic Corruption and How to Buy Olympic Medals* (New York: Pocket Books, 1996); Alan Tomlinson and Garry Whannel, *Five Ring Circus: Money, Power, and Politics at the Olympic Games* (London: Pluto Press, 1984).

7. For more on Coubertin's ideological influence on Olympic policy, see David C. Young, *The Modern Olympics: A Struggle for Revival* (Baltimore, MD: Johns Hopkins University

Press, 1996); John J. MacAloon, *This Great Symbol: Pierre de Coubertin and the Origins of the Modern Olympic Games* (Chicago, IL: University of Chicago Press, 1981).

8. Roland Barthes, *Mythologies* (New York: Hill and Wang, 1972), 11.

9. James S. Duncan and Nancy G. Duncan, "Ideology and Bliss: Roland Barthes and the Secret Histories of Landscape," *Postmodernism: Disciplinary Texts* 3 (1998): 45.

10. Antonio Gramsci, *Further Selections from the Prison Notebook*, trans. Derek Boothman (Minneapolis: University of Minnesota Press, 1995), 291.

11. Barthes, *Mythologies*, 159.

12. Deconstructionist historians of sport have long warned of the epistemological dangers of relying on archive materials formed, framed, and preserved by major sport organizations and bureaucracies. See Douglas Booth, "Sites of Truth or Metaphors of Power? Refiguring the Archive," *Sport in History* 26, no. 1 (2006): 91–109; Douglas Booth, *The Field: Truth and Fiction in Sports History* (London: Routledge, 2006).

13. The authors share Martin Johnes's methodological opinion that even though our caution in interrogating archives is not always obvious, we understand that archives are not straightforward repositories from which truths can be retrieved. See Martin Johnes, "Archives, Truths and the Historian at Work: A Reply to Douglas Booth's 'Refiguring the Archive,'" *Sport in History* 27, no. 1 (2007): 127–35.

14. Eric Hobsbawm and Terence Ranger, *The Invention of Tradition* (Cambridge: Cambridge University Press, 1983).

15. Examples of Olympic-themed scholarship are far too many to cite. In sport history alone, two academic journals are dedicated exclusively to the history of the Olympic Games. See *Olympika: International Journal of Olympic Studies* and the *Journal of Olympic History*.

16. There is an outdated and historically problematic exception to this claim. See Eugene A. Glader, *Amateurism and Athletics* (West Point, NY: Leisure Press, 1978). Admittedly, historians have long examined the social origins of amateurism within Victorian Britain. For example, see Norman Baker, "Whose Hegemony? The Origins of the Amateur Ethos in Nineteenth Century English Society," *Sport in History* 24, no: 1 (2004): 1–16; Richard Holt, "Amateurism and Its Interpretation: The Social Origins of British Sport," *Innovation in Social Science Research* 5, no. 4 (1992): 19–31. David Young also wrote a monograph exposing the myth of ancient Greek amateurism. See David Young, *The Olympic Myth of Greek Amateur Athletics* (Chicago, IL: Ares, 1984).

17. Richard Holt, a doyen of sport historians, has long bemoaned the absence of a comprehensive book monograph dedicated exclusively to the subject of amateurism. See Holt, "Amateurism and Its Interpretation," 19–31.

18. Richard Holt, "The Amateur Body and the Middle-Class Man: Work, Health and Style in Victorian Britain," *Sport in History* 26, no. 3 (December 2006): 352–69.

Chapter 1. *The Anatomy of Olympic Amateurism*

1. "Le Congrès de Paris," *Revue Olympique* 1 (July 1896): 1–4. For a contextualized overview, see Raymond Gafner, *The International Olympic Committee, One Hundred Years: The Idea, the Presidents, the Achievements, 1894–1994*, vol. 1 (Lausanne, Switzerland: International Olympic Committee, 1994), 52–55.

2. David Young, "Demetrius Vikelas: First President of the IOC," *Stadion* 14 (1988): 85–102.

3. George Eisen, "The 'Budapest Option': The Hungarian Alternative to the First Modern Olympic Games," *International Journal of the History of Sport* 8 (1991): 124–32.

4. For an excellent biography of Coubertin, see John J. MacAloon, *This Great Symbol: Pierre de Coubertin and the Origins of the Modern Olympic Games* (Chicago, IL: University of Chicago Press, 1981).

5. John Hoberman, *The Olympic Crisis: Sports, Politics and the Moral Order* (New York: Aristide D. Caratzas, 1986), 33–42.

6. Thomas Hughes, *Tom Brown's School Days*, rev. ed. (Oxford: Oxford University Press, 1999).

7. MacAloon, *This Great Symbol*, 63–64.

8. Academic histories on the British Empire abound. For some contemporary examples, see Piers Brendon, *The Decline and Fall of the British Empire, 1781–1997* (London: Alfred A. Knopf, 2008); Lawrence James, *The Rise and Fall of the British Empire* (New York: St. Martin's Press, 1997); and Niall Ferguson, *Empire: The Rise and Demise of the British World Order and the Lessons for Global Power* (New York: Basic Books, 2004).

9. Allen Guttmann, *The Olympics: A History of the Modern Games*, 2nd ed. (Champaign: University of Illinois Press, 2002), 10.

10. For pre-Coubertinian Olympic festivals, see Martin Polley, *The British Olympics: British Olympic Heritage 1612–2012* (London: English Heritage, 2011); Joachim K. Rühl, "Olympic Games before Coubertin," In *Encyclopedia of the Modern Olympic Movement*, edited by John E. Findling and Kimberly D. Pelle, 3–16 (Westport, CT: Greenwood Press, 2004).

11. David C. Young, *The Modern Olympics: A Struggle for Revival* (Baltimore: Johns Hopkins University Press, 1996), especially 68–80. Young claims that William Penny Brookes was the driving force behind Pierre de Coubertin's Olympic revival ambitions. Young argues that prior to Coubertin's interactions with Brookes, the baron had never even conceived of reviving the Olympics.

12. Hoberman, *Olympic Crisis*, 134.

13. Dikaia Chatziefstathiou and Ian Henry, *Discourses of Olympism: From Sorbonne 1894 to London 2012* (Hampshire, U.K.: Palgrave Macmillan, 2012).

14. John Hoberman, "Toward a Theory of Olympic Internationalism," *Journal of Sport History* 22 (Spring 1995): 1–37.

15. A vast body of critical scholarship exists addressing the exclusionary nature of the modern Olympic Movement. For some excellent contemporary examples, see Helen Lenskyj, *Gender Politics and the Olympic Industry* (Hampshire, U.K.: Palgrave Macmillan, 2012); Gyozo Molnar and Alan Bairner, *The Politics of the Olympics: A Survey* (London: Routledge, 2010).

16. Gafner, *International Olympic Committee*, 54.

17. David Young, *The Olympic Myth of Greek Amateur Athletics* (Chicago, IL: Ares, 1984).

18. Lincoln Allison, *Amateurism in Sport: An Analysis and a Defence* (London: Frank Cass, 2001), 3.

19. Norman Baker, "Whose Hegemony? The Origins of the Amateur Ethos in Nineteenth Century English Society," *Sport in History* 24, no. 1 (2004): 1–16; Richard Gruneau, "Amateurism as a Sociological Problem: Some Reflections Inspired by Eric Dunning," *Sport in Society* 9, no. 4 (2006): 559–82; Richard Holt, "Amateurism and Its Interpretation:

The Social Origins of British Sport," *Innovation in Social Science Research* 5, no. 4 (1992): 19–31.

20. Mike Huggins, *Victorians and Sport* (London: Hambledon Continuum, 2004).

21. Wray Vamplew, *Play Up and Play the Game: Professional Sport in Britain, 1875–1914* (Cambridge: Cambridge University Press, 1988).

22. Christiane Eisenberg, "Playing the Market Game: Cash Prizes, Symbolic Awards and the Professional Ideal in British Amateur Sport," *Sport in History* 31, no. 2 (2011): 197–217.

23. Jack Williams, "'The *Really* Good Professional Has *Never* Been Seen!': Perceptions of the Amateur/Professional Divide in County Cricket, 1900–39," *Sport in History* 26, no. 3 (December 2006): 429–49.

24. Wray Vamplew, "Playing with the Rules: Influences on the Development of Regulation in Sport," *International Journal of the History of Sport* 24, no. 7 (2007): 843–71; Allen Guttmann, *From Ritual to Record: The Nature of Modern Sports*, 2nd ed. (New York: Columbia University Press, 2004).

25. Vamplew, *Play Up*, 33–44.

26. Ibid., 51–72; Tony Collins, *Rugby's Great Split: Class, Culture and the Origins of Rugby League Football*, 2nd ed. (London: Routledge, 2006), 23–51.

27. Collins, *Rugby's Great Split*, 31–32.

28. J. A. Mangan, *The Games Ethic and Imperialism: Aspect of the Diffusion of an Ideal* (London: Frank Cass, 1998).

29. Mike Huggins and J. A. Mangan, eds., *Disreputable Pleasures: Less Virtuous Victorians at Play* (London: Routledge, 2004).

30. Tony Collins, "Violence, Gamesmanship and the Amateur Ideal in Victorian Middle-Class Rugby," in *Disreputable Pleasures: Less Virtuous Victorians at Play*, ed. Mike Huggins and J.A. Mangan (London: Routledge, 2004): 172–84.

31. Collins, *Rugby's Great Split*, 32–41. For horse racing, see Mike Huggins, *Flat Racing and British Society, 1790–1914: A Social and Economic History* (London: Routledge, 1999).

32. David Cannadine, *The Rise and Fall of Class in Britain* (New York: Columbia University Press, 1999).

33. For the classic social history of the emergence of the working class in Victorian Britain, see E. P. Thompson, *The Making of the English Working Class* (New York: Vintage Books, 1966).

34. Tony Collins, *A Social History of English Rugby Union* (London: Routledge, 2009), 30; Ross McKibbin, *The Ideologies of Class: Social Relations in Britain, 1880–1950* (Oxford: Oxford University Press, 1990).

35. For more on middle-class fears of class revolt and social disorder, see E. H. H. Green, *The Crisis of Conservatism: The Politics, Economics and Ideology of the Conservative Party, 1880–1914* (London: Routledge, 1996); Franz Coetzee, *For Party or Country: Nationalism and the Dilemmas of Popular Conservatism in Edwardian England* (Oxford: Oxford University Press, 1990); and Rhodri Williams, *Defending the Empire: The Conservative Party and the British Defence Policy, 1899–1915* (New Haven, CT: Yale University Press, 1991).

36. Holt, "Amateurism," 19–22.

37. Peter Lovesey, *The Official Centenary History of the Amateur Athletic Association* (Enfield, U.K.: Guinness Superlatives, 1979), 19–23.

38. Martin Crotty, "'Separate and Distinct'? The Manual Labour Distinction in Nineteenth Century Victorian Rowing," *International Journal of the History of Sport* 15, no. 2 (1998): 152–63.

39. Collins, *Rugby's Great Split*, 43.

40. C. Love, "Social Class and the Swimming World: Amateurs and Professionals," *International Journal of the History of Sport* 24, no. 5 (May 2007): 603–19.

41. Collins, *Rugby's Great Split*, 48–51. For a classic account of the professionalization of association football, see Tony Mason, *Association Football and English Society, 1863–1915* (Brighton, U.K.: Branch Line, 1982).

42. Mike Huggins, "More Sinful Pleasures? Leisure, Respectability and the Male Middle Classes in Victorian England," *Journal of Social History* 33, no. 3 (Spring 2000): 585–600.

43. Vamplew, *Play Up*, 44–47.

44. Baker, "Whose Hegemony?" 1–16.

45. Richard Holt, "The Amateur Body and the Middle-Class Man: Work, Health and Style in Victorian Britain," *Sport in History* 26, no. 3 (December 2006): 352–69.

46. Ibid., 360.

47. Ibid., 363.

48. Neil Carter, "From Knox to Dyson: Coaching, Amateurism and British Athletics, 1912–1947," *Sport in History* 30, no. 1 (March 2010): 55–81; Martin Polley, "'The Amateur Rules': Amateurism and Professionalism in Post-War British Athletics," in *Amateurs and Professionals in Post-War British Sport*, edited by Adrian Smith and Dilwyn Porter (London: Frank Cass, 2000), 81–114.

49. Holt, "Amateur Body," 363–66. On amateur playing styles in tennis and cricket, see Robert Lake, "Stigmatized, Marginalized, Celebrated: Developments in Lawn Tennis Coaching, 1870–1939," *Sport in History* 30, no. 1 (March 2010): 82–103; and Richard Holt, "Cricket and Englishness: The Batsman as Hero," *International Journal of the History of Sport* 13, no. 1 (March 1996): 48–70.

50. John Hargreaves, *Sport, Power, and Culture: A Social and Historical Analysis of Popular Sports in Britain* (London: Palgrave Macmillan, 1986).

51. Eric Dunning and Kenneth Sheard, *Barbarians, Gentlemen and Players: A Sociological Study of the Development of Rugby Football*, 2nd ed. (London: Routledge, 2005).

52. For these outdated and more simplistic perspectives, see Johan Huizinga, *Homo Ludens: A Study of the Play Element in Culture* (Boston: Beacon Press, 1955), notably 195–213; and Gregory P. Stone, "American Sports: Play and Dis-Play," *Chicago Review* 9, no. 3 (1955): 83–100.

53. For a broad examination of Britain's role in the diffusion of modern sport, see Allen Guttmann, *Games and Empires: Modern Sports and Cultural Imperialism* (New York: Columbia University Press, 1994); Maarten Van Bottenburg, *Global Games* (Urbana: University of Illinois Press, 2001).

54. This claim runs contrary to the thesis proposed by historian Steve W. Pope; see Pope, "Amateurism and American Sports Culture: The Invention of an Athletic Tradition in the United States," *International Journal of the History of Sport* 13, no. 3 (1996): 290–309; Pope, *Patriotic Games: Sporting Traditions in the American Imagination, 1876–1926* (Oxford: Oxford University Press, 1997).

55. Ronald A. Smith has forcefully revealed the true extent of "shamateurism" afflicting late-nineteenth- and early-twentieth-century U.S. collegiate athletics; see Smith, *Sports*

and Freedom: The Rise of Big-Time College Athletics (Oxford: Oxford University Press, 1988); for track and field, see Joseph M. Turrini, *The End of Amateurism in American Track and Field* (Urbana: University of Illinois Press, 2010).

56. Tony Mason, *Passion of the People? Football in South America* (London: Verso, 1994); Allison, *Amateurism in Sport,* 18.

57. Dikaia Chatziefstathiou and Ian Henry, "Hellenism and Olympism: Pierre de Coubertin and the Greek Challenge to the Early Olympic Movement," *Sport in History* 27, no. 1 (2007): 25.

58. For an impassioned philosophical defense of amateurism, see Allison, *Amateurism in Sport.*

59. Robert J. Paddick, "Amateurism: An Idea of the Past or a Necessity for the Future?" *Olympika* 3 (1994): 1–15; Gruneau, "Amateurism as a Sociological Problem," 575–78.

60. Hoberman, *Olympic Crisis,* 35.

61. MacAloon, *This Great Symbol,* 72–74; Stephen Wassong, *Pierre de Coubertin's American Studies and Their Importance for the Analysis of His Early Educational Campaign* (Würzberg, Germany: Ergon Verlag, 2002), 32–42; Gafner, *International Olympic Committee,* 40–45.

62. Hoberman, *Olympic Crisis,* 34.

63. Pierre de Coubertin, *Olympism: Selected Writings* (Lausanne, Switzerland: International Olympic Committee, 1997), 298–99.

64. Pierre de Coubertin, *Olympic Memoirs,* rev. ed. (Lausanne, Switzerland: International Olympic Committee, 1997), 14–16.

65. Ibid., 16–17 and 21.

66. Ibid., 115.

67. As cited in Guy-Lionel Loew, "Amateurism and the Olympic Movement: The Stakes of the Definition of Amateurism under the Light of the Case of Karl Schranz; 1972 Winter Games Sapporo, Japan," *Journal of Olympic History* 13 (January 2005): 25.

68. Eric Hobsbawm and Terrance Ranger, eds., *The Invention of Tradition* (Cambridge: Cambridge University Press, 1983). Quoted phrase appears on p. 2.

69. Chatziefstathiou and Henry, "Hellenism and Olympism," 24–43.

70. Young, *Olympic Myth.*

71. Wassong, *Coubertin's American Studies,* 30.

72. MacAloon, *This Great Symbol,* 64.

73. Hughes, *Tom Brown's School Days.* For a detailed examination of the philosophy of Olympism, see Chatziefstathiou and Henry, *Discourses of Olympism.*

74. Jim Parry, "Sport and Olympism: Universals and Multiculturalism," *Journal of the Philosophy of Sport* 33, no. 2 (2006): 188–204 (quote, 190); Mike McNamee, "Olympism, Eurocentrism, and Transcultural Virtues," *Journal of the Philosophy of Sport* 33, no. 2 (2006): 174–87.

75. As cited in Arnd Krüger, "The Origins of Pierre de Coubertin's *Religio Athletae,*" *Olympika* 2 (1993): 91.

76. Joseph Maguire, *Global Sport: Identities, Societies, Civilizations* (Cambridge, U.K.: Polity, 1999).

77. Maurice Roche, *Mega-Events and Modernity: Olympics and Expos in the Growth of Global Culture* (London: Routledge, 2000).

78. Even Coubertin heralded the games as a "great innovation for the time." See Coubertin, *Olympic Memoirs*, 46.

79. Karl Lennartz and Stephen Wassong, "Athens 1896," in *Encyclopaedia of the Modern Olympic Movement*, 17–26, ed. John E. Findling and Kimberly D. Pelle (Westport, CT: Greenwood Press, 2004).

80. Bill Mallon and Ture Widlund, *The 1896 Olympic Games: Results for All Competitors in All Events, with Commentary* (Jefferson, NC: McFarland, 1997); Richard D. Mandell, *The First Modern Olympics* (Berkeley: University of California Press, 1976).

81. Gafner, *International Olympic Committee*, 118.

82. International Athletic Congress of Paris, "Commission on Amateurism," Commission d'Amateurisme, 204768 (1894–1971), IOC Archives.

83. Ibid.

84. Ibid.

85. Lennartz and Wassong, "Athens 1896," 17–26.

86. Ibid., 23; Young, *Modern Olympics*, 153.

87. Guttmann, *The Olympics*, 21–22.

88. Coubertin, *Olympic Memoirs*, 69.

89. Reverend Robert S. de Courcy Laffan to Pierre de Coubertin, 28 December 1902, MBR-COURCY-CORR, 0056930 (1902–1929), IOC Archives.

90. "New Olympic Games," *National Observer* 15, no. 385 (April 1896): 613. For early British criticisms, see Matthew P. Llewellyn, *Rule Britannia: Nationalism, Identity and the Modern Olympic Games* (London: Routledge, 2012).

91. Gruneau, "Amateurism as a Sociological Problem," 573.

92. Guttmann, *The Olympics*, 22.

93. "The Paris International Meeting," *The Field*, 21 July 1900, 155; "Paris International Championship," *London Daily Telegraph*, 17 July 1900, 7; "Swimming," *The Times of London*, 11 August 1900, 5.

94. Guttmann, *The Olympics*, 20–24.

95. André Drevon, "Paris 1900," in *Encyclopedia of the Modern Olympic Movement*, 27–32, ed. John E. Findling and Kimberly D. Pelle (Westport, CT: Greenwood Press, 2004).

96. "The Controversial Questions! The Games of the Second Olympiad in Paris 1900," *Journal of Olympic History* (Special Issue, December 2008): 2–91.

97. Historian Bill Mallon has marginalized the status of these events by applying modern standards of interpretation. Such an approach is deeply flawed and ahistorical. If we discredit specific events because they fall outside modern conceptions of what constitutes an Olympic event, then we must also reduce the entire 1900 Paris Games to non-Olympic status. See Bill Mallon, *The 1900 Olympic Games: Results for All Competitors in All Events, with Commentary* (Jefferson, NC: McFarland, 1998). For a contemporary analysis supporting the legitimacy of these events, see "The Controversial Questions," 6.

98. Mallon, *1900 Olympic Games*.

99. Robert K. Barney, "Born from Dilemma: America Awakens to the Modern Olympic Games, 1901–1903," *Olympika* 1 (1992): 92–135. Barney contends that the transfer of the 1904 Olympics had to do with Henry Fuber's unwillingness to stand up to St. Louis authorities, who threatened to overshadow his Olympic event in Chicago with their plans for the Louisiana Purchase Exposition.

100. Mark Dyreson, *Making the American Team: Sport, Culture, and the Olympic Experience* (Urbana: University of Illinois Press, 1998), 73–77.

101. Susan Brownell, *The 1904 Anthropology Days and Olympic Games: Sport, Race, and American Imperialism* (Lincoln: University of Nebraska Press, 2008); Dyreson, *Making the American Team*.

102. C. Robert Barnett, "St. Louis 1904," in *Encyclopaedia of the Modern Olympic Movement*, ed. John E. Findling and Kimberly D. Pelle (Westport, CT: Greenwood Press, 2004), 33–40.

103. "Gold Watch for Hicks," *Boston Daily Globe*, 16 September 1904, 4.

104. "Questionnaire," *Revue Olympique* 8 (April 1902): 4.

105. Coubertin, *Olympic Memoirs*, 115.

106. Congress of the International Olympic Committee, Brussels 1905, 7, IOC Archives.

107. For a far more specific and detailed discussion of this entire episode, see Karl Lennartz, "The 2nd International Olympic Games in Athens 1906," *Journal of Olympic History* (March 2002): 3–25.

108. For an excellent examination of the 1906 Intercalated Games, see Alexander Kitroeff, *Wrestling with the Ancients: Modern Greek Identity and the Olympics* (New York: Greekworks, 2004).

Chapter 2. A Universal Dilemma

1. As cited in International Olympic Committee, "Amateurism and Professionalism—The Olympic Games" [pamphlet], International Olympic Committee Archives, Lausanne, Switzerland (hereafter cited as IOC Archives).

2. For a scholarly discussion of the social origins of amateurism, see Norman Baker, "Whose Hegemony? The Origins of the Amateur Ethos in Nineteenth Century English Society," *Sport in History* 24, no. 1 (2004): 1–16; Richard Holt, "Amateurism and Its Interpretation: The Social Origins of British Sport," *Innovation in Social Science Research* 5, no. 4 (1992): 19–31.

3. For a detailed list of early-twentieth-century English amateur codes, see Theodore Andrea Cook, *The Fourth Olympiad: Being the Official Report of the Olympic Games of 1908 Celebrated in London under the Patronage of His Most Gracious Majesty King Edward VII* (London: International Olympic Committee, 1908), 763–71; Amateur Athletic Federation Los Angeles (LA84), Los Angeles, CA, http://library.la84.org/6oic/OfficialReports/1908/1908.pdf.

4. The English Rugby Football Union (RFU) never had a definition of an amateur; they simply defined who was a "professional." Still, the RFU evidently had a very clear sense of what constituted an amateur, as the "broken-time" issue and the development of Northern Rugby League demonstrates.

5. Robert J. Paddick, "Amateurism: An Idea of the Past or a Necessity for the Future?" *Olympika* 3 (1994): 1–15.

6. J. A. Maguire, *Global Sport: Identities, Societies, Civilizations* (Cambridge, U.K.: Polity Press, 1999).

7. This theory was first raised by Murray G. Philips, "Diminishing Contrast and Increasing Varieties: Globalization Theory and 'Reading' Amateurism in Australian Sport," *Sporting Traditions* 18, no. 1 (2001): 19–32.

8. Matthew P. Llewellyn, *Rule Britannia: Nationalism, Identity and the Modern Olympic Games* (London: Routledge, 2011); and Llewellyn, "Rule Britannia—Nationalism, Identity and the Modern Olympic Games," Special Issue, *International Journal of the History of Sport* 28, no. 5 (2011): 639–841.

9. Matthew P. Llewellyn, "The British Olympics," *International Journal of the History of Sport* 28, no. 5 (April 2011): 683–701.

10. Amateur Athletic Association, General Committee Minutes, 2 February 1907, AAA/1/2/2/4; British Olympic Association, Council Minutes, 24 October 1907, British Olympic Foundation Archives, 60 Charlotte Street, London W1T2NU, U.K.

11. Theodore Andrea Cook, *International Sport: A Short History of the Olympic Movement from 1896 to the Present Day, Containing the Account of a Visit to Athens in 1906, and of the Olympic Games of 1908 in London, Together with the Code of Rules for Twenty Different Forms of Sport and Numerous Illustrations* (London: Archibald Constable, 1909).

12. Cook, *Fourth Olympiad*, 761.

13. "The Games: Athletes of the World to Gather in July," *London Daily News*, 11 May 1908, Lord Desborough Press Cuttings, Hertfordshire Archives and Local Studies, Register Office Block, County Hall, Pegs Lane, Hertford, SG13 8EJ, England, DE/Rv/F25.

14. Cook, *Fourth Olympiad*, 527.

15. Ibid., 624.

16. Ibid., 764.

17. Ibid., 768.

18. Ibid., 767–68.

19. Ibid., 763.

20. Ibid., 763–71.

21. For French and Belgian amateur codes, see ibid., 763–71.

22. Mark Dyreson, "'To Construct a Better and More Peaceful World' or 'War minus the Shooting'? The Olympic Movement's Second Century," in *Onward to the Olympics: Historical Perspectives on the Olympic Games*, ed. Gerald P. Schaus and Stephen R. Wenn (Waterloo, ON, Canada: Wilfrid Laurier University Press, 2007), 337–51.

23. Bruce Kidd, *Tom Longboat* (Markham, ON, Canada: Fitzhenry and Whiteside, 2004); Jack Battan, *The Man Who Ran Faster Than Everyone: The Story of Tom Longboat* (Toronto: Tundra, 2002).

24. British Olympic Association, General Council Minutes, 15 July 1908, BOF Archives.

25. "The Attempt to Bar Out Longboat Analyzed by James G. Merrick," *Montreal Daily Star*, 9 July 1908, 1.

26. Minutes of the 25th Annual Meeting of the Canadian Amateur Athletic Union, Toronto, 9 November 1908, Amateur Athletic Union of Canada folder, M3209, Library and Archives, Ottawa, ON, Canada.

27. Ibid.

28. Anonymous, "The Olympic Games: An Answer to Mr. Francis Peabody, Jr., and 'A Member of the British Olympic Committee,' by a Member of the American Olympic Committee," n.p., 1908, 18, CIO MA 910, IOC Archives.

29. Sigfrid Edström to Members of the International Olympic Committee, 7 April 1932, Commission d'Amateurisme (1933–1934), ID Chemise: 204758, IOC Archives.

30. Matthew P. Llewellyn, "The Battle of Shepherds Bush," *International Journal of the History of Sport* 28, no. 5 (April 2011): 702–23; Matthew McIntire, "National Status, the 1908 Olympic Games and the English Press," *Media History* 15 (August 2009): 271–86.

31. American and British charges and countercharges were thoroughly documented in competing publications, for example, Anonymous, "The Olympic Games: An Answer to Mr. Francis Peabody, Jr., and 'A Member of the British Olympic Committee,' by a Member of the American Olympic Committee," n.p., 1908, CIO MA 910, IOC Archives; Theodore Andrea Cook, "The Olympic Games of 1908 in London: A Reply to Certain Criticisms Made by Some of the American Officials," London, U.K.: British Olympic Association, 1908, BOF Archives.

32. Casper Whitney, "The View-Point: Olympic Games American Committee Report," *Outing* 53 (November 1908): 244–49; Anonymous, "The Olympic Games: An Answer."

33. Mark Dyreson, *Making the American Team: Sport, Culture, and the Olympic Experience* (Urbana: University of Illinois Press, 1998); S. W. Pope, *Patriotic Games: Sporting Traditions in the American Imagination, 1876–1926* (Oxford: Oxford University Press, 1997).

34. Roberta J. Park, "Athletes and Their Training in Britain and America, 1800–1914," in *Sport and Exercise Science: Essays in the History of Sports Medicine*, ed. Jack W. Berryman and Roberta J. Park (Urbana: University of Illinois Press, 1992), 57–108.

35. Pope, *Patriotic Games*, 46.

36. Mark Dyreson, *Crafting Patriotism for Global Dominance: America at the Olympics* (London: Routledge, 2010), esp. chapter four.

37. Photocopied clipping, "Amateurism: An Attempt at Standardisation," *Sporting Life*, 16 October 1908 (hereafter cited as SL Amateur Definition), Avery Brundage Collection, University of Illinois Archives, Urbana, IL (hereafter cited as Brundage Archives), box 11, "Amateurism," folder "Amateur for Olympic Games, Definition of an: Sporting Life." *Sporting Life* ran a series of articles on the topic with the same title during 1908 and 1909, all of which are in the Brundage Archives in box 11, "Amateurism," folder "Amateur for Olympic Games, Definition of an: Sporting Life." The folder contains copies of the articles collated by *Sporting Life* as the document "The Definition of an Amateur for Olympic Games: An Inquiry into the Question of a Standard Definition, or Definitions, of an Amateur for Olympic Purposes, Conducted by the Editor of the 'Sporting Life' and Presented to Members of the International Olympic Committee with a Respectful Request to Consider the Matter" and presented to the IOC.

38. Matthew P. Llewellyn, "'Viva l'Italia! Viva l'Italia!' Dorando Pietri and the North American Professional Marathon Craze, 1908–1910," *International Journal of the History of Sport* 25 (May 2008): 710–36.

39. SL Amateur Definition, 6 January 1909, Brundage Archives.

40. SL Amateur Definition, 23 October 1908, Brundage Archives.

41. For more on the divide between the English Amateur Rowing Association and the National Amateur Rowing Association, see Eric Halladay, *Rowing in England: A Social History* (Manchester, U.K.: Manchester University Press, 1990); Stephen Wagg, "'Base Mechanic Arms'? British Rowing, Some Ducks and the Shifting Politics of Amateurism," *Sport in History* 26, no. 3 (December 2006): 520–39.

42. For more on divide between the FA and AFA, see Dilwyn Porter, "Revenge of the Crouch End Vampires: The AFA, the FA and English Football's 'Great Split,' 1907–14," *Sport in History* 26, no. 3 (December 2006): 406–28.

43. SL Amateur Definition, 23 October 1908, Brundage Archives.

44. SL Amateur Definition, 18 November 1908, Brundage Archives.

45. SL Amateur Definition, 24 January 1909, Brundage Archives.

46. E. H. H. Green, *The Crisis of Conservatism: The Politics, Economics and Ideology of the Conservative Party, 1880–1914* (London: Routledge, 1996); David Cannadine, *The Decline and Fall of the British Aristocracy* (New Haven, CT: Yale University Press, 1990); Franz Coetzee, *For Party or Country: Nationalism and the Dilemmas of Popular Conservatism in Edwardian England* (Oxford: Oxford University Press, 1990); Matthew Forde, *Conservatism and Collectivism, 1886–1914* (Edinburgh, U.K.: Edinburgh University Press, 1990).

47. SL Amateur Definition, 30 October 1908, Brundage Archives.

48. Peter Jorgensen, "'Order, Discipline and Self-Control': The Breakthrough for the Danish Sports Federation and Sport, 1896–1918," *International Journal of the History of Sport* 13, no. 3 (1996): 340–55.

49. "What Is an Amateur? The World's Definitions," *Sporting Life*, 26 January 1909, SL Amateur Definition, Brundage Archives.

50. Mr. Will (managing editor of *Sporting Life*) to Pierre de Coubertin, 27 April 1909, Commission d'Amateurisme: Correspondence (1894–1968), ID Chemise: 204767, IOC Archives.

51. Raymond Gafner, *The International Olympic Committee, One Hundred Years: The Idea, the Presidents, the Achievements, 1894–1994,* vol. 1 (Lausanne, Switzerland: International Olympic Committee, 1994), 117–18.

52. SL Amateur Definition, 28 November 1908, Brundage Archives.

53. "Rapport sur la Question de l'Amateurisme," *Révue Olympique* 45 (September 1909): 115–18; "L' Enquête sur l'Amateurisme," *Révue Olympique* 42 (June 1909): 90–91.

54. Commission d'Amateurisme: *Questionnaires sur l'Amateurisme* (1909–1926), ID Chemise: 204769, IOC Archives.

55. For a full, detailed report of the IOC's findings, see IOC Annual Meeting Minutes, 11–13 June 1910, Luxembourg, 32–38, IOC Archives. Also see Captain Johan Sverre to Pierre de Coubertin, 26 April 1910; Federazione Atletica Italiana to Jules de Musza, 17 December 1909; Sports-Club d'Alexandrie to Jules de Musza, 10 January 1910; Fédération Belge de Gymnastique to Jules de Musza, 4 January 1910; Nederlandsch Amateur-Schermbond to Jules de Musza, 2 January 1910; Nederlandsch Gymnastiek to Jules de Musza, 3 March 1910; Association Suisse de Football to Jules de Musza, 19 February 1910; Dansk Idraets-Forbund to Theodore Andrea Cook, 19 February 1910; Fédération Suisse de Natation to Jules de Musza, 10 November 1909, Commission d'Amateurisme: *Questionnaires sur l'Amateurisme* (1909–1926), ID Chemise: 204769, IOC Archives.

56. For more on Cook, see Matthew P. Llewellyn, "Advocate or Antagonist? Sir Theodore Andrea Cook and the British Olympic Movement," *Sport in History* 32, no. 2 (June 2012): 183–203. On British Olympic apathy, see Llewellyn, *Rule Britannia*.

57. Pierre de Coubertin, *Olympic Memoirs*, rev. ed. (Lausanne, Switzerland: International Olympic Committee, 1997), 120.

58. IOC Annual Meeting Minutes, 11–13 June 1910, Luxembourg, 32–38, IOC Archives.

59. Coubertin, *Olympic Memoirs*, 120.

60. IOC Annual Meeting Minutes, 11–13 June 1910, Luxembourg, 32–38, IOC Archives.

61. Sports-Club d'Alexandrie to Jules de Musza, 10 January 1910, Commission d'Amateurisme: *Questionnaires sur l'Amateurisme* (1909–1926), ID Chemise: 204769, IOC Archives.

62. Captain Johan Sverre to Pierre de Coubertin, 26 April 1910, Commission d'Amateurisme: *Questionnaires sur l'Amateurisme* (1909–1926), ID Chemise: 204769, IOC Archives.

63. Federazione Atletica Italiana to Jules de Musza, 17 December 1909, Commission d'Amateurisme: *Questionnaires sur l'Amateurisme* (1909–1926), ID Chemise: 204769, IOC Archives.

64. IOC Annual Meeting Minutes, 11–13 June 1910, Luxembourg, 32–38, IOC Archives.

65. Association Suisse de Football to Jules de Musza, 19 February 1910, Commission d'Amateurisme: *Questionnaires sur l'Amateurisme* (1909–1926), ID Chemise: 204769, IOC Archives.

66. Sports-Club d'Alexandrie to Jules de Musza, 10 January 1910, Commission d'Amateurisme: *Questionnaires sur l'Amateurisme* (1909–1926), ID Chemise: 204769, IOC Archives.

67. IOC Annual Meeting Minutes, 11–13 June 1910, Luxembourg, 32–38, IOC Archives.

68. Ibid., 32–33.

69. Dyreson, *Making the American Team*, 128–29.

70. IOC Annual Meeting Minutes, 11–13 June 1910, Luxembourg, 33, IOC Archives.

71. Barbara Keys, *Globalizing Sport: National Rivalry and International Community in the 1930s* (Cambridge, MA: Harvard University Press, 2006), 40–62; Pierre Arnaud and James Riordan, *Sport and International Politics: The Impact of Fascism and Communism on Sport* (London: E. and F. N. Spon, 1998), 14–30.

72. George W. Hearn, International Amateur Swimming Federation, to Pierre de Coubertin, 1 September 1909, Commission d'Amateurisme: *Questionnaires sur l'Amateurisme* (1909–1926), ID Chemise: 204769, IOC Archives.

73. George W. Hearn, International Amateur Swimming Federation, to Pierre de Coubertin, 14 September 1909, Commission d'Amateurisme: *Questionnaires sur l'Amateurisme* (1909–1926), ID Chemise: 204769, IOC Archives; Mr. Will (managing editor of *Sporting Life*) to Pierre de Coubertin, 3 August 1909, Commission d'Amateurisme: Correspondence (1894–1968), ID Chemise: 204767, IOC Archives.

74. Keys, *Globalizing Sport*, 40–63.

75. Coubertin, *Olympic Memoirs*, 115–21.

76. Robert S. de Courcy Laffan to Pierre de Coubertin, 23 December 1912, IOC Archives, Grande-Bretagne Correspondence (1892–1923), OU MO 01 14 36.

77. British Olympic Association, General Council Minutes, 2 August 1908, BOF Archives.

78. For an excellent biography of Jim Thorpe, see Bill Crawford, *All-American: The Rise and Fall of Jim Thorpe* (Hoboken, NJ: John Wiley and Sons, 2005).

79. John Lucas, "Early Olympic Antagonists: Pierre de Coubertin versus James E. Sullivan," *Stadion* 3 (1977): 261–68.

80. "The Thorpe Case Shifts to New York," *New York Times*, 27 January 1913, 10.

81. James Thorpe to James E. Sullivan, 26 January 1913, "Jim Thorpe, 1912–1913, 1948," OU MO 01 14 36, IOC Archives.

82. Gustavus T. Kirby, James E. Sullivan, and Bartow S. Weeks, "Statement by the Amateur Athletic Union of the United States in Regard to Jim Thorpe," to Kristian Hellström, 27 January 1913, "Jim Thorpe, 1912–1913, 1948," OU MO 01 14 36, IOC Archives.

83. Dyreson, *Making the American Team*.

84. Erik Bergvall, *The Fifth Olympiad. The Official Report of the Olympic Games of Stockholm 1912* (Stockholm: Wahlström and Widstrand, 1913), 95–98.

85. "Encore l'Affaire Thorpe," *Revue Olympique* (April 1913): 58–59.

86. Ibid.

87. "Solutions Diverses," *Revue Olympique* (November 1913): 179–80.

88. Ibid.

89. Gordon MacDonald, "A History of Relations between the International Olympic Committee and the International Sports Federations, 1891–1968," unpublished PhD diss., University of Western Ontario, London, ON, Canada, 1998, 29.

90. "American Olympic Fund Is Started," *New York Times*, 20 January 1914, 7.

91. "The Athletic Epidemic Spreads in Europe," *Current Opinion* 55 (1913): 310. Also see Arnd Krüger, "'Buying Victories Is Positively Degrading': European Origins of Government Pursuit of National Prestige through Sport," in *Tribal Identities: Nationalism, Europe, Sport*, ed. J. A. Mangan (London: Frank Cass, 1996), 191.

92. "Athletic Epidemic," 310.

93. "$100,000 for Olympic Fund," *New York Times*, 25 April 1914, 16.

94. Matthew P. Llewellyn, "Dominion Nationalism or Imperial Patriotism? Citizenship, Race, and the Proposed British Empire Olympic Team," *Journal of Sport History* 39, no. 1 (Spring 2012): 45–62; Matthew P. Llewellyn, "A Nation Divided: Great Britain and the Pursuit of Olympic Excellence 1912–1914," *Journal of Sport History* 35, no. 1 (Spring 2008): 73–97.

95. Benedict R. Anderson, *Imagined Communities: Reflections on the Origin and Spread of Nationalism* (London: Verso, 1983); Eric Hobsbawm, *Nations and Nationalism since 1780: Programme, Myth, Reality* (Cambridge, U.K.: Canto, 1991).

96. "Nouveaux Aspects du Problème," *Revue Olympique* (November 1913): 178–79.

97. "La Question d'Argent," *Revue Olympique* (December 1913): 183–85.

Chapter 3. The Rise of the Shamateur

1. Modris Eksteins, *Rites of Spring: The Great War and the Birth of the Modern Age* (New York: Houghton Mifflin, 1989); Eric Hobsbawm, *The Age of Empire: 1875–1914* (London: Vintage, 1989).

2. Isabel V. Hull, *Absolute Destruction: Military Culture and the Practices of War in Imperial Germany* (Ithaca, NY: Cornell University Press, 2005).

3. John Hoberman, "Toward a Theory of Olympic Internationalism," *Journal of Sport History* 22, no. 1 (Spring 1995): 1–37.

4. Roland Renson, *The VIIth Olympiad Antwerp 1920* (Ghent, Belgium: Pandora-Snoeck-Ducaju and Zoon, Leuven Pandora, 1996).

5. Raymond Gafner, *The International Olympic Committee, One Hundred Years: The Idea, the Presidents, the Achievements, 1894–1994*, vol. 1 (Lausanne, Switzerland: International Olympic Committee, 1994).

6. Adam Gregory, *The Last Great War: British Society and the First World War* (Cambridge: Cambridge University Press, 2008).

7. David Cannadine, *The Decline and Fall of the British Aristocracy* (New Haven, CT: Yale University Press, 1990).

8. Quoted phrase is from Barbara J. Keys, "Spreading Peace, Democracy, and Coca-Cola: Sport and American Cultural Expansion in the 1930s," *Diplomatic History*, 28, no. 2 (April 2004): 165. Also see Barbara J. Keys, "The Internationalization of Sport, 1890–1939," in *The Cultural Turn: Essays in the History of U.S. Foreign Relations*, ed. Frank A. Ninkovich and Liping Bu (Chicago, IL: Imprint, 2001): 201–20.

9. P. F. McDevitt, *May the Best Man Win: Sport, Masculinity, and Nationalism in Great Britain and the Empire, 1880–1935* (New York: Palgrave Macmillan, 2008).

10. Tony Mason and Eliza Riedi, *Sport and the Military: The British Armed Forces, 1880–1960* (Cambridge: Cambridge University Press, 2010); Mike Huggins and Jack Williams, *Sport and the English, 1918–1939* (London: Routledge, 2006).

11. Christopher Young, "When Pierre Met Adolph? The Olympic Games in the Age of Technical Reproduction," paper presented at the Conference on Globalization and Sport in Historical Context, University of California, San Diego, March 2005, 3.

12. For a broad examination of the diffusion of modern sport, see Allen Guttmann, *Games and Empires: Modern Sports and Cultural Imperialism* (New York: Columbia University Press, 1994); Maarten Van Bottenburg, *Global Games* (Urbana: University of Illinois Press, 2001).

13. Barbara J. Keys, *Globalizing Sport: National Rivalry and International Community in the 1930s* (Cambridge, MA: Harvard University Press, 2006), 40–63; Pierre Arnaud, "Sport and International Relations before 1918," in *Sport and International Politics: The Impact of Fascism and Communism on Sport*, ed. Pierre Arnaud and James Riordan (London: E. and F. N. Spon, 1998), 14–30.

14. Federation Internationale de Football Association, *Minutes of the 16th Annual Congress*, Helsinki, 3–5 June 1927, 3, box 102; "International Olympic Committee Subject File," folder "Broken Time—Background Material," Avery Brundage Collection, University of Illinois Archives, Urbana, IL (hereafter, Brundage Archives); Paul Dietschy, "Making Football Global? FIFA, Europe, and the non-European Football World, 1912–74," *Journal of Global History* 8, no. 2 (July 2013): 279–98.

15. Pierre de Coubertin, *Pierre de Coubertin: Textes Choisis*, 4 vols. (Zurich, Switzerland: Weidmann, 1986), 1:394.

16. Cesar Torres, "The Latin American 'Olympic Explosion' of the 1920s: Causes and Consequences," *International Journal of the History of Sport* 23 (November 2006) 1088–1111.

17. Keys, *Globalizing Sport*, 60.

18. Larry Gerlach, ed., *The Winter Olympics: From Chamonix to Salt Lake* (Salt Lake City: University of Utah Press, 2004).

19. Olympic Movement, *Amsterdam 1928* [webpage]. Retrieved from http://www.olympic.org/amsterdam-1928-summer-olympics.

20. G. Van Rossem, *The Ninth Olympiad, Being the Official Report of the Olympic Games of 1928 Celebrated at Amsterdam*, 17–19 (Amsterdam, Holland: International Olympic Committee, 1928), http://library.la84.org/6oic/OfficialReports/1928/1928p1 .pdf. Paul Ziffren Sports Library, Amateur Athletic Federation Los Angeles, Los Angeles, CA.

21. Keys, *Globalizing Sport*, 45–49; Allen Guttmann, *Games and Empires*, 120–40.

22. Florence Carpentier and Jean-Pierre Lefevre, "The Modern Olympic Movement, Women's Sport and the Social Order during the Inter-war Period," *International Journal of the History of Sport* 23, no. 7 (November 2006): 1112–27; Susan J. Bandy, "Politics of Gender through the Olympics: The Changing Nature of Women's Involvement in the Olympics," in *The Politics of the Olympics: A Survey*, ed. Alan Bairner and Gyozo Molnar (London: Routledge, 2010): 41–57.

23. Mary A. Leigh and Thérèse M. Bonin, "The Pioneering Role of Madame Alice Milliat and the FSFI in Establishing International Trade [sic] and Field Competition for Women," *Journal of Sport History* 4 (1977): 76–77.

24. For a broader examination of these issues, see Helen Jefferson Lenskyj, *Gender Politics and the Olympic Industry* (Houndmills, U.K.: Palgrave Macmillan, 2012).

25. Andrew M. Guest, "The Diffusion of Development-through-Sport: Analysing the History and Practice of the Olympic Movement's Grassroots Outreach to Africa," *Sport in Society* 12, no. 10 (December 2009): 1336–52; quote, 1337.

26. Dikaia Chatziefstathiou, Ian Henry, Eleni Theodoraki, and Mansour Al-Tauqi, "Cultural Imperialism and the Diffusion of Olympic Sport in Africa: A Comparison of Pre– and Post–Second World War Contexts," in *Cultural Imperialism in Action, Critiques in the Global Olympic Trust*, ed. Nigel B. Crowther, Robert K. Barney, Michael K. Heine, Cesar R. Torres, and Wanda Ellen Wakefield (London, ON, Canada: International Centre for Olympic Studies, 2006), 283.

27. John Hoberman, "Olympic Universalism and the Apartheid Issue," paper presented at Sport, the Third Millennium Symposium, Quebec City, Canada, 21–25 May 1990.

28. Chatziefstathiou et al., "Cultural Imperialism," 283.

29. Ian Henry and Mansour Al-Tauqi, "The Development of Olympic Solidarity: West and Non-West (Core and Periphery) Relations in the Olympic World," *International Journal of the History of Sport* 25, no. 3 (February 2008): 355–69; quote 359.

30. Glenn Warner, "Statement in Regard to James Thorpe," 1912–1913, 1948, OU MO 01 14 36, IOC Archives.

31. Colin Tatz, *Obstacle Race: Aborigines in Sport* (Sydney, Australia: University of New South Wales Press, 1996), 88.

32. Susan Grant, *Physical Culture and Sport in Soviet Society: Propaganda, Acculturation, and Transformation in the 1920s and 30s* (London: Routledge, 2013); Keys, *Globalizing Sport*, 158–64.

33. Jenifer Parks, "Red Sport, Red Tape: The Olympic Games, the Soviet Sports Bureaucracy, and the Cold War, 1952–1980," PhD diss., University of North Carolina at Chapel Hill, 2009, 23 and 42.

34. For regional examinations of the Workers' Movement, see Stephen Jones, *Sport, Politics and the Working Class: Organised Labour and Sport in Inter-War Britain* (Manchester, U.K.:

Manchester University Press, 1989); Bruce Kidd, "'We Must Maintain a Balance between Propaganda and Serious Athletics'—The Workers' Sport Movement in Canada, 1924–1936," *Sport in Society* 16, no. 4 (2013): 565–77.

35. Robert Wheeler, "Organized Sport and Organized Labor: The Workers' Sports Movement," *Journal of Contemporary History* 13, no. 2 (April 1978): 191–210.

36. "L.F.A. Suspension Exposes Sham Amateurism," *Daily Worker* (U.K.), 4 January 1930, 12.

37. "Awards to Dynamic Puzzle Soccer Big Chiefs," *Daily Worker* (U.K.), 19 December 1925, 4.

38. James Riordan, "The Worker Sports Movement," in *The International Politics of Sport in the 20th Century*," ed. Jim Riordan and Arnd Krüger (London: E. and F. N. Spon, 1999), 105–20. A third Worker's Olympics was scheduled for Barcelona in 1936, but it was canceled because of the outbreak of the Spanish Civil War. It was eventually held in Antwerp in 1937.

39. "Worse Than Ever," *London Daily Express*, 30 August 1920, 4.

40. Osii Viita, *Suden hetkiä. Amerikansuomalainen olympiavoittaja Ville Ritola* (Peräseinäjoki, Finland: Siirtolaisinstituutti, 1997), 126–27, 140–42.

41. David Colquhoun, ed., *As if Running on Air: The Journals of Jack Lovelock* (Nelzon, NZ: Craig Potton, 2008).

42. For an exhaustive discussion of these growing commercial trends, see Robert Knight Barney, Stephen R. Wenn, and Scott G. Martyn, *Selling the Five Rings: The International Olympic Committee and the Rise of Olympic Commercialism* (Salt Lake City: University of Utah Press, 2002).

43. Barney et al., *Selling the Five Rings*; Mark Dyreson, "Aggressive America: Media Nationalism and the 'War' over Olympic Pictures in Sport's 'Golden Age,'" *International Journal of the History of Sport* 22, no. 6 (November 2005): 974–89.

44. John Gleaves and Matthew P. Llewellyn, "Charlie Paddock and the Shifting State of Olympic Amateurism," *Olympika* 21 (2012): 1–32.

45. For more extended discussions of these issues, see Mark Dyreson, *Crafting Patriotism for Global Domination: America at the Olympic Games* (London: Routledge, 2009); Mark Dyreson, "'Imperishable Sports History'? Interpreting El Ouafi in the United States and Mexico," *Journal of Sport History* 36, no. 1 (Spring 2009), 19–42; Mark Dyreson, "Introduction: The 1928 Olympic Marathon," *Journal of Sport History* 36, no. 1 (Spring 2009), 1–2; Mark Dyreson, "Icons of Liberty or Objects of Desire? American Women Olympians and the Politics of Consumption," *Journal of Contemporary History* 38, no. 3 (July 2003), 435–60; Mark Dyreson, "Globalizing the Nation-Making Process: Modern Sport in World History," *International Journal of the History of Sport* 20, no. 1 (March 2003), 91–106; Mark Dyreson, "Selling American Civilization: The Olympic Games of 1920 and American Culture," *Olympika* 8 (1999), 1–41; Mark Dyreson, "Scripting the American Olympic Story-Telling Formula: The 1924 Paris Olympic Games and the American Media," *Olympika* 5 (1996), 45–80.

46. Richard Gruneau, "When Amateurism Mattered: Class, Moral Entrepreneurship and the Winter Olympics," in *The Winter Olympics: From Chamonix to Salt Lake*, ed. Larry Gerlach (Salt Lake City: University of Utah Press, 2004), 127–54.

47. IOC Annual Session, Antwerp, August 1920, IOC Archives.

48. "Amateurs in Rowing," *Manchester Guardian*, 2 July 1919, 6; "The Olympic Games," *The Times* (London), 18 August 1920, 6; For more on "Jack" Kelly, see John A. Lucas, "The Kelly Family of Philadelphia: From 'Rags to Riches,'" *Journal of Olympic History* 18, no. 2 (2010): 50–55.

49. "Athletes and Gentlemen," *New York Times*, 30 April 1922, 36; "More Amateur Ethics," *New York Times*, 9 November 1923, 16.

50. "Professionalism in Lawn Tennis," *Times of India*, 26 April 1923, 6.

51. As quoted in "Cost of Sending Team to 1932 Olympiad in U.S. Is Vexing Problem," *Lethbridge Herald* (Alberta), 29 May 1929, 3.

52. Henri Desgrange, "Vers une Formule Honnête d'Amateurisme," *L'Auto*, 1925 (undated clipping), ID chemise: 204765, IOC Archives.

53. Keys, *Globalizing Sport*, 48.

54. International Olympic Committee, *Olympic Charter*. Retrieved from http://www .olympic.org/Documents/Olympic%20Charter/Olympic_Charter_through_time/1920 -Charte_Olympique.pdf. This policy, which was first ratified at the 1914 Olympic Congress in Paris, had been reaffirmed at the first postwar congress in Lausanne in 1921.

55. United States Olympic Committee, *Report of the American Olympic Committee: Seventh Olympic Games, Antwerp, Belgium, 1920* (New York: Condé Nast, 1921).

56. International Amateur Athletic Federation, Minutes of the Fourth Congress, Antwerp, 22 August 1920; Gordon MacDonald, "A History of Relations between the International Olympic Committee and the International Sports Federations, 1891–1968," unpublished PhD diss., International Centre for Olympic Studies, University of Western Ontario, London, ON, Canada, 1998, 45–102.

57. "Obsolete Laws Are Killing Amateur Sport," *Referee* (Sydney), 20 July 1932, 1.

58. Alfred Senn, *Power, Politics, and the Olympic Games: A History of the Power Brokers, Events, and Controversies That Shaped the Games* (Champaign, IL: Human Kinetics, 1999), 38–39.

59. IOC Executive Committee Meeting, Paris, 12, 17, 18, and 23 July 1922, 5–7, IOC Archives.

60. IOC Annual Session, Rome, 7–12 April 1923, 21–23, IOC Archives.

61. Norbert Müller, ed., *Pierre de Coubertin, Olympism: Selected Writings* (Lausanne, Switzerland: International Olympic Committee, 2000), 651–53.

62. Matthew P. Llewellyn, "Olympic Games Doomed," *International Journal of the History of Sport* 28, no. 5 (April 2011): 773–95.

63. British Olympic Association, Chairman's Annual Statement, 1924, British Olympic Foundation Archives; F. G. L. Fairlie, *The Official Report of the VIIIth Olympiad, Paris 1924* (London: British Olympic Association, 1925), 39–41, British Olympic Foundation Archives.

64. "Olympic Games Doomed: Failure of the Ideal," *Times* (London), 22 July 1924, 14.

65. Minutes of the Technical Olympic Congress, Prague, 29 May–4 June 1925, 15–16, Box 75 "IOC Meetings," folder "Technical Olympic Congress," Brundage Archives.

66. MacDonald, "History of Relations."

67. Guy Schultz, *The IAAF and IOC: Their Relationship and Its Impact on Women's Participation in Track and Field at the Olympic Games, 1912–1932*, unpublished M.A. thesis,

International Centre for Olympic Studies, University of Western Ontario, London, ON, Canada, 2000.

68. Yoan Grosset and Michaël Attali, "The French Initiative towards the Creation of an International Sports Movement 1908–1925: An Alternative to the International Olympic Committee," *Journal of Sport History* 36, no. 2 (Summer 2009): 245–62. After the international federations failed to rival the Olympic Movement, they actively sought a place on the IOC.

69. Matthew P. Llewellyn, *Rule Britannia: Nationalism, Identity and the Modern Olympic Games* (London: Routledge, 2011), 174–76.

70. Bill Murray, *The World's Game: A History of Soccer* (Urbana: University of Illinois Press, 1998).

71. Minutes of the Technical Olympic Congress, Prague, 29 May–4 June 1925, 27, box 75, "IOC Meetings," folder "Technical Olympic Congress," Brundage Archives.

72. Ibid., p. 9.

73. Ibid.

74. Gustavus T. Kirby, "Some Remarks upon the Olympic and Pedagogic Congress, Prague, Czecho-Slovakia, 1925," 2, BOF Archives.

75. Minutes of the Technical Olympic Congress, Prague, 29 May–4 June 1925, 27, box 75, "IOC Meetings," folder "Technical Olympic Congress," Brundage Archives.

76. Karl Lennartz, "Difficult Times: Baillet-Latour and Germany, 1931–1942," *Olympika* 3 (1994): 99–106.

77. Robert Gallay to Comte Baillet-Latour, 22 March 1926, International Tennis Federation Correspondence (1914–1974), OU MO 01 14 33, IOC Archives. For a more comprehensive discussion of this debate, see MacDonald, "History of Relations," 72–79.

78. For an example of the IOC president's letter campaign, see Count Henri de Baillet-Latour, Circular Letter to National Tennis Federations, 28 December 1926, International Tennis Federation Correspondence (1914–1974), OU MO 01 14 33, IOC Archives.

79. Fédération Internationale de Football Association, *Minutes of the 15th Annual Congress,* Rome, 2–3 May 1926, 8–9, box 102, folder 21, Brundage Archives.

80. Fédération Internationale de Football Association, Official Communications, 13 January 1927, box 102, "International Olympic Committee Subject File," folder "Broken Time—Background Material," Brundage Archives.

81. Charles Hirschman to Sigfrid Edström, 25 February 1927, Commission d'Amateurisme Correspondence (1894–1968), ID Chemise: 204767, IOC Archives.

82. A. W. Betteley to Sigfrid Edström, 1 January 1927, Commission d'Amateurisme Correspondence (1894–1968), ID Chemise: 204767, IOC Archives.

83. "Is This Our Last March Past? If Great Britain Withdraws from the Olympic Games," *Athletic News,* 7 November 1927, Olympic Scrapbook 1925–1930, BOF Archives.

84. Meeting of the Annual IOC Session, Lisbon, 3–7 May 1926, IOC Archives; *Official Bulletin of the International Olympic Committee* 3 (July 1926): 15.

85. Meeting of the IOC Executive Committee, Paris, 8 August 1927, IOC Archives; *Official Bulletin of the International Olympic Committee* 2, no. 8 (September 1927): 12.

86. Ibid.

87. Henri de Baillet-Latour to P. de Borman, 14 May 1927; A. G. Berdez to R. Gallay, 7 April 1926, International Lawn Tennis Federation Correspondence (1914–1974), OU MO 01 14 33, IOC Archives.

88. Lord Rochdale to Comte Baillet-Latour, 22 August 1927, Grande-Bretagne Correspondence (1925–27), OU MO 01 14 36, IOC Archives.

89. James Taylor to the International Olympic Committee, 17 August 1927, Grande-Bretagne Correspondence (1925–27), OU MO 01 14 36, IOC Archives.

90. Minutes of the Fortieth Annual Meeting of the Amateur Athletic Union of Canada, Edmonton, AB, Canada, 1–3 December 1927, 4–5, Amateur Athletic Union of Canada folder, M3209, Library and Archives Canada, Ottawa, ON.

91. Ira G. Emery to A. Berdez, 12 October 1927, IOC Archives, Grande-Bretagne Correspondence (1925–27), OU MO 01 14 36.

92. "A.A.U. Opposes Football Association's 'Broken Time' Ruling for 1928 Olympics: American Authorities Will Not Accept Plan," *Hartford Courant*, 23 November 1927, 13.

93. Llewellyn, *Rule Britannia*.

94. "Not Allow Broken-Time Payments?" *Athletic News*, 3 September 1927, Olympic Scrapbook 1925–1930, BOF Archives.

95. "Part Time and the Olympic Games," *The Field*, 8 August 1927, Olympic Scrapbook 1925–1930, BOF Archives.

96. Tony Mason, *Association Football and English Society, 1863–1915* (Brighton, U.K.: Harvester Press, 1980)

97. Wray Vamplew, *Play Up and Play the game: Professional Sport in Britain, 1875–1914* (Cambridge: Cambridge University Press, 1988); John M. Carroll, *Red Grange and the Rise of Modern Football* (Urbana: University of Illinois Press, 2004).

98. Comte Baillet-Latour to Lord Rochdale, 24 September 1927, Grande-Bretagne Correspondence (1925–27), OU MO 01 14 36, IOC Archives.

99. British Olympic Association, "Meeting Convened by the BOA of the Representatives of the Sporting Associations of Great Britain Whose Sport Is Included in the Olympic Games of Amsterdam," 12 November 1927, BOF Archives.

100. "The Olympic Games," *Times* (London), 29 October 1927, 7.

101. Peter J. Beck, *Scoring for Britain: International Football and International Politics, 1900–1939* (London: Frank Cass, 1999), 108–13.

102. "Lever for 1932? Subsidised Amateur Means Knell of a Great Principle," *Athletic News*, 7 November 1927, Olympic Scrapbook 1925–1930, BOF Archives.

103. IOC Congress, 25–30 May 1930, Berlin, IOC Archives; "Joint Report of the Delegates Representing the Olympic Association of Great Britain, New Zealand and South Africa at the Berlin Olympic Congress" (London: British Olympic Association, 1930), BOF Archives.

104. Murray, *World's Game*, chapter three.

105. For more on the contradictory nature of Olympic ideology, see Dikaia Chatziefstathiou, "Paradoxes and Contestations of Olympism in the History of the Modern Olympic Movement," *Sport in Society* 14, no. 3 (April 2011): 332–44.

106. Rossem, *Ninth Olympiad*, Appendix V.

Chapter 4. *"Ambassadors in Tracksuits"*

1. Sean Dinces, "Padres on Mount Olympus: Los Angeles and the Production of the 1932 Olympic Mega-Event," *Journal of Sport History* 32 (Summer 2005): 137–66.

2. Barbara J. Keys, "Spreading Peace, Democracy, and Coca Cola: Sport and American Cultural Expansion in the 1930s," *Diplomatic History* 28, no. 2 (April 2004): 165–96.

3. Jeremy White, "The Los Angeles Way of Doing Things: The Olympic Village and the Practice of Boosterism," *Olympika* 11 (2000): 79–116.

4. Mark Dyreson and Matthew P. Llewellyn, "Los Angeles Is the Olympic City: Legacies of 1932 and 1984," *International Journal of the History of Sport* 25 (December 2008): 1991–2018.

5. Pierre Arnaud and James Riordan, *Sport and International Politics: The Impact of Fascism and Communism on Sport* (London: E. and F. N. Spon, 1998).

6. Barbara J. Keys, *Globalizing Sport: National Rivalry and International Community in the 1930s* (Cambridge, MA: Harvard University Press, 2006), 52.

7. Mark Dyreson, *Crafting Patriotism for Global Domination: America at the Olympic Games* (London: Routledge, 2009).

8. Keys, *Globalizing Sport*, 75.

9. "Meeting of the Executive Committee of the International Olympic Committee and of the Council of Delegates of the International Federations," *Official Bulletin of the International Olympic Committee* No. 25 (September 1933): 1–3.

10. Ibid.

11. IOC Executive Board Meeting, Vittel, 23–25 July 1929, IOC Archives.

12. For an excellent analysis of the entire Nurmi affair, see Leif Yttergren, "J. Sigrid Edström and the Nurmi Affair of 1932: The Struggle of the Amateur Fundamentalists against Professionalism in the Olympic Movement," *Journal of Olympic History* 15, no. 3 (2007): 111–26.

13. Daniel A. Nathan, "'The Nonpareil, the Runner of the Ages': Paavo Nurmi and His 1925 American Exhibition Tour," *Sport History Review* 43, no. 1 (May 2012): 43–71.

14. As cited in Allen Guttmann, *The Olympics: A History of the Modern Games*, 2nd ed. (Urbana: University of Illinois Press, 2002), 51.

15. Avery Brundage to Lauri Pihkala, 6 June 1932, box 33, "Individuals," folder "Paavo, Nurmi," Brundage Archives.

16. Yttergren, "J. Sigrid Edström," 116.

17. J. Sigfrid Edström to IAAF Members, 8 April 1932; unknown writer to Fr. Hasseler, Secretary General of the German Athletic Association, (n.d.), box 33, "Individuals," folder "Paavo, Nurmi," Brundage Archives.

18. "A Triumph for Diplomatic Plots," *Uusi Suomi*, 30 July 1932; "A Miscarriage of Justice," *Uusi Suomi*, 31 July 1932.

19. "A Slap in Our Face, a Major Insult towards Nurmi and Finland," *Helsingin Sanomat*, 30 July 1932.

20. See Urho Kekkonen to IAAF, 18 April 1932, 6 May 1932, and 2 June 1932, box 33, "Individuals," folder "Paavo, Nurmi," Brundage Archives.

21. Lauri Pihkala to Avery Brundage, 9 April 1932, box 33, "Individuals," folder "Paavo, Nurmi," Brundage Archives.

22. Minutes of the Eleventh Congress of the International Amateur Athletic Federation, Los Angeles, California, 29 July and 8–9 August 1932, IAAF Archives.

23. Sigfrid Edström to Avery Brundage, 9 April 1934, box 42, "IOC Presidents and Secretariat," folder "Edstrom, J. Sigfrid," Brundage Archives.

24. "Meeting of the Executive Committee of the International Olympic Committee and of the Council of Delegates of the International Federations," *Official Bulletin of the International Olympic Committee* No. 25 (September 1933): 1–3.

25. Sigfrid Edström to members of the International Olympic Committee, 7 April 1932; "Proposals of the International Amateur Athletic Federation regarding the Basic Principles of Amateurism to Be Uniformly Adopted by All International Federations," Vienna, June 1933, Commission d'Amateurisme (1933–1934), ID Chemise: 204758, IOC Archives.

26. Memo, Vienna, 1933, Commission d'Amateurisme (1933–1973), ID Chemise: 204857, IOC Archives.

27. Arnaud and Riordan, *Sport and International Politics*; Keys, *Globalizing Sport*.

28. For an excellent treatment of Mussolini's rise to power, see Simon Martin, *Sport Italia: The Italian Love Affair with Sport* (London: I. B. Tauris, 2011); Simon Martin, *Football and Fascism: The National Game under Mussolini* (New York: Berg, 2004).

29. Arnd Krüger, "Strength through Joy: The Culture of Consent under Fascism, Nazism and Francoism," in *The International Politics of Sport in the Twentieth Century*, ed. James Riordan and Arnd Krüger (London: E. and F. N. Spon, 1999), 78.

30. Angela Teja, "Italian Sport and International Relations under Fascism," in *Sport and International Politics: The Impact of Fascism and Communism on Sport*, ed. Pierre Arnaud and James Riordan (London: E. and F. N. Spon, 1998), 147–70.

31. Krüger, "Strength through Joy," 71–77.

32. Sarah Morgan, "Mussolini's Boys (and Girls): Gender and Sport in Fascist Italy," *History Australia* 3, no. 1 (2006), 04.1–12, http://journals.publishing.monash.edu/ojs/index.php/ha/article/viewFile/417/429.

33. Krüger, "Strength through Joy," 78; Martin, *Sport Italia*, 56.

34. Luigi Ferrario, "Olympiaidi. Gli Azzurri Ambasciatori dello Sport Fascista sul Teatro della X Olympiade," *La Gazzetta dello Sport*, 18 July 1932, 3.

35. "Il Primo Saluto agli Azzurri Reduci da Los Angeles," *La Stampa*, 1 September 1932, 7.

36. Morgan, "Mussolini's Boys (and Girls)," 04.2.

37. Arnd Krüger, "The Influence of the State Sport of Fascist Italy on Nazi Germany, 1928–1936," in *Sport, Culture, Society*, ed. James A. Mangan and Robert B. Small (London: E. & F. N. Spon, 1986), 145–65.

38. Vic Duke and Liz Crolley, *Football, Nationality and the State* (London: Longman, 1996), 32; Duncan Shaw, *Fútbol y Franquismo* (Madrid: Alianza Editorial, 1987); Hunter Shobe, "Place, Identity and Football: Catalonia, Catalanisme and Football Club Barcelona, 1899–1975," *National Identities* 10, no. 3 (September 2008): 329–43.

39. Keys, *Globalizing Sport*, 109.

40. Masaji Kiyokawa, "My Olympic Golden Moment: Swimming into History," *Journal of Olympic History* 5 (1997): 10–14; Mark Dyreson and Thomas Rorke, "A Powerful False Positive: Nationalism, Science and Public Opinion in the 'Oxygen Doping' Allegations against Japanese Swimmers at the 1932 Olympics," *International Journal of the History of Sport*, 31, no. 8 (2014): 854–70.

41. Avery Brundage, "Report to President Baillet-Latour on Conditions in South America," n.d., box 42, "IOC Presidents and Secretariat," folder "Edstrom, J. Sigfrid," Brundage Archives.

42. "Traveling Expenses Already Raised for Strong Aggregation," *Los Angeles Examiner*, n.d., box 151, "Olympic Games," folder "Newspaper Clippings, 1928, 1931–32," Brundage Archives; Arnd Krüger, "'Buying Victories Is Positively Degrading': The European Origins of Government Pursuit of National Prestige through Sports," *International Journal of the History of Sport* 12, no. 2 (1995): 201–18. The *Los Angeles Examiner* reported that 450,000 Kroner converted to approximately $100,000.

43. "Olympic Executive Reports on Europe," *New York Times*, 17 July 1923, 17; for France, see Phil Dine, "Sport and State in Contemporary France: From la Charte des Sportes to Decentralization," *Modern and Contemporary France* 6, no. 3 (1998): 301–11.

44. "Wishes Expressed at the I.O.C. Meeting of Prague," *Official Bulletin of the International Olympic Committee* (January 1926): 18.

45. Kay Schiller and Christopher Young, *The 1972 Munich Olympics and the Making of Modern Germany* (Berkeley: University of California Press, 2010), quote on 58.

46. John Hoberman, "Towards a Theory of Olympic Internationalism," *Journal of Sport History* 22, no. 1 (Spring 1995): 17.

47. Keys, *Globalizing Sport*, 136.

48. A substantial body of excellent scholarly literature exists on the 1936 Berlin games. A few of the best examples include Richard Mandell, *The Nazi Olympics* (Urbana: University of Illinois Press, 1987); David Clay Large, *Nazi Olympics* (New York: W. W. Norton, 2007); Duff Hart-Davis, *Hitler's Games: The 1936 Olympics* (New York: Harper and Row, 1986); and Arnd Krüger, *Die Olympischen Spiele 1936 und die Weltmeinung* (Berlin: Bartels and Wernitz, 1972).

49. Keys, *Globalizing Sport*, 142.

50. Arnd Krüger and William Murray, eds., *The Nazi Olympics: Sport, Politics, and Appeasement in the 1930s* (Urbana: University of Illinois Press, 2003).

51. Guttmann, *The Olympics*, 56.

52. Arnd Krüger, "United States of America: The Crucial Battle," in *The Nazi Olympics: Sport, Politics, and Appeasement in the 1930s*, ed. Arnd Krüger and William Murray (Urbana: University of Illinois Press, 2003), 51.

53. Hans von Tschammer und Osten to Henri Baillet-Latour, 24 September 1935, box 42, "IOC Presidents and Secretariat," folder "Baillet-La Tour, Count Henri," Brundage Archives.

54. Krüger, "The Influence of the State Sport of Fascist Italy on Nazi Germany," 145–65.

55. Walter Citrine, *Under the Heel of Hitler: The Dictatorship over Sport in Nazi Germany* (London: Trades Union Congress General Council, 1936), British Olympic Foundation Archives.

56. International Olympic Committee, *Berlin 1936 Olympic Games* [webpage], http://www.olympic.org/berlin-1936-summer-olympics.

57. As the historian Arnd Krüger has revealed, future IOC president Avery Brundage masterminded the effort to persuade both the AAU and American Olympic Committee to reverse their initial decisions and begrudgingly compete. See Krüger, "United States of America," 44–69.

58. Keys, *Globalizing Sport*, 141.

59. Large, *Nazi Olympics*, 116–18.

60. Keys, *Globalizing Sport*, 142.

61. Mandell, *Nazi Olympics*; Large, *Nazi Olympics*; Hart-Davis, *Hitler's Games*; Krüger, *Olympischen Spiele 1936*.

62. As cited in Christopher Young, "Berlin 1936," in *The Politics of the Olympics: A Survey*, ed. Alan Bairner and Gyozo Molnar (London: Routledge, 2010): 102.

63. John Hoberman, "Primacy of Performance: Superman not Superathlete," *International Journal of the History of Sport* 16, no. 2 (1999): 69.

64. Young, "Berlin 1936," 93.

65. It is important to note that no direct archival or material evidence is provided to support any of these claims. In almost every instance, historians cite only unsubstantiated secondary scholarship. See Arnd Krüger, "Germany: The Propaganda Machine," in *The Nazi Olympics: Sport, Politics and Appeasement in the 1930s*, ed. Arnd Krüger and William Murray (Urbana: University of Illinois Press 2003), 17–43; Arnd Krüger, "Breeding, Rearing and Preparing the Aryan Body: Creating Superman the Nazi Way," *International Journal of the History of Sport* 16, no. 2 (1999): 59; Keys, *Globalizing Sport*, 129 and 153; Krüger, "Strength through Joy," 71–72; Benoît Heimermann, *Les Champions d'Hitler* (Paris: Éditions Stock, 2014).

66. Krüger, "Buying Victories," 189–96.

67. For a discussion of scholars who have asserted these claims, see Paul Dimeo, *A History of Drug Use in Sport: 1876–1976* (London: Routledge, 2007), 5.

68. "Lessons of the Olympic Games," *The Times* (London), 21 August 1936, 11; "We Fail in Games—But We Can Feel Proud," *London Daily Mirror*, 13 August 1936, 3.

69. "English the International Tongue with Berlin's Polyglot Visitors," *New York Times*, 7 August 1936, 12.

70. "Nazi Jew-Baiting and the Olympics: Some Things They Can't Hide Away," *Daily Worker* (U.K.), 3 February 1936, 5.

71. "Goering on the Nazi Olympics," *Daily Worker* (U.K.), 30 June 1936, 6.

72. *Deutsche Diplomatische-Politische Korrespondenz*, August 1936, as cited and translated in British Foreign Office Memorandum, 4 August 1936, FO/371/19940/5677, National Archives, Kew, Richmond, Surrey, TW9 4DU, United Kingdom.

73. Theodor Lewald to Henri Baillet-Latour, 5 April 1935, COMMI-ADMIS-CORR, ID Chemise: 204767, IOC Archives.

74. Allen Guttmann, *The Games Must Go On: Avery Brundage and the Olympic Movement* (New York: Columbia University Press, 1983).

75. Henri Baillet-Latour to Avery Brundage, 4 December 1935, box 42, "IOC Presidents and Secretariat," folder "Baillet-La Tour, Count Henri," Brundage Archives; for an examination of *L'Auto's* campaign against Nazi sport, see William J. Murray, "France, Coubertin and the Nazi Olympics: The Response," *Olympika* 1 (1996): 53.

76. Previous scholarship on the subject is undermined by a reliance on either non-German newspaper reports or secondary scholarly accounts. In some instances, no documentation whatsoever is provided to validate such controversial claims.

77. Hoberman, "Primacy of Performance," 69–85.

78. Krüger, "Buying Victories," 189–96.

79. The Germans employed a "Reichstrainer," at least in athletics, as early as the 1928 Olympic Games in Amsterdam. See K. Sturm, "Die Vorbereitung auf die Spiele," in *Welt-Olympia 1928 in Wort und Bild. Deutsches Erinnerungswerk über die Olympischen Spiele*

Amsterdam 1928 gewidmet der Deutschen Sportjugend zur Belehrung und Begeisterung, ed. Josef Von Waitzer and Wilhelm Dörr (Berlin: Conzett and Huber, 1928), 170–72.

80. Emanuel Hübner, *Das Olympische Dorf von 1936: Planung, Bau und Nutzungsgeschichte* (Paderborn, Ger.: Ferdinand Schöningh, 2015).

81. Christian Strauch, *Sport Jahrbuch für die Wehrmacht 1938/39* (Berlin: Sport- und Turnverlag K. F. Bräutigam, 1943), 47, 58–59, 69.

82. The authors acknowledge that this is not the final word on the subject. A detailed examination of German federal and local archives would help to shed crucial light on the question.

83. For a refutation of these beliefs in Nazi doping, see Marcel Reinold and John Hoberman, "The Myth of the Nazi Steroid," *International Journal of the History of Sport* 31, no. 8 (2014): 871–83.

84. Gordon MacDonald, "A History of Relations between the International Olympic Committee and the International Sports Federations, 1891–1968," unpublished PhD diss. International Centre for Olympic Studies, University of Western Ontario, London, ON, Canada, 1998, 131.

85. Sigfrid Edström to Avery Brundage, 28 May 1935, box 42, "IOC Presidents and Secretariat," folder "Edstrom, J. Sigfrid," Brundage Archives.

86. IOC Annual Session, Athens, 16–23 May 1934, 7, IOC Archives.

87. "Speech of the President of the IOC at the Opening of the Meeting of the Delegates of the International Federations," *Official Bulletin of the International Olympic Committee* (September 1934): 3.

88. IOC Annual Session, Berlin, 28–31 July 1936, IOC Archives.

89. MacDonald, "International Olympic Committee and the International Sports Federations," 104.

90. Avery Brundage to Henri Baillet-Latour, 21 April 1936, CIO-COMMI-ADMIS-GENER 204766, IOC Archives.

91. Carl Diem to Henri Baillet-Latour, 9 July 1935, CIO-COMMI-ADMIS-GENER 204766, IOC Archives.

92. Count Adam Zamoyski to Henri Baillet-Latour, 8 August 1936, CIO-COMMI-ADMIS-GENER 204766, IOC Archives.

93. "Report of the Meeting of the IOC," *Official Bulletin of the International Olympic Committee* (May 1935): 9.

94. MacDonald, "International Olympic Committee and the International Sports Federations," 134.

95. Ibid., 137.

96. Richard Gruneau, "When Amateurism Mattered: Class, Moral Entrepreneurship, and the Winter Olympics," in *The Winter Olympics: From Chamonix to Salt Lake City,* ed. Larry Gerlach (Salt Lake City: University of Utah Press, 2004), 143.

97. IOC Annual Session, 13–19 March 1938, Cairo, IOC Archives.

98. James Merrick to Henri Baillet-Latour, 27 April 1937, CIO COMMI-ADMIS-GENER, ID 204766, IOC archives.

99. IOC Annual Session, 6–15 June 1937, Warsaw, IOC Archives.

100. Henri Baillet-Latour to Avery Brundage, 6 April 1937, box 44, IOC Archives.

101. Henri Baillet-Latour, "Essay on Amateurism," n.d. (probably mid- to late 1937), box 42, "IOC Presidents and Secretariat," folder "Baillet-La Tour, Count Henri," Brundage Archives.

102. Ibid.

103. IOC Annual Session, Warsaw, 6–15 June 1937, 5–6, IOC Archives.

104. Avery Brundage to Henri Baillet-Latour, 11 January 1938, box 42, "IOC Presidents and Secretariat," folder "Baillet-La Tour, Count Henri," Brundage Archives.

105. "Report of Special Commission appointed by the International Olympic Committee to study certain questions relating to the status of amateurs in general and to the application of qualifying rules in particular," n.d., box 42, "IOC Presidents and Secretariat," folder "Baillet-La Tour, Count Henri," Brundage Archives.

106. "International Olympic Committee, 1938 Session, Cairo," *Official Bulletin of the International Olympic Committee* (July 1938): 29–31.

107. Schiller and Young, *1972 Munich Olympics*, 58.

108. Martin, *Sport Italia*, 56.

109. *Sportsmedizin und Olympische Spiele 1936*, JO-1936W Medic, folder "Médecine des Sports," IOC Archives.

110. John Gleaves, "Enhancing the Odds: Horse Racing, Gambling and the First Anti-Doping Movement in Sport, 1889—1911," *Sport in History* 32, no. 1 (2012): 26–52.

111. Henri Baillet-Latour, "Essay on Amateurism," n.d. (probably mid- to late 1937), box 42, "IOC Presidents and Secretariat," folder "Baillet-La Tour, Count Henri," Brundage Archives.

112. Paul Anspach to Henri Baillet-Latour, 29 September 1937, CIO COMMI-ADMIS-GENER, ID 204766, IOC Archives; Albert Berdez to Paul Anspach, 12 October 1937, CIO COMMI-ADMIS-GENER, ID 204766, IOC Archives; report of Dr. E. Galfre, 1937, "Du Doping," ID Chemise: 204766 CIO COMMI-ADMIS 1935–1967, IOC Archives; unsigned report, n.d., "Rapport sur le Doping," ID Chemise: 204766 CIO COMMI-ADMIS 1935–1967, IOC Archives; report of Dott. Giuseppe Poggi-Longostrevi, 1938, "Relation sur la Question des 'Excitants,'" ID Chemise: 204766 CIO COMMI-ADMIS 1935–1967, IOC Archives.

113. Avery Brundage, handwritten note, n.d., box 75, "IOC Meetings," folder "35th Session, Cairo, March 1938," Brundage Archives.

114. International Olympic Committee, *Olympic Charter 1946*, http://www.olympic.org/Documents/Olympic%20Charter/Olympic_Charter_through_time/1946-Olympic_Charter.pdf.

115. "Meeting minutes for the 75th Session of the International Olympic Committee," Vienna, 21–24 October 1974, IOC Archives.

116. "International Olympic Committee, 1938 Session, Cairo," *Official Bulletin of the International Olympic Committee* (July 1938): 21–31.

117. Ibid., 24.

118. Coubertin's 29 August 1936 interview in *L'Auto* was recited by French IOC member Marquis de Polignac during the 1947 IOC session. See IOC Annual Session, Stockholm, 19–21 June 1947, IOC Archives; this interview also is cited in Murray, "France, Coubertin and the Nazi Olympics," 53.

Chapter 5. *The Amateur Apostle and the Cold War Games*

1. Stephen Wenn, "Rivals and Revolutionaries: Avery Brundage, the Marquess of Exeter and Olympic Television Revenue," *Sport in History* 32, no. 2 (June 2012): 257–78.

2. For example, Allen Guttmann, *The Games Must Go On: Avery Brundage and the Olympic Movement* (New York: Columbia University Press, 1983); Roger Butterfield, "Self-Made Millionaire and Hell-and-Toe Champion, He Is the Irascible High Priest of Amateurism in Sports," *Life Magazine*, 14 June 1948, 115.

3. Arthur Daley, "What Price Amateurism?" *New York Times*, 11 June 1972, S2.

4. William Johnson, "Defender of the Faith," *Sports Illustrated*, 24 July 1972; Frank Litsky, "Avery Brundage of the Olympics Dies," *New York Times*, 9 May 1975, 1.

5. John Hoberman, *The Olympic Games: Sports, Politics and the Moral Order* (New York: Aristide D. Caratzas, 1986), 51.

6. Guttmann, *Games Must Go On*, 129.

7. Avery Brundage, "Amateur Sport and Broken Time," *World Sports*, November 1948, box 102, "International Olympic Committee Subject File," folder "Broken Time," Brundage Archives.

8. Avery Brundage, "Memorandum" [n.d.], box 102, "International Olympic Committee Subject File," folder "Broken Time," Brundage Archives.

9. Guttmann, *Games Must Go On*, 123.

10. Ibid., 110.

11. Hoberman, *Olympic Games*, 57.

12. Allen Guttmann, *The Olympics: A History of the Modern Games* (Urbana: University of Illinois Press, 2002), 98–103.

13. IOC Executive Committee Meeting, Lausanne, Switzerland, 1–3 September 1946, IOC Archives.

14. Avery Brundage to Lord Aberdare, 5 April 1945, box 50, "IOC Members," folder "Aberdare, Lord Clarence," Brundage Archives.

15. International Meeting of the Danish, Finish, Norwegian, and Swedish Sporting Associations, January 1946, box 156, "Olympic Games," folder "Amateurism," Brundage Archives.

16. Proposal of *La Ligue Belge d'Athlétisme* at the Congress of the I.A.A.F. at Oslo, 1946, box 156, "Olympic Games," folder "Amateurism," Brundage Archives.

17. Bo Ekelund to Avery Brundage, 27 March 1946, box 54, "IOC Members," folder "Ekelund, Bo," Brundage Archives; Avery Brundage to Sigfrid Edström, 5 February 1947, box 42, "IOC Presidents and Secretariat," folder "Edstrom, J. Sigfrid," Brundage Archives; "Men from 45 Olympic Nations Expected to Attend Amateur Congress," *New York Times*, 6 June 1946, 29.

18. Guttmann, *Games Must Go On*, 116.

19. Avery Brundage to Sigfrid Edström, 5 February 1947, box 42, "IOC Presidents and Secretariat," folder "Edstrom, J. Sigfrid," Brundage Archives.

20. Avery Brundage, "Amateur Sport and Broken Time," *World Sports*, November 1948, box 102, "International Olympic Committee Subject File," folder "Broken Time," Brundage Archives.

21. Avery Brundage to Sigfrid Edström, 23 April 1946, box 42, "IOC Presidents and Secretariat," folder "Edstrom, J. Sigfrid," Brundage Archives.

22. Avery Brundage to Sigfrid Edström, November 1947, box 42, "IOC Presidents and Secretariat," folder "Edstrom, J. Sigfrid," Brundage Archives.

23. Avery Brundage to Sigfrid Edström, 27 December 1947, box 42, "IOC Presidents and Secretariat," folder "Edstrom, J. Sigfrid," Brundage Archives.

24. International Amateur Athletic Federation, "Amateur Status Rules Revised," 27 August 1947, box 102, "International Olympic Committee Subject File," folder "Broken Time," Brundage Archives.

25. Avery Brundage to Sigfrid Edström, 1 June 1946, box 42, "IOC Presidents and Secretariat," folder "Edstrom, J. Sigfrid," Brundage Archives.

26. Ibid.

27. Avery Brundage to Lord Aberdare, 27 September 1945, box 50, "IOC Members," folder "Aberdare, Lord Clarence," Brundage Archives.

28. Avery Brundage to Sigfrid Edström, 21 April 1947, box 42, "IOC Presidents and Secretariat," folder "Edstrom, J. Sigfrid," Brundage Archives; Janie Hampton, *The Austerity Olympics: When the Games came to London in 1948* (London: Aurum, 2008).

29. Gordon MacDonald, "A Colossal Embroglio: Control of Amateur Ice-Hockey in the United States and the 1948 Olympic Winter Games," *Olympika* 7 (1998): 43–60; John Soares, "'Very Correct Adversaries': The Cold War on Ice from 1947 to the Squaw Valley Olympics," *International Journal of the History of Sport* 30, no. 13 (2013): 1536–53.

30. Avery Brundage to Sigfrid Edström, 8 April 1946, box 42, "IOC Presidents and Secretariat," folder "Edstrom, J. Sigfrid," Brundage Archives.

31. Avery Brundage to M. C. Nater, 7 January 1948, box 156, "Olympic Games," folder "Amateurism," Brundage Archives.

32. MacDonald, "Colossal Embroglio," 43–60; Soares, "Very Correct Adversaries," 1536–53.

33. *Olympic Charter 1946*, http://www.olympic.org/Documents/Olympic%20Charter/ Olympic_Charter_through_time/1946-Olympic_Charter.pdf.

34. Avery Brundage to Sigfrid Edström, 7 May 1946, box 42, "IOC Presidents and Secretariat," folder "Edstrom, J. Sigfrid," Brundage Archives; Avery Brundage to Sigfrid Edström, 23 April 1946, box 42, "IOC Presidents and Secretariat," folder "Edstrom, J. Sigfrid," Brundage Archives.

35. Sigfrid Edström to *Fédération Internationale de Ski*, 9 July 1946, box 42, "IOC Presidents and Secretariat," folder "Edstrom, J. Sigfrid," Brundage Archives.

36. Raymond Gafner, *The International Olympic Committee, One Hundred Years: The Idea, the Presidents, the Achievements, 1894–1994*, vol. 2 (Lausanne, Switzerland: International Olympic Committee, 1994), 42; *Fédération Internationale de Ski* to Its Members, regarding the Qualification of the Ski-Competitors for the Olympic Winter Games, 1952, Circular Letter No. 8 [n.d.], box 70, "Circular Letters," Brundage Archives.

37. Sigfrid Edström to Avery Brundage, 27 February 1950, box 42, "IOC Presidents and Secretariat," folder "Edstrom, J. Sigfrid," Brundage Archives.

38. IOC, *Olympic Charter 1949*, http://www.olympic.org/Documents/Olympic%20 Charter/Olympic_Charter_through_time/1949-Olympic_Charter.pdf.

39. IOC, *Olympic Charter 1946*, http://www.olympic.org/Documents/Olympic%20 Charter/Olympic_Charter_through_time/1946-Olympic_Charter.pdf.

40. "Report on the Commission of Amateurism," IOC Session, Stockholm, 19–21 June 1947, IOC Archives.

41. 45th IOC Session, Copenhagen, 14–18 May 1950, IOC Archives.

42. Avery Brundage, "Stop, Look and Listen," *IOC Bulletin* 5, no. 2 (1950): 20–21; quote, 21.

43. "Fifteenth Olympic Games," *Komsomol Pravda*, 17 July 1952, 7, as cited and translated in British Foreign Office, Soviet Press Clippings, FO/371/100898, The National Archives, Kew.

44. Barbara J. Keys, *Globalizing Sport: National Rivalry and International Community in the 1930s* (Cambridge, MA: Harvard University Press, 2007).

45. Susan Grant, *Physical Culture and Sport in Soviet Society: Propaganda, Acculturation, and Transformation in the 1920s and 1930s* (London: Routledge, 2012); Vassil Girginov, "Capitalist Philosophy and Communist Practice: The Transformation of Eastern European Sport and the International Olympic Committee," *Sport in Society* 1, no. 1 (May 1998): 122.

46. Jenifer Parks, "Red Sport, Red Tape: The Olympic Games, the Soviet Sports Bureaucracy, and the Cold War, 1952–1980," PhD diss., University of North Carolina at Chapel Hill, 2009.

47. With that said, amateur violations in the form of under-the-table payments to athletes were a common feature of pre–World War II Soviet sport. See Robert Edelman, *Serious Fun: A History of Spectator Sports in the USSR* (Oxford: Oxford University Press, 1993); Robert Edelman, *Spartak Moscow: A History of the People's Team in the Workers' State* (Ithaca, NY: Cornell University Press, 2009).

48. Evelyn Mertins, "Presenting Heroes: Athletes as Role Models for the New Soviet Person," *International Journal of the History of Sport* 26, no. 4 (2009): 469–83.

49. Parks, "Red Sport, Red Tape," 18.

50. Guttmann, *Games Must Go On*, 133.

51. Vassil Girginov, "Eastern European Sport: Nomen," *International Journal of the History of Sport* 21, no. 5 (2004): 690–709.

52. Avery Brundage to Sigfrid Edström, 4 March 1947, box 42, "IOC Presidents and Secretariat," folder "Edstrom, J. Sigfrid," Brundage Archives.

53. Avery Brundage to Lord Aberdare, 5 April 1945, box 50, "IOC Members," folder "Aberdare, Lord Clarence," Brundage Archives; Lord Aberdare to Avery Brundage, 26 May 1945, box 50, "IOC Members," folder "Aberdare, Lord Clarence," Brundage Archives; Avery Brundage to Sigfrid Edström, 29 October 1945, box 42, "IOC Presidents and Secretariat," folder "Edstrom, J. Sigfrid," Brundage Archives; Sigfrid Edström to Avery Brundage, 4 December 1946, box 42, "IOC Presidents and Secretariat," folder "Edstrom, J. Sigfrid," Brundage Archives; P. W. Scharroo to Sigfrid Edström, 12 November 1947, box 62, "IOC Members," folder "Scharroo, Col. Peter W.," Brundage Archives.

54. James Riordan, "The USSR and Olympic Boycotts," *International Journal of the History of Sport* 5, no. 3 (1988): 349–59.

55. James Riordan, "Russia and Eastern Europe in the Future of the Modern Olympic Movement," in *Critical Reflections on Olympic Ideology* (London: University of Western Ontario, International Center for Olympic Studies, 1994): 1–9.

56. Sigfrid Edström to Avery Brundage, 4 December 1946, box 42, "IOC Presidents and Secretariat," folder "Edstrom, J. Sigfrid," Brundage Archives.

57. Sigfrid Edström to Avery Brundage, 12 November 1947, box 149, "National Olympic Committees," folder "Union of Soviet Socialist Republics," Brundage Archives.

58. Avery Brundage to Sigfrid Edström, 21 January 1947, box 42, "IOC Presidents and Secretariat," folder "Edstrom, J. Sigfrid," Brundage Archives.

59. Avery Brundage to Sigfrid Edström, 16 April 1946, box 42, "IOC Presidents and Secretariat," folder "Edstrom, J. Sigfrid," Brundage Archives.

60. Sigfrid Edström to Avery Brundage, 4 December 1946, box 42, "IOC Presidents and Secretariat," folder "Edstrom, J. Sigfrid," Brundage Archives.

61. Sigfrid Edström to Nikolai Romanov, 25 November 1946, box 42, "IOC Presidents and Secretariat," folder "Edstrom, J. Sigfrid," Brundage Archives.

62. Sigfrid Edström to Avery Brundage, 4 December 1946, box 42, "IOC Presidents and Secretariat," folder "Edstrom, J. Sigfrid," Brundage Archives; Lord Aberdare to Avery Brundage, 26 December 1946, box 50, "IOC Members," folder "Aberdare, Lord Clarence," Brundage Archives.

63. Parks, "Red Sport, Red Tape."

64. Mertins, "Presenting Heroes."

65. Nikolai Romanov to Lord David Burghley, 29 January 1947, box 42, "IOC Presidents and Secretariat," folder "Edstrom, J. Sigfrid," Brundage Archives.

66. Sigfrid Edström to Avery Brundage, 11 March 1947, box 42, "IOC Presidents and Secretariat," folder "Edstrom, J. Sigfrid," Brundage Archives.

67. Lord David Burghley to Sigfrid Edström, 31 July 1947, box 54, "IOC Members," folder "Exeter, Marquess David," Brundage Archives.

68. Arthur E. Porrit to Avery Brundage, 24 July 1947, box 130, "National Olympic Committees," folder "Great Britain," Brundage Archives.

69. Richard Espy, *The Politics of the Olympic Games* (Berkeley: University of California Press, 1981), 28.

70. Sigfrid Edström to Avery Brundage, 25 April 1951, box 42, "IOC Presidents and Secretariat," folder "Edstrom, J. Sigfrid," Brundage Archives; Parks, "Red Sport, Red Tape."

71. Sigfrid Edström to Avery Brundage, 25 April 1951, box 42, "IOC Presidents and Secretariat," folder "Edstrom, J. Sigfrid," Brundage Archives.

72. Avery Brundage to Sigfrid Edström, 27 September 1948, box 43, "IOC Presidents and Secretariat," folder "Edstrom, J. Sigfrid," Brundage Archives.

73. Avery Brundage to Sigfrid Edström, 15 November 1947, box 149, "National Olympic Committees," folder "Union of Soviet Socialist Republics," Brundage Archives.

74. Ibid.

75. "Financial Resources of the National Olympic Committees," by the Belgian national Olympic committee, June 1952, box 70, "Circular Letters," Brundage Archives.

76. Alfredo Benavides to Brundage, 13 December 1951, box 51, "IOC Members," folder "Benavides, Alfredo," Brundage Archives.

77. Avery Brundage, Report on the Commission to Study Conditions in Latin America, 1950 IOC Session, Copenhagen, 14–18 May 1950, IOC Archives.

78. "State Amateurs," IOC Session, meeting with national Olympic committees, Athens, 10–11 May 1954, IOC Archives.

79. Parks, "Red Sport, Red Tape," 117.

80. Ibid., 53.

81. Girginov, "Eastern European Sport," 694.

82. Barbara J. Keys, "The Early Cold War Olympics, 1952–1960: Political, Economic and Human Rights Dimensions," in *The Palgrave Handbook of Olympic Studies*, ed. Stephen Wagg and Helen Lenskyj (London: Palgrave Macmillan, 2012), 72.

83. IOC Executive Session, Mexico, 15–16 April 1963, IOC Archives.

84. Parks, "Red Sport, Red Tape."

85. "Fifteenth Olympic Games: Before the Opening Ceremony," *Literaturnaya Gazeta*, 19 July 1952, as cited and translated in British Foreign Office, Soviet Press Clippings, FO/371/100898, The National Archives, Kew.

86. Riordan, "Russia and Eastern Europe," 4.

87. Avery Brundage to Konstantin Andrianov, 28 July 1955, box 50, "IOC Members," folder "Andrianov, Konstantin," Brundage Archives.

88. Konstantin Andrianov to Avery Brundage, 22 October 1955, box 50, "IOC Members," folder "Andrianov, Konstantin," Brundage Archives.

89. Parks, "Red Sport, Red Tape," 47.

90. Ibid., 92.

91. Lord David Burghley to Avery Brundage, 10 September 1954, box 54, "IOC Members," folder "Exeter, Marquess David," Brundage Archives.

92. Avery Brundage to Lord David Burghley, 16 September 1954, box 54, "IOC Members," folder "Exeter, Marquess David," Brundage Archives.

93. "The XV Olympic Games Have Ended: Soviet Union's Sportsmen Have Taken First Place," *Pravda*, 4 August 1952, as cited and translated in British Foreign Office, Soviet Press Clippings, FO/371/100898, The National Archives, Kew.

94. "Victory of Soviet Sportsmen," *Sovetsky Sport*, 5 August 1952, as cited and translated in British Foreign Office, Soviet Press Clippings, FO/371/100898, The National Archives, Kew.

95. Jenifer Parks, "'Nothing but Trouble': The Soviet Union's Push to 'Democratise' International Sports during the Cold War, 1959–1962," *International Journal of the History of Sport* 30, no. 13 (2013), 1554–67.

96. Girginov, "Capitalist Philosophy and Communist Practice," 118–48.

97. Avery Brundage to Dr. Jerzy Loth, 17 June 1953, box 59, Brundage Archives; Avery Brundage to Dr. Jerzy Loth, 20 October 1953, box 59, "IOC Members," folder "Loth, Dr. Jerzy," Brundage Archives; Avery Brundage to General Vladimir Stoytchev, 3 September 1954, box 63, "IOC Members," folder "Stoytchev, Gen. Vladimir," Brundage Archives; Avery Brundage to General Vladimir Stoytchev, 18 January 1965, box 63, "IOC Members," folder "Stoytchev, Gen. Vladimir," Brundage Archives.

98. Dr. Jerzy Loth to Avery Brundage, 10 August 1953, box 59, "IOC Members," folder "Loth, Dr. Jerzy," Brundage Archives.

99. Avery Brundage to IOC members on Rule No. 25, Circular Letter No. 27, 12 February 1954, box 70, "Circular Letters," Brundage Archives; IOC, *Olympic Charter 1954*, http://www.olympic.org/Documents/Olympic%20Charter/Olympic_Charter_through_time/1954-Olympic_Charter-Olympic_Rule_Nr25.pdf.

100. IOC Session, Paris, 13–17 June 1955, box 91, "IOC Minutes, 1954–1960," folder "IOC 50th Session," Brundage Archives.

101. Riordan, "Russia and Eastern Europe," 4; R. G. Osterhoudt, "Capitalist and Socialist Interpretations of Modern Amateurism: An Essay on the Fundamental Difference," in *Olympism*, ed. Jeffrey Segrave and Donald Chu (Champaign, IL: Human Kinetics, 1981), 42–47.

102. Avery Brundage, "I Must Admit—Russian Athletes Are Great!" *Saturday Evening Post*, 30 April 1955, 28.

103. Avery Brundage, "Questionnaire, the Problem of Amateur Status," Association of Sport Editors of Switzerland, box 102, "International Olympic Committee Subject File," folder "Broken Time," Brundage Archives.

104. "The 'Cold War' about the Olympic Amateur Statute," *Neue zürcher Zeitung* (Zurich), 7 May 1954, box 102, "International Olympic Committee Subject File," folder "Broken Time," Brundage Archives.

105. "The Soviet Athletes Who Devote Half the Year to Sport Are No More Amateurs," *World Athletic Service* No. 47, 24 November 1954, box 102, "International Olympic Committee Subject File," folder "Broken Time," Brundage Archives.

106. Avery Brundage to Lord David Burghley, 21 September 1954, box 54, "IOC Members," folder "Exeter, Marquess David," Brundage Archives; Otto Mayer to Konstantin Andrianov, 18 August 1961, box 50, "IOC Members," folder "Andrianov, Konstantin," Brundage Archives; Avery Brundage to Konstantin Andrianov, 31 October 1961, box 50, "IOC Members," folder "Andrianov, Konstantin," Brundage Archives; Konstantin Andrianov to Avery Brundage, 31 May 1960, box 50, "IOC Members," folder "Andrianov, Konstantin," Brundage Archives.

107. IOC Session, Paris, 13–17 June 1955, box 91, "IOC Minutes, 1954–1960," folder "IOC 50th Session," Brundage Archives.

108. Ibid.

109. E. J. H. Holt to Avery Brundage, 10 November 1952, box 26, "Individuals," folder "Holt, E. J. H."; Avery Brundage to E. J. H. Holt, 21 November 1952, box 26, "Individuals," folder "Holt, E. J. H.," Brundage Archives; Avery Brundage to Comité Olímpico Argentino, 19 June 1952, box 116, "National Olympic Committees," folder "Comite Olímpico Argentino," Brundage Archives.

110. Avery Brundage to Donald Hull, 8 October 1963, box 1, "Amateur Athletic Union," folder "1963," Brundage Archives; Donald Hull to Avery Brundage, 10 October 1963, box 1, "Amateur Athletic Union," folder "1963," Brundage Archives.

111. IOC Session, Rome, 21–27 April 1949, box 90, "IOC Minutes, 1914–1953," folder "IOC, Rome," Brundage Archives.

112. Avery Brundage to Sigfrid Edström, 12 April 1947, box 42, "IOC Presidents and Secretariat," folder "Edstrom, J. Sigfrid," Brundage Archives; Barbara Schrodt, "Ice Queen in Hot Seat: The Gift of a Sporty New Buick Gave Canada's Sweetheart Some Grief," *The Beaver* (1 December 2009), http://www.highbeam.com/doc/1G1-227182620.html.

113. IOC Session, Melbourne, November 1956, box 91, "IOC Minutes, 1954–1960," folder "IOC 52nd Session," Brundage Archives; IOC Executive Board meeting, Lausanne, Switzerland, 3–4 October 1956, box 91, "IOC Minutes, 1954–1960," folder "Executive Board, Lausanne," Brundage Archives.

114. IOC Session, meeting with national Olympic committees, Athens, 10–11 May 1954, IOC Archives.

115. Avery Brundage, "Amateur Sport and Broken Time," *World Sports*, November 1948, box 102, "International Olympic Committee Subject File," folder "Broken Time," Brundage Archives.

116. Avery Brundage to IOC Members, Circular Letter No. 114, 7 December 1957, box 70, "Circular Letters," Brundage Archives.

Chapter 6. *The Global Games and the Intransigent Dictator*

1. Phil Pilley, "Halt This Amateur Sham," *World Sports* (April 1960), box 149, "National Olympic Committees," folder "Union of Soviet Socialist Republics—Newspaper Clippings," Brundage Archives.

2. Irving Jaffee, "Why America Can't Win: The 1960 Olympics," *American Weekly*, 17 January 1960, box 149, "National Olympic Committees," folder "Union of Soviet Socialist Republics—Newspaper Clippings," Brundage Archives.

3. "Olympics Must Become 'Open Event,'" *Montreal Gazette*, 15 March 1956, 29; Pilley, "Amateur Sham."

4. Charles W. Thayer, "A Question of the Soul," *Sports Illustrated* (15 August 1960): 73–83; quote, 73.

5. Ken Doherty, "A Modern View of Amateurism," *Amateur Athlete* (February 1961): 32–34; quote, 32.

6. 56th IOC Session, San Francisco, 15–16 February 1960, IOC Archives.

7. A. Sidney Dawes to Avery Brundage, 15 March 1956, box 53, "IOC Members," folder "Dawes, A. Sidney," Brundage Archives.

8. Konstantin Andrianov to Avery Brundage, 31 May 1960, box 149, "National Olympic Committees," folder "Union of Soviet Socialist Republics," Brundage Archives.

9. David F. Gerrard, "Playing Foreign Policy Games: States, Drugs and Other Olympian Vices," *Sport in Society* 11, no. 4 (July 2008): 459–66; Paul Dimeo, Thomas M. Hunt, and Richard Horbury, "The Individual and the State: A Social Historical Analysis of the East German 'Doping System,'" *Sport in History* 31, no. 2 (June 2011): 218–37.

10. Otto Mayer to Avery Brundage, 9 July 1956, box 130, "National Olympic Committees," folder "Nationales Olympisches Komitee der Deutschen Demokratischen Republik," Brundage Archives.

11. "Mr Ewald Drops His Mask: Political Demonstration at the Third Sports Conference of the Soviet Zone at Chemnitz," November 1956, box 130, "National Olympic Committees," folder "Nationales Olympisches Komitee der Deutschen Demokratischen Republik," Brundage Archives.

12. Uta Andrea Balbier, "'A Game, a Competition, an Instrument?' High Performance, Cultural Diplomacy and German Sport from 1950 to 1972," *International Journal of the History of Sport* 26, no. 4 (March 2009): 539–55; G. A. Carr, "The Use of Sports in the German Democratic Republic for the Promotion of National Consciousness and International Prestige," *Journal of Sport History* 1 (1974): 123–36.

13. *Leipziger Volkszeitung* (Leipzig), No. 286, 10 December 1954, box 130, "National Olympic Committees," folder "Nationales Olympisches Komitee der Deutschen Demokratischen Republik," Brundage Archives.

14. As cited in Raymond Gafner, *The International Olympic Committee, One Hundred Years: The Idea, the Presidents, the Achievements, 1894–1994*, vol. 2 (Lausanne, Switzerland: International Olympic Committee, 1994), 95.

15. Ibid., 93–99.

16. Steven Ungerleider, *Faust's Gold: Inside the East German Doping Machine* (New York: Macmillan, 2001).

17. Mike Dennis and Jonathan Grix, *Sport under Communism: Behind the East German Sports 'Miracle'* (New York: Palgrave Macmillan, 2012).

18. "Eastern Zone Athletes Compete for Money," *Das Bild*, 30 September 1960, in Avery Brundage to Heinz Schöbel, 28 September 1962, box 62, "IOC Members," folder "Schöbel, Heinz," Brundage Archives.

19. "Interview with Former East German Athlete," No. 138 of the Document Roll, 16 October 1962, box 149, "National Olympic Committees," folder "Union of Soviet Socialist Republics," Brundage Archives.

20. Otto Mayer to Avery Brundage, 9 July 1956, box 130, "National Olympic Committees," folder "Nationales Olympisches Komitee der Deutschen Demokratischen Republik," Brundage Archives.

21. For example, see Avery Brundage to Nationales Olympisches Komitee der Deutschen Demokratischen Republik, 27 October 1965, box 130, "National Olympic Committees," folder "Nationales Olympisches Komitee der Deutschen Demokratischen Republik," Brundage Archives; Avery Brundage to Heinz Schöbel, 13 January 1964, box 62, "IOC Members," folder "Schöbel, Heinz," Brundage Archives.

22. Avery Brundage to Heinz Schöbel, 26 January 1963, box 62, "IOC Members," folder "Schöbel, Heinz," Brundage Archives.

23. Heinz Schöbel to Avery Brundage, 24 January 1964, box 62, "IOC Members," folder "Schöbel, Heinz," Brundage Archives.

24. "Olympic Malaise," *Neue zürcher Zeitung* (Zurich), 24 May 1963, box 149, "National Olympic Committees," folder "Union of Soviet Socialist Republics—Newspaper Clippings," Brundage Archives.

25. Allen Guttmann, *The Games Must Go On: Avery Brundage and the Olympic Movement* (New York: Columbia University Press, 1983), 130.

26. IOC Executive Board meeting with IOC members of Eastern Europe, Athens, 16 June 1961, IOC Archives.

27. Ibid.

28. Avery Brundage to Julio Gerlein Comelin, 28 December 1965, box 53, "IOC Members," folder "Comelin, Julio Gerlein," Brundage Archives; Avery Brundage to Armand Massard, 9 July and 15 September 1966, box 60, "IOC Members," folder "Massard, Armand," Brundage Archives; J. W. Westerhoff to Avery Brundage, 17 August 1967, box 44, "IOC Presidents and Secretariat," folder "Westerhoff, Johann," Brundage Archives; Avery Brundage to General Gustav Dyrssen and Gunnar Ericsson, 30 June 1967, box 54, "IOC Members," folder "Dryssen, Gen. Gustav," Brundage Archives.

29. Toby Rider, "The Olympic Games and the Secret Cold War: The U.S. Government and the Propaganda Campaign against Communist Sport, 1950–1960," PhD diss., University of Western Ontario, 2011.

30. Guttmann, *Games Must Go On*, 127.

31. As cited in Charles W. Thayer, "A Question of the Soul," *Sports Illustrated* (15 August 1960): 73–83; quote, 82.

32. Avery Brundage to David Burghley, 14 August 1961, box 54, "IOC Members," folder "Exeter, Marquess David," Brundage Archives.

33. IOC Executive Board meeting, Lausanne, Switzerland, 5 June 1963, IOC Archives.

34. Otto Mayer to Prince Axel of Denmark, 15 April 1955, Union Cycliste Int (1894–1962, OU Mo 01 14 33, IOC Archives.

35. nd IOC Session, Tokyo, 7–9 October 1964, IOC Archives.

36. "The Olympic Oath," *Toronto Globe and Mail*, 26 May 1962, 8.

37. Albert Mayer, "Amateurism—Project No. 2, Official Interpretation of Art. 26 of the Olympic Rules," in Circular Letter No. 184, 28 November 1961, box 70, "Circular Letters," Brundage Archives.

38. Albert Mayer to Avery Brundage, 16 May 1960, box 60, "IOC Members," folder "Mayer, Albert," Brundage Archives.

39. 57th IOC Session, Rome, 20–24 August 1960, Annex 3, IOC Archives.

40. Avery Brundage to members of the IOC, Circular Letter No. 184, 28 November 1961, box 70, "Circular Letters," Brundage Archives.

41. Albert Mayer to Avery Brundage, 23 June 1960, box 60, "IOC Members," folder "Mayer, Albert," Brundage Archives.

42. IOC Executive Board meeting with delegates of South Africa, Rome, 24 August 1960, IOC Archives.

43. 58th IOC Session, Athens, 19–21 June 1961, Annex 5, IOC Archives.

44. Ibid.

45. Konstantin Andrianov and Aleksei Romanov to Avery Brundage, 8 April 1961, box 149, "National Olympic Committees," folder "Union of Soviet Socialist Republics," Brundage Archives.

46. 58th IOC Session, Athens, 19–21 June 1961, Annex 5, IOC Archives.

47. "Stop, Look and Listen," 15 November 1961, box 102, "International Olympic Committee Subject File," folder "Broken Time," Brundage Archives; Avery Brundage to members of the IOC, Circular Letter No. 184, 28 November 1961, box 70, "Circular Letters," Brundage Archives. The quote appears in both items.

48. Avery Brundage, "The Olympic Amateur Code," IOC Executive Board meeting with amateur commission in Lausanne, Switzerland, 2–3 March 1962, Commission d'Amateurisme: Correspondence 1894–1968, CIO COMMI-ADMIS-CORR, ID Chemise: 204764, IOC Archives.

49. Avery Brundage to François Piétri, 16 April 1962, Commission d'Amateurisme: Correspondence 1894–1968, CIO COMMI-ADMIS-CORR, ID Chemise: 204767, IOC Archives.

50. Avery Brundage to members of the IOC Executive Committee, Circular Letter No. 197, 4 April 1962, box 70, "Circular Letters," Brundage Archives.

51. 59th IOC Session, Moscow, 5–8 June 1962, IOC Archives.

52. IOC, *Olympic Charter 1962*, http://www.olympic.org/Documents/Olympic%20 Charter/Olympic_Charter_through_time/1962-Eligibility_rules_of_the_IOC.pdf.

53. Avery Brundage to AAU, 27 September 1962, box 1, "Amateur Athletic Union," folder "1962," Brundage Archives.

54. Otto Mayer to Avery Brundage, n.d. Commission d'Amateurisme: Correspondence 1894–1968, CIO COMMI-ADMIS-CORR, ID Chemise: 204767, IOC Archives.

55. "L'Athlète Payée N'Est Pas un Sportif," *Monde des Sport*, undated clipping, box 102, "International Olympic Committee Subject File," folder "Broken Time," Brundage Archives.

56. Avery Brundage to National Olympic Committees, Circular Letter No. 203, 1 September 1962, box 70, "Circular Letters," Brundage Archives.

57. Gafner, *International Olympic Committee*, 152.

58. Allen Guttmann, *Games Must Go On*, 213–22.

59. Robert K. Barney, Stephen R. Wenn, and Scott G. Martyn, *Selling the Five Rings: The International Olympic Committee and the Rise of Olympic Commercialism*, rev. ed. (Salt Lake City: University of Utah Press, 2004). When the Olympics were held in Los Angeles in 1932, Paul Helms successfully sought out the exclusive contract to supply bread to the Olympic Village in Baldwin Hills. A smart entrepreneur, Helms took legal steps to ensure that he had the authority to utilize Olympic symbols in advertising. With no precedents blocking his action, he was granted authorization and immediately set out to capitalize on his Olympic affiliation. Avery Brundage publicly denounced Helms and his "Official Olympic Bakers." Brundage accused Helms of exploiting the Olympics for his own personal gain. The case was finally settled in 1950: Helms agreed to remove the symbols from his ads, despite possessing the legal authorization to utilize the symbols. Scholars argue that this event spurred the Olympic Movement toward seeking the protection of Olympic trademarks.

60. IOC Session, Melbourne, 19–21 November 1956, box 78, "IOC Meetings, October, 1956–May 19, 1959, folder "52nd Session, Melbourne," Brundage Archives; Stephen Wenn, "Rivals and Revolutionaries: Avery Brundage, the Marquess of Exeter and Olympic Television Revenue," *Sport in History* 32, no. 2 (June 2012): 263.

61. Marquess of Exeter to Avery Brundage, 16 April 1958, Athlétisme, Correspondance 1914–1966, CIO FI OU MO 01 14 22, IOC Archives.

62. "Threaten to Set Up 2nd Olympics," *Chicago Daily Sun-Times*, 9 April 1958, 68.

63. Avery Brundage to Otto Mayer, 2 March 1957, box 47, "IOC Presidents and Secretariat," folder "Mayer, Otto(Chancellor)," Brundage Archives.

64. As cited in Wenn, "Rivals and Revolutionaries," 267.

65. Avery Brundage, "Mr. Brundage's Answer to the Marquess of Exeter," box 54, "IOC Members," folder "Exeter, Marquess David," Brundage Archives.

66. Jenifer Parks, "'Nothing but Trouble': The Soviet Union's Push to 'Democratise' International Sports during the Cold War, 1959–1962," *International Journal of the History of Sport* 30, no. 13 (2013): 1554–67.

67. IOC Executive Board meeting, Tehran, 2–8 May 1967, IOC Archives; Gafner, *International Olympic Committee*, 145–46.

68. Terry Vaios Gitersos, "The Sporting Scramble for Africa: GANEFO, the IOC and the 1965 African Games," *Sport in Society* 14, no. 5 (June 2011): 648–49.

69. Ian Henry and Mansour Al-Tauqi, "The Development of Olympic Solidarity: West and Non-West (Core and Periphery) Relations in the Olympic World," *International Journal of the History of Sport* 25, no. 3 (February 2008): 355–69.

70. John Hoberman, "Olympic Universalism and the Apartheid Issue," in *Sport, the Third Millennium: Proceedings of the International Symposium* (Sainte-Foy, Canada: Presses de l'Université Laval, 1991): 523–34. For more on late nineteenth- and early twentieth-century

racial attitudes, see Edward Beasley, *The Victorian Reinvention of Race* (London: Routledge, 2010).

71. Andrew M. Guest, "The Diffusion of Development-through-Sport: Analysing the History and Practice of the Olympic Movement's Grassroots Outreach to Africa," *Sport in Society* 12, no. 10 (December 2009): 1336–52.

72. For an examination of the IOC's handling of South African apartheid, see Christopher Hill, *Olympic Politics: Athens to Atlanta, 1896–1996* (Manchester, U.K.: Manchester University Press, 1996), 198–240. For Rhodesia, see Andrew Novak, "Rhodesia's 'Rebel and Racist' Olympic Team: Athletic Glory, National Legitimacy and the Clash of Politics and Sport," *International Journal of the History of Sport* 23, no. 8 (2006): 1369–88.

73. Guttmann, *Games Must Go On*, 223–55.

74. Avery Brundage to members of the IOC, Circular Letter No. 179, 20 March 1961, box 70, "Circular Letters," Brundage Archives.

75. Ibid.

76. IOC Executive Board meeting, Lausanne, Switzerland, 9 February 1963, IOC Archives.

77. Reginald Alexander, *The All-Africa Sub-Committee of the IOC,* report presented to the full session in Rome, 24–30 April 1966, IOC Archives.

78. Avery Brundage, Olympic Aid Committee, 28 August 1962, box 51, "IOC Members," folder "de Beaumont, Count Jean," Brundage Archives.

79. Henry and Al-Tauqi, "Development of Olympic Solidarity," 355–69.

80. See IOC Executive Board meeting, Lausanne, 5 June 1963, IOC Archives and 60th IOC Session, Baden-Baden, Germany, 16–20 October 1963, IOC Archives.

81. Avery Brundage, Olympic Aid Committee, 28 August 1962, box 51, "IOC Members," folder "de Beaumont, Count Jean," Brundage Archives.

82. Vijay Prashad, *The Darker Nations: A People's History of the Third World* (London: New Press, 2007).

83. Richard Espy, *The Politics of the Olympic Games* (Berkeley: University of California Press, 1981), 93–117.

84. Chris A. Connolly, "The Politics of the Games of the New Emerging Forces (GANEFO)," *International Journal of the History of Sport* 29, no. 9 (June 2012): 1311–24; Gitersos, "Sporting Scramble for Africa," 648–49; Amanda Shuman, "Elite Competitive Sport in the People's Republic of China 1958–1966: The Games of the New Emerging Forces (GANEFO)," *Journal of Sport History* 40, no. 2 (summer 2013): 258–83.

85. Barbara J. Keys, "The Early Cold War Olympics, 1952–1960: Political, Economic and Human Rights Dimensions," in *The Palgrave Handbook of Olympic Studies*, ed. Stephen Wagg and Helen Lenskyj (New York: Palgrave Macmillan, 2012), 72–83.

86. Gafner, *International Olympic Committee.*

87. There was no competition in Europe among rival networks. The European Broadcasting Union received favorable deals from the IOC in the absence of opposing bids. See Barney et al., *Selling the Five Rings*, 79–102.

88. Ibid.

89. Guttmann, *The Olympics*, 115–123.

90. "Report of the Meeting of the Co-Ordinating and Study Committee of National Olympic Committees," as cited in 64th IOC session, Rome, 24–30 April 1966, Annex 6, IOC Archives.

91. Avery Brundage to Hugh Weir and members of the Sub-Committee on the Amateur Rule, 23 February 1966, Commission d'Amateurisme: Correspondence 1894–1968, CIO COMMI-ADMIS-CORR, ID Chemise: 204767, IOC Archives.

92. Hugh Weir, "Amateurism," Preliminary Report of Sub-Committee, Commission d'Amateurisme: Correspondence 1894–1968, CIO COMMI-ADMIS-CORR, ID Chemise: 204767, IOC Archives.

93. Avery Brundage to members of the IOC, Circular Letter No. 313, 23 April 1966, box 70, "Circular Letters," Brundage Archives.

94. IOC Executive Board meeting, Mexico City, 22 October 1966, IOC Archives; J. W. Westerhoff to Hugh Weir, 11 September 1968, Commission d'Amateurisme: Correspondence 1894–1968, CIO COMMI-ADMIS-CORR, ID Chemise: 204767, IOC Archives.

95. "Olympism Looking for the Superman," *Die Welt*, 28 January 1966, as cited in Avery Brundage to members of the IOC, Circular Letter No. 309, 31 March 1966, box 70, "Circular Letters," Brundage Archives.

96. IOC Executive Board meeting, Lausanne, Switzerland, 11 and 14 April 1965, IOC Archives.

97. Avery Brundage to National Olympic Committee of Germany, n.d., box 128, "National Olympic Committees," folder "Nationales Olympisches Komitee fur Deutschland," Brundage Archives; Willie Daume to Ivan Vind, 31 January 1966, box 128, "National Olympic Committees," folder "Nationales Olympisches Komitee fur Deutschland," Brundage Archives.

98. IOC Executive Board meeting, Paris, 9–10 July 1965, IOC Archives.

Chapter 7. Selling Out the Amateur Ideal

1. For an examination of the 1968 Mexico City Games, see Kevin Witherspoon, *Before the Eyes of the World: Mexico and the 1968 Olympic Games* (Chicago: Northern Illinois University Press, 2008); Keith Brewster, ed., *Reflections of Mexico '86* (Hoboken, NJ: Wiley-Blackwell, 2010).

2. "Free Huey" became a Black Panthers chant to protest the imprisonment of Black Panthers member Huey Newton. Marianne DeKoven, *The Sixties and the Emergence of the Postmodern* (Durham, NC: Duke University Press, 2004); Arthur Marwick, *The Sixties: Cultural Revolution in Britain, France, Italy, and the United States, c. 1958–c. 1974* (Oxford: Oxford University Press, 1998).

3. For a comprehensive description of the 1960s political events around the world, see James S. Baugess and Abbe Allen DeBolt, *Encyclopedia of the Sixties: A Decade of Culture and Counterculture* (Santa Barbara, CA: Greenwood Press, 2011).

4. David Zang, *Sports Wars: Athletes in the Age of Aquarius* (Fayetteville: University of Arkansas Press, 2001); Dave Zirin, *What's My Name, Fool? Sports and Resistance in the United States* (Chicago, IL: Haymarket Books, 2005); Douglas Hartman, *Race, Culture, and the Revolt of the Black Athlete: The 1968 Olympic Protests and Their Aftermath* (Chicago, IL: University of Chicago Press, 2004).

5. Susan Cahn, *Coming on Strong: Gender and Sexuality in Twentieth-Century Women's Sports* (Cambridge, MA: Harvard University Press, 1998); Jaime Schultz, *Qualifying Times: Points of Change in U.S. Women's Sport* (Urbana: University of Illinois Press, 2014).

6. Amy Bass, *Not the Triumph But the Struggle: 1968 Olympics and the Making of the Black Athlete* (Minneapolis: University of Minnesota Press, 2002).

7. Allen Guttmann, *The Games Must Go On: Avery Brundage and the Olympic Movement* (New York: Columbia University Press, 1983), 180–83.

8. "Speech by Mr. Giulio Onesti of the National Olympic Committees," IOC Annual Session, Grenoble, 2–5 February 1968, IOC Archives.

9. Giulio Onesti, "Report—Visit to Africa," 20 December–6 January 1969, box 61, "IOC Members," folder "Onesti, Giullo," Brundage Archives.

10. Giulio Onesti to the IOC, 17 July 1969, IOC Executive Board meeting, Dubrovnik, Yugoslavia, 23–27 October 1969, Annex 27, box 94, "IOC Minutes, October 7–11, 1968," folder "Executive Board and National Olympic Committees," Brundage Archives.

11. Avery Brundage to Hugh Weir, 8 January 1968, box 98, "IOC Commissions and Committees," folder "Eligibility Commission, Hugh Weir," Brundage Archives; Avery Brundage to Hugh Weir, 29 August 1968, box 98, "IOC Commissions and Committees," folder "Eligibility Commission, Hugh Weir," Brundage Archives.

12. IOC Annual Session, Mexico City, 7–11 October 1968, IOC Archives.

13. To accurately gauge the impact of the television on sport, see Garry Whannel, *Fields in Vision: Television Sport and Cultural Transformation* (London: Routledge, 2005). Also see Ronald A. Smith, *Play by Play: Radio, Television, and Big-Time College Sport* (Baltimore, MD: Johns Hopkins University Press, 2001).

14. Robert K. Barney, Stephen R. Wenn, and Scott G. Martyn, *Selling the Five Rings: The International Olympic Committee and the Rise of Olympic Commercialism*, rev. ed. (Salt Lake City: University of Utah Press, 2004), 58.

15. Ibid., 104. Also see Raymond Gafner, *The International Olympic Committee, One Hundred Years: The Idea, the Presidents, the Achievements, 1894–1994*, vol. 3 (Lausanne, Switzerland: International Olympic Committee, 1994), 167–79.

16. Barney et al., *Selling the Five Rings*, 99–100.

17. For more on the television battles preceding the 1968 Games, see Stephen Wenn, "An Olympian Squabble: The Distribution of Olympic Television Revenue, 1960–1966," *Olympika* 3 (1994): 27–47.

18. John Underwood, "No Goody Two-Shoes," *Sports Illustrated,* 10 March 1969, 14–23.

19. Ibid., 23.

20. Joseph M. Turrini, *The End of Amateurism in American Track and Field* (Urbana: University of Illinois Press, 2010), 92.

21. "Tingeln durch Europa," *Die Zeit*, 8 October 1976, 21.

22. A. Strenk, "Amateurism: Myth and Reality," in *Olympism*, ed. Jeffrey Segrave and Donald Chu (Champaign, IL: Human Kinetics, 1981): 57–75.

23. Underwood, "No Goody Two-Shoes," 23.

24. P. Putnam, "Victory over Germany but a Loss to the AAU," *Sports Illustrated*, 27 July 1970, 48.

25. J. B. Strasser and Laurie Becklund, *Swoosh: The Unauthorized Story of Nike and the Men Who Played There* (New York: Harper Business, 1993), 18.

26. Barbara Smit, *Sneaker Wars: The Enemy Brothers Who Founded Adidas and Puma and the Family Feud That Forever Changed the Business of Sports* (New York: Harper Perennial, 2009), 41–45.

27. Archived photographs taken during the games reveal that all athletes wore Adidas shoes while competing at the 1956 Olympic Games. See *Life* magazine, 10 December 1956 cover image, box 176, "Olympic Games," folder "Commercial Use of Olympiad, Shoe Scandal," Brundage Archives.

28. Smit, *Sneaker Wars*, 46.

29. Underwood, "No Goody Two-Shoes," 17.

30. Ibid., 17.

31. Ibid., 18.

32. Puma aggressively lobbied the IOC to void Adidas's exclusive contract with the Mexico Olympic Organizing Committee. See Puma Sportschuhfabriken KG to J. W. Westerhoff, 28 December 1967, box 176, "Olympic Games," folder "Commercial Use of Olympiad, Shoe Scandal," Brundage Archives; Avery Brundage to General José de J. Clark, 8 July 1967, box 176, "Olympic Games," folder "Commercial Use of Olympiad, Shoe Scandal," Brundage Archives; Armin A. Dassler to International Olympic Committee, 24 May 1967, box 176, "Olympic Games," folder "Commercial Use of Olympiad, Shoe Scandal," Brundage Archives.

33. Underwood, "No Goody Two-Shoes."

34. See box 176, "Olympic Games," folder "Commercial Use of Olympiad, Shoe Scandal," Brundage Archives, for contents of letters sent between Brundage, Adidas, Puma, and the Mexico City Olympic Organizing Committee. For example, Horst Dassler to Avery Brundage, 5 September 1967; Pedro Ramírez Vásquez to Avery Brundage, 18 September 1967; Pedro Ramírez Vásquez to Avery Brundage, 18 July 1967.

35. Underwood, "No Goody Two-Shoes."

36. Ibid.

37. As cited in Turrini, *End of Amateurism*, 88.

38. Deux Cents Athlètes Auraient Reçu de l'Argent de Fabricants de Chaussures aux Jeux de Mexico," *Tribune de Lausanne*, 7 March 1969, box 176, "Olympic Games," folder "Commercial Use of Olympiad, Shoe Scandal," Brundage Archives.

39. Charles Maher, "Wide Olympic Payoffs Hinted," *Los Angeles Times,* 24 October 1968, 1.

40. Robert Lipsyte, "Sport of the Times: Shoes in the Machinery" *New York Times,* 24 October 1968, 60.

41. Avery Brundage to Pedro Ramírez Vásquez, 8 April 1969, box 176, "Olympic Games," folder "Commercial Use of Olympiad, Shoe Scandal," Brundage Archives; Daniel J. Ferris to Jesse Pardue, 23 April 1969, box 176, "Olympic Games," folder "Commercial Use of Olympiad, Shoe Scandal," Brundage Archives; Shirley Povich, "Olympic Scandal: U.S. May Give Up Some Medals," *Los Angeles Times,* 23 October 1968, 1.

42. Claire Brewster and Keith Brewster, *Representing the Nation: Sport and Spectacle in Post-Revolutionary Mexico* (London: Routledge, 2010), 141.

43. Turrini, *End of Amateurism*, 89.

44. Daniel J. Ferris to Jesse Pardue, 23 April 1969, box 176, "Olympic Games," folder "Commercial Use of Olympiad, Shoe Scandal," Brundage Archives.

45. Underwood, "No Goody Two-Shoes," 22.

46. Both companies argued that this reported sum was inflated. See "L'Affaire des Chaussures," *Tribune de Genève,* 7 May 1969. The *Chicago Daily News* provides an even

higher estimate: $100,000 in cash and $350,000 in free equipment. See "$450,000 Olympic Payoff Charged," *Chicago Daily News*, 5 March 1969, box 176, "Olympic Games," folder "Commercial Use of Olympiad, Shoe Scandal," Brundage Archives.

47. "Only White Shoes on the Track," *The Guardian* (London), May 1969, box 176, "Olympic Games," folder "Commercial Use of Olympiad, Shoe Scandal," Brundage Archives.

48. Puma Sportschuhfabriken KG to Avery Brundage, 22 January 1969, box 176, "Olympic Games," folder "Commercial Use of Olympiad, Shoe Scandal," Brundage Archives.

49. International Amateur Athletic Federation, minutes of the IAAF Congress, 1 September 1970, Amateurisme, Athle Gener Notice: 0074964, IOC Archives.

50. Christopher Hill, *Olympic Politics* (Manchester, U.K.: Manchester University Press, 1992), 84–88. Also see Thomas Turner, "German Sports Shoes, Basketball, and Hip Hop: The Consumption and Cultural Significance of the Adidas 'Superstar,' 1966—1988," *Sport in History* 35, no. 1 (2015): 127–55.

51. For examples of advertisements starring Killy and Shranz, see "Notice SKI 0087372, Correspondence 1960–1970," IOC Archives.

52. Avery Brundage, "Olympic Games in Danger," IOC Annual Session, Amsterdam, 12–16 May 1970, Annex 1, IOC Archives.

53. Newspaper headlines are cited in ibid.

54. Allen Guttmann, *The Olympics: A History of the Modern Games* (Urbana: University of Illinois Press, 2002), 128; Stephen Wenn, "Television, Corporate Sponsorship, and the Winter Olympics," in *The Winter Olympics: From Chamonix to Salt Lake City*, ed. Larry Gerlach (Salt Lake City: University of Utah Press, 2002), 155–84.

55. The newspaper article quoted was a clipping included in a letter from Avery Brundage to International Ski Federation president Marc Hodler: Brundage to Hodler, 4 March 1964, Notice SKI 0087372, Correspondence 1960–1970, IOC Archives.

56. "The Amateurs Know How to Look after Themselves Too!" *The Minute*, 19 February 1970, 23.

57. IOC Annual Session, Grenoble, 1–5 February 1968, IOC Archives.

58. Mark Katz, "Alpine Skiing: The Shadow under the Table," *International Herald Tribune*, 20 February 1970, box 98, "IOC Commissions and Committees," folder "Eligibility Commission, Hugh Weir," Brundage Archives; Guttmann, *Games Must Go On*, 220.

59. "Olympics: Hero in the Dock," *Time*, 15 March 1968, http://content.time.com/time/magazine/article/0,9171,838032,00.html; Guttmann, *Games Must Go On*, 198.

60. Gafner, *International Olympic Committee*, 160.

61. Avery Brundage to members of the IOC Executive Board, EB/545, 18 March 1970, IOC Archives.

62. Witherspoon, *Before the Eyes of the World*; Hartman, *Race, Culture, and the Revolt of the Black Athlete*; Christopher Hill, *Olympic Politics: Athens to Atlanta, 1896–1996* (Manchester, U.K.: Manchester University Press, 1996), 198–240.

63. Brundage, "Olympic Games in Danger."

64. Ibid.

65. "Report from Joint Commission II on Eligibility," in IOC Annual Session, Warsaw, 6–10 June 1969, Annex 15, box 94, "IOC Minutes, October 7–11, 1968–1969," folder "IOC 68th Session, Warsaw," Brundage Archives.

66. "Report of the Activity of Joint Commission II on Eligibility," IOC Executive Board meeting, Dubrovnik, Yugoslavia, 23–27 October 1969, Annex 11, box 94, "IOC Minutes, October 7–11, 1968–1969," folder "Executive Board and National Olympic Committees, Dubrovnik," Brundage Archives.

67. "Report from Joint Commission II on Eligibility," IOC Annual Session," Warsaw, 6–10 June 1969, Annex 15, box 94, "IOC Minutes, October 7–11, 1968–1969," folder "IOC 68th Session, Warsaw," Brundage Archives; "Report of the Activity of Joint Commission II on Eligibility," IOC Executive Board meeting, Dubrovnik, Yugoslavia, 23–27 October 1969, Annex 11, box 94, "IOC Minutes, October 7–11, 1968–1969," folder Executive Board and National Olympic Committees, Dubrovnik," Brundage Archives.

68. Avery Brundage to Hugh Weir, 10 February 1970, box 98, "IOC Commissions and Committees," folder "Eligibility Commission, Hugh Weir," Brundage Archives.

69. Avery Brundage to members of the Eligibility Committee, 2 March 1970, box 98, "IOC Commissions and Committees," folder "Eligibility Commission, Hugh Weir," Brundage Archives; IOC Annual Session, Amsterdam, Holland, 12–16 May 1970, IOC Archives.

70. Standing Eligibility Commission, "Comparative Study," October 1970, box 98, "IOC Commissions and Committees," folder "Eligibility Commission, Hugh Weir," Brundage Archives.

71. Gafner, *International Olympic Committee*, 160.

72. IOC, *Olympic Charter 1971*, http://www.olympic.org/Documents/Olympic%20Charter/Olympic_Charter_through_time/1971-Olympic_Charter-Olympic_rules_and_regulations .pdf.

73. Avery Brundage to Hugh Weir, 25 March 1971, box 98, "IOC Commissions and Committees," folder "Eligibility Commission, Hugh Weir," Brundage Archives.

74. Ibid.

75. Hugh Weir to Avery Brundage, April 1971, box 98, "IOC Commissions and Committees," folder "Eligibility Commission, Hugh Weir," Brundage Archive.

76. Hugh Weir to Avery Brundage, 26 October 1971, box 98, "IOC Commissions and Committees," folder "Eligibility Commission, Hugh Weir," Brundage Archive.

77. IOC, Minutes of the IOC Eligibility Commission, Luxembourg, 13 September 1971, IOC Archives.

78. Brundage devoted a considerable portion of his opening address at the 1970 annual IOC session to Karl Schranz and his shamateur exploits. See Brundage, "Olympic Games in Danger."

79. For a comprehensive media examination of the Karl Schranz affair, see Guy-Lionel Loew, "Karl Schranz and the International Debate on Amateurism, Sapporo 1972," *Olympika* 17 (2008): 153–68; Guy-Lionel Loew, "Amateurism and the Olympic Movement: The Stakes of the Definition of Amateurism under the Light of the Case of Karl Schranz—1972 Winter Games Sapporo, Japan," *Journal of Olympic History* 13 (January 2005): 24–30.

80. Brundage, "Olympic Games in Danger."

81. IOC, Minutes of the meeting of the Executive Board of the International Olympic Committee, Lausanne, Switzerland, 1–2 February 1969, 4, IOC Archives.

82. "Report from the President of the FIS," IOC Executive Board meeting, Lausanne, Switzerland, 4 October 1970, IOC Archives.

83. Marc Hodler to Avery Brundage, 2 December 1971, Corr 1970, FED INT SKI File 0087372, IOC Archives.

84. Avery Brundage to members of the IOC Executive Board, EB/545, 18 March 1970, IOC Archives.

85. Avery Brundage to the IOC, Circular Letter No. 573, 27 August 1970. box 71, "Circular Letters," Brundage Archives.

86. Arthur Takac to Hugh Weir, 1 December 1971, box 98, "IOC Commissions and Committees," folder "Eligibility Commission, Hugh Weir," Brundage Archives.

87. "Françoise Macchi Prend la Tête dans la Coupe du Monde," *L'Équipe*, 21 December 1971, box 98, "IOC Commissions and Committees," folder "Eligibility Commission, Hugh Weir," Brundage Archives.

88. "France's Annie Famose Suspended from Games," *Spokesman-Review*, 10 February 1972, 27.

89. "Sportsmen also Insure with the Zurich," *Kurier*, 15 February 1972, as cited in Artur Takac to Jean Weymann, 29 March 1972, box 98, "IOC Commissions and Committees," folder "Eligibility Commission, Hugh Weir," Brundage Archives.

90. See International Olympic Committee File ID Chemise 204801 CIO COMMI-ADMIS-LITG 1972, IOC Archives, for specific files following this frequent pattern, including skiers Marie-Therese Nadig (Switzerland), Bernard Russi (Switzerland), and Gustabo Thoeni (Italy). Also see IOC Eligibility Committee, box 98, "IOC Commissions and Committees," folder "Eligibility Commission, Hugh Weir," Brundage Archives.

91. Comte Jean de Beaumont letter of resignation, 8 December 1971, IOC Executive Board meeting, 29 January–1 February 1972, Tokyo-Sapporo, Annex 2, IOC Archives.

92. Avery Brundage to IOC, Circular Letter, M/C/676, 29 December 1971, box 71, "Circular Letters," Brundage Archives.

93. Avery Brundage to Hugh Weir, 5 January 1972, box 98, "IOC Commissions and Committees," folder "Eligibility Commission, Hugh Weir," Brundage Archives.

94. Barney et al., *Selling the Five Rings*, 104. Also see Gafner, *International Olympic Committee*, 167–79.

95. Hugh Weir to Avery Brundage, 18 December 1971, box 98, "IOC Commissions and Committees," folder "Eligibility Commission, Hugh Weir," Brundage Archives.

96. See Hugh Weir to Lord Killanin, 5 January 1972, box 98, "IOC Commissions and Committees," folder "Eligibility Commission, Hugh Weir," Brundage Archives; IOC Annual Session, Munich, Germany, 21–24 August and 5 September 1972, IOC Archives.

97. IOC Executive Board meeting, 29 January 1972, Tokyo, IOC Archives.

98. "Les Enseignements de Val d'Isère ou les Contradictions du Ski," *Tribune de Lausanne*, 14 December 1971, box 98, "IOC Commissions and Committees," folder "Eligibility Commission, Hugh Weir," Brundage Archives.

99. Artur Takac to *Oesterreichisches Olympisches Komitee*, 16 December 1971, box 98, "IOC Commissions and Committees," folder "Eligibility Commission, Hugh Weir," Brundage Archives.

100. Deposition by Karl Schranz, 23 December 1971, box 98, "IOC Commissions and Committees," folder "Eligibility Commission, Hugh Weir," Brundage Archives; deposition by Heinrich Messner, 28 December 1971, box 98, "IOC Commissions and Committees," folder "Eligibility Commission, Hugh Weir," Brundage Archives.

101. Franz Kneissl to Heinz Klee, n.d., box 98, "IOC Commissions and Committees," folder "Eligibility Commission, Hugh Weir," Brundage Archives.

102. Report by Heinz Pruckner to Hugh Weir, 31 December 1971, box 98, "IOC Commissions and Committees," folder "Eligibility Commission, Hugh Weir," Brundage Archives.

103. IOC press release, 31 January 1972, 20612, JG-1972-AMATE, IOC Archives.

104. IOC Executive Board meeting, Sapporo, 29 January–1 February1972, Annex 9, IOC Archives.

105. IOC Annual Session, Sapporo, Japan, 31 January–1 February 1972, IOC Archives.

106. Ibid.

107. See newspaper clippings, box 181, "Olympic Games," folder "Protests: Karl Schranz 1972–73," Brundage Archives.

108. IOC Annual Session, Sapporo, Japan, 31 January–1 February 1972, IOC Archives.

109. "Brundage Droht Ganz Österreich mit Olympia-Ausschlub," *Oberösterreichische Nachrichten,* box 181, "Olympic Games," folder "Protests: Karl Schranz 1972–73," Brundage Archives.

110. Guttmann, *Games Must Go On,* 120.

111. Joan Sweeney, "Just for the Fun of It," *Los Angeles Times,* 8 December 1972, 16.

112. As cited in "The Karl Schranz Case," *Sie und Er* (Zurich), 22 February 1972, box 181, "Olympic Games," folder "Protests: Karl Schranz 1972–73," Brundage Archives.

113. "Brundage: None of the Skiers Was Qualified at Sapporo," *Mainichi Shimbun,* 16 February 1972, box 181, "Olympic Games," folder "Protests: Karl Schranz 1972–73," Brundage Archives.

114. "Austria to Compete," *Los Angeles Times,* 2 February, 1972, D1; Jim Murray, "Honest Ave Umbrage," *Los Angeles Times,* 3 February 1972, B6; Arthur Daley, "The Abominable Snowman Wins Again," *New York Times,* 3 February 1972, 39; "Brundage Ranks as IOC's Top Pro," *Washington Post,* 5 February 1972, E2.

115. Gafner, *International Olympic Committee,* 47, 50.

116. Roger Butterfield, "Self-Made Millionaire and Heel-and-Toe Champion, He Is the Irascible High Priest of Amateurism in Sports," *Life,* 14 June 1948, 115.

117. Smit, *Sneaker Wars,* 103–6.

118. Kay Schiller and Christopher Young, *The 1972 Munich Olympics and the Making of Modern Germany* (Berkeley: University of California Press, 2010).

119. Meeting minutes, PV sur la Préparation du Congrès—Minutes on the Preparation of the Congress—1972, IOC Archives.

120. "A.A.U. Board Endorses Liberalized Amateur Code," *New York Times,* 4 December 1972, 61.

121. "USOC to Ask for Changes in Olympics," *New York Herald Tribune,* 9 May 1973, ID Chemise 204833 CIO COMMI-ADMIS-CORR, SD 3: Art. De presse et sa corr. 1972–1974, IOC Archives.

122. IOC, *Official Report, Olympic Congress, Varna, Bulgaria, 1973,* 21, IOC Archives.

123. Ibid., 25.

124. Ibid., 25.

125. This conclusion is based on a summary of the official report and correspondence with Killanin from 1973 to 1974. Commission d'Admission: Correspondences et Divers Documents 1972–74 ID Chemise: 204833 CIO COMMI-ADMIS-CORR, IOC Archives.

126. Circular letter Lord Killian to IOC members, ref M/F/855, 16 October 1973, Annex 1, ID Chemise 204833 CIO COMMI-ADMIS-CORR, SD 1: Corr. Oct.–Dec. 1973, IOC Archives.

127. Ibid.

128. Ibid.

129. The national Olympic committees and the national sports federations were the only two authorized providers of the broken-time payments.

130. IOC Annual Session, Vienna, Austria, 21–24 October 1974, IOC Archives. For clear comparisons, see the *Olympic Charter*'s Rule 26 in its 1973 and 1975 editions, IOC Archives, 13. IOC, 1975 Olympic statutes (provisional), section B, bye-laws I, 26, 41.

Chapter 8. *The Ultimate Move*

1. For examples of critical press reports discussing the IOC's handling of the Karl Schranz affair, see Jim Murray, "Dollars Don't Do It," *Los Angeles Times,* 16 November 1973, E1; Leonard Shapiro, "Moneymen Glow after a Victory," *Washington Post,* 8 February 1976, 41; Dave Anderson, "The Olympic Flame of Hypocrisy," *New York Times,* 3 February 1976, 25.

2. IOC Executive Board meeting, Lausanne, 20–22 February 1975, IOC Archives.

3. IOC Annual Session, Innsbruck, 2–3 February 1976, IOC Archives.

4. IOC Annual Session, Prague, 15–18 June 1977, IOC Archives.

5. IOC Annual Session, Athens, 17–20 May 1978, IOC Archives.

6. Ibid.

7. IOC Annual Session, Lake Placid, New York, 10–13 February 1980, IOC Archives, 49.

8. Ibid.

9. Dave Day, *Professionals, Amateurs, and Performance: Sports Coaching in England, 1789–1914* (Bern: Peter Lang, 2012), 55–84; Neil Carter, "From Knox to Dyson: Coaching, Amateurism and British Athletics, 1912—1947," *Sport in History* 30, no. 1 (2010): 55–81.

10. Allen Guttmann, *From Ritual to Record: The Nature of Modern Sports* (New York: Columbia University Press, 1978).

11. Day, *Professionals, Amateurs, and Performance*, 113–42; John Hoberman, *Mortal Engines: The Science of Performance and the Dehumanization of Sport* (New York: Free Press, 1992), 62–99.

12. Hoberman, *Mortal Engines*, 62–99; Vanessa Heggie, *A History of British Sports Medicine* (Manchester, U.K.: Manchester University Press, 2011), chapter 2.

13. Larry Owens, "Pure and Sound Government: Laboratories, Playing Fields, and Gymnasia in the Nineteenth-Century Search for Order," *Isis* 76, no. 2 (1985): 182–94.

14. For the development of sport science including specific research, see John D. Massengale and Richard A. Swanson, *The History of Exercise and Sport Science* (Champaign, IL: Human Kinetics, 1997); Heggie, *British Sports Medicine*.

15. Alison Wrynn, "The Human Factor: Science, Medicine and the International Olympic Committee, 1900–70," *Sport in Society,* 7, no. 2 (2004): 211–31; Alison Wrynn, "'A Debt Was Paid Off in Tears': Science, IOC Politics and the Debate about High Altitude in the

1968 Mexico City Olympics," *International Journal of the History of Sport* 23, no. 7 (2006): 1152–72.

16. For the development of anabolic steroids in the postwar era, see Paul Dimeo, *A History of Drug Use in Sport, 1876–1976: Beyond Good and Evil* (London: Routledge, 2007), 87–104. For the development of blood transfusions, see John Gleaves, "Manufactured Dope: How the 1984 US Olympic Cycling Team Rewrote the Rules on Drugs in Sports," *International Journal for the History of Sport* 32, no. 1 (2015): 89–107.

17. Heggie, *British Sports Medicine*, chapter 4; Dimeo, *Drug Use in Sport*, 87–104.

18. For a fuller discussion of sport and its cultural importance, see David Caute, *The Dancer Defects: The Struggle for Cultural Supremacy during the Cold War* (Oxford: Oxford University Press, 2003); Stephen Wagg and David L. Andrews, eds., *East Plays West: Sport and the Cold War* (London, U.K.: Routledge, 2006).

19. Kalevi Heinila, "The Totalization Process in International Sport," in *Sport in Social Context*, ed. Kalevi Heinila (Jyvaskyla, Finland: University of Jyvaskyla Press, 1984), 123–40.

20. Thomas Hunt, *Drug Games: The International Olympic Committee and the Politics of Doping, 1960–2008* (Austin: University of Texas Press, 2011), 61–86.

21. Michael Kalinski, "State-Sponsored Research on Creatine Supplements and Blood Doping in Elite Sport," *Perspectives in Biology and Medicine* 46, no. 3 (2003): 445–51.

22. For a detailed examination of sport in the GDR, see Mike Dennis and Jonathan Grix, *Sport under Communism: Behind the East German Sports 'Miracle'* (New York: Palgrave Macmillan, 2012); Hoberman, *Mortal Engines*, 222.

23. Dennis and Grix, *Sport under Communism*, 48.

24. Ibid., 52.

25. Thomas Hunt, Paul Dimeo, Florian Hemme, and Anne Mueller, "The Health Risks of Doping during the Cold War: A Comparative Analysis of the Two Sides of the Iron Curtain," *International Journal for the History of Sport* 31, no. 17 (2014): 2230–44.

26. Alison Wrynn, "The Athlete in the Making: The Scientific Study of American Athletic Performance, 1920–1932," *Sport in History* 30, no. 1 (2010): 121–37.

27. Thomas Hunt, "Sport, Drugs, and the Cold War: The Conundrum of Olympic Doping Policy, 1970–1979," *Olympika* 16 (2007): 19–41.

28. "Effect of Drugs to Aid Athletes Studied by U.S.," *New York Times*, 22 August 1976, 176.

29. Gerald R. Ford, "In Defense of the Competitive Urge," *Sports Illustrated*, 8 July 1974, 17.

30. Thomas Hunt, "Countering the Soviet Threat in the Olympic Medal Race: The Amateur Sports Act of 1978 and American Athletics Policy Reform," *International Journal for the History of Sport* 24, no. 6 (June 2007): 796–818.

31. J. B. Strasser and Laurie Becklund, *Swoosh: The Unauthorized Story of Nike and the Men Who Played There* (New York: Harper Business, 1993).

32. For the creation of Athletics West, see Strasser and Becklund, *Swoosh*, 273.

33. Hunt, "Sport, Drugs, and the Cold War," 19–41.

34. Michael Kruger and Christian Becker, "Doping and Anti-Doping in the Process of German Reunification," *Sport in History* 34, no. 4 (2014): 620–43.

35. For more on doping in East Germany in the 1970s, see Hunt et al., "Health Risks of Doping," 2230–44; Steven Ungerleider, *Faust's Gold: Inside the East German Doping Machine* (New York: Macmillan, 2001).

36. Dennis and Grix, *Sport under Communism*, 119; Michael Krüger, Christian Becker, and Stefan Nielsen, *German Sports, Doping, and Politics: A History of Performance Enhancement* (Washington, DC: Rowman and Littlefield, 2015).

37. "Effect of Drugs to Aid Athletes Studied by U.S.," *New York Times*, 22 August 1976, 176.

38. Gleaves, "Manufactured Dope," 89–107.

39. For more on the Medical Commission and the organization of antidoping rules and amateurism, see John Gleaves and Matthew Llewellyn, "Sport, Drugs, and Amateurism: Tracing the Real Cultural Origins of Anti-Doping Rules in International Sport," *International Journal for the History of Sport* 31, no. 8 (2014): 839–53; Wrynn, "Human Factor," 211–31.

40. International Olympic Committee, *Olympic Charter 1975*, IOC Archives, http://www.olympic.org/Documents/Olympic%20Charter/Olympic_Charter_through_time/1975-Olympic_Charter-Olympic_Rules.pdf.

41. Hunt, *Drug Games.*

42. For a fuller defense of this claim, see Dimeo, *History of Drug Use*, 105–20.

43. John Holt, "Eligibility for the Olympic Games," *Official Report of the 11th Olympic Congress in Baden-Baden 1981*, vol. 1, 64, IOC Archives.

44. David Miller, "Juggling Acts of the Olympic Circus," *New York Times*, 28 February 1984, 10.

45. Ian Thatcher, "Brezhnev as Leader," in *Brezhnev Reconsidered*, ed. Edwin Bacon and Mark Sandle (New York: Palgrave, 2002), 33.

46. IOC Annual Session, Lake Placid, New York, 10–13 February 1980, IOC Archives, 21.

47. Ibid., 49–50.

48. IOC Executive Board meeting, Lausanne, Switzerland, 1–3 June 1974, IOC Archives, 12.

49. Arthur Daley, "What Price Amateurism?" *New York Times*, 11 June 1972, S2.

50. "In a Changing World, the Lords of Amateurism Stand Still," *Washington Post*, 8 May 1975, E5.

51. Gerald R. Ford: "Executive Order 11868—President's Commission on Olympic Sports," 19 June 1975, "The American Presidency Project," http://www.presidency.ucsb.edu/ws/?pid=23939.

52. "4 Former Olympians Rap U.S. Amateurism," *Washington Post*, 10 September 1975, D6.

53. "The Final Report on the President's Commission on Olympic Sports," January 1977, vol. 1, 4, http://hdl.handle.net/2027/mdp.39015005350619.

54. Hunt, "Countering the Soviet Threat," 796–818.

55. Stanley Rous, *Football Worlds: A Lifetime in Sport* (London: Faber and Faber, 1978), 123.

56. Lincoln Alison, *Amateurism in Sport: An Analysis and Defence* (London: Frank Cass, 2001), 55.

57. Donald Macintosh and David Whitson, *The Game Planners: Transforming Canada's Sport System* (Montreal, QC, Canada: McGill-Queen's University Press, 1990).

58. Erik Nielsen, "Flights to Empire: Australia's Imperial Engagement with the Olympic Games, 1900–1938," *Sport in Society* 18, no. 7 (September 2015): 783–99.

59. Uta Andrea Balbier, "'A Game, a Competition, an Instrument?' High Performance, Cultural Diplomacy and German Sport from 1950 to 1972," *International Journal for the History of Sport* 26, no. 4 (2009): 539–55; Von Gunter Deister, "Wer Hilft der Sporthilfe?" *Die Zeit*, 15 April 1977, http://www.zeit.de/1977/16/wer-hilft-der-sporthilfe.

60. "Address of Mr. Willi Daume at the Opening of the 73rd Session of the I.O.C.," http://library.la84.org/OlympicInformationCenter/OlympicReview/1972/ore59/ore59f.pdf.

61. IOC Annual Session, Athens, 17–20 May 1978, IOC Archives.

62. IOC Annual Session, Lake Placid, New York, 10–13 February 1980, IOC Archives, 49–50.

63. Garry Whannel, *Fields in Vision: Television Sport and Cultural Transformation* (London: Routledge, 1992).

64. Michael MacCambridge, *America's Game: The Epic Story of How Pro Football Captured a Nation* (New York: Random House, 2004); Dan Daly, *The National Forgotten League: Entertaining Stories and Observations from Pro Football's First Fifty Years* (Lincoln: University of Nebraska Press, 2012); Benjamin G. Rader, *Baseball: A History of America's Game* (Urbana: University of Illinois Press, 2008).

65. For a history of tennis and the increase in its interest, see Herbert Warren Wind, *Game, Set, and Match: The Tennis Boom of the 1960's and 70's* (New York: Dutton, 1979).

66. At its height, a single ITA meet received higher ratings than any other show in its time slot, which included Johnny Carson's iconic *Tonight Show*, a popular late night show for U.S. audiences. Pat Putnam, "Pros Are Beginning to Look Professional," *Sports Illustrated*, 6 May 1974.

67. Annie Gilbert Coleman, *Ski Style: Sport and Culture in the Rockies* (Lawrence: University Press of Kansas, 2004).

68. IOC Annual Session, Lake Placid, New York, 10–13 February 1980, IOC Archives, 49–50.

69. This term is taken from the IOC president Jacques Rogge, who claimed in 2011 that "the 1981 Congress marked the start of a revolution—the 'Samaranch Revolution.'" Jacques Rogge, "Return to Baden-Baden, Remarks from the President of the International Olympic Committee," IOC Olympic Congress, 2011, http://www.olympic.org/documents/conferences_forums_and_events/2011-baden-baden/rogge_congress_baden-baden-30_anniversary_speech.pdf.

70. Scarlett Cornelissen, "Resolving 'the South Africa Problem': Transnational Activism, Ideology and Race in the Olympic Movement, 1960–91," *International Journal of the History of Sport* 28, no. 1 (2001): 153–67; Douglas Booth, "Hitting Apartheid for Six? The Politics of the South African Sports Boycott," *Journal of Contemporary History* 38, no. 3 (2003): 477–93.

71. Nicholas Evan Sarantakes, *Dropping the Torch: Jimmy Carter, the Olympic Boycott, and the Cold War* (Cambridge: Cambridge University Press, 2010).

72. Wayne Wilson, "Los Angeles 1984," in *Historical Dictionary of the Modern Olympic Movement*, ed. John E. Findling and Kimberly D. Pelle (Westport, CT: Greenwood Press,

1996), 169–77; Mark Dyreson and Matthew P. Llewellyn, "Los Angeles Is the Olympic City: Legacies of 1932 and 1984," *International Journal of the History of Sport* 25 (December 2008): 1991–2018.

73. IOC Annual Session, Moscow, 15 July–3 August 1980, IOC Archives, 49–50.

74. For a thorough critique of Samaranch's presidency, see Robert K. Barney, Stephen R. Wenn, and Scott G. Martyn, *Selling the Five Rings: The International Olympic Committee and the Rise of Olympic Commercialism*, rev. ed. (Salt Lake City: University of Utah Press, 2004); Christopher A. Shaw, *Five Ring Circus: Myths and Realities of the Olympic Games* (New Society, 2008); Andrew Jennings, *The New Lord of the Rings: Olympic Corruption and How to Buy Olympic Medals* (New York: Pocket Books, 1996).

75. Comparison of IOC membership from the 1972 presidential election to the 1980 presidential election. IOC Annual Session, Munich, 21–24 August and 5 September 1972, IOC Archives; IOC Annual Session, Moscow, 15 July–3 August 1980, IOC Archives.

76. Comparison of IOC membership from the 1972 presidential election and the 1952 presidential election. IOC Annual Session, Munich, 21–24 August and 5 September 1972, IOC Archives; IOC Annual Session, Helsinki, 16–18 and 28 July 1952, IOC Archives.

77. Admittedly, the IOC would remain an almost exclusively male-run, patriarchal organization. See Helen Lenskyj, *Gender Politics and the Olympic Industry* (New York: Palgrave Pivot, 2012).

78. IOC Executive Board meeting, Los Angeles, 23–24 February 1981, IOC Archives.

79. IOC Executive Board meeting, Lausanne, Switzerland, 4 June 1981, IOC Archives.

80. Juan Antonio Samaranch, "Remarks," *Official Report of the 11th Olympic Congress in Baden-Baden 1981*, vol. 1, 32, IOC Archives.

81. See "Final Report of the Working Group for the Study of the Congress Presented by Mr. Vitaly Smirnov," IOC Executive Board meeting, New Delhi, India, 23–24 March 1983, IOC Archives.

82. IOC Annual Session, Baden-Baden, Germany, 29 September–2 October 1981, IOC Archives.

83. Joseph M. Turrini, *The End of Amateurism in American Track and Field* (Urbana: University of Illinois Press, 2010), 149–68.

84. IOC Executive Board meeting, Lausanne, Switzerland, 10–13 October 1982, IOC Archives.

85. IOC Annual Session, New Delhi, India, 26–28 March 1983, IOC Archives.

86. IOC Executive Board meeting, Lausanne, Switzerland, 29–30 January 1979, IOC Archives.

87. Ibid., Annex 4.

88. Ibid.

89. Harry Cavan, "FIFA and Eligibility," *Official Report of the 11th Olympic Congress in Baden-Baden 1981*, vol. 1, 69, IOC Archives.

90. IOC Executive Board meeting, Lausanne, 10–13 October 1982, IOC Archives.

91. IOC Executive Board meeting, Helsinki, Finland, 5 August 1983, IOC Archives.

92. In qualifying rounds, many teams openly admitted to using professional players who had not competed in the World Cup. All sixteen teams that qualified used professionals, and many of these same players appeared in the Olympic tournament. Grahame Jones, "IOC Won't Make a New Ruling on Pros in Soccer," *Los Angeles Times*, 7 April 1984, E15;

Jane Leavy, "W. German Pros Olympic Bound," *Washington Post*, 15 June 1984, D2; George Vecsey, "The Year of the Pro," *New York Times*, 20 July 1984, A21.

93. Barney et al., *Selling the Five Rings*, 193–96. Technical costs reflected the financial resources that an Olympic Organizing Committee had to expend in order to build a media center, and provide equipment and key media infrastructure.

94. Richard S. Gruneau and David Whitson, *Hockey Night in Canada: Sport, Identities, and Cultural Politics* (Toronto, ON, Canada: Garamond Press, 1993).

95. Barney et al., *Selling the Five Rings*, 183–91.

96. IOC Executive Board meeting, Lausanne, Switzerland, 10–13 October 1982, IOC Archives.

97. Robert Lake, *A Social History of Tennis Britain* (London: Routledge, 2014), 266.

98. Wind, *Game, Set, and Match*.

99. IOC Executive Board meeting, Lausanne, Switzerland, 9–10 March 1979, IOC Archives.

100. IOC Executive Board meeting, Lausanne, Switzerland, 9–10 March 1979, IOC Archives; IOC Executive Board meeting, Montevideo, Uruguay, 3–4 and 6 April 1979, IOC Archives.

101. IOC Annual Session, 15 June–3 July 1980, IOC Archives; IOC Executive Board meeting, Lausanne, Switzerland, 31 October 1980, IOC Archives.

102. IOC Executive Board meeting, Lausanne, 24–25 November 1983, IOC Archives.

103. Frank Litsky, "The Olympics Is No Place for Amateurs," *New York Times*, 29 July 1984, E24.

104. John Dreyfuss, "The Olympics as a Pro-Am Tourney," *Los Angeles Times*, 20 May 1984, G1.

105. "The Games They Play," *Economist*, 9 August 1980, 13–14.

106. Dreyfuss, "Pro-Am Tourney," G1.

107. David Young, *The Olympic Myth of Greek Amateur Athletics* (Chicago, IL: Ares, 1984).

108. For a fuller discussion of the legacy of the 1984 Los Angeles Olympics, see Stephen Wenn, "Peter Ueberroth's Legacy: How the 1984 Los Angeles Olympics Changed the Trajectory of the Olympic Movement," *International Journal for the History of Sport* 32, no. 1 (2015): 157–71; Wayne Wilson, "Sports Infrastructure, Legacy and the Paradox of the 1984 Olympic Games," *International Journal for the History of Sport* 32, no. 1 (2015): 144–56; Mark Dyreson, "Global Television and the Transformation of the Olympics: The 1984 Los Angeles Games," *International Journal for the History of Sport* 32, no. 1 (2015): 172–84.

109. Barney et al., *Selling the Five Rings*, 153–180.

110. Dyreson, "Global Television," 172–84; Susan Brownell, "Why 1984 Medalist Li Ning Lit the Flame at the Beijing 2008 Olympics: The Contribution of the Los Angeles Olympics to China's Market Reform," *International Journal for the History of Sport* 32, no. 1 (2015): 128–43.

111. Grahame Jones, "Confusion Reigns over Issue of Professionalism in Olympic Soccer," *Los Angeles Times*, 25 January 1984, B10; Terry Shepard, "Norway's Amateur Soccer Players Stand Out in an Olympic Field," *Los Angeles Times*, 31 July 1984, H21.

112. IOC Annual Session, Berlin, 4–6 June 1985, IOC Archives.

113. Summary of these proposed changes is taken from Daume's official report "Annex 7," IOC Annual Session, Berlin, 4–6 June 1985, IOC Archives.

114. Such concessions proved poorly thought out, as broken-time payments, endorsements, and the usual funding allotted to an national Olympic committee's athlete would still apply. Nevertheless, the ITF was eager to show that its professionals could behave like amateurs for two weeks while at the Olympics.

115. IOC Annual Session, Lausanne, Switzerland, 12–17 October 1986, IOC Archives.

116. Ibid.

117. Ibid.

118. IOC Annual Session, Istanbul, Turkey, 5–9 August 1987, IOC Archives.

119. Ibid.

120. "Olympic Players Also Demonstrate Proper Etiquette on the Courts," *Los Angeles Times*, 14 August 1984, H27.

121. Hunt, *Drug Games*.

Epilogue

1. Ian Thomsen, "The Dream Team Is Finished, but Its Legacy Will Linger," *New York Times,* 10 August 1992, http://www.nytimes.com/1992/08/10/sports/10iht-hoop_6.html.

2. Ibid.

3. Miquel de Moragas, "Barcelona 1992," in *Encyclopedia of the Modern Olympic Movement*, ed. John E. Findling and Kimberly D. Pelle (Westport, CT: Greenwood Press, 2004), 225–34.

4. IOC Annual Session, 30 August–1 September 1898, San Juan, Puerto Rico, IOC Archives.

5. IOC, Annual Session, 17–20 September 1990, Tokyo, IOC Archives.

6. International Olympic Committee, *Olympic Charter* (Lausanne, Switzerland: International Olympic Committee, 1991), http://www.olympic.org/Documents/Olympic%20 Charter/Olympic_Charter_through_time/1991-Olympic_Charter_June91.pdf.

7. Though it is often referred to as Rule 26, for much of its life the amateur eligibility requirement moved around the *Olympic Charter*. Only in 1956 did it first occupy the 26 position. It ceased to be Rule 26 in the 1991 edition of the *Charter*.

8. IOC Annual Session, Rome, 24–30 April 1966, IOC Archives.

9. IOC Annual Session, Moscow, 15 July–3 August 1980, 49–50, IOC Archives.

10. IOC Executive Board meeting, Lausanne, Switzerland, 30–31 October 1980, 49, IOC Archives.

11. Robert Helmick, "Remarks," *Official Report of the 11th Olympic Congress in Baden-Baden 1981*, vol. 1, 40; Primo Nebiolo, "The Olympic Movement and Athletics, *Official Report of the 11th Olympic Congress in Baden-Baden 1981*, vol. 1, 77.

12. International Olympic Committee, *Olympic Charter* (Lausanne, Switzerland: International Olympic Committee, 1991), http://www.olympic.org/Documents/Olympic%20 Charter/Olympic_Charter_through_time/1991-Olympic_Charter_June91.pdf.

13. IOC Annual Session, Courchevel, France, 5–6 February 1992, IOC Archives.

14. London Olympic Games Organizing Committee, *London 2012 Marketing Report* (Lausanne, Switzerland: International Olympic Committee, 2012), http://www.olympic.org/

Documents/IOC_Marketing/London_2012/LR_IOC_MarketingReport_medium_res1
.pdf.

15. London Olympic Games Organizing Committee, *London 2012 Olympic Games Global Broadcasting Report* (Lausanne, Switzerland: International Olympic Committee, 2012), http://www.olympic.org/Documents/IOC_Marketing/Broadcasting/London_2012 _Global_%20Broadcast_Report.pdf.

16. According to the IOC's own marketing research in 2001, the public associates the Olympic Games with "a peaceful and festive forum for cultural exchange and fair play," with the "ideals of equality, tradition, honour and excellence." Benoît Séguin and Norman Reilly, "The Olympic Brand, Ambush Marketing and Clutter," *International Journal for Sport Management and Marketing* 4, no.1 (2008): 65.

17. As the IOC reminds its sponsors, "these [Olympic] symbols and ideals that they embody are the cornerstones of all Olympic marketing programs." IOC, *Final Report on the XXVIIth Olympiad: 1997–2000*, http://www.olympic.org/Documents/Reports/EN/ en_report_677.pdf.

18. International Olympic Committee, *Olympic Charter* (Lausanne, Switzerland: International Olympic Committee, 2015), http://www.olympic.org/documents/olympic_charter _en.pdf.

19. Ian Ritchie, "The Construction of a Policy: The World Anti-Doping Code's 'Spirit of Sport' Clause," *Performance Enhancement and Health* 2 (2013): 194–200.

20. Dikaia Chatziefstathiou and Ian Henry, *Discourses of Olympism: From Sorbonne 1894 to London 2012* (Hampshire, U.K.: Palgrave Macmillan, 2012).

21. Bill Crawford, *All American: The Rise of Jim Thorpe* (Hoboken, NJ: Wiley, 2005), 236–37.

22. Even the IOC's own website makes no mention of Nurmi's past transgressions: http://www.olympic.org/paavo-nurmi.

23. International Association of Athletics Federations, *Hall of Fame Profile: Paavo Nurmi* [webpage], http://www.iaaf.org/news/news/hall-of-fame-profile-paavo-nurmi-finland.

24. IOC Executive Board meeting, Vienna, 7–8 December 1988, Annexes 8, 7, 10, 63–65, as cited in Raymond Gafner, *The International Olympic Committee, One Hundred Years: The Idea, the Presidents, the Achievements*, vol. 3 (Lausanne, Switzerland: International Olympic Committee, 1996); "Executive Board of the IOC: Programme, Doping and Apartheid on the Agenda," *Olympic Review* No. 255–56 (January–February 1989): 16.

25. Karl Schranz, *Mein 'Olympiasieg'* (Munich, Germany: Herbig, 2002), 196; Guy-Lionel Loew, "Amateurism and the Olympic Movement: The Stakes of the Definition of Amateurism under the Light of the Case of Karl Schranz—1972 Winter Games Sapporo, Japan," *Journal of Olympic History* 13 (January 2005): 24–30.

INDEX

MATTHEW P. LLEWELLYN and JOHN GLEAVES are associate professors of kinesiology at California State University, Fullerton.

SPORT AND SOCIETY

The University of Illinois Press
is a founding member of the
Association of American University Presses.

Composed in 10.5/13 Adobe Minion Pro
at the University of Illinois Press
Manufactured by Cushing Malloy, Inc.

University of Illinois Press
1325 South Oak Street
Champaign, IL 61820-6903
www.press.uillinois.edu

THE RISE AND FALL
OF
OLYMPIC AMATEURISM

SPORT AND SOCIETY

Series Editors
Randy Roberts
Aram Goudsouzian
Founding Editors
Benjamin G. Rader
Randy Roberts

A list of books in the series appears at the end of this book.